BLACKGUARD

5

RYO HANADA

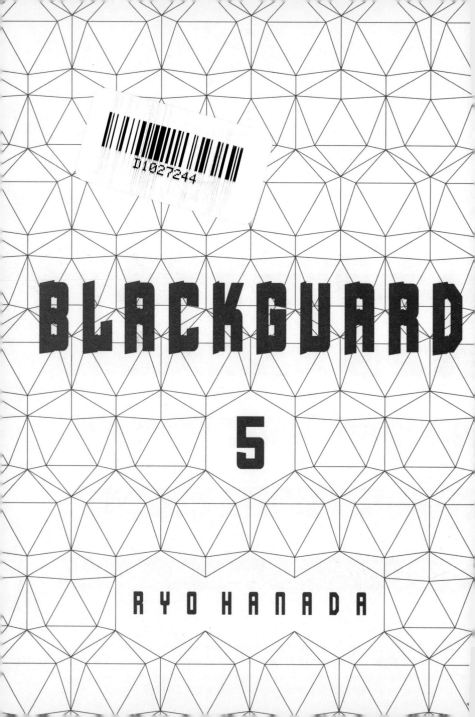

CONTENTS

WARNING: This volume contains references to suicide. If you or someone you know has suicidal thoughts or feelings, you are not alone, and there is free, 24/7 help.

National Suicide Prevention Lifeline offers confidential support for those in crisis or emotional distress. You can call 988 or go to SuicidePreventionLifeline.org for free, 24/7 help.

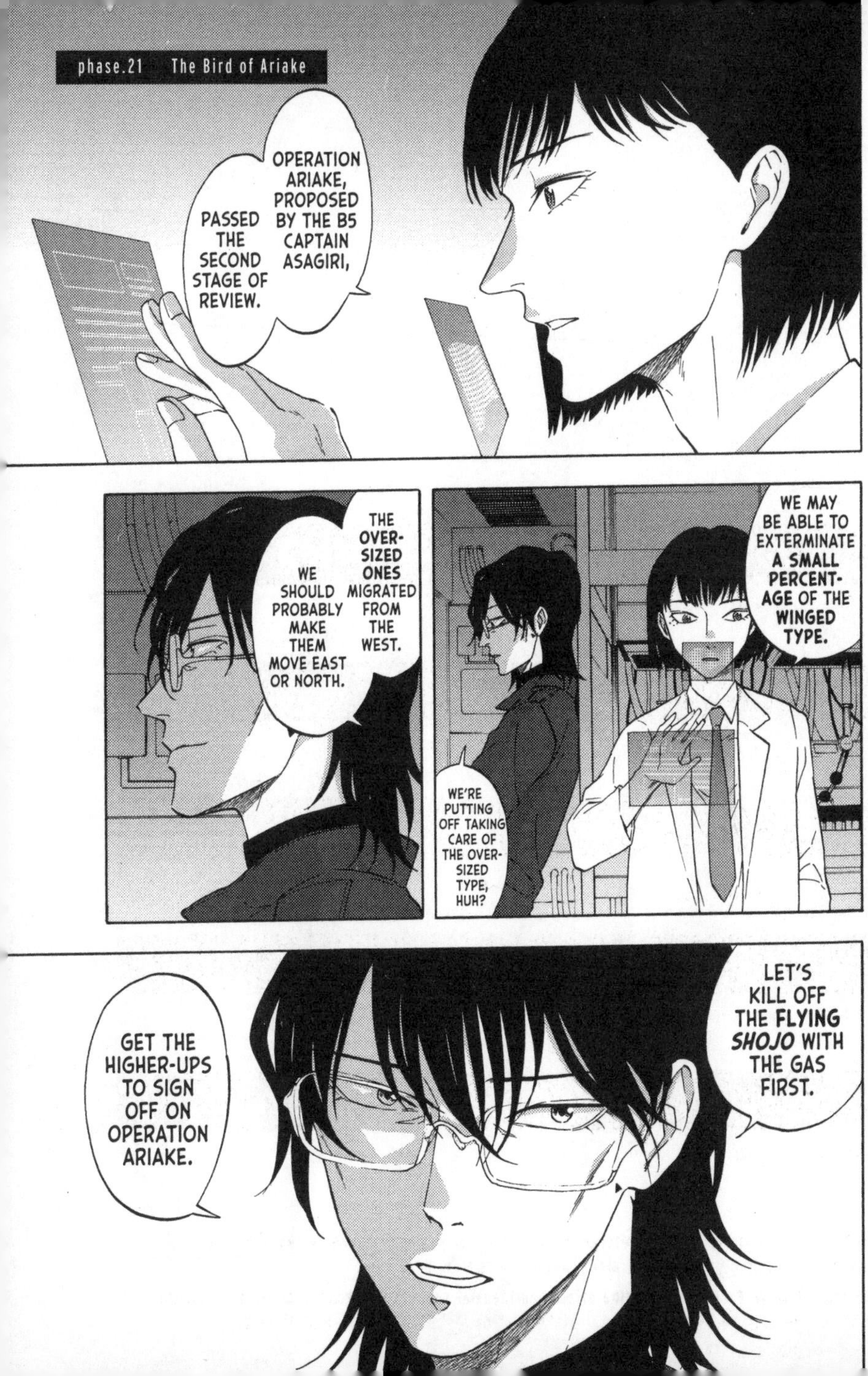
phase.21 The Bird of Ariake
OPERATION ARIAKE, PROPOSED BY THE B5 CAPTAIN ASAGIRI,
PASSED THE SECOND STAGE OF REVIEW.
WE MAY BE ABLE TO EXTERMINATE A SMALL PERCENTAGE OF THE WINGED TYPE.
WE'RE PUTTING OFF TAKING CARE OF THE OVERSIZED TYPE, HUH?
THE OVERSIZED ONES MIGRATED FROM THE WEST.
WE SHOULD PROBABLY MAKE THEM MOVE EAST OR NORTH.
LET'S KILL OFF THE FLYING SHOJO WITH THE GAS FIRST.
GET THE HIGHER-UPS TO SIGN OFF ON OPERATION ARIAKE.

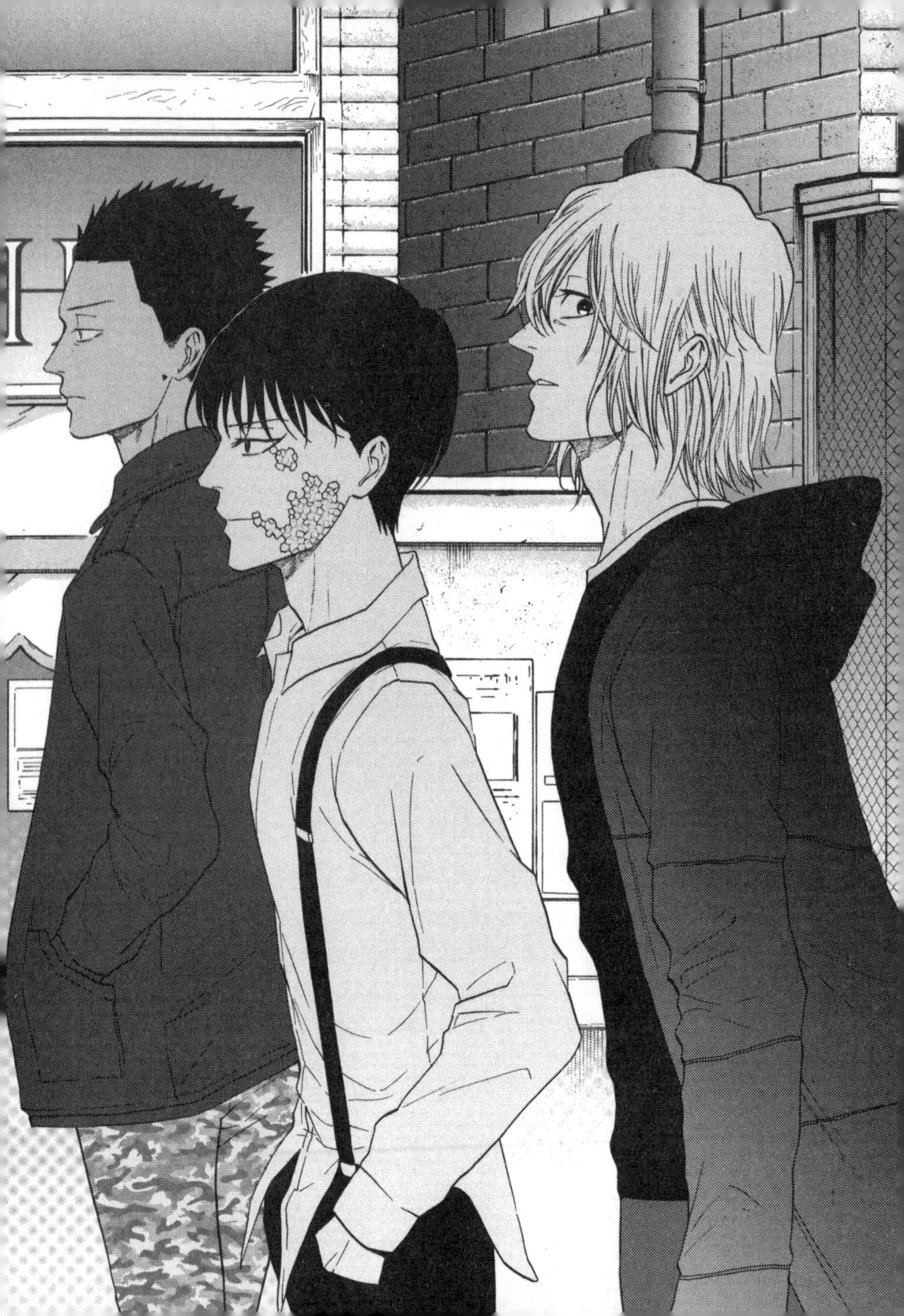

phase.21 The Bird of Ariake

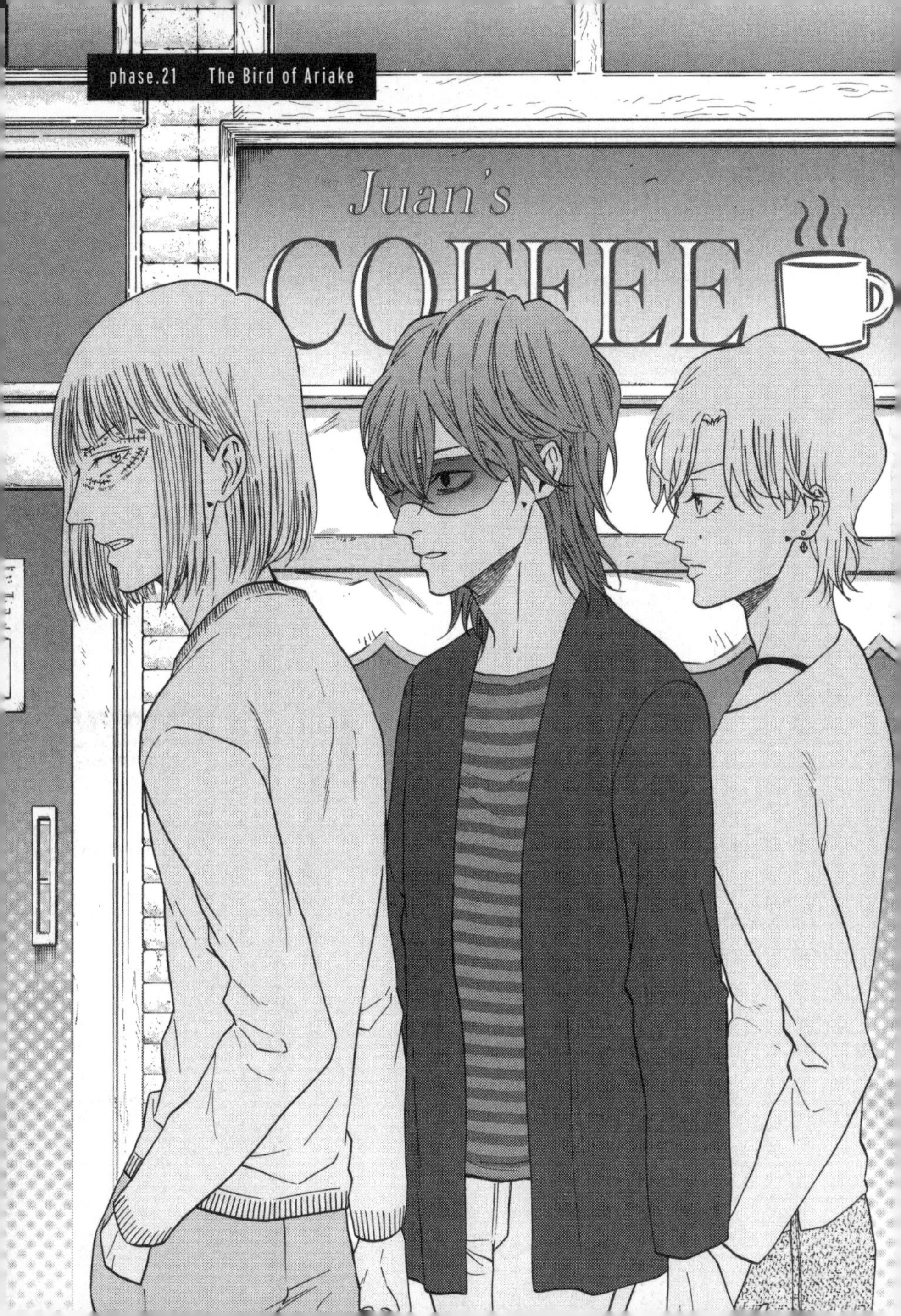
Juan's
COFFEE

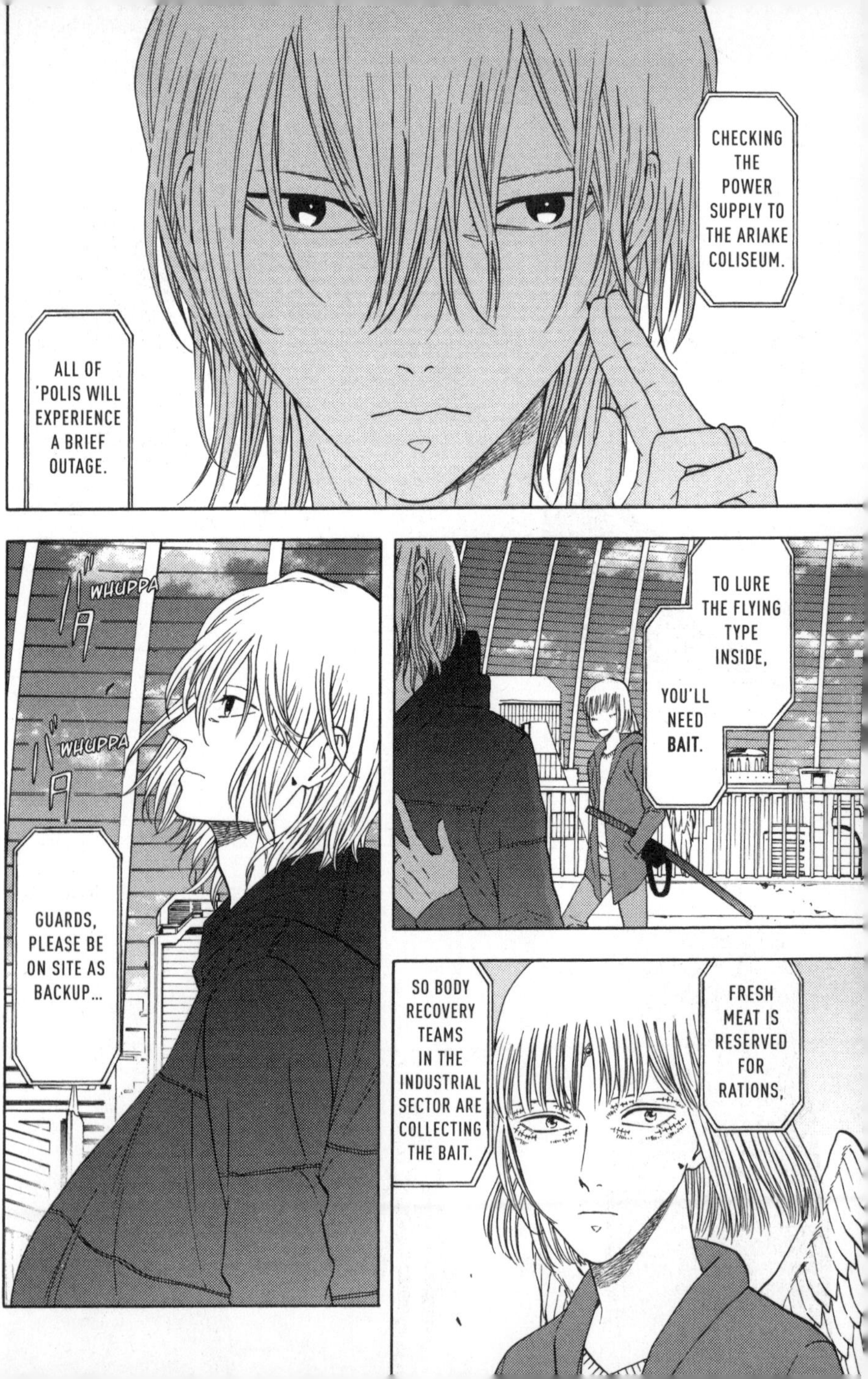
CHECKING THE POWER SUPPLY TO THE ARIAKE COLISEUM.
ALL OF 'POLIS WILL EXPERIENCE A BRIEF OUTAGE.
TO LURE THE FLYING TYPE INSIDE,
YOU'LL NEED **BAIT**.
FRESH MEAT IS RESERVED FOR RATIONS,
SO BODY RECOVERY TEAMS IN THE INDUSTRIAL SECTOR ARE COLLECTING THE BAIT.
WHUPPA
WHUPPA
GUARDS, PLEASE BE ON SITE AS BACKUP...

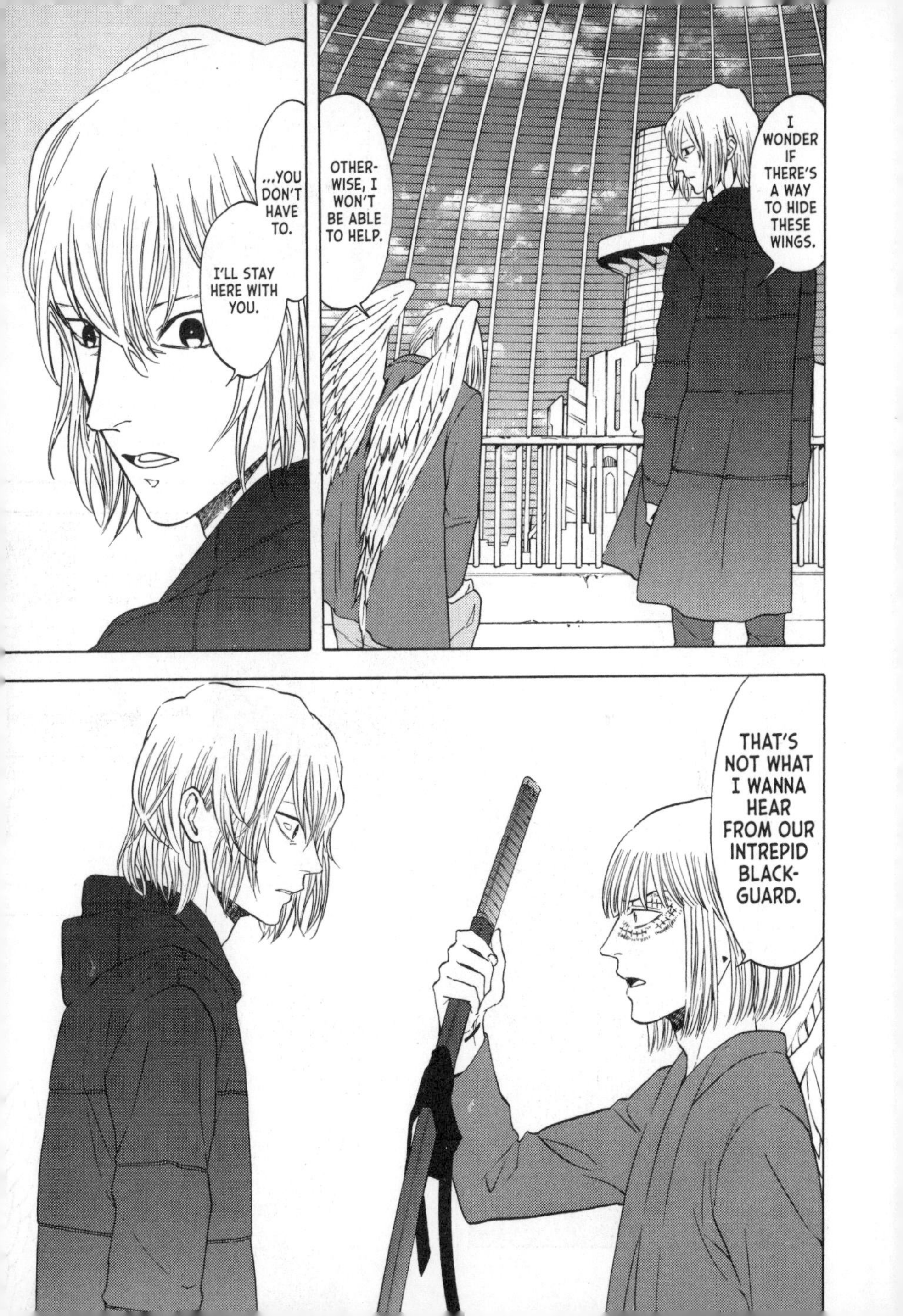
I WONDER IF THERE'S A WAY TO HIDE THESE WINGS.
OTHER-WISE, I WON'T BE ABLE TO HELP.
...YOU DON'T HAVE TO.
I'LL STAY HERE WITH YOU.
THAT'S NOT WHAT I WANNA HEAR FROM OUR INTREPID BLACK-GUARD.

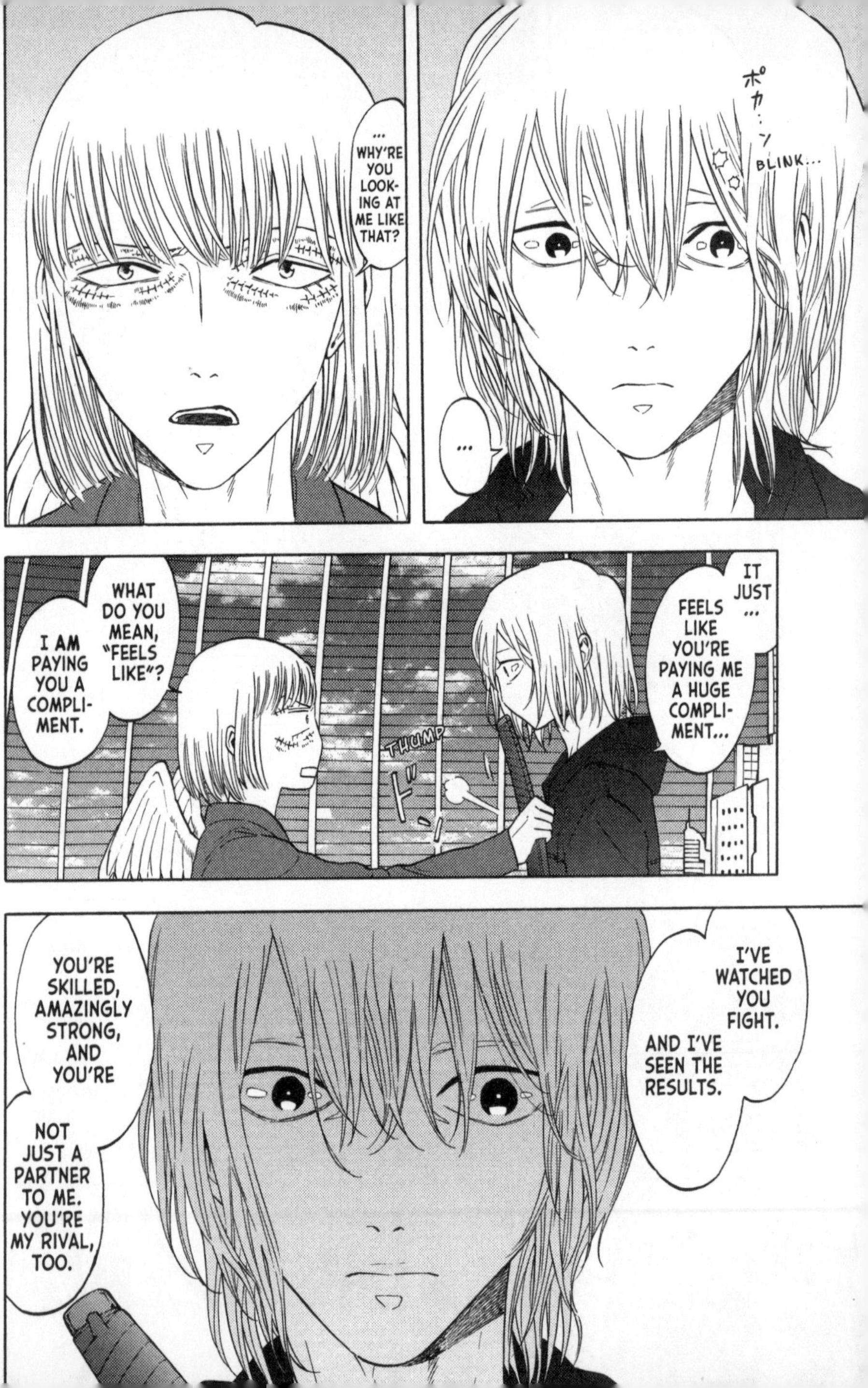
ポカ‥ン
BLINK...
...
... WHY'RE YOU LOOKING AT ME LIKE THAT?
IT JUST ... FEELS LIKE YOU'RE PAYING ME A HUGE COMPLIMENT...
THUMP
ド
WHAT DO YOU MEAN, "FEELS LIKE"?
I **AM** PAYING YOU A COMPLIMENT.
I'VE WATCHED YOU FIGHT.
AND I'VE SEEN THE RESULTS.
YOU'RE SKILLED, AMAZINGLY STRONG, AND YOU'RE
NOT JUST A PARTNER TO ME. YOU'RE MY RIVAL, TOO.

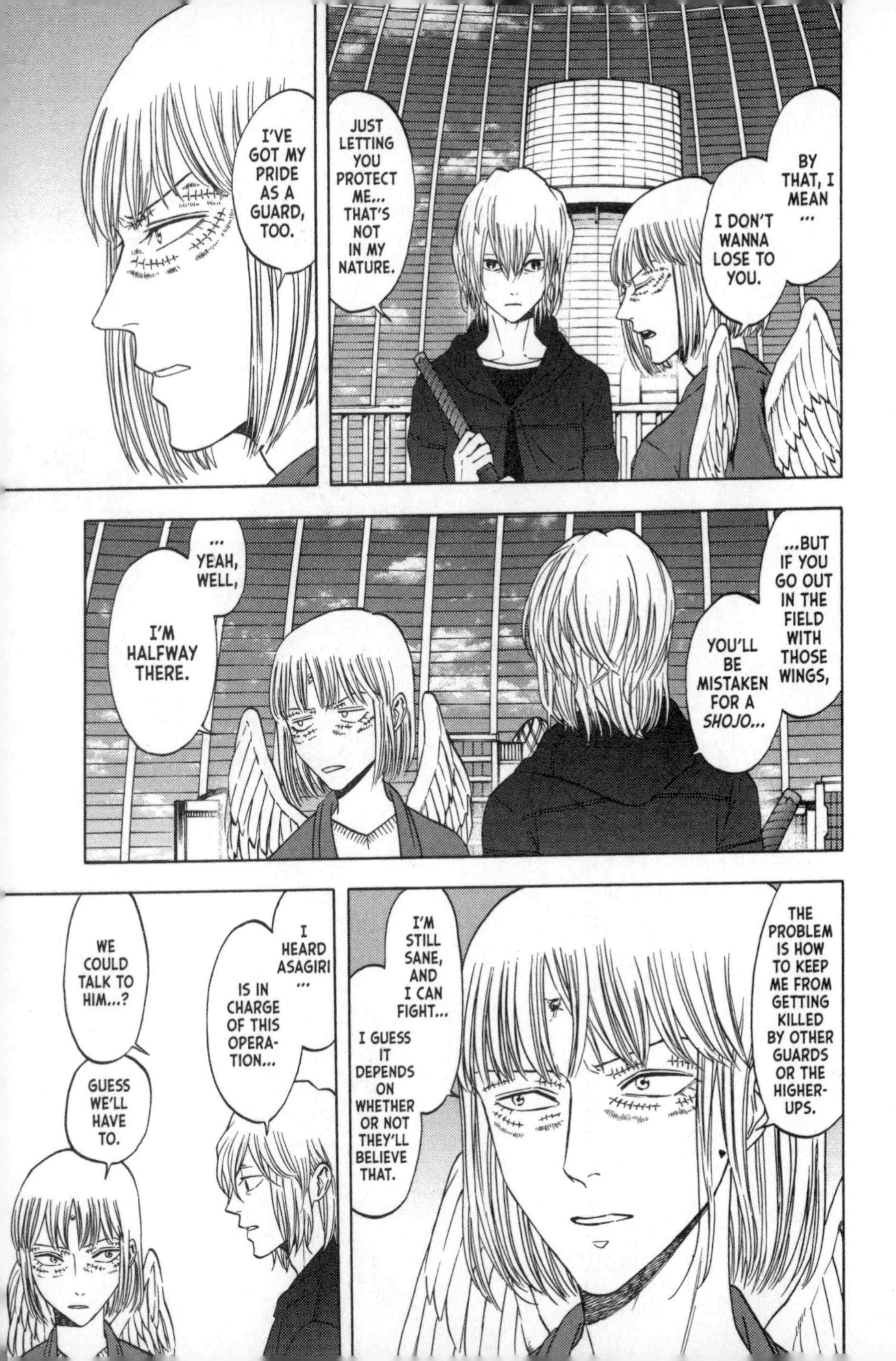
BY THAT, I MEAN ...
I DON'T WANNA LOSE TO YOU.
JUST LETTING YOU PROTECT ME... THAT'S NOT IN MY NATURE.
I'VE GOT MY PRIDE AS A GUARD, TOO.
...BUT IF YOU GO OUT IN THE FIELD WITH THOSE WINGS,
YOU'LL BE MISTAKEN FOR A *SHOJO*...
... YEAH, WELL,
I'M HALFWAY THERE.
THE PROBLEM IS HOW TO KEEP ME FROM GETTING KILLED BY OTHER GUARDS OR THE HIGHER-UPS.
I'M STILL SANE, AND I CAN FIGHT...
I GUESS IT DEPENDS ON WHETHER OR NOT THEY'LL BELIEVE THAT.
I HEARD ASAGIRI ...
IS IN CHARGE OF THIS OPERATION...
WE COULD TALK TO HIM...?
GUESS WE'LL HAVE TO.

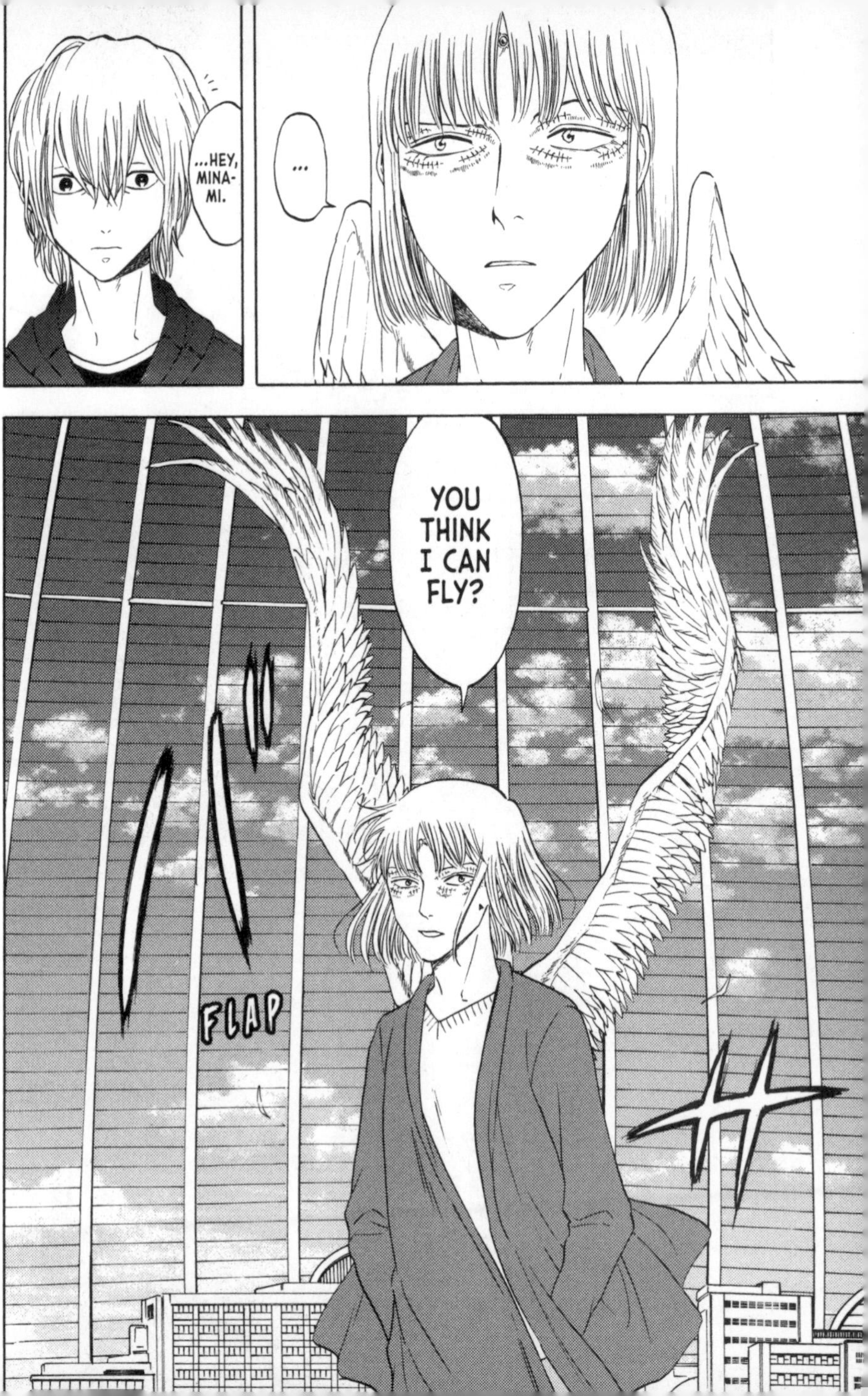
...
...HEY, MINA-MI.
YOU THINK I CAN FLY?
FLAP

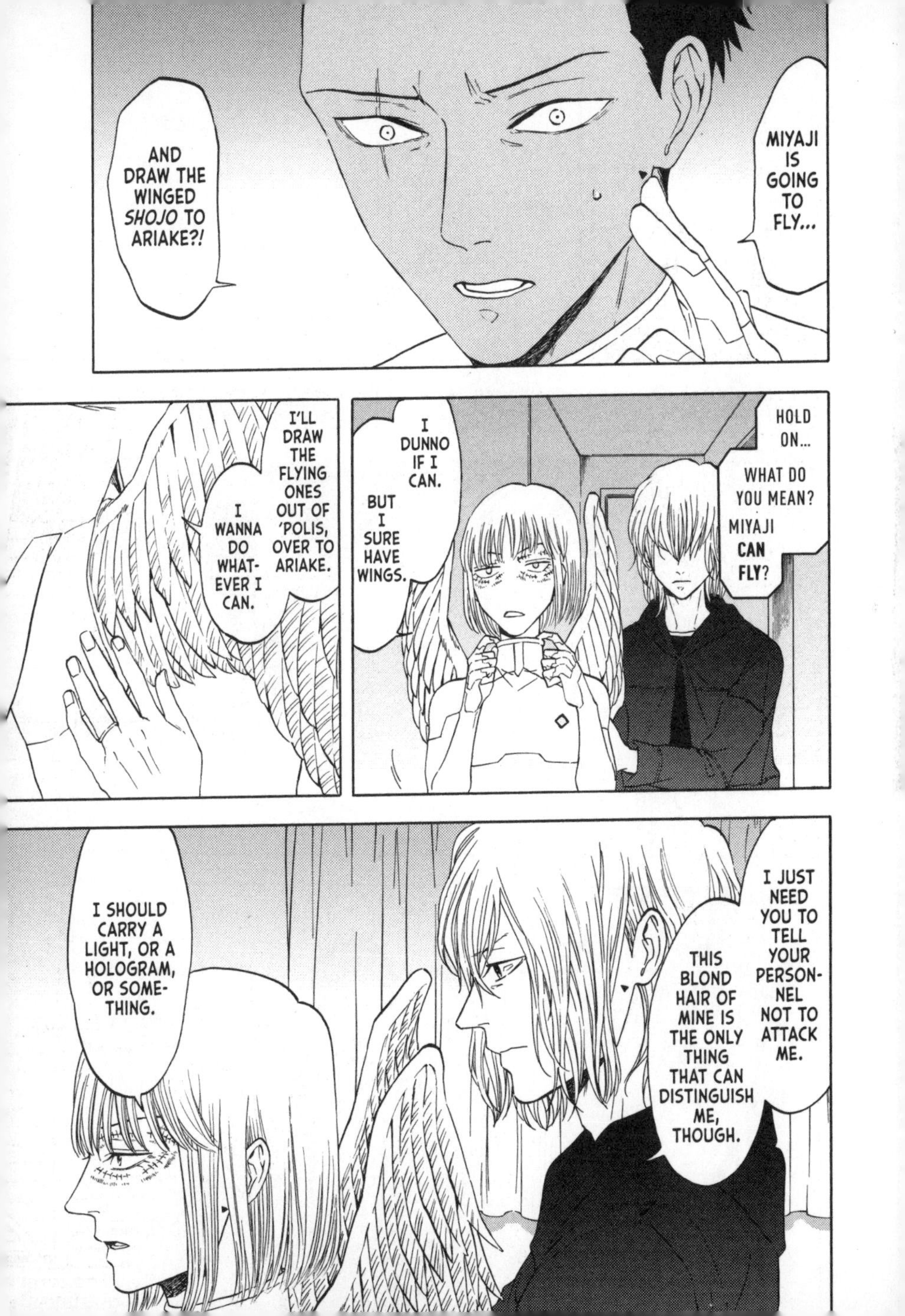
MIYAJI IS GOING TO FLY...
AND DRAW THE WINGED *SHOJO* TO ARIAKE?!
HOLD ON...
WHAT DO YOU MEAN?
MIYAJI **CAN FLY**?
I DUNNO IF I CAN.
BUT I SURE HAVE WINGS.
I'LL DRAW THE FLYING ONES OUT OF 'POLIS, OVER TO ARIAKE.
I WANNA DO WHATEVER I CAN.
I JUST NEED YOU TO TELL YOUR PERSONNEL NOT TO ATTACK ME.
THIS BLOND HAIR OF MINE IS THE ONLY THING THAT CAN DISTINGUISH ME, THOUGH.
I SHOULD CARRY A LIGHT, OR A HOLOGRAM, OR SOMETHING.

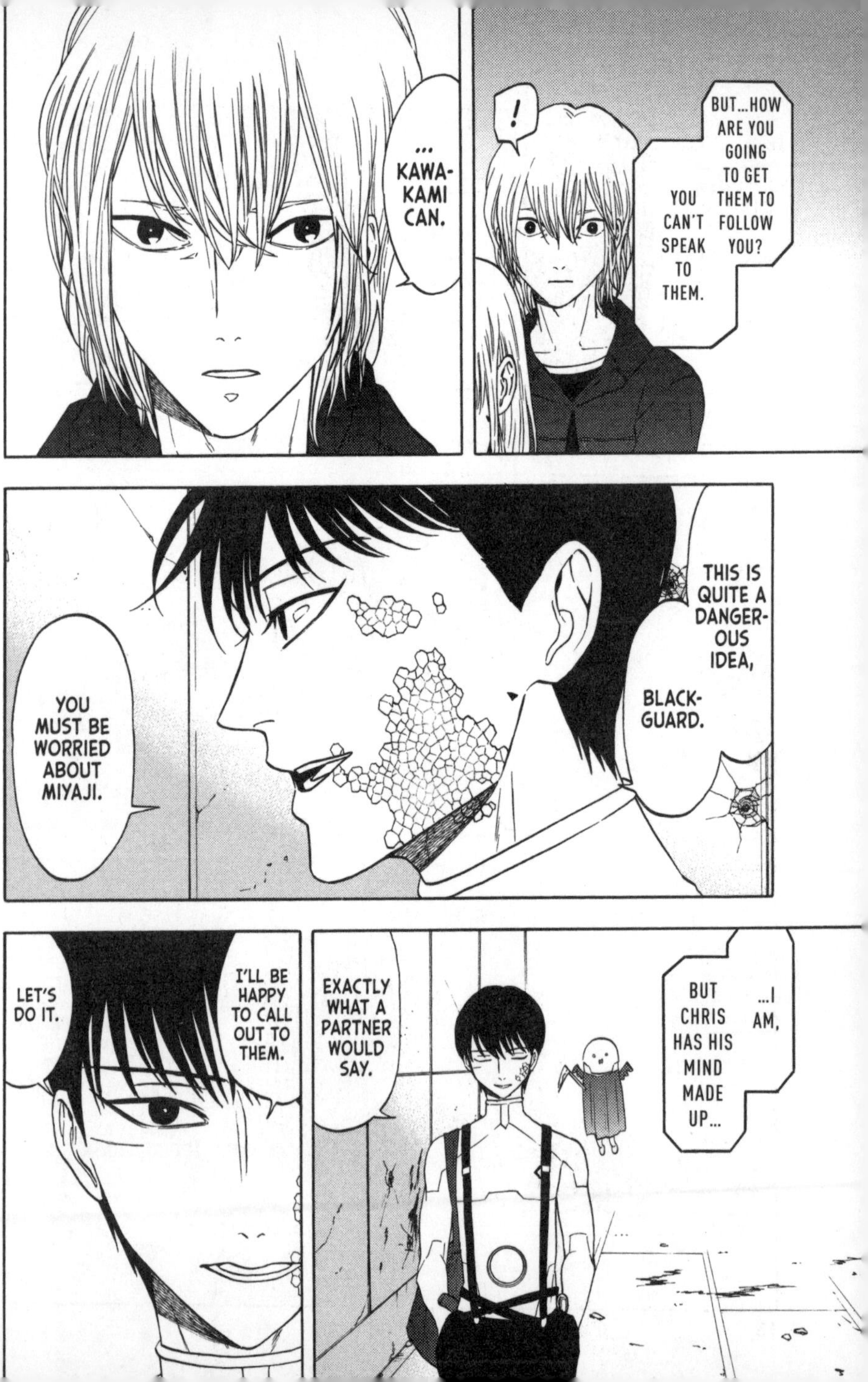
!
BUT...HOW ARE YOU GOING TO GET THEM TO FOLLOW YOU?
YOU CAN'T SPEAK TO THEM.
...KAWAKAMI CAN.
THIS IS QUITE A DANGEROUS IDEA,
BLACKGUARD.
YOU MUST BE WORRIED ABOUT MIYAJI.
...I AM,
BUT CHRIS HAS HIS MIND MADE UP...
EXACTLY WHAT A PARTNER WOULD SAY.
I'LL BE HAPPY TO CALL OUT TO THEM.
LET'S DO IT.

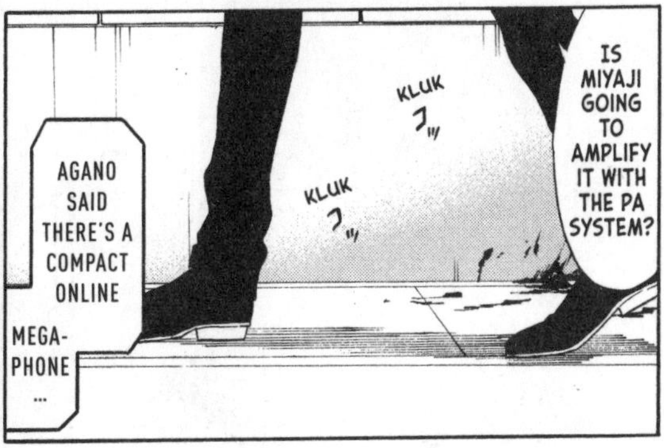
IS MIYAJI GOING TO AMPLIFY IT WITH THE PA SYSTEM?
KLUK
KLUK
AGANO SAID THERE'S A COMPACT ONLINE MEGAPHONE ...

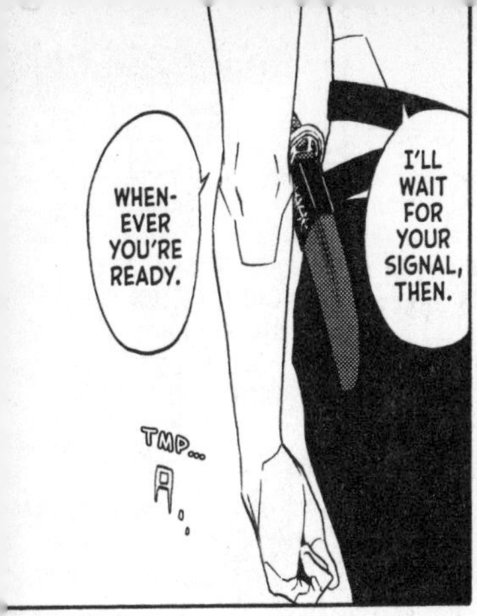
I'LL WAIT FOR YOUR SIGNAL, THEN.
WHEN-EVER YOU'RE READY.
TMP...

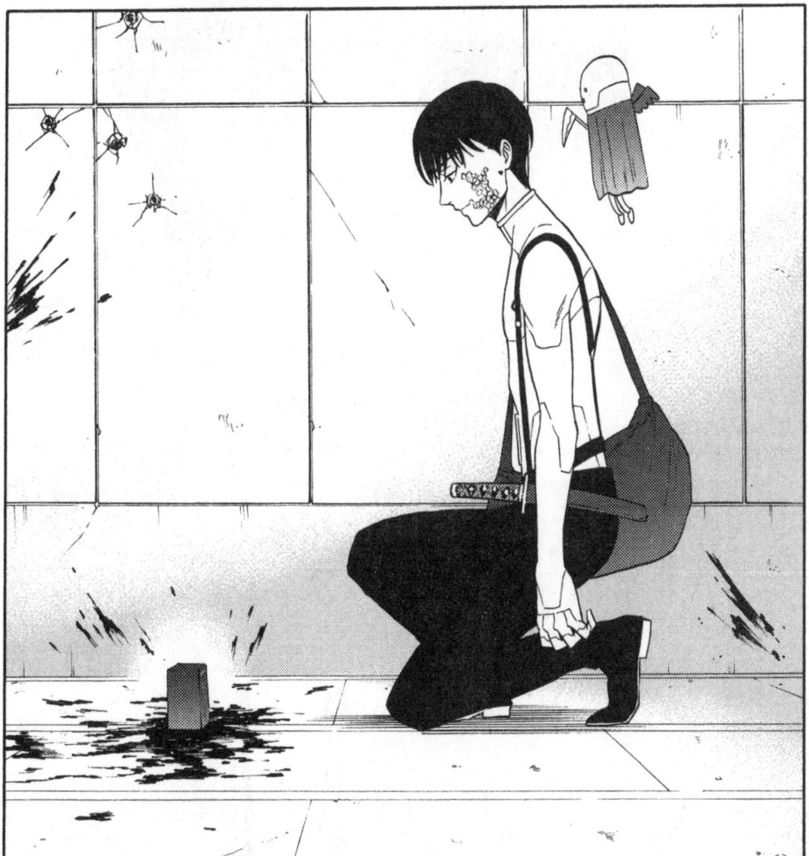

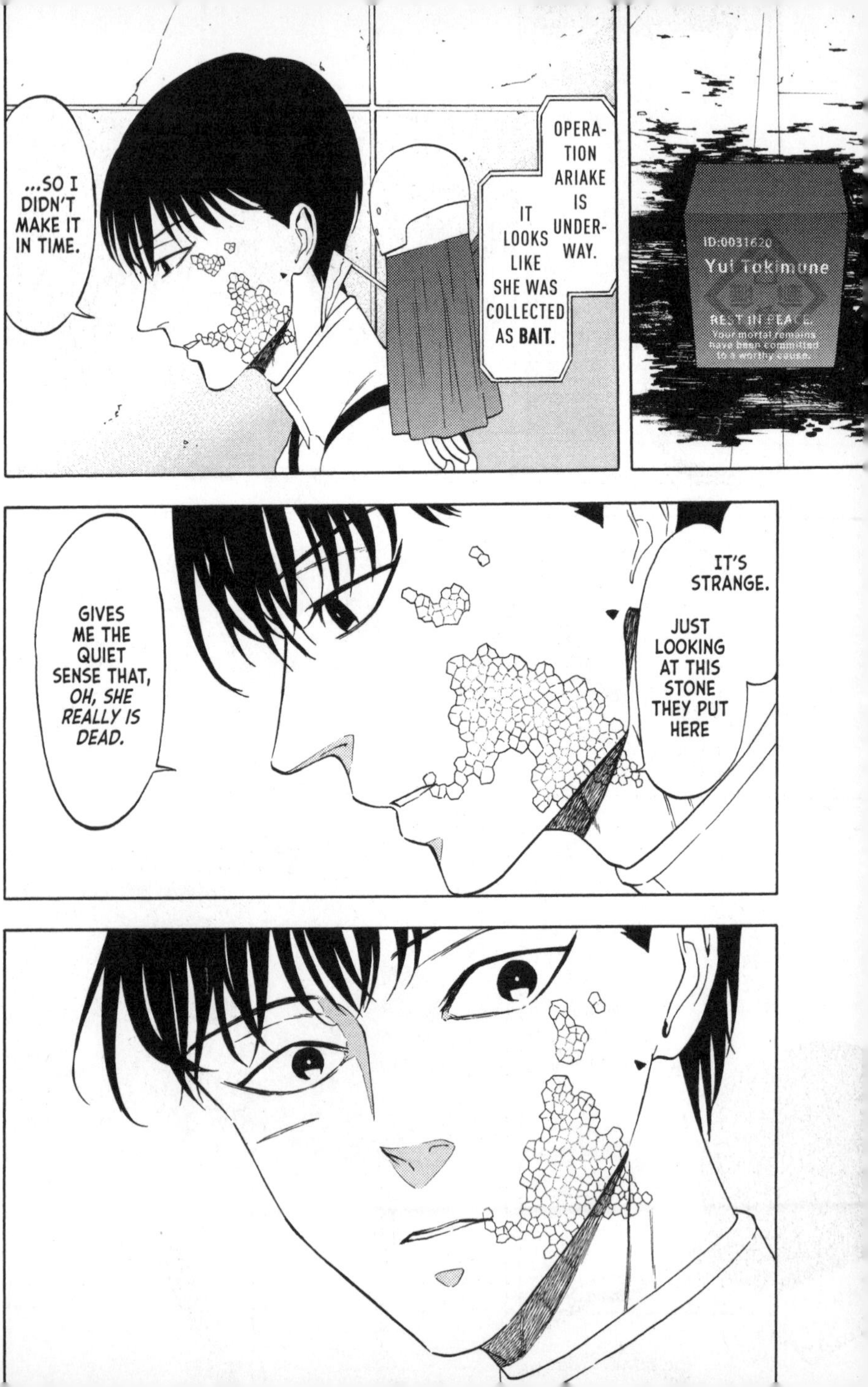
ID:0031620
Yui Tokimune
REST IN PEACE.
Your mortal remains have been committed to a worthy cause.
OPERATION ARIAKE IS UNDERWAY.
IT LOOKS LIKE SHE WAS COLLECTED AS **BAIT.**
...SO I DIDN'T MAKE IT IN TIME.
IT'S STRANGE.
JUST LOOKING AT THIS STONE THEY PUT HERE
GIVES ME THE QUIET SENSE THAT, *OH, SHE REALLY IS DEAD.*

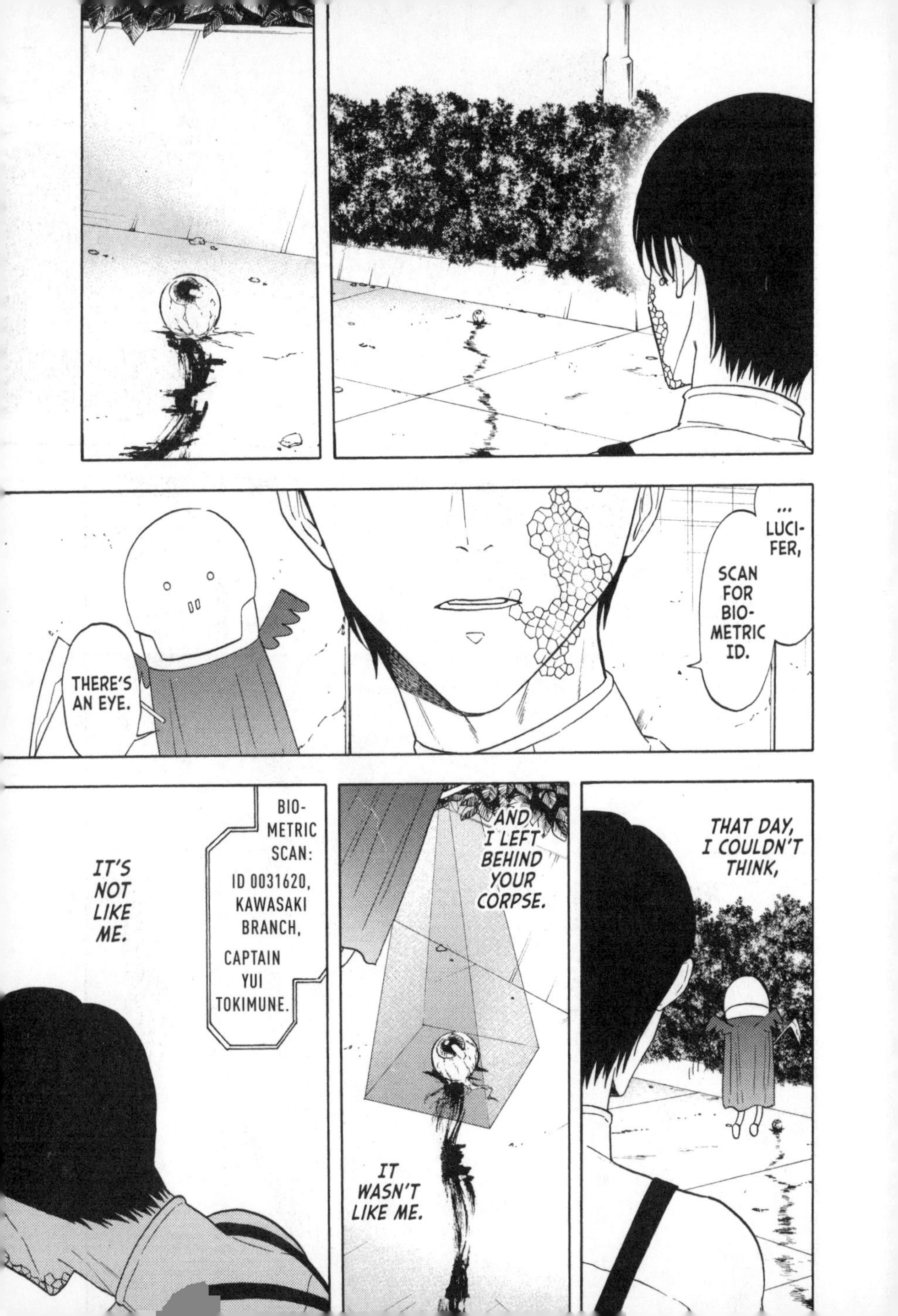
... LUCI-FER, SCAN FOR BIO-METRIC ID.
THERE'S AN EYE.
THAT DAY, I COULDN'T THINK,
AND I LEFT BEHIND YOUR CORPSE.
IT WASN'T LIKE ME.
BIO-METRIC SCAN: ID 0031620, KAWASAKI BRANCH, CAPTAIN YUI TOKIMUNE.
IT'S NOT LIKE ME.

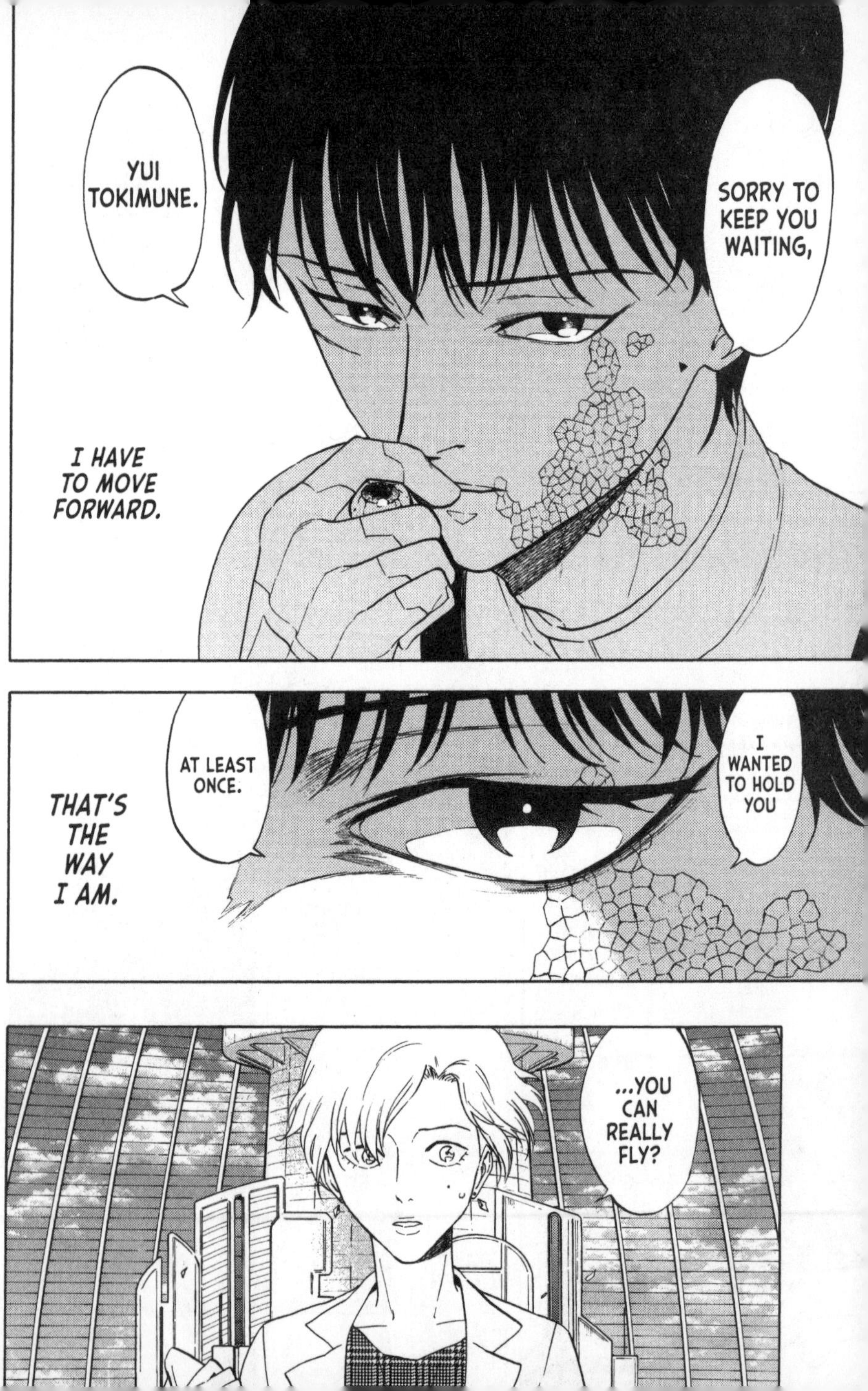
SORRY TO KEEP YOU WAITING,
YUI TOKIMUNE.
I HAVE TO MOVE FORWARD.
I WANTED TO HOLD YOU
AT LEAST ONCE.
THAT'S THE WAY I AM.
...YOU CAN REALLY FLY?

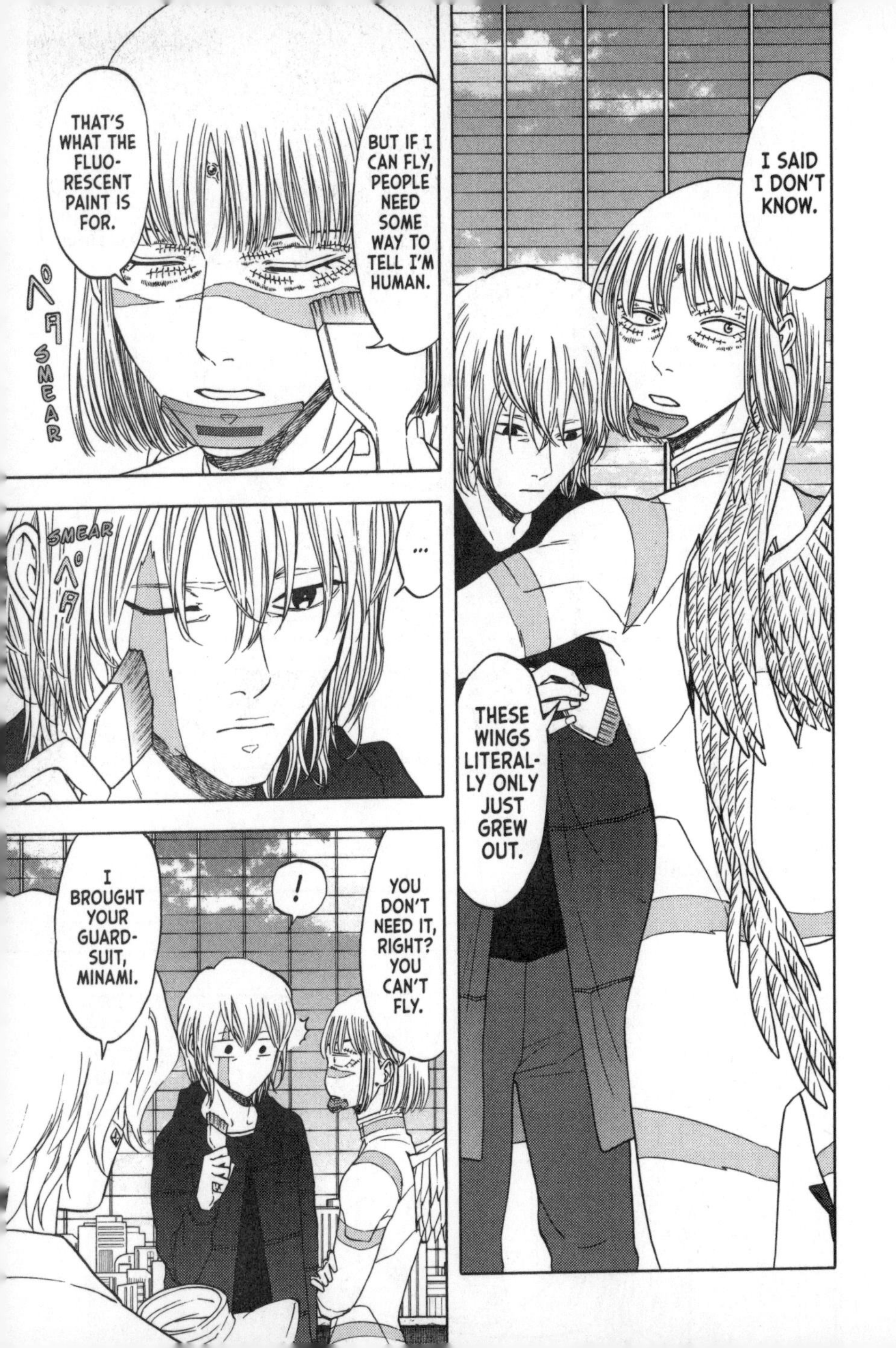
I SAID I DON'T KNOW.
THESE WINGS LITERALLY ONLY JUST GREW OUT.
BUT IF I CAN FLY, PEOPLE NEED SOME WAY TO TELL I'M HUMAN.
THAT'S WHAT THE FLUORESCENT PAINT IS FOR.
ペタ SMEAR
...
SMEAR ペタ
YOU DON'T NEED IT, RIGHT? YOU CAN'T FLY.
!
I BROUGHT YOUR GUARDSUIT, MINAMI.

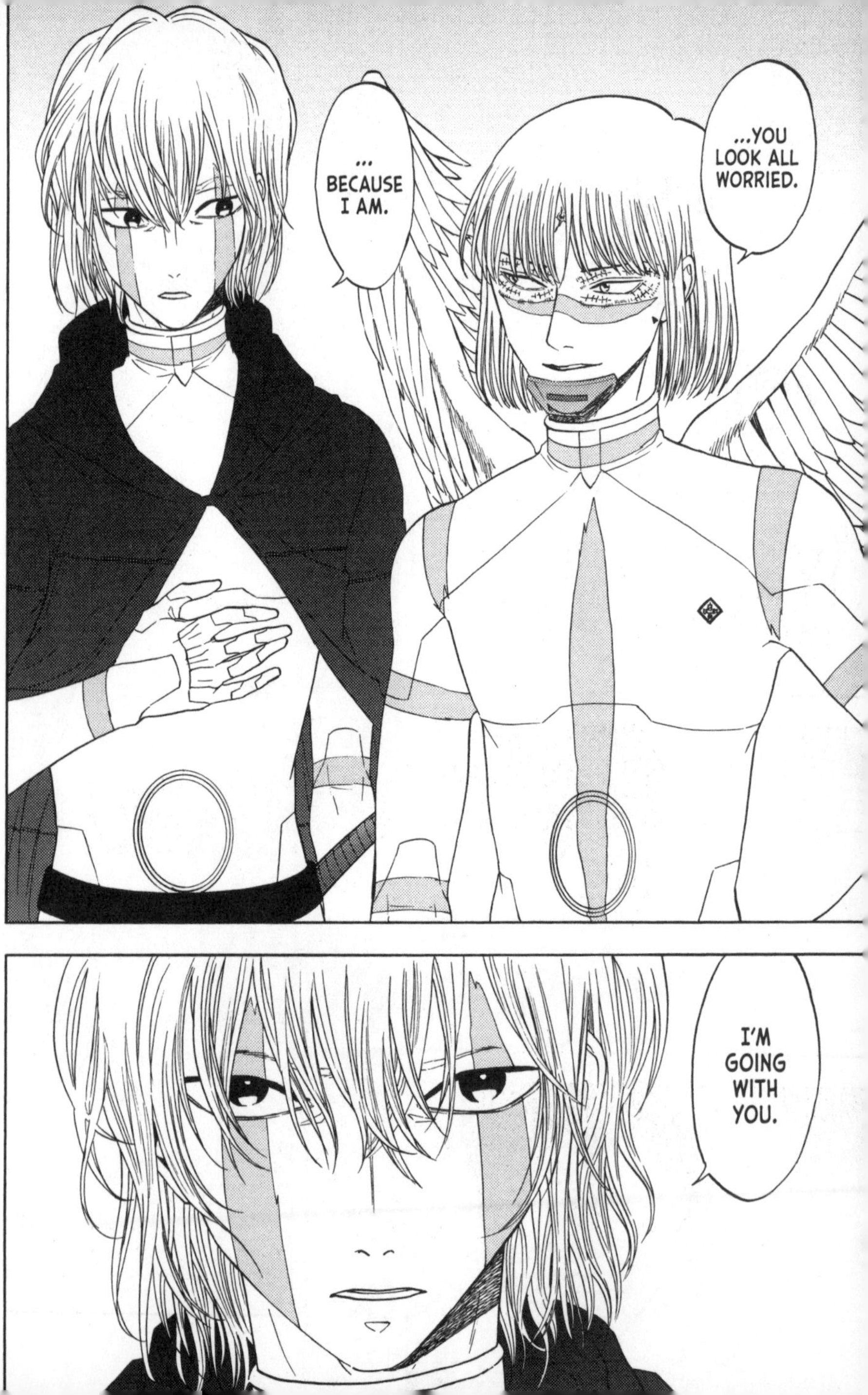
...YOU LOOK ALL WORRIED.
... BECAUSE I AM.
I'M GOING WITH YOU.

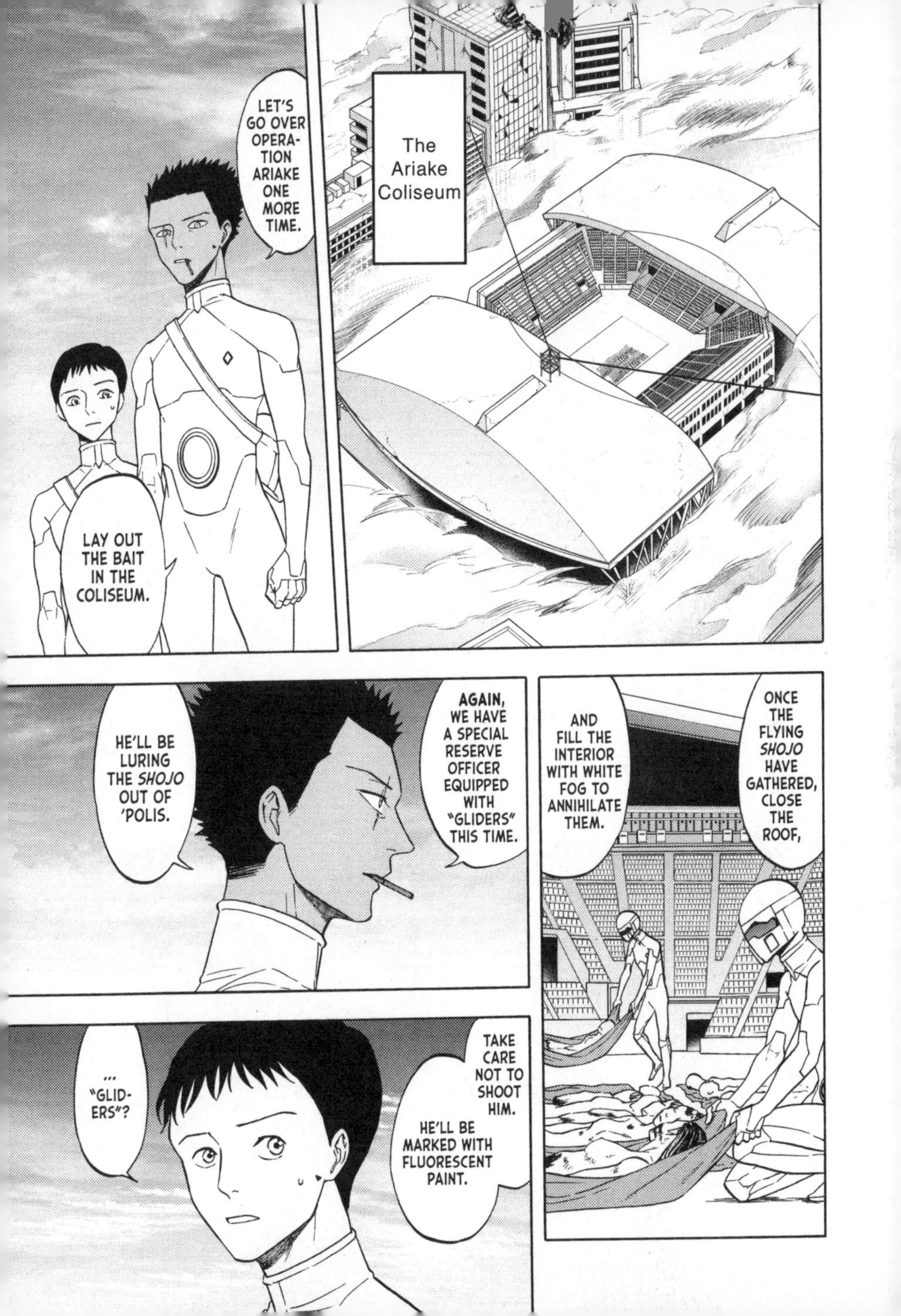
The Ariake Coliseum
LET'S GO OVER OPERATION ARIAKE ONE MORE TIME.
LAY OUT THE BAIT IN THE COLISEUM.
ONCE THE FLYING *SHOJO* HAVE GATHERED, CLOSE THE ROOF,
AND FILL THE INTERIOR WITH WHITE FOG TO ANNIHILATE THEM.
AGAIN, WE HAVE A SPECIAL RESERVE OFFICER EQUIPPED WITH "GLIDERS" THIS TIME.
HE'LL BE LURING THE *SHOJO* OUT OF 'POLIS.
TAKE CARE NOT TO SHOOT HIM.
HE'LL BE MARKED WITH FLUORESCENT PAINT.
... "GLIDERS"?

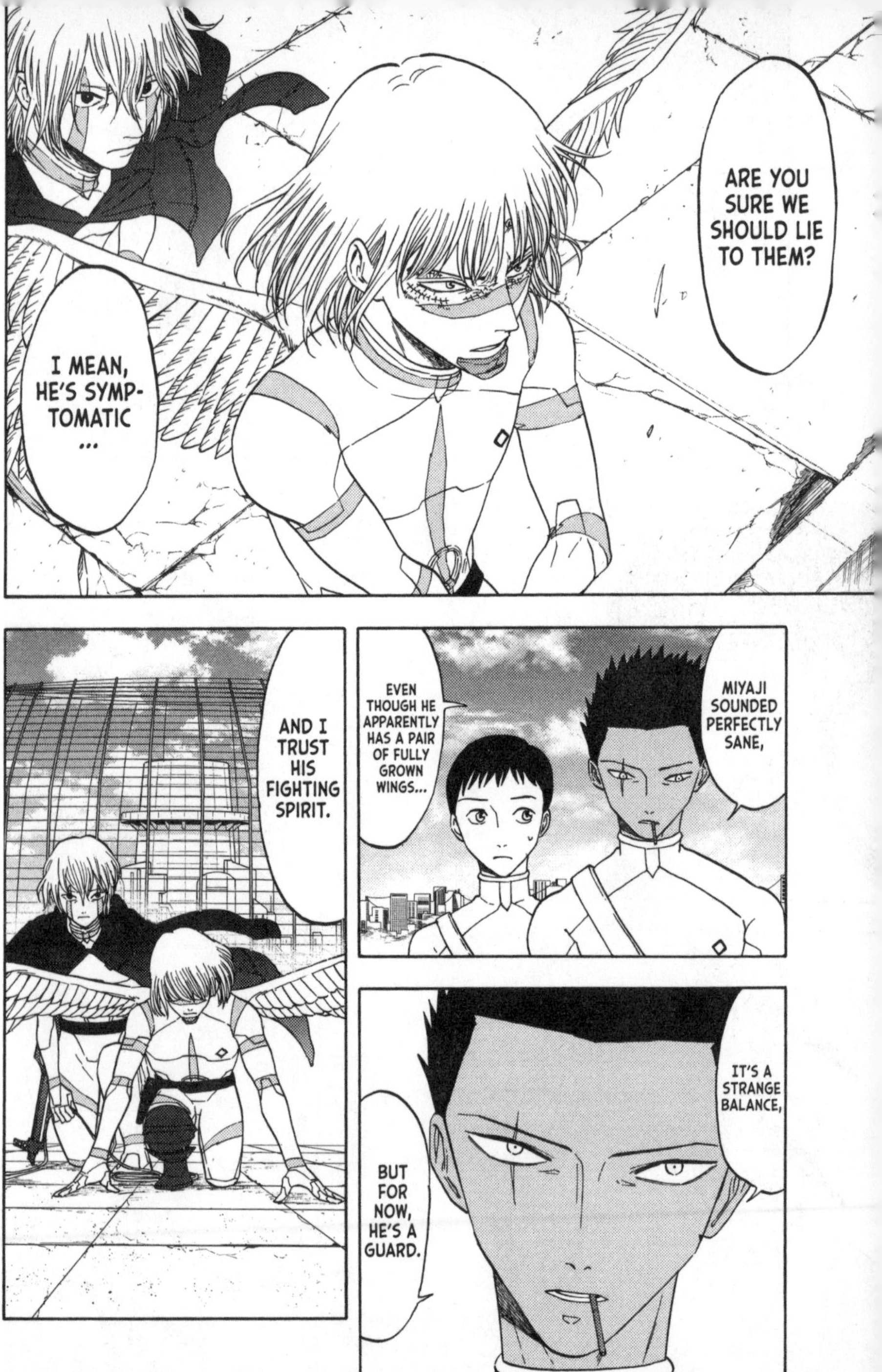
ARE YOU SURE WE SHOULD LIE TO THEM?
I MEAN, HE'S SYMP-TOMATIC ...
MIYAJI SOUNDED PERFECTLY SANE,
EVEN THOUGH HE APPARENTLY HAS A PAIR OF FULLY GROWN WINGS...
IT'S A STRANGE BALANCE,
BUT FOR NOW, HE'S A GUARD.
AND I TRUST HIS FIGHTING SPIRIT.

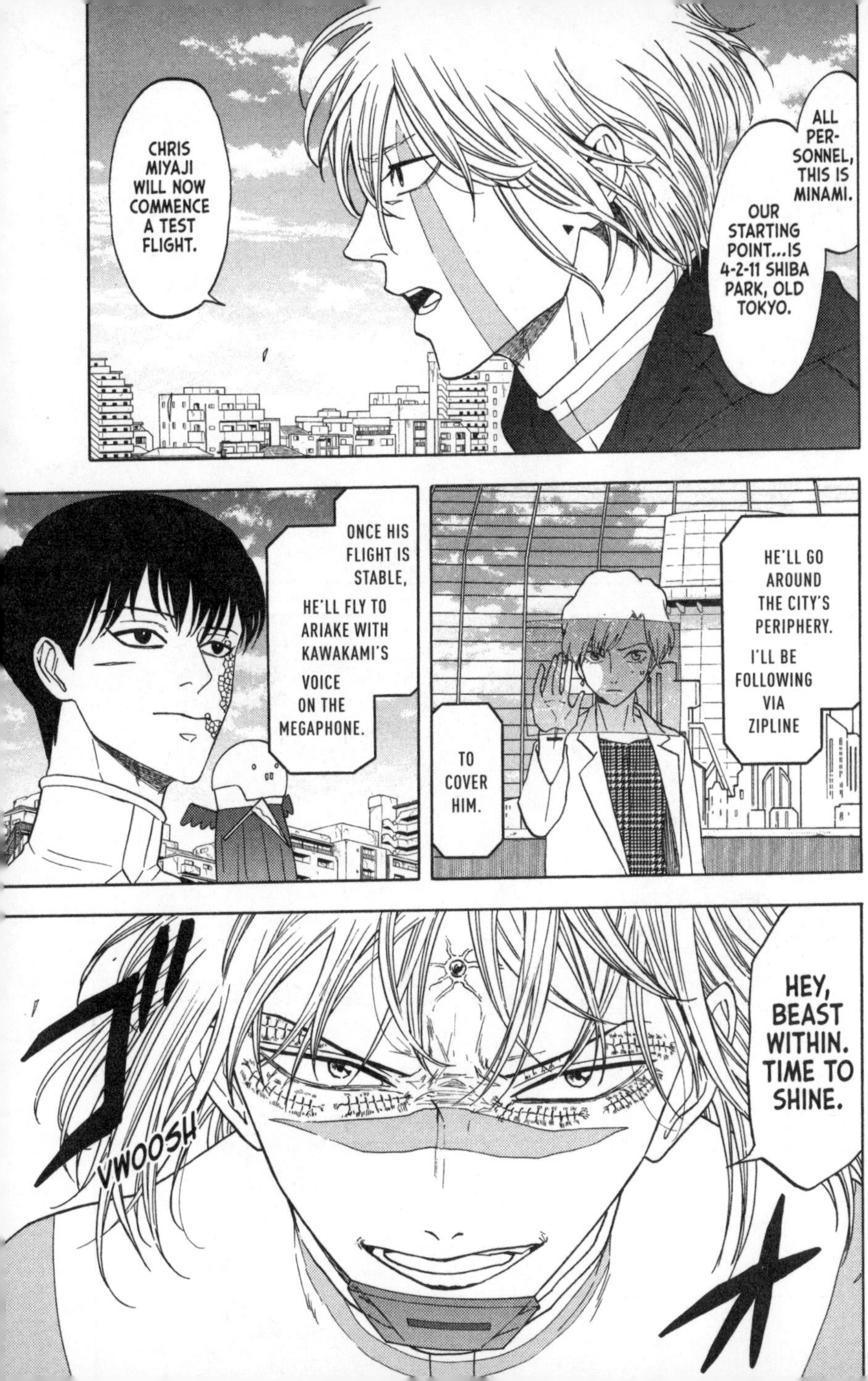
ALL PER-SONNEL, THIS IS MINAMI.
OUR STARTING POINT...IS 4-2-11 SHIBA PARK, OLD TOKYO.
CHRIS MIYAJI WILL NOW COMMENCE A TEST FLIGHT.
HE'LL GO AROUND THE CITY'S PERIPHERY.
I'LL BE FOLLOWING VIA ZIPLINE
TO COVER HIM.
ONCE HIS FLIGHT IS STABLE,
HE'LL FLY TO ARIAKE WITH KAWAKAMI'S
VOICE ON THE MEGAPHONE.
HEY, BEAST WITHIN. TIME TO SHINE.
VWOOSH

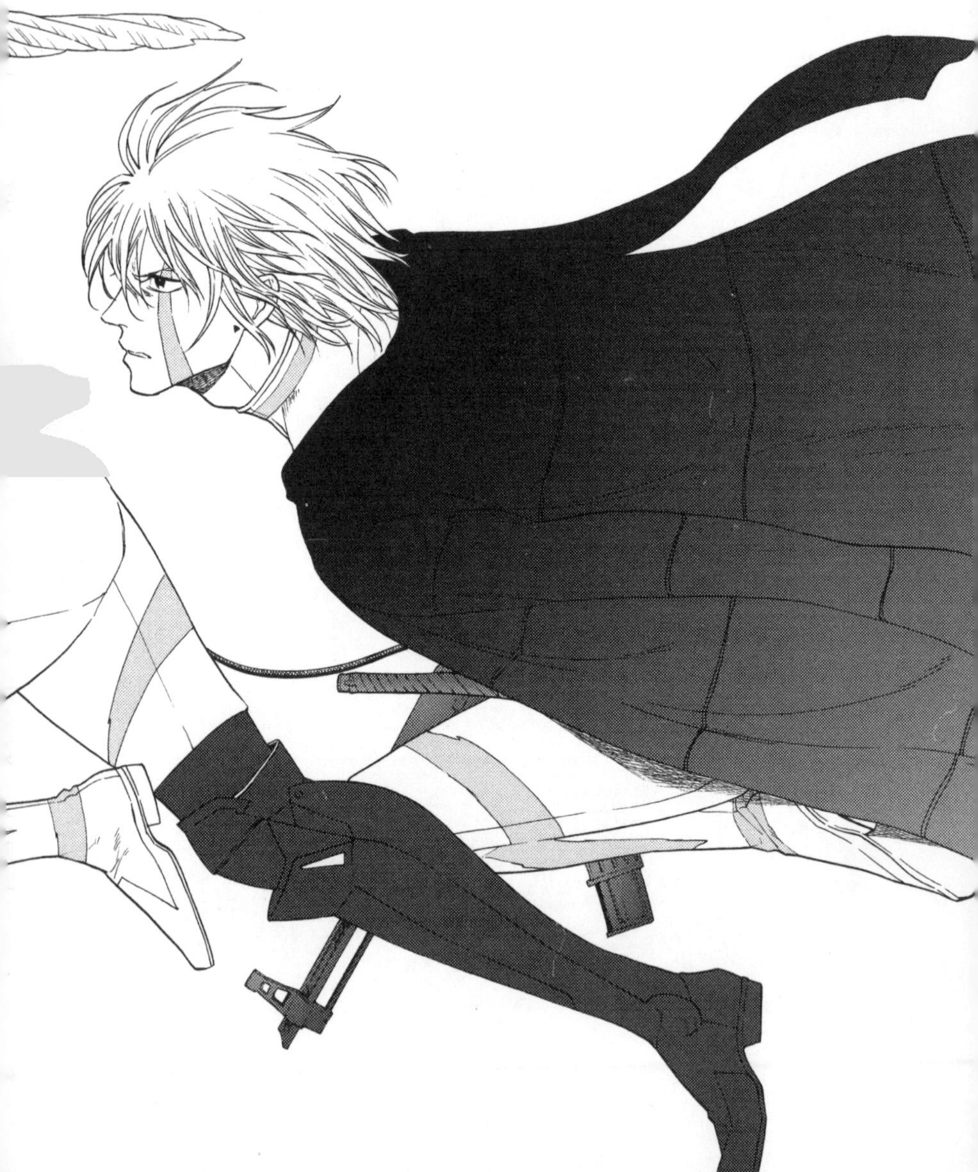

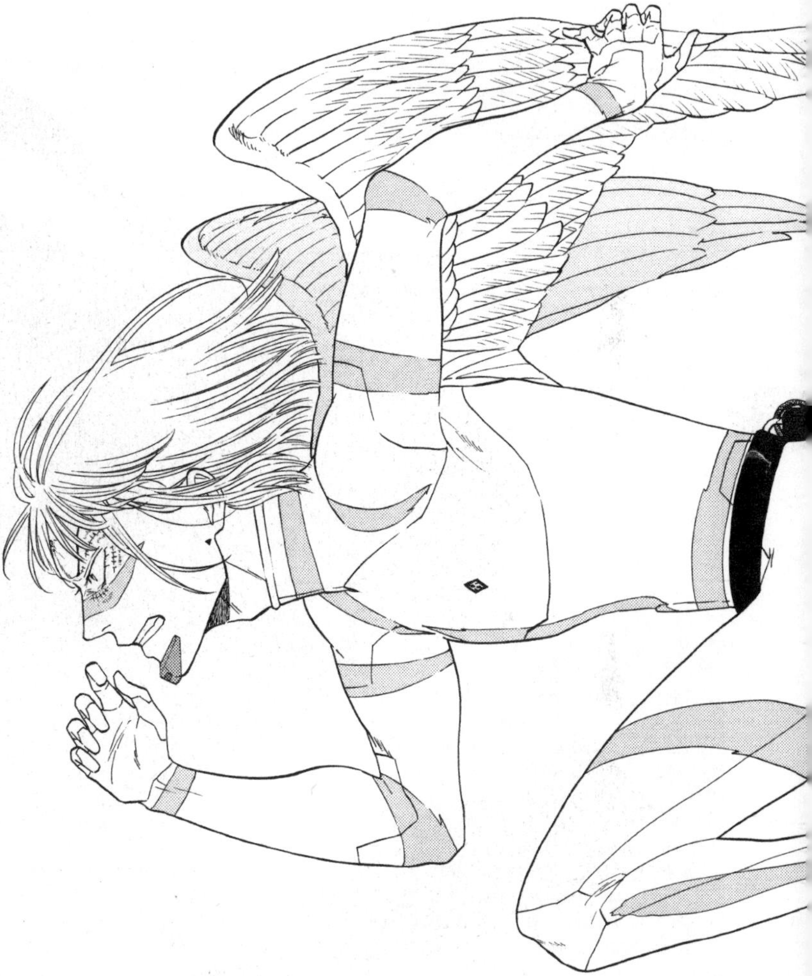

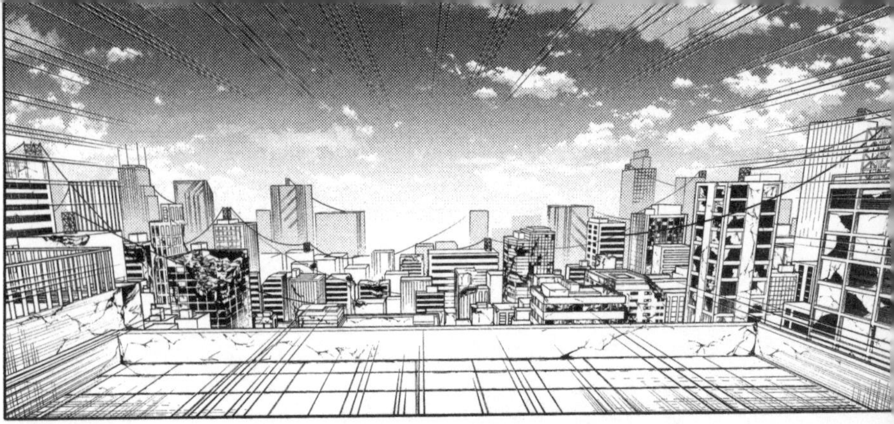
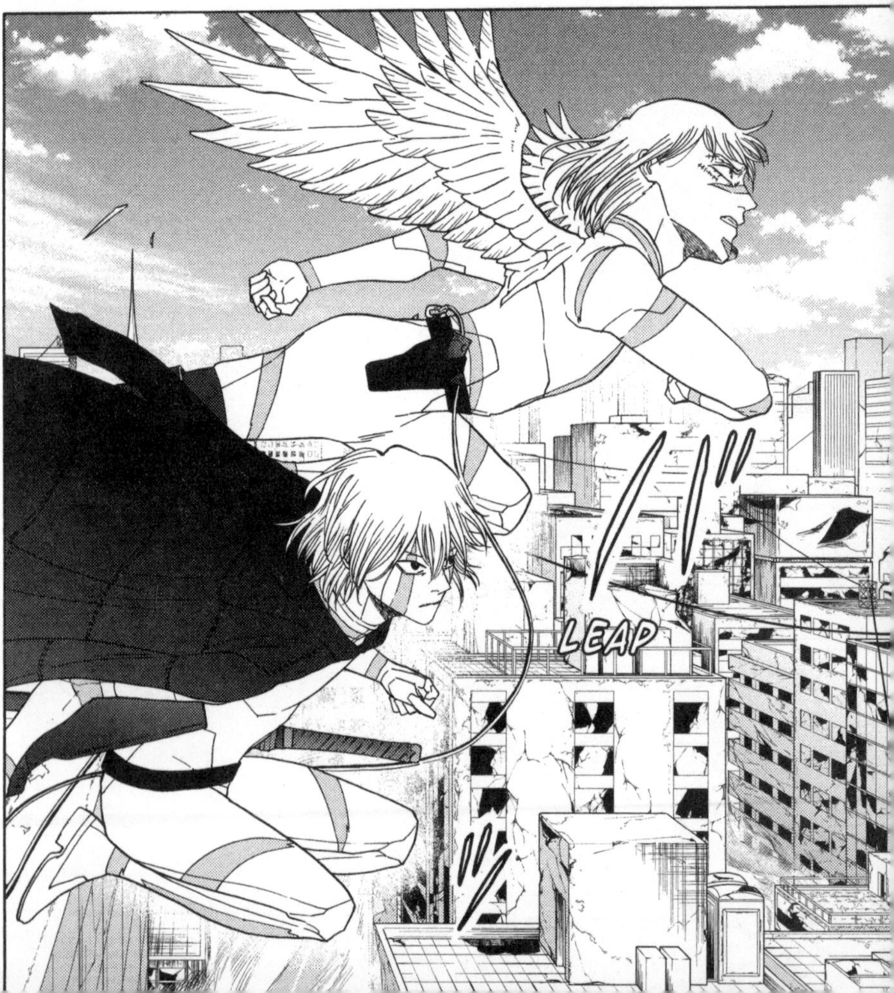
LEAP

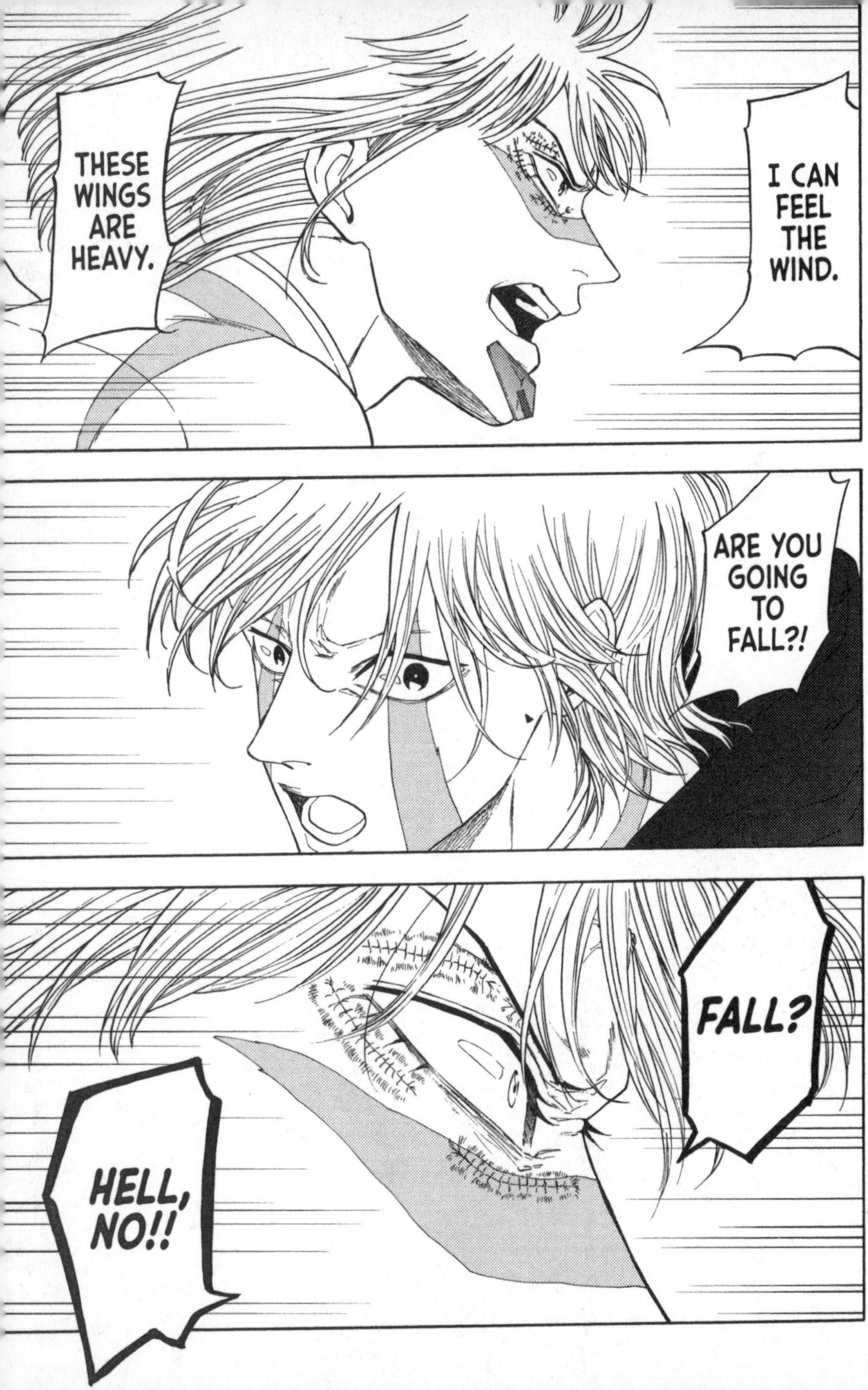
I CAN FEEL THE WIND.
THESE WINGS ARE HEAVY.
ARE YOU GOING TO FALL?!
FALL?
HELL, NO!!

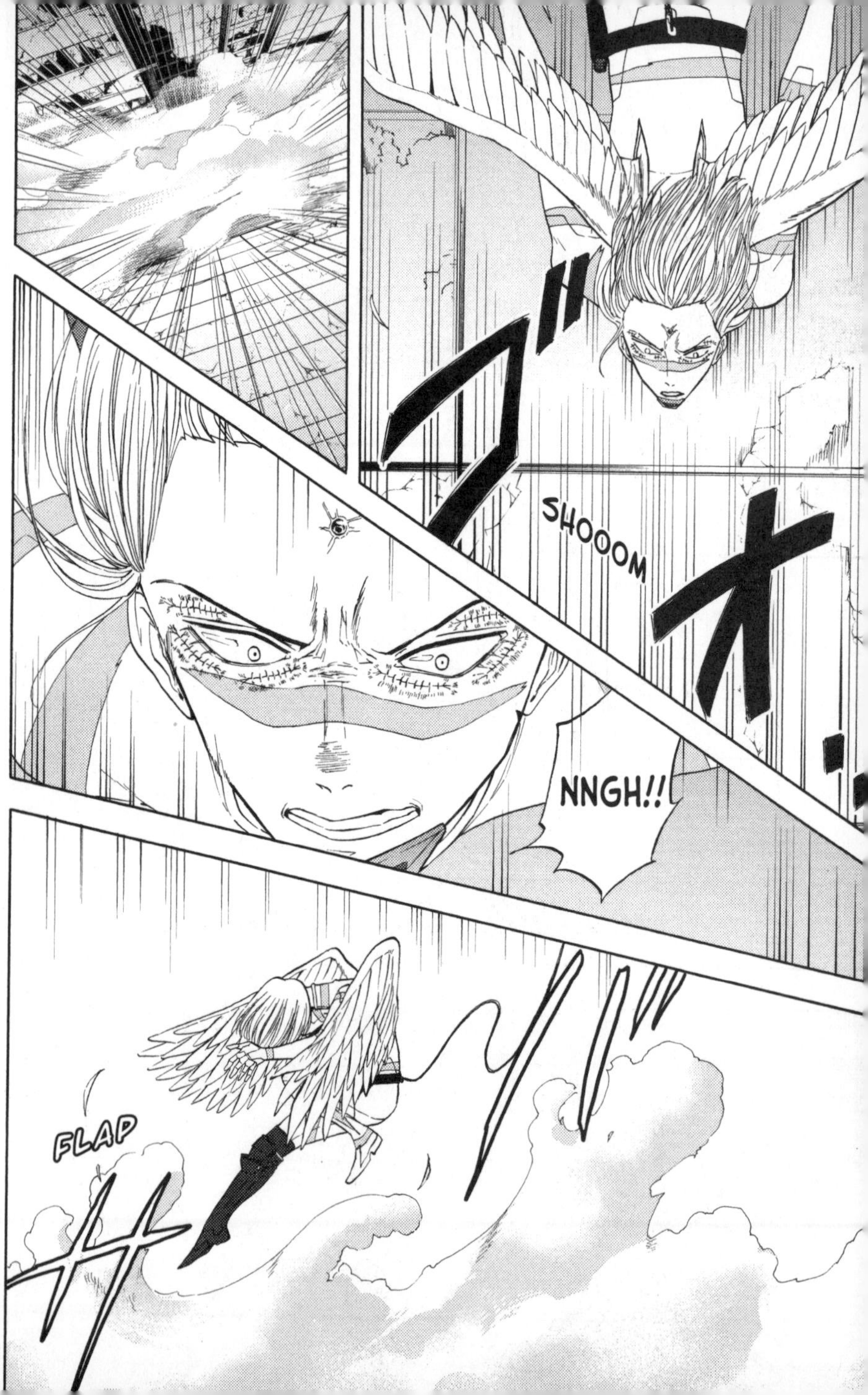
SHOOOM
NNGH!!
FLAP

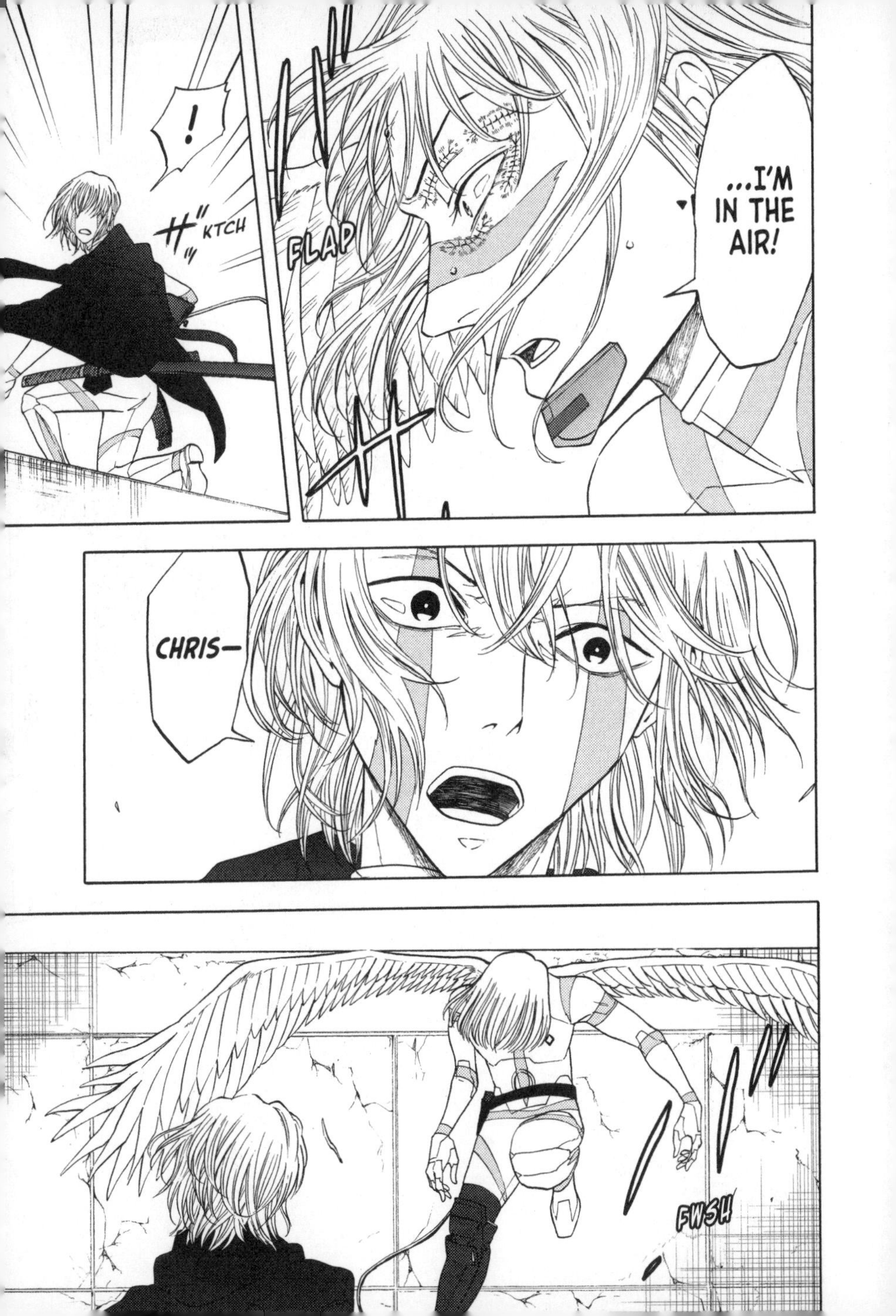
...I'M IN THE AIR!
FLAP
!
KTCH
CHRIS—
FWSH

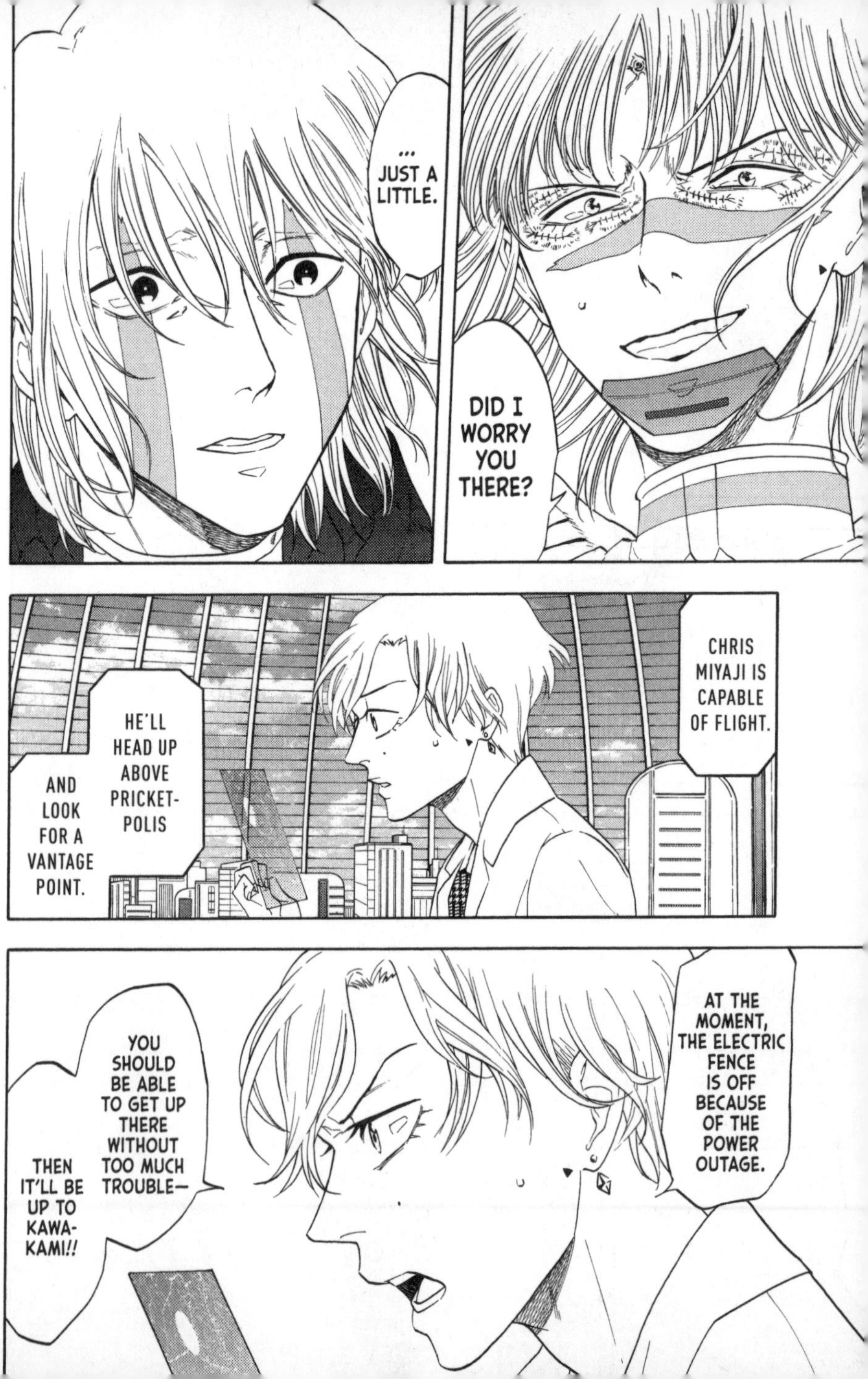
DID I WORRY YOU THERE?
... JUST A LITTLE.
CHRIS MIYAJI IS CAPABLE OF FLIGHT.
HE'LL HEAD UP ABOVE PRICKETPOLIS
AND LOOK FOR A VANTAGE POINT.
AT THE MOMENT, THE ELECTRIC FENCE IS OFF BECAUSE OF THE POWER OUTAGE.
YOU SHOULD BE ABLE TO GET UP THERE WITHOUT TOO MUCH TROUBLE—
THEN IT'LL BE UP TO KAWAKAMI!!

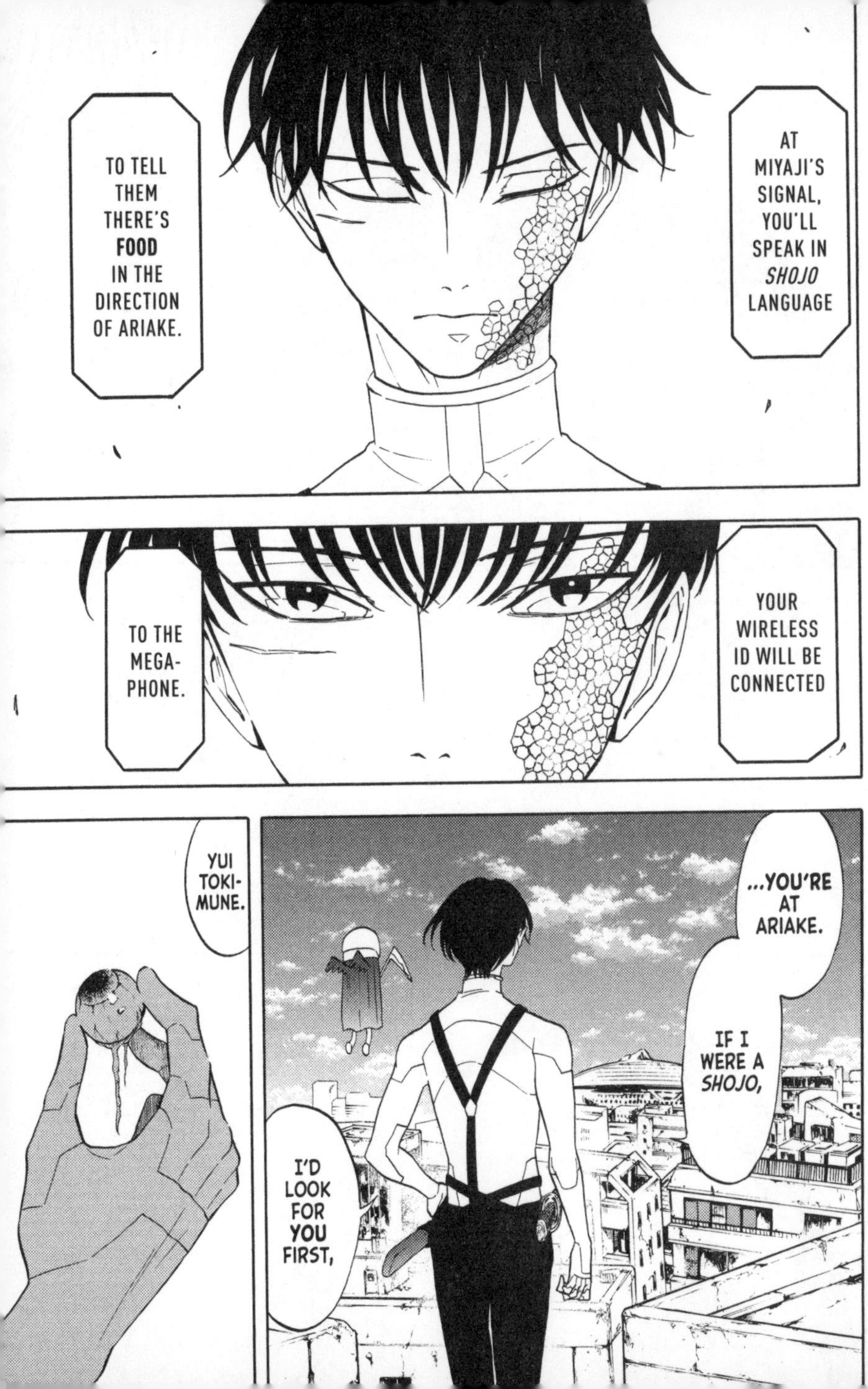
AT MIYAJI'S SIGNAL, YOU'LL SPEAK IN *SHOJO* LANGUAGE
TO TELL THEM THERE'S **FOOD** IN THE DIRECTION OF ARIAKE.
YOUR WIRELESS ID WILL BE CONNECTED
TO THE MEGA-PHONE.
...YOU'RE AT ARIAKE.
IF I WERE A *SHOJO*,
I'D LOOK FOR **YOU** FIRST,
YUI TOKI-MUNE.

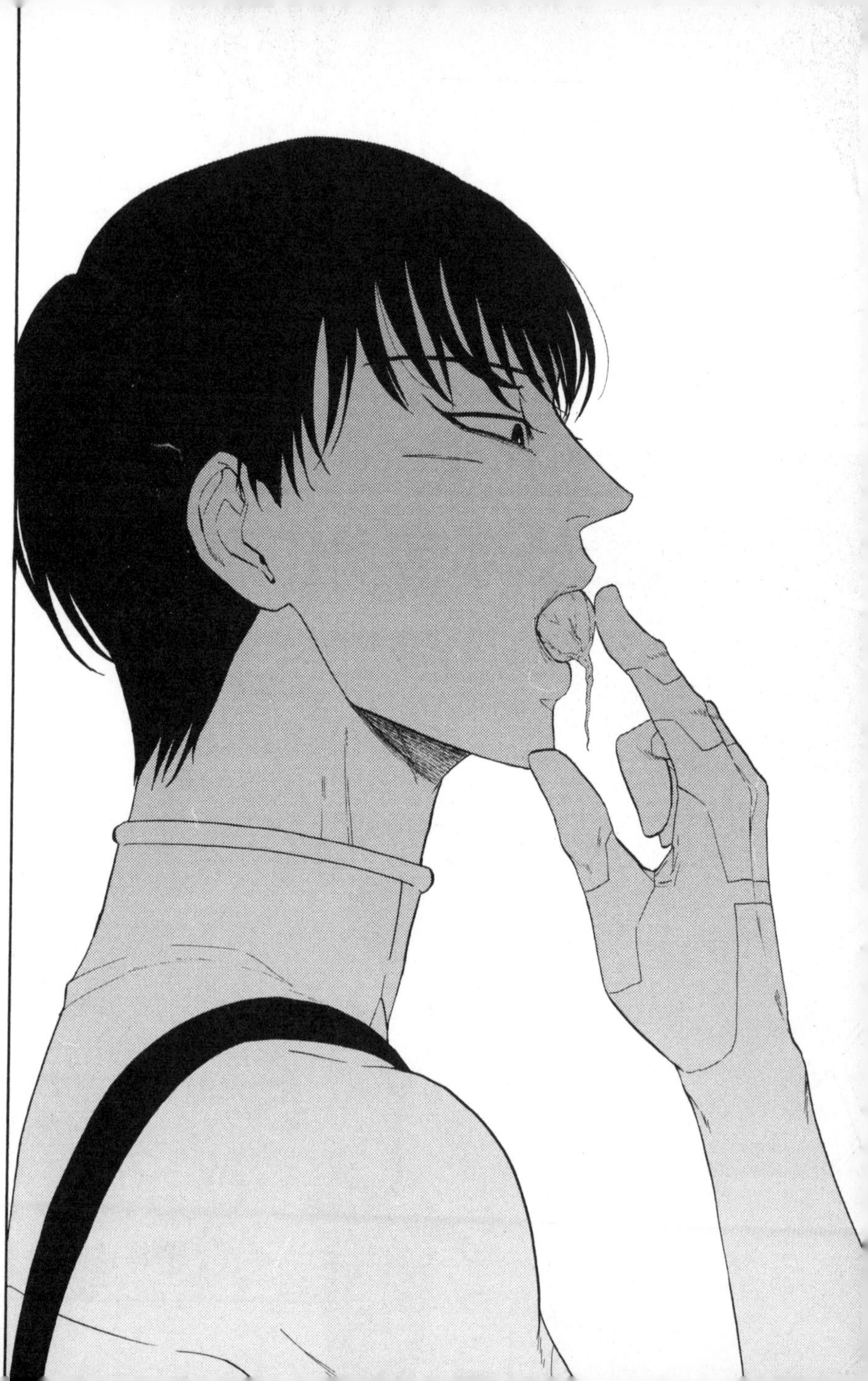

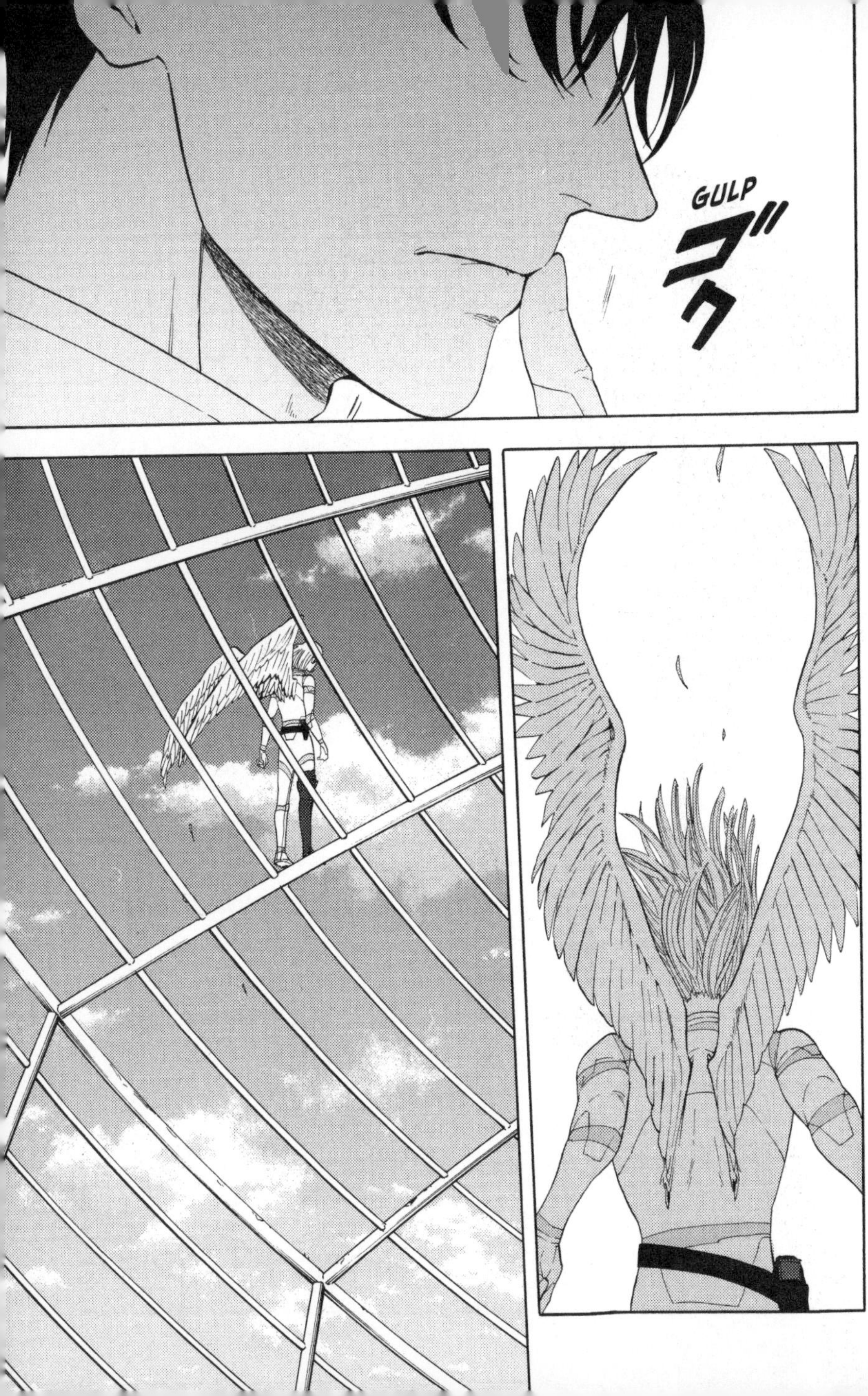
GULP
ゴク

ALL RIGHT, KAWA-KAMI.

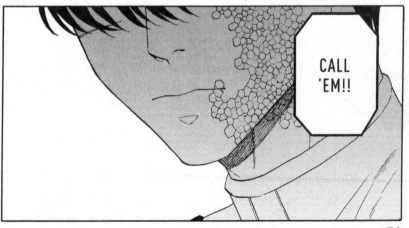

CALL 'EM!!

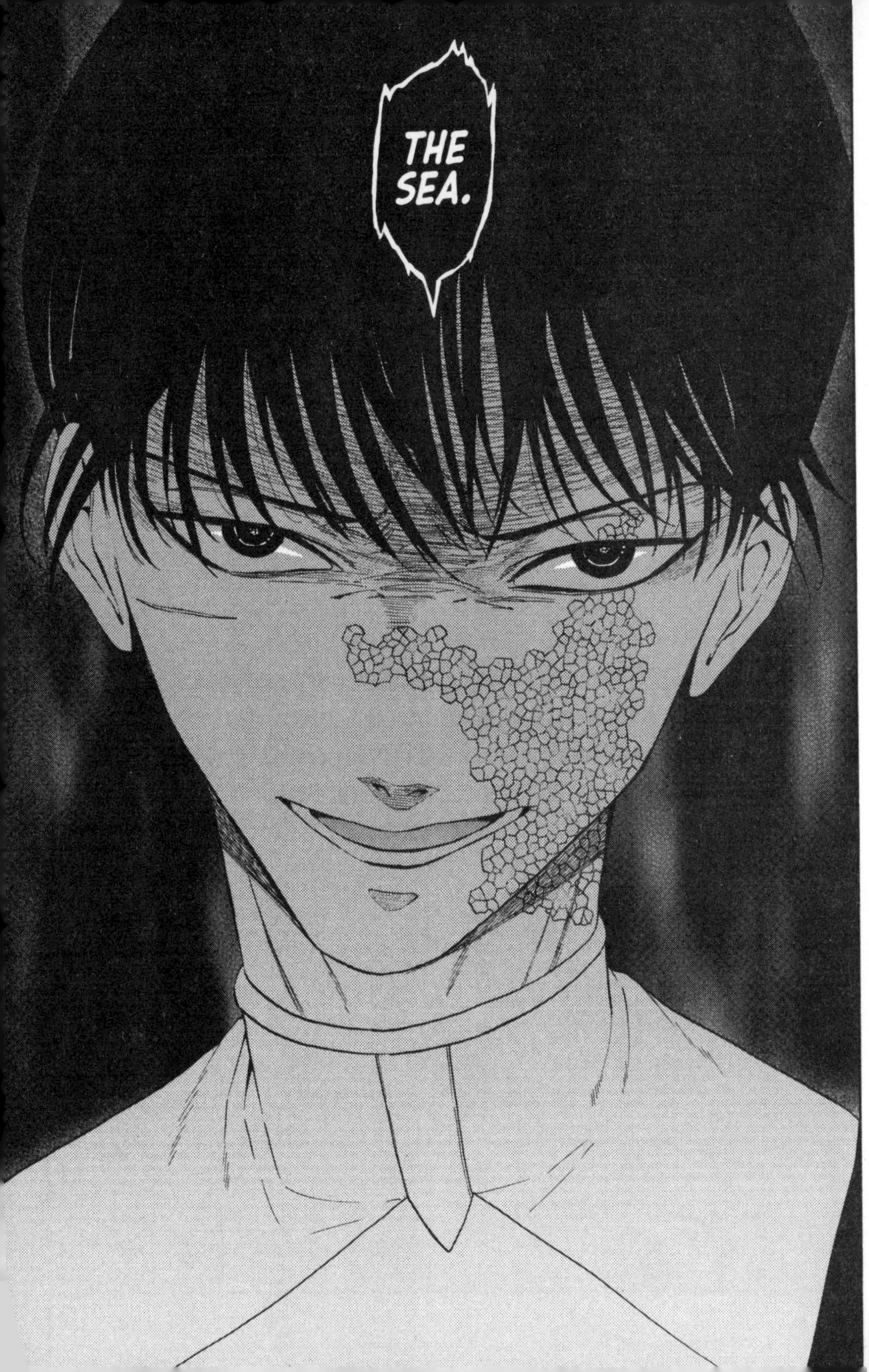
THE SEA.

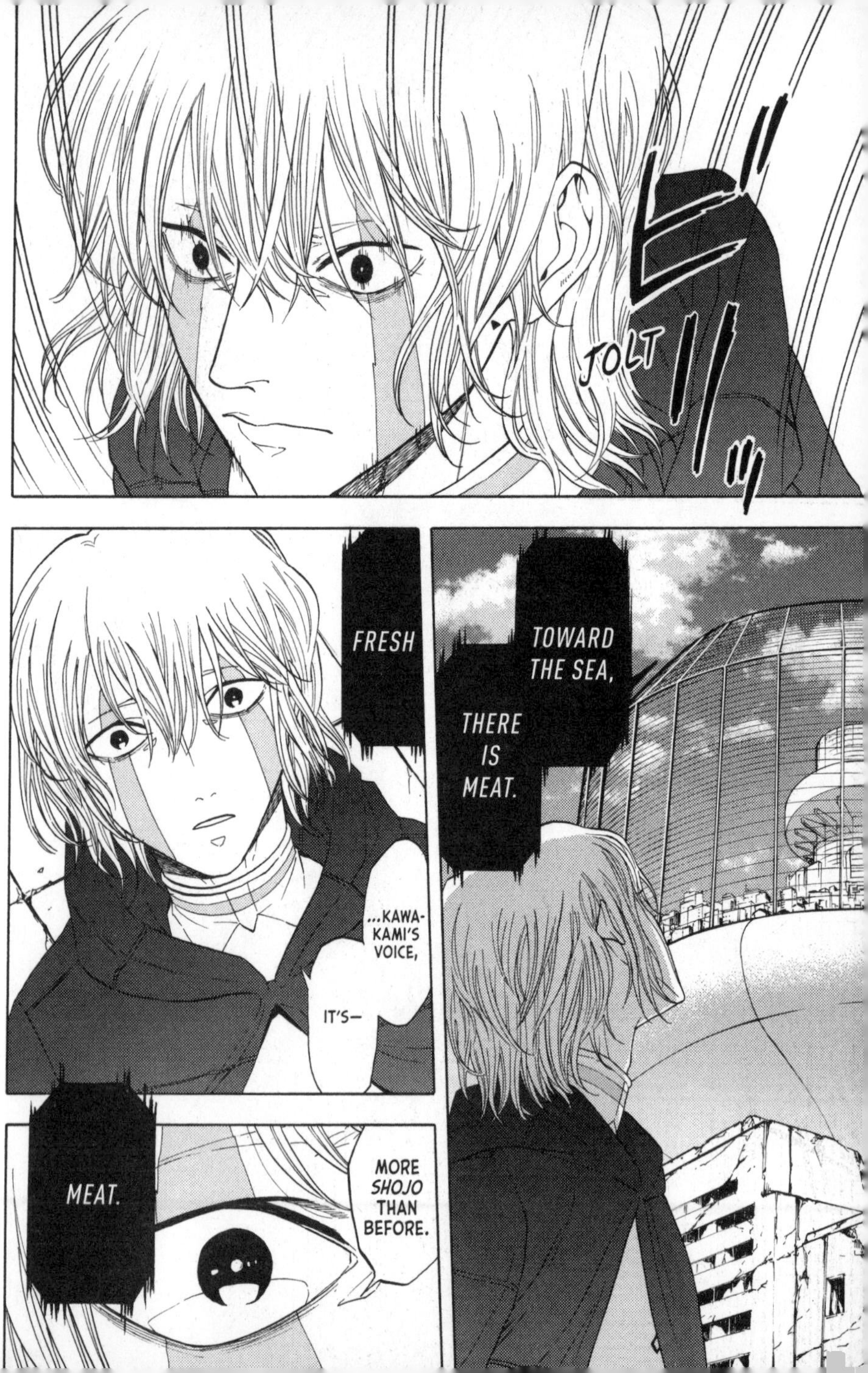
JOLT
TOWARD THE SEA,
THERE IS MEAT.
FRESH
...KAWA-KAMI'S VOICE,
IT'S—
MEAT.
MORE SHOJO THAN BEFORE.

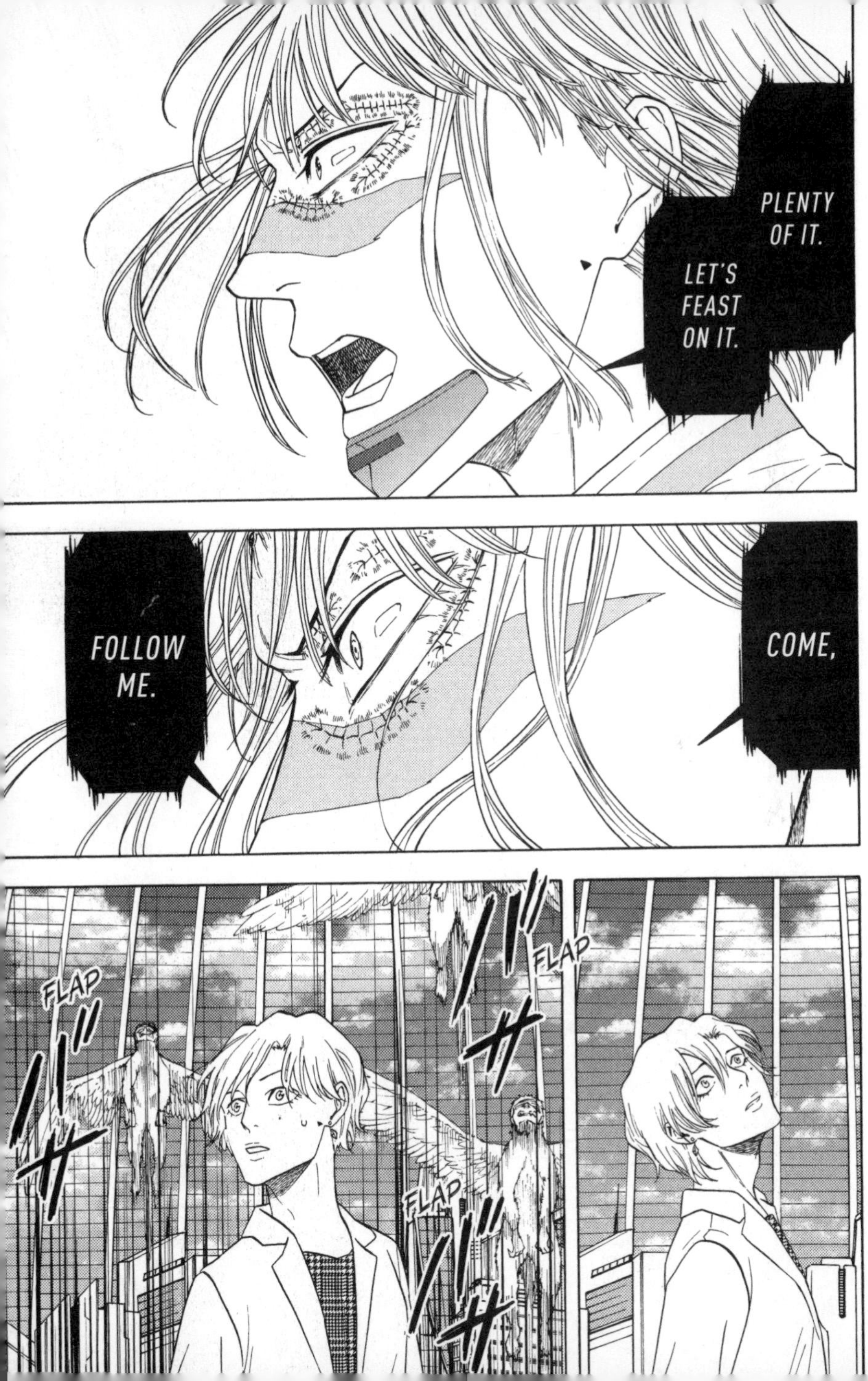
PLENTY OF IT.
LET'S FEAST ON IT.
COME,
FOLLOW ME.
FLAP
FLAP
FLAP

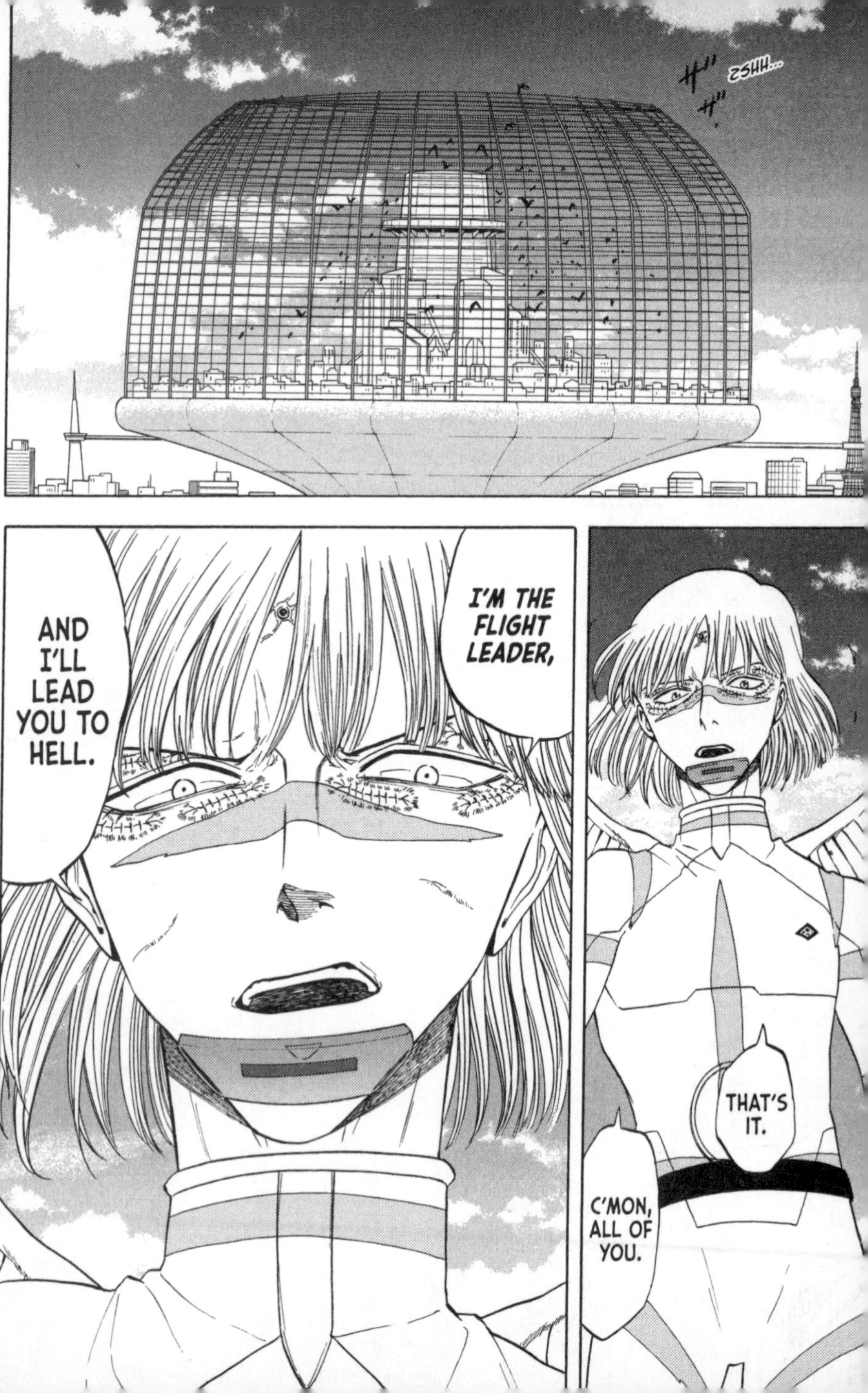
ZSHH...
THAT'S IT.
C'MON, ALL OF YOU.
I'M THE FLIGHT LEADER,
AND I'LL LEAD YOU TO HELL.

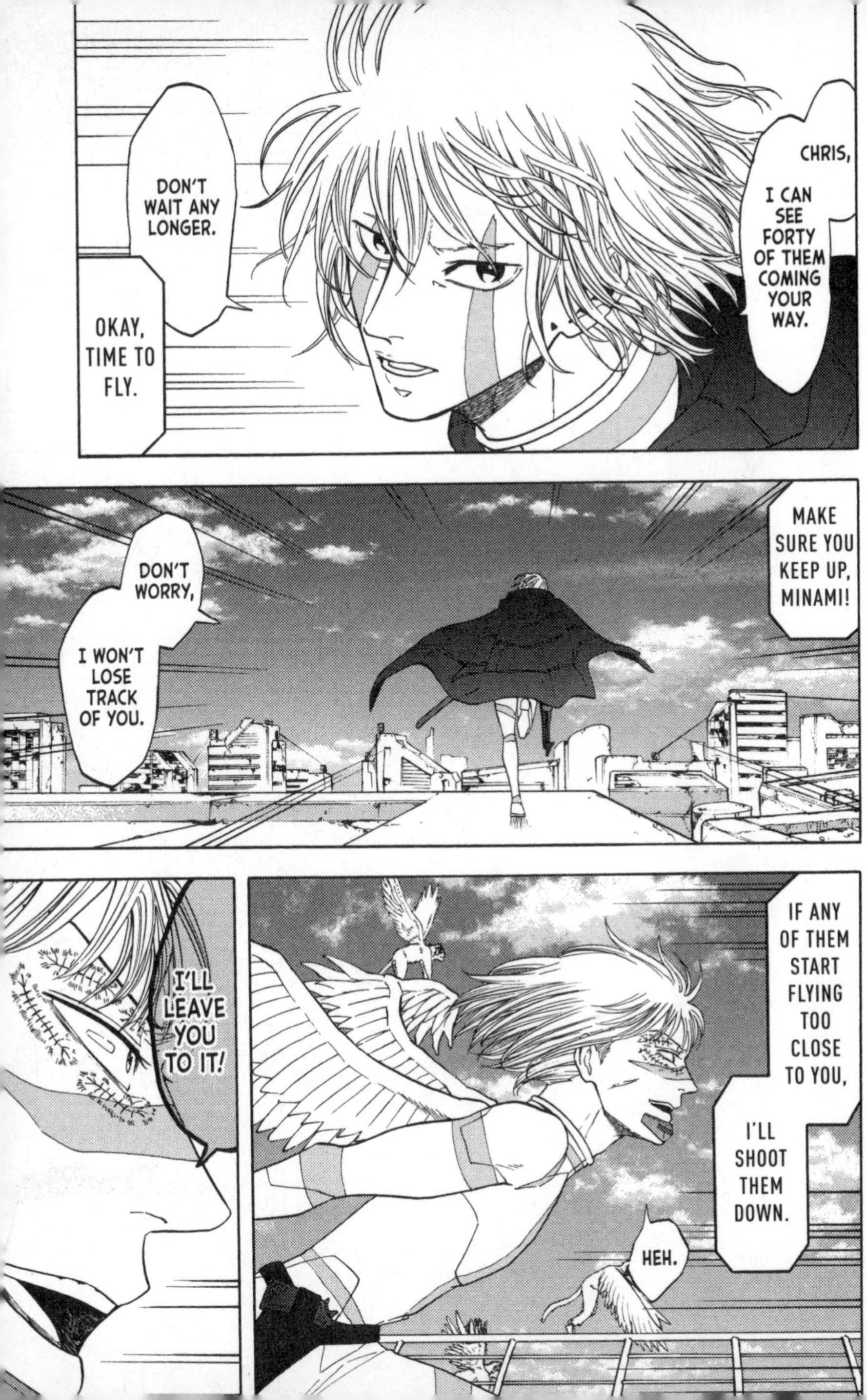
CHRIS,
I CAN SEE FORTY OF THEM COMING YOUR WAY.
DON'T WAIT ANY LONGER.
OKAY, TIME TO FLY.
MAKE SURE YOU KEEP UP, MINAMI!
DON'T WORRY,
I WON'T LOSE TRACK OF YOU.
IF ANY OF THEM START FLYING TOO CLOSE TO YOU,
I'LL SHOOT THEM DOWN.
HEH.
I'LL LEAVE YOU TO IT!

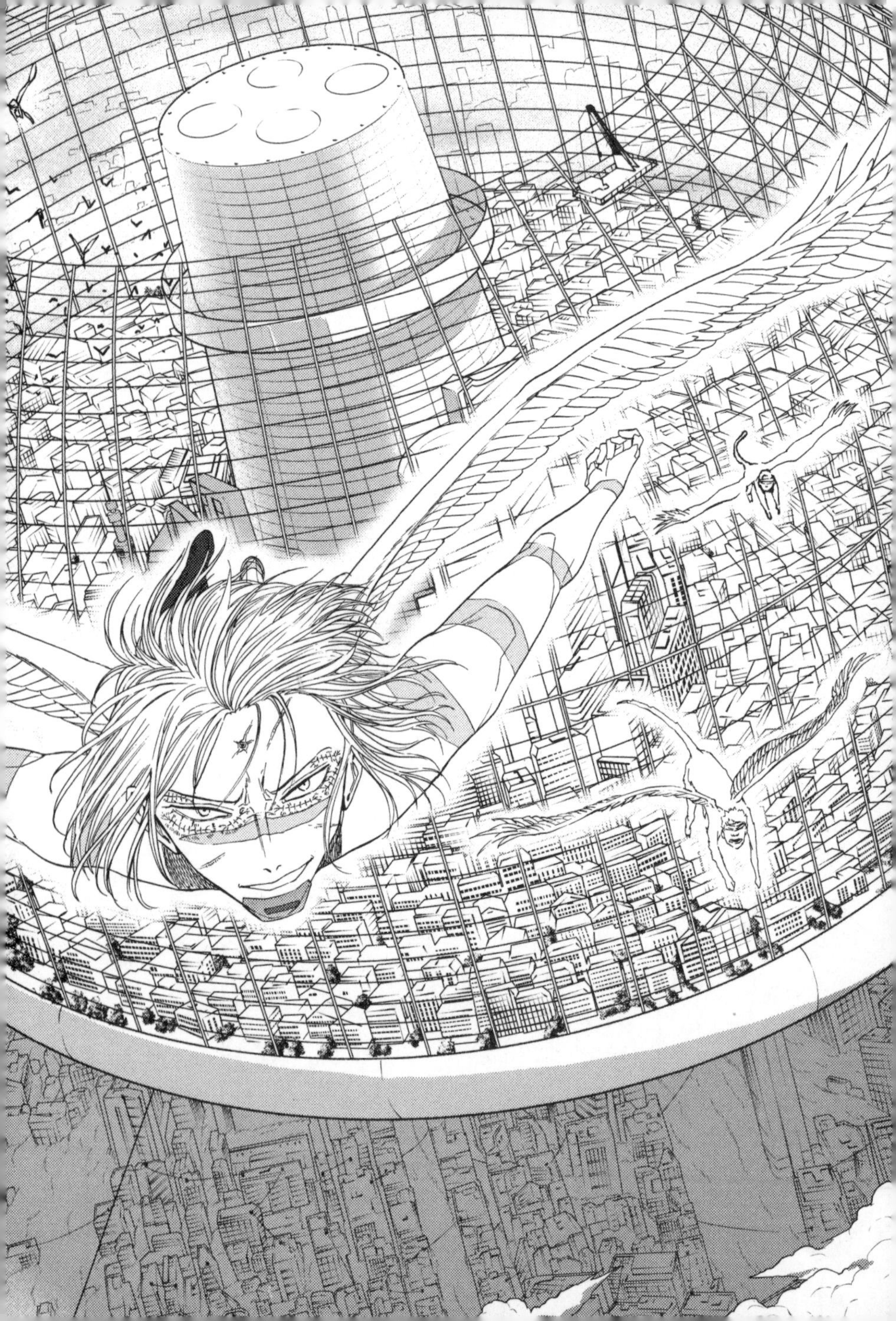

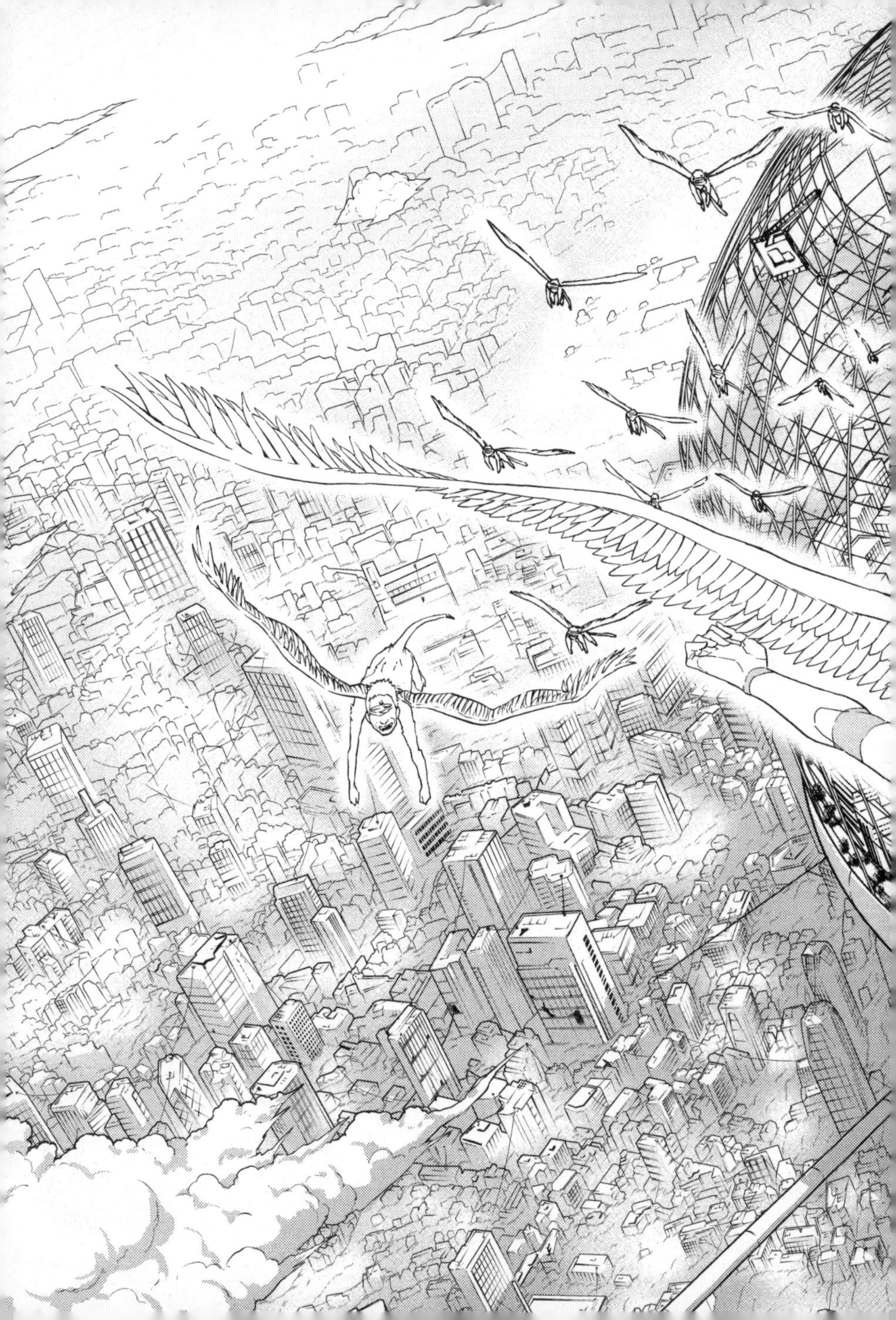

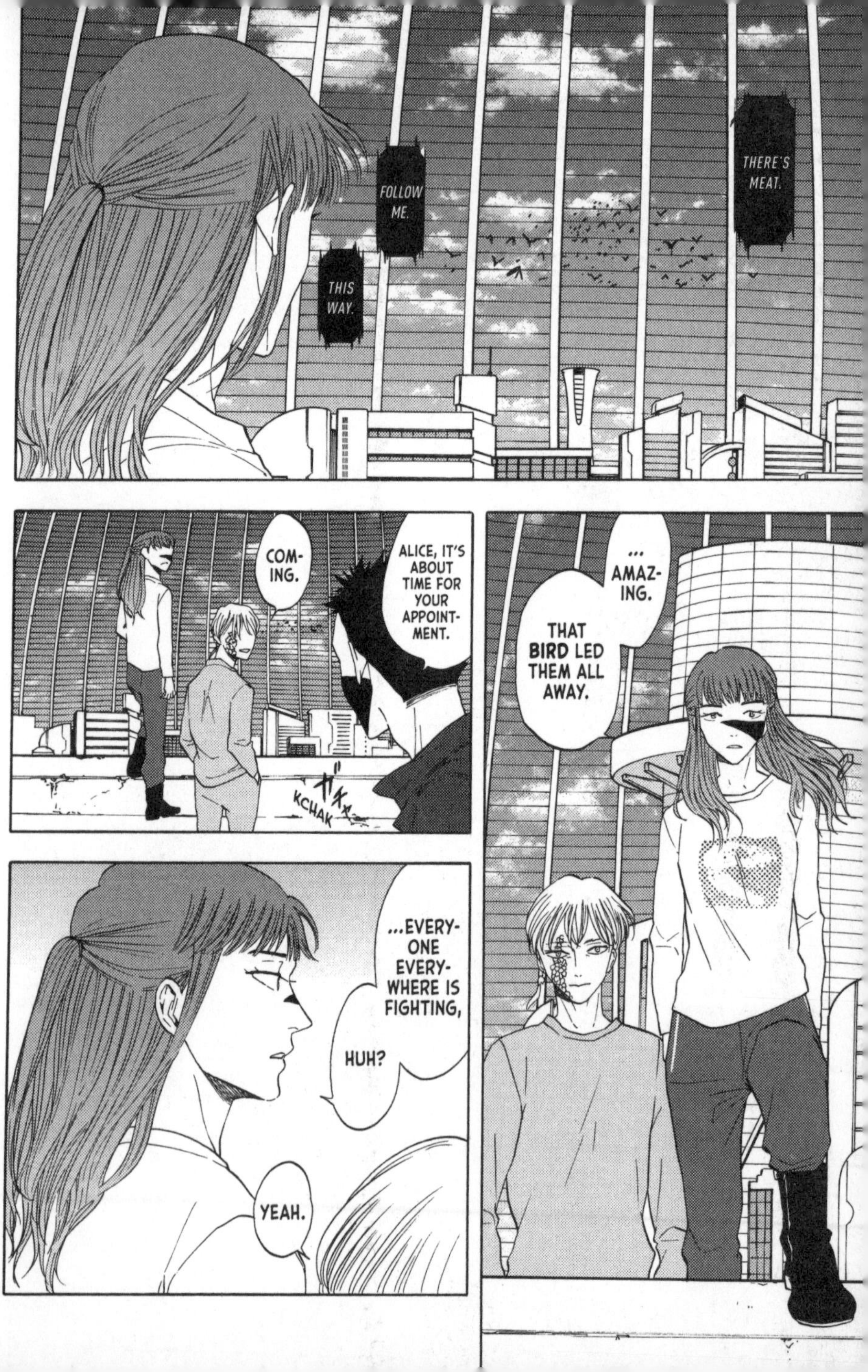
THERE'S MEAT.
FOLLOW ME.
THIS WAY.
...AMAZ-ING.
THAT BIRD LED THEM ALL AWAY.
ALICE, IT'S ABOUT TIME FOR YOUR APPOINT-MENT.
COM-ING.
KCHAK
...EVERY-ONE EVERY-WHERE IS FIGHTING,
HUH?
YEAH.

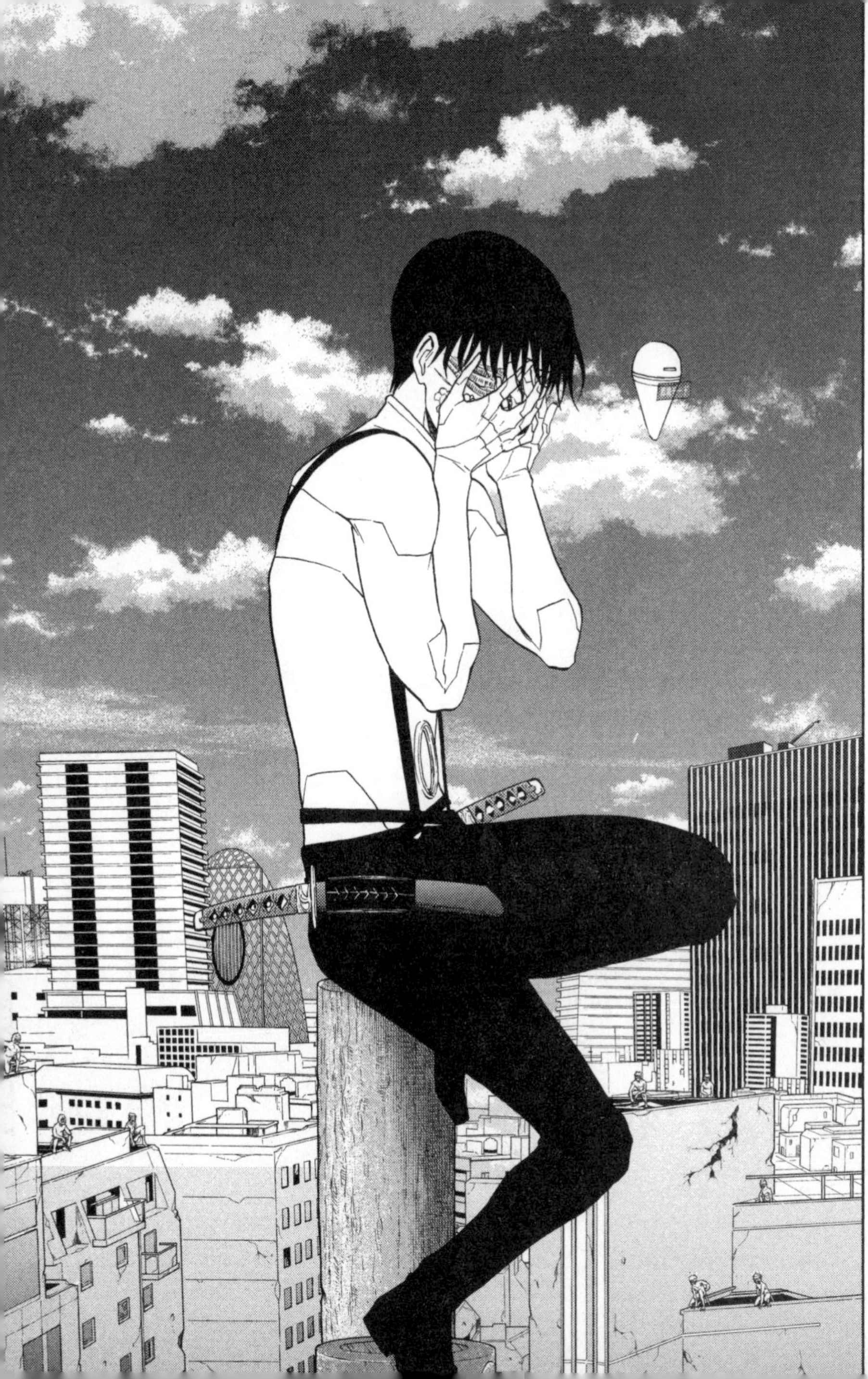

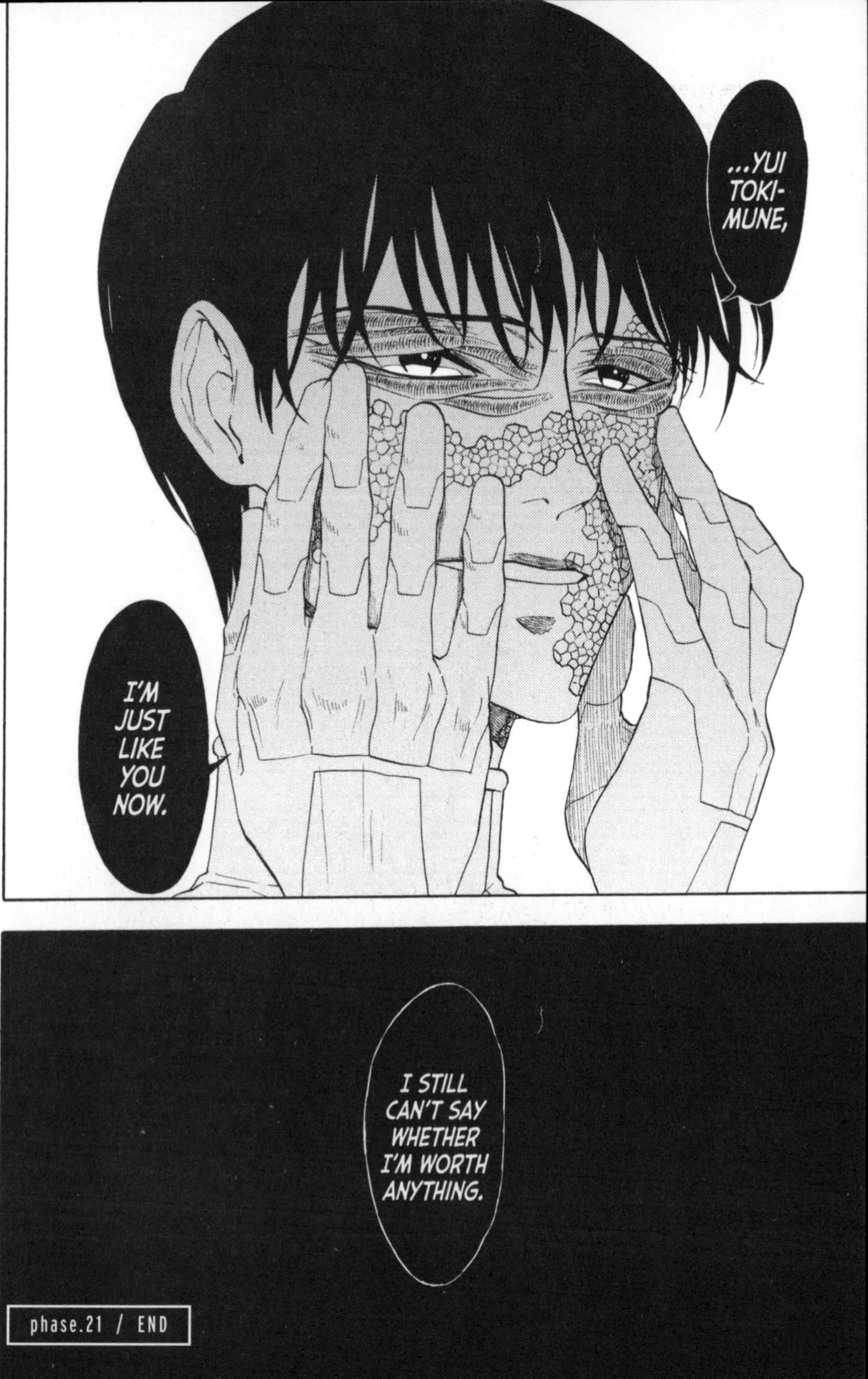
...YUI TOKI-MUNE,
I'M JUST LIKE YOU NOW.
I STILL CAN'T SAY WHETHER I'M WORTH ANYTHING.
phase.21 / END

phase.22 The Wish to Protect

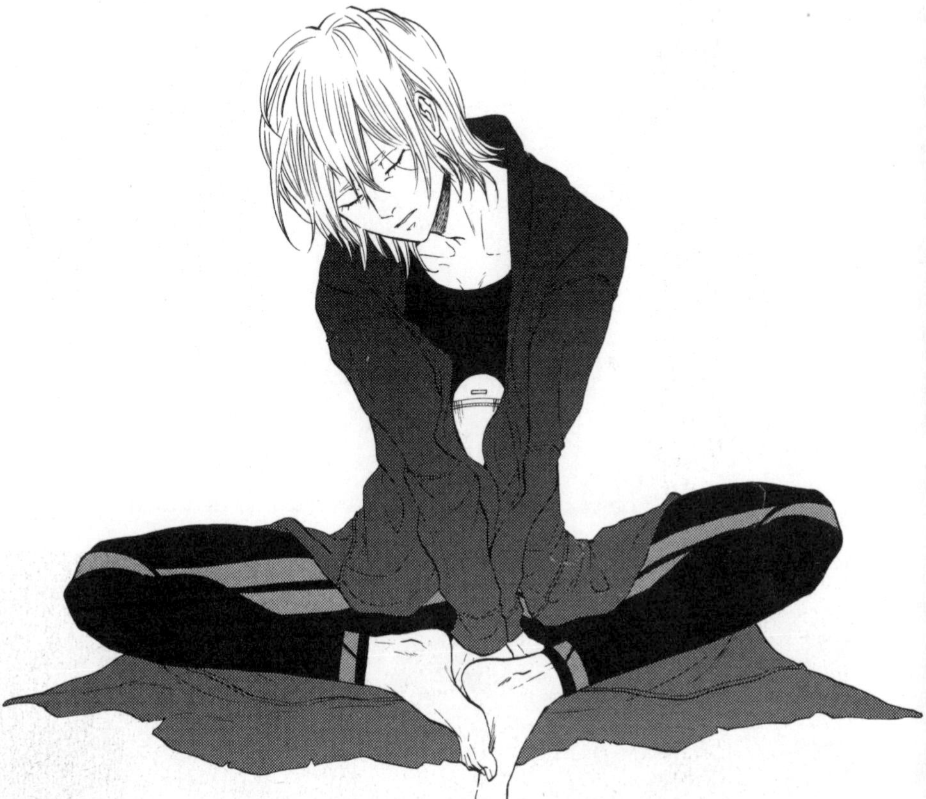

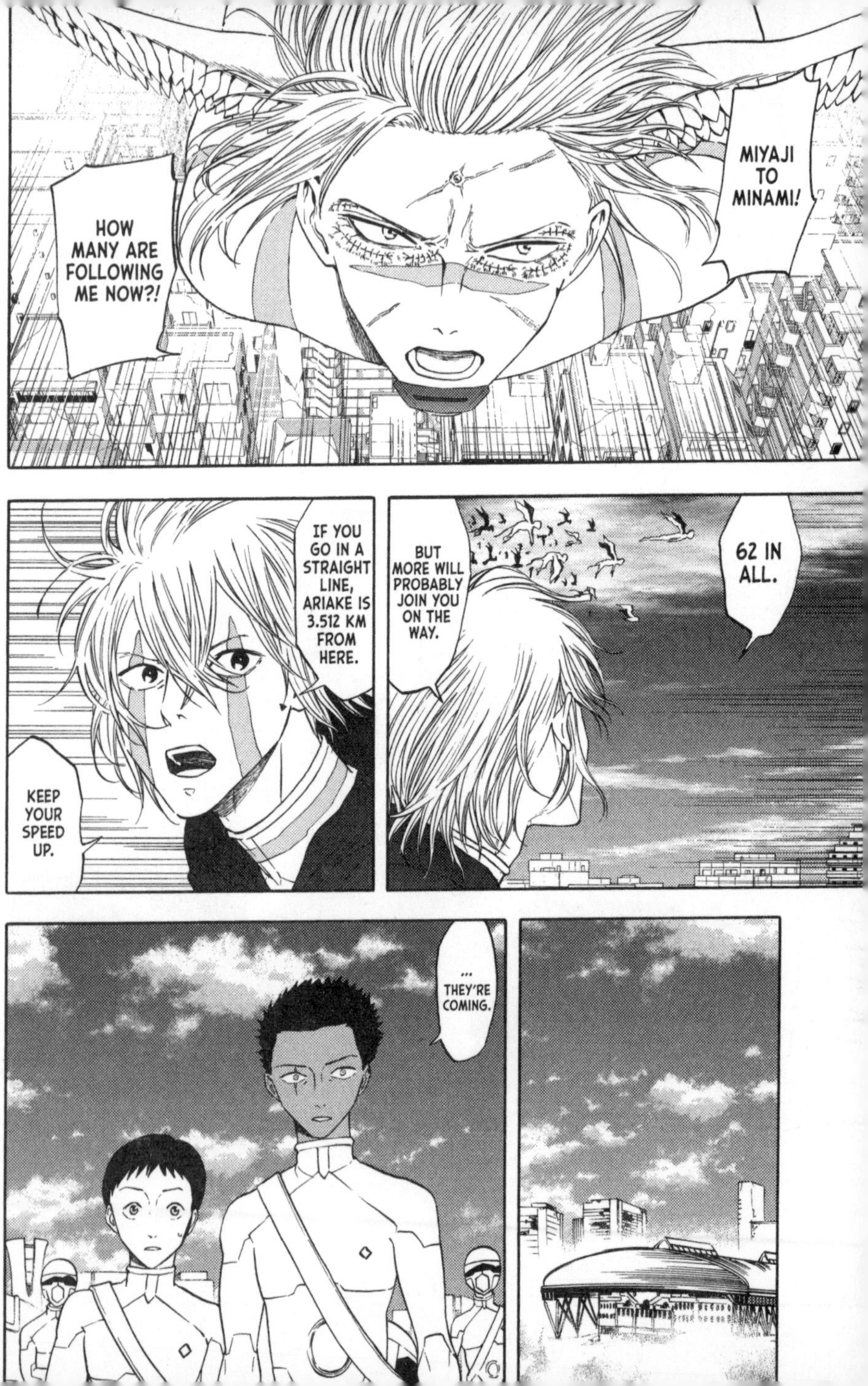
MIYAJI TO MINAMI!
HOW MANY ARE FOLLOWING ME NOW?!
62 IN ALL.
BUT MORE WILL PROBABLY JOIN YOU ON THE WAY.
IF YOU GO IN A STRAIGHT LINE, ARIAKE IS 3.512 KM FROM HERE.
KEEP YOUR SPEED UP.
... THEY'RE COMING.

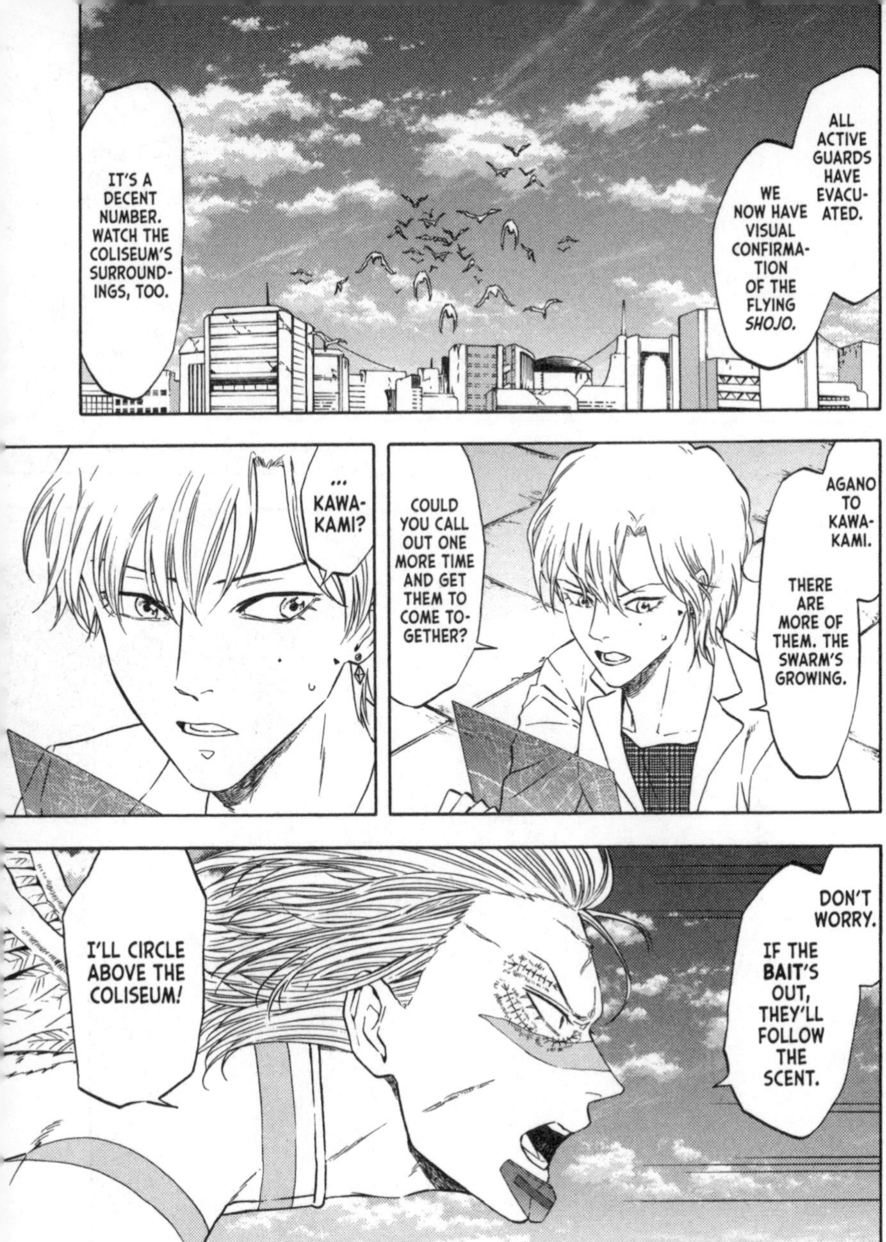
ALL ACTIVE GUARDS HAVE EVACU-ATED.
WE NOW HAVE VISUAL CONFIRMA-TION OF THE FLYING *SHOJO.*
IT'S A DECENT NUMBER. WATCH THE COLISEUM'S SURROUND-INGS, TOO.
AGANO TO KAWA-KAMI.
THERE ARE MORE OF THEM. THE SWARM'S GROWING.
COULD YOU CALL OUT ONE MORE TIME AND GET THEM TO COME TO-GETHER?
... KAWA-KAMI?
DON'T WORRY.
IF THE **BAIT**'S OUT, THEY'LL FOLLOW THE SCENT.
I'LL CIRCLE ABOVE THE COLISEUM!

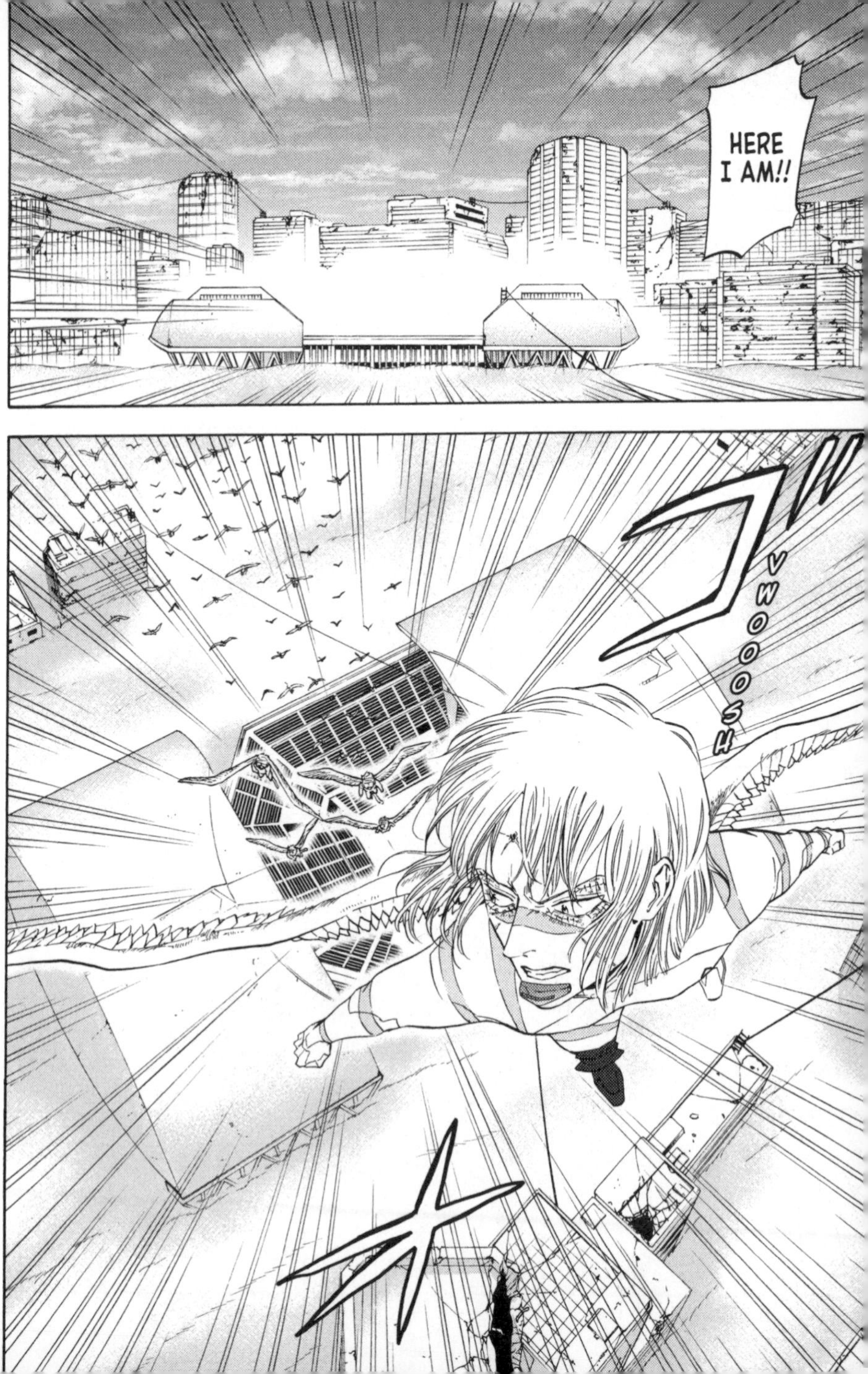
HERE I AM!!
VWOOOOSH

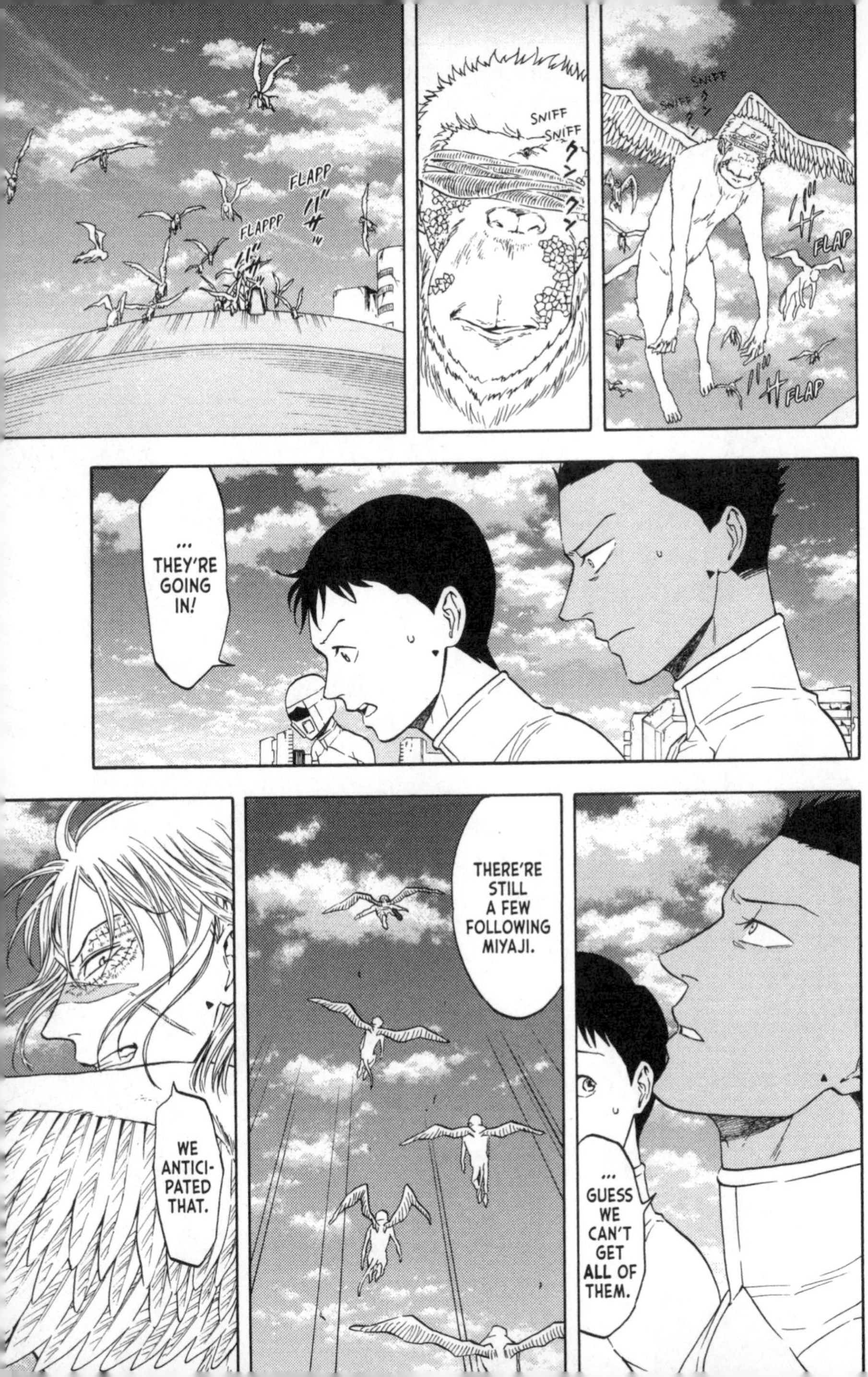
SNIFF
SNIFF
FLAP
FLAP
SNIFF
SNIFF
FLAPP
FLAPP
... THEY'RE GOING IN!
... GUESS WE CAN'T GET ALL OF THEM.
THERE'RE STILL A FEW FOLLOWING MIYAJI.
WE ANTICI-PATED THAT.

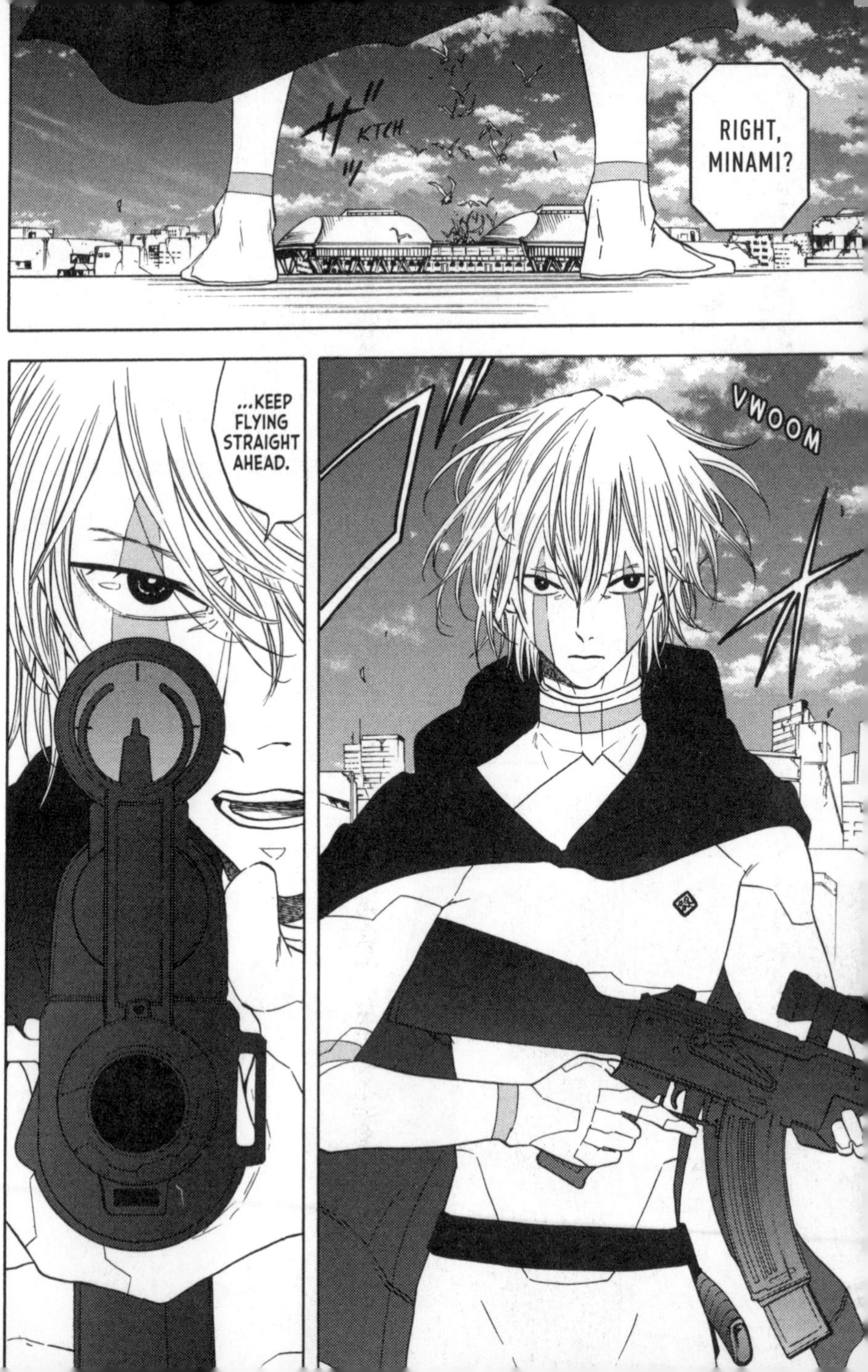
KTCH
RIGHT, MINAMI?
VWOOM
...KEEP FLYING STRAIGHT AHEAD.

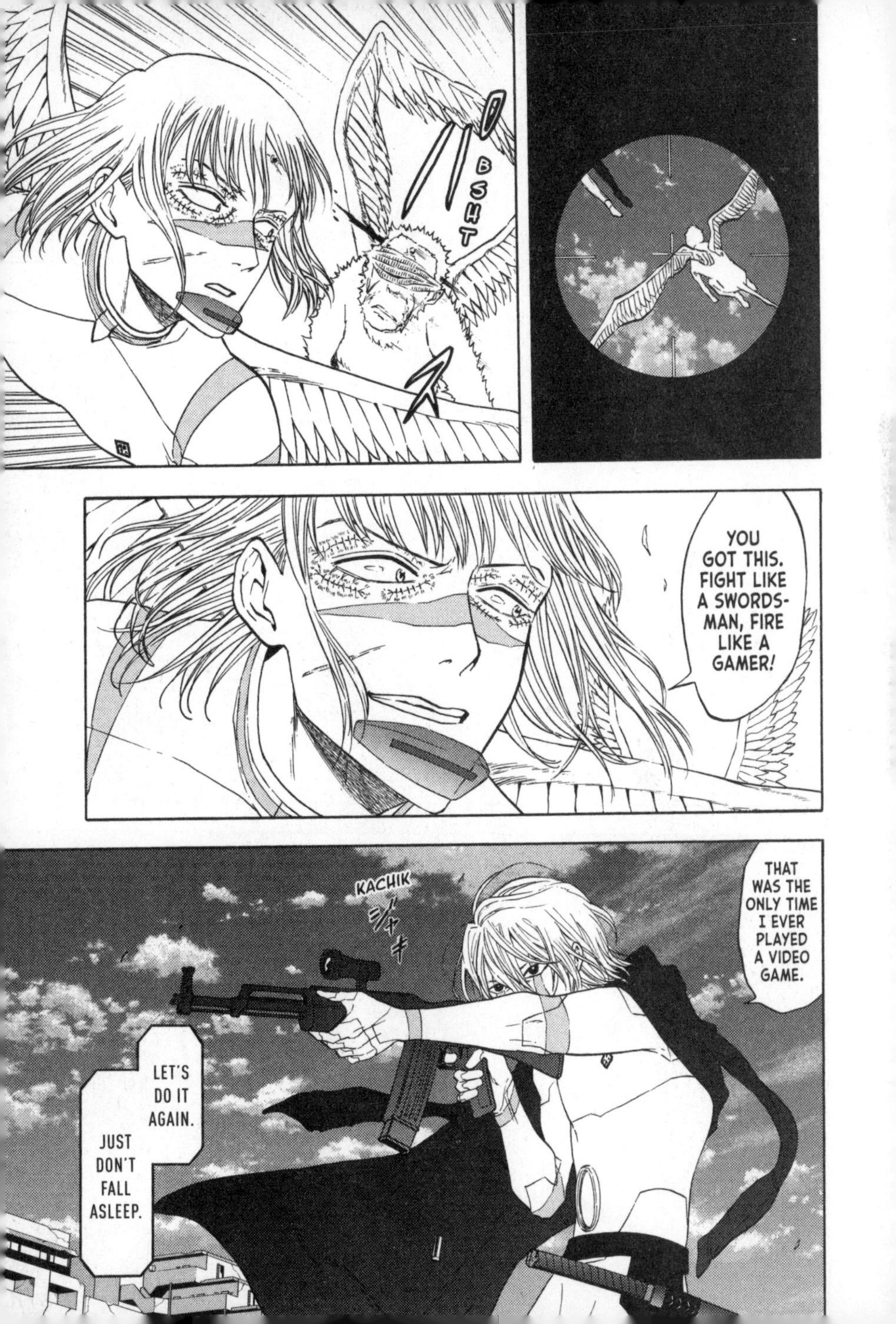
BSHT
YOU GOT THIS. FIGHT LIKE A SWORDS-MAN, FIRE LIKE A GAMER!
THAT WAS THE ONLY TIME I EVER PLAYED A VIDEO GAME.
KACHIK
ジャキ
LET'S DO IT AGAIN.
JUST DON'T FALL ASLEEP.

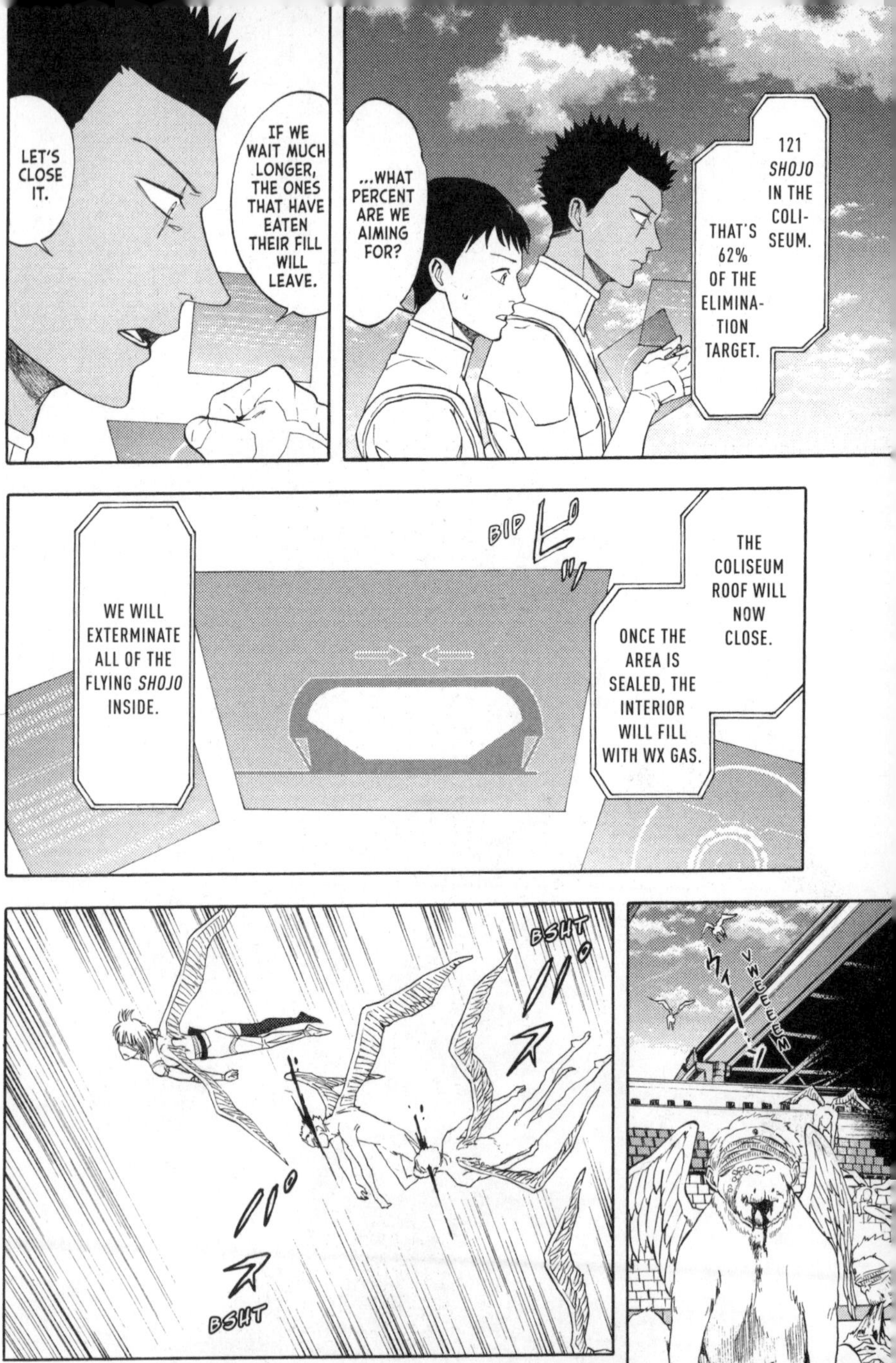
121 *SHOJO* IN THE COLISEUM.
THAT'S 62% OF THE ELIMINATION TARGET.
...WHAT PERCENT ARE WE AIMING FOR?
IF WE WAIT MUCH LONGER, THE ONES THAT HAVE EATEN THEIR FILL WILL LEAVE.
LET'S CLOSE IT.
BIP
THE COLISEUM ROOF WILL NOW CLOSE.
ONCE THE AREA IS SEALED, THE INTERIOR WILL FILL WITH WX GAS.
WE WILL EXTERMINATE ALL OF THE FLYING *SHOJO* INSIDE.
VWEEEEM
BSHT
BSHT

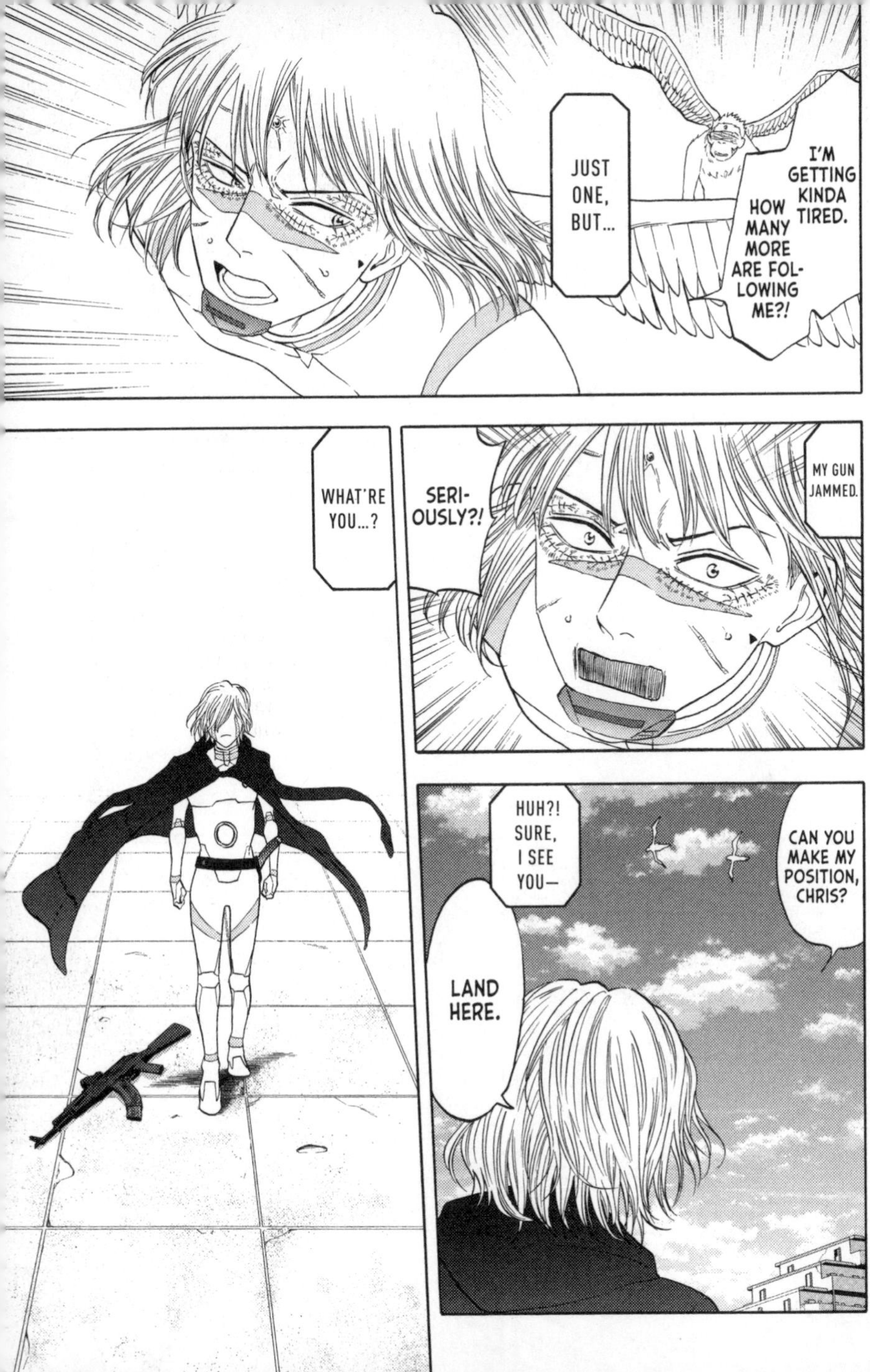
I'M GETTING KINDA TIRED.
HOW MANY MORE ARE FOL-LOWING ME?!
JUST ONE, BUT...
MY GUN JAMMED.
SERI-OUSLY?!
CAN YOU MAKE MY POSITION, CHRIS?
HUH?! SURE, I SEE YOU—
LAND HERE.
WHAT'RE YOU...?

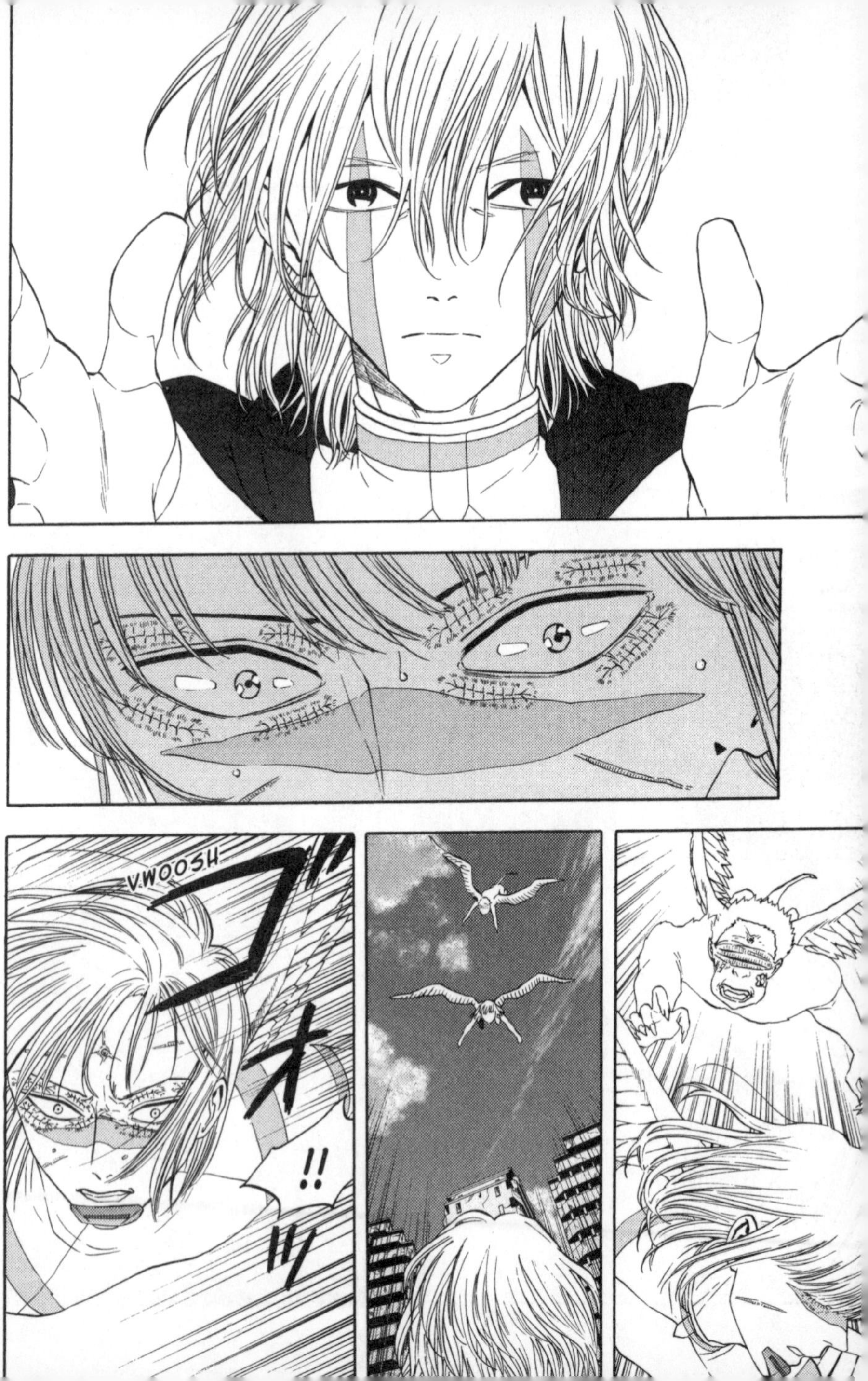
VWOOSH
!!

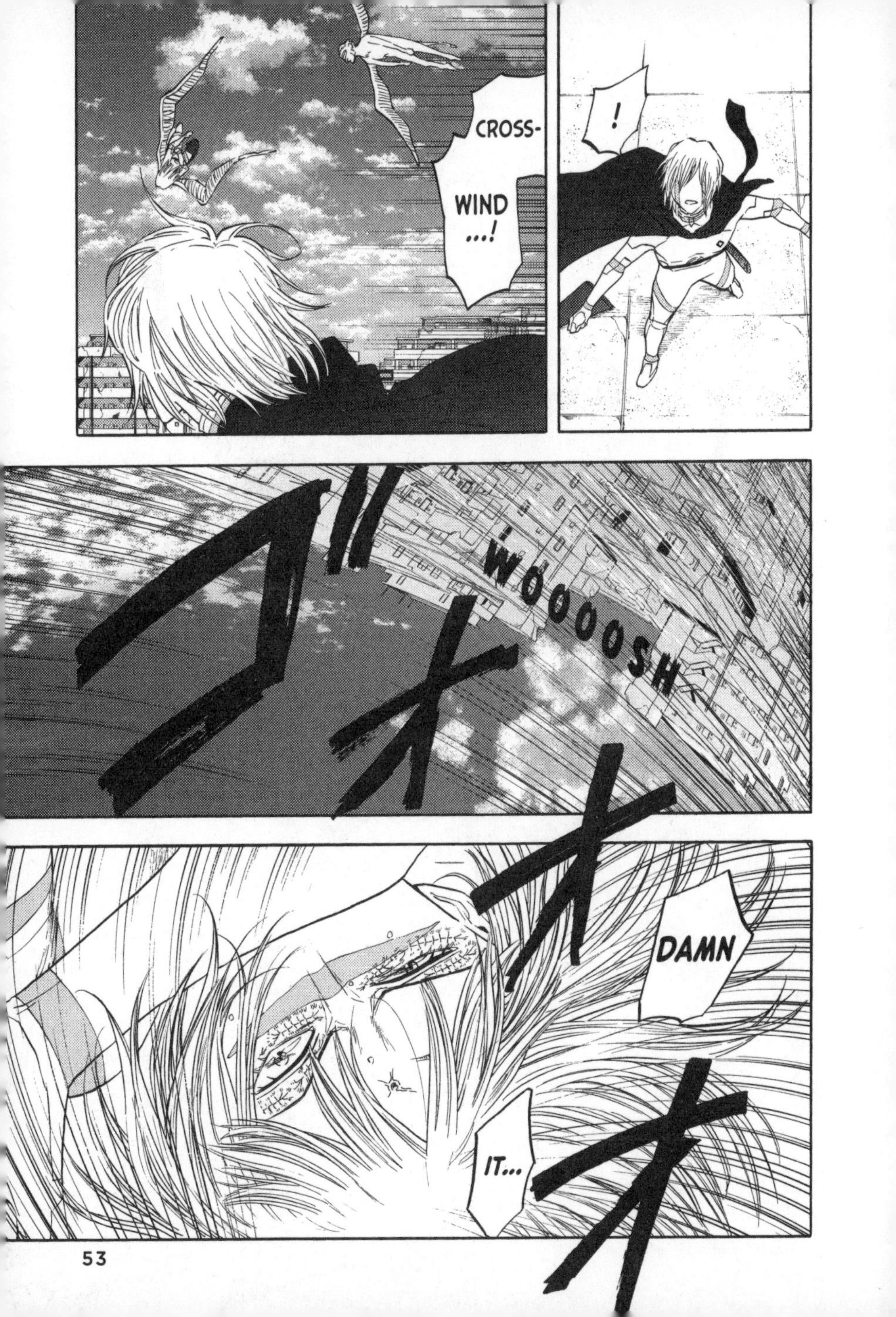
!
CROSS-
WIND
...!
WOOOOSH
DAMN
IT...

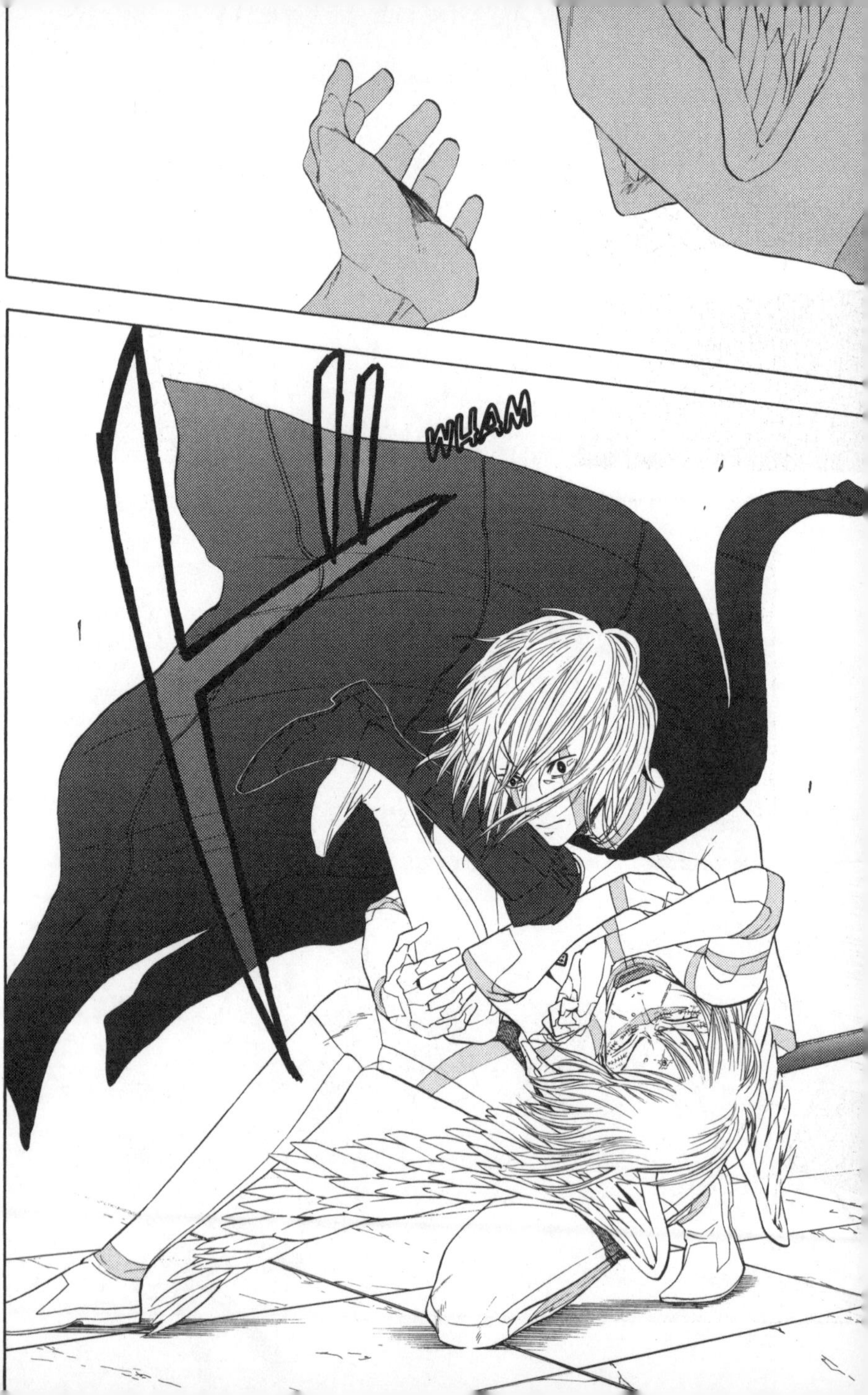
WHAM

SKREEEEE

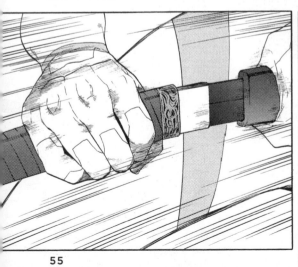

MINA-
MI...

GET
DOWN.

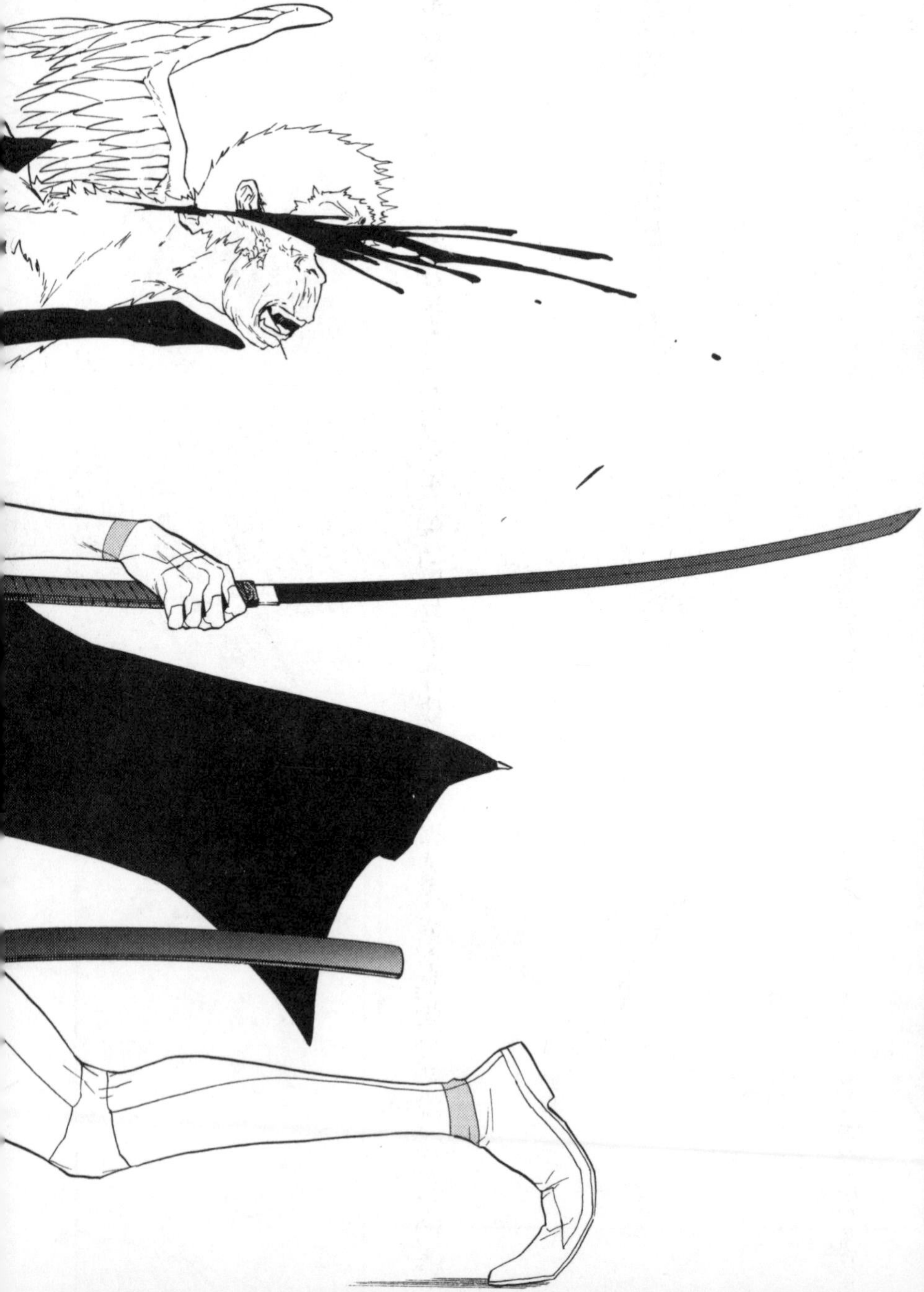

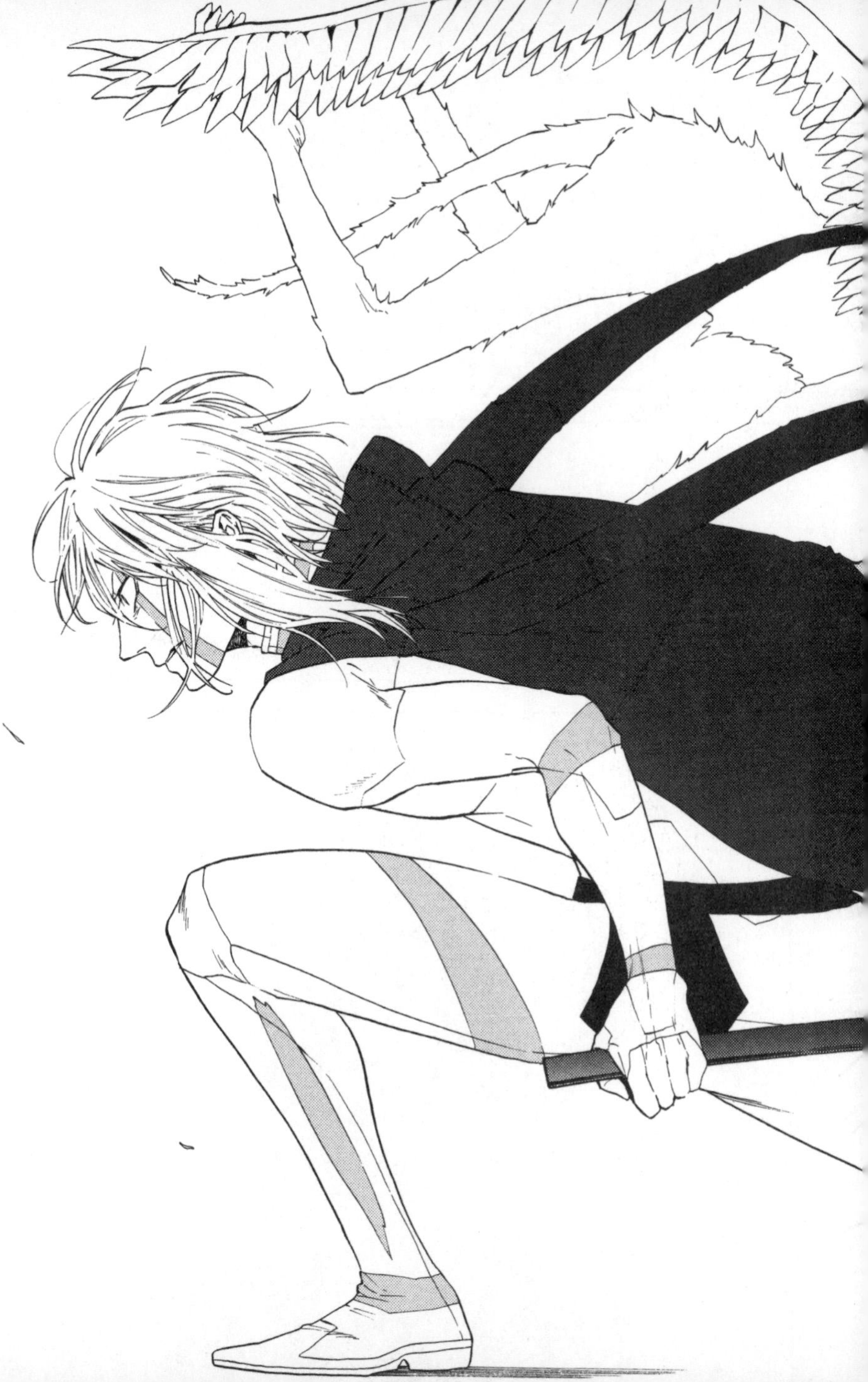

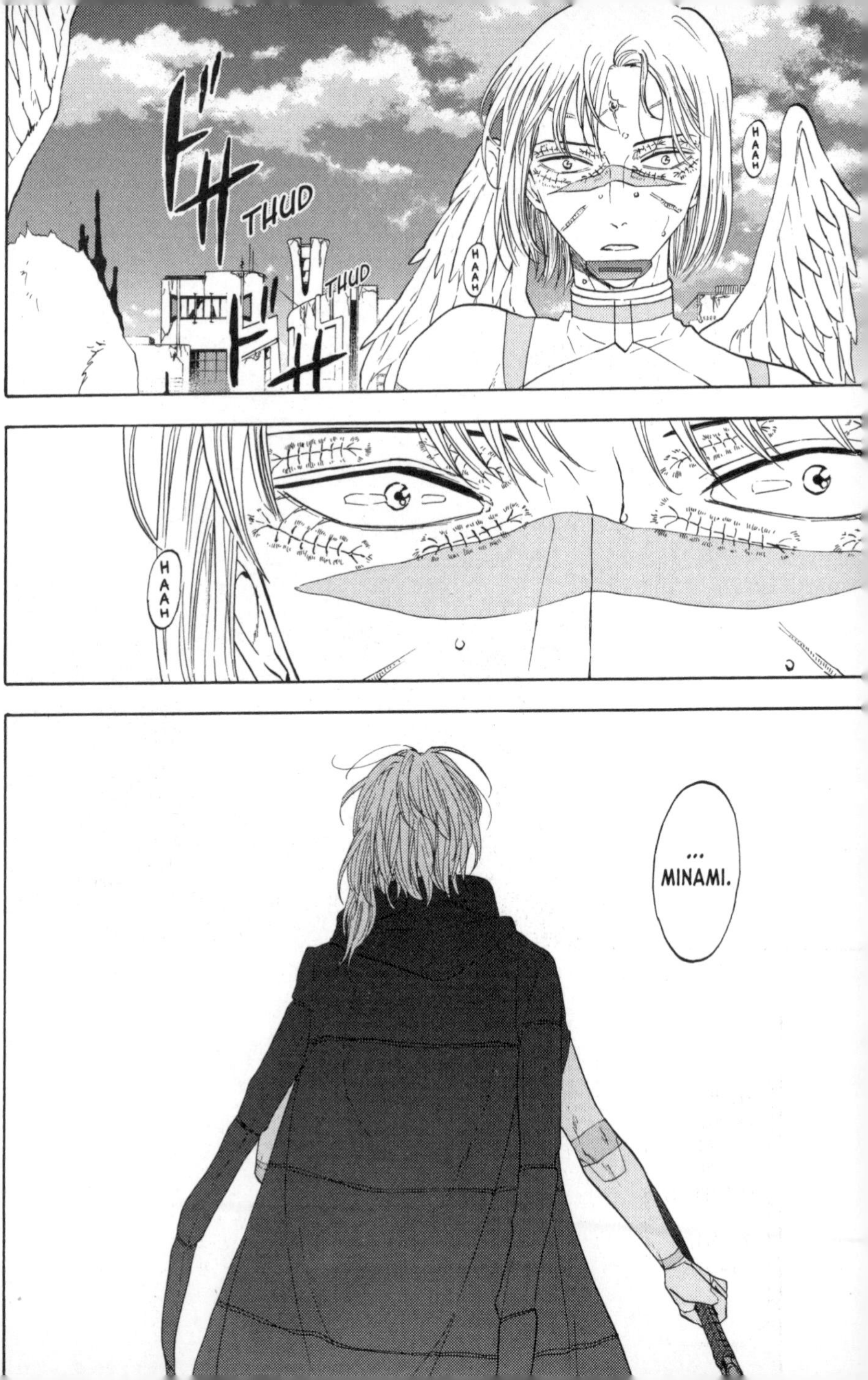
HAAH
THUD
HAAH
THUD
HAAH
... MINAMI.

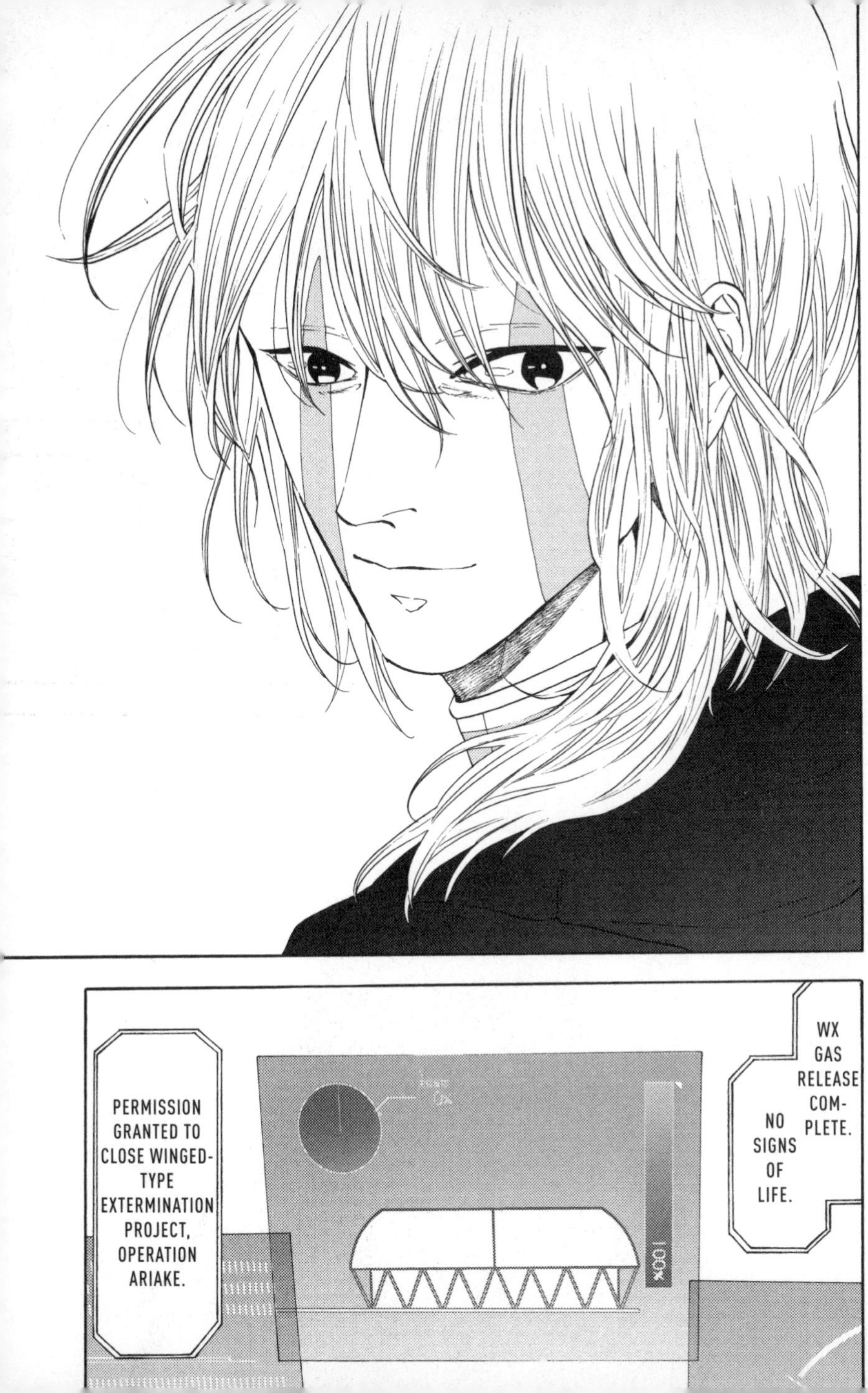
WX GAS RELEASE COMPLETE.
NO SIGNS OF LIFE.
PERMISSION GRANTED TO CLOSE WINGED-TYPE EXTERMINATION PROJECT, OPERATION ARIAKE.

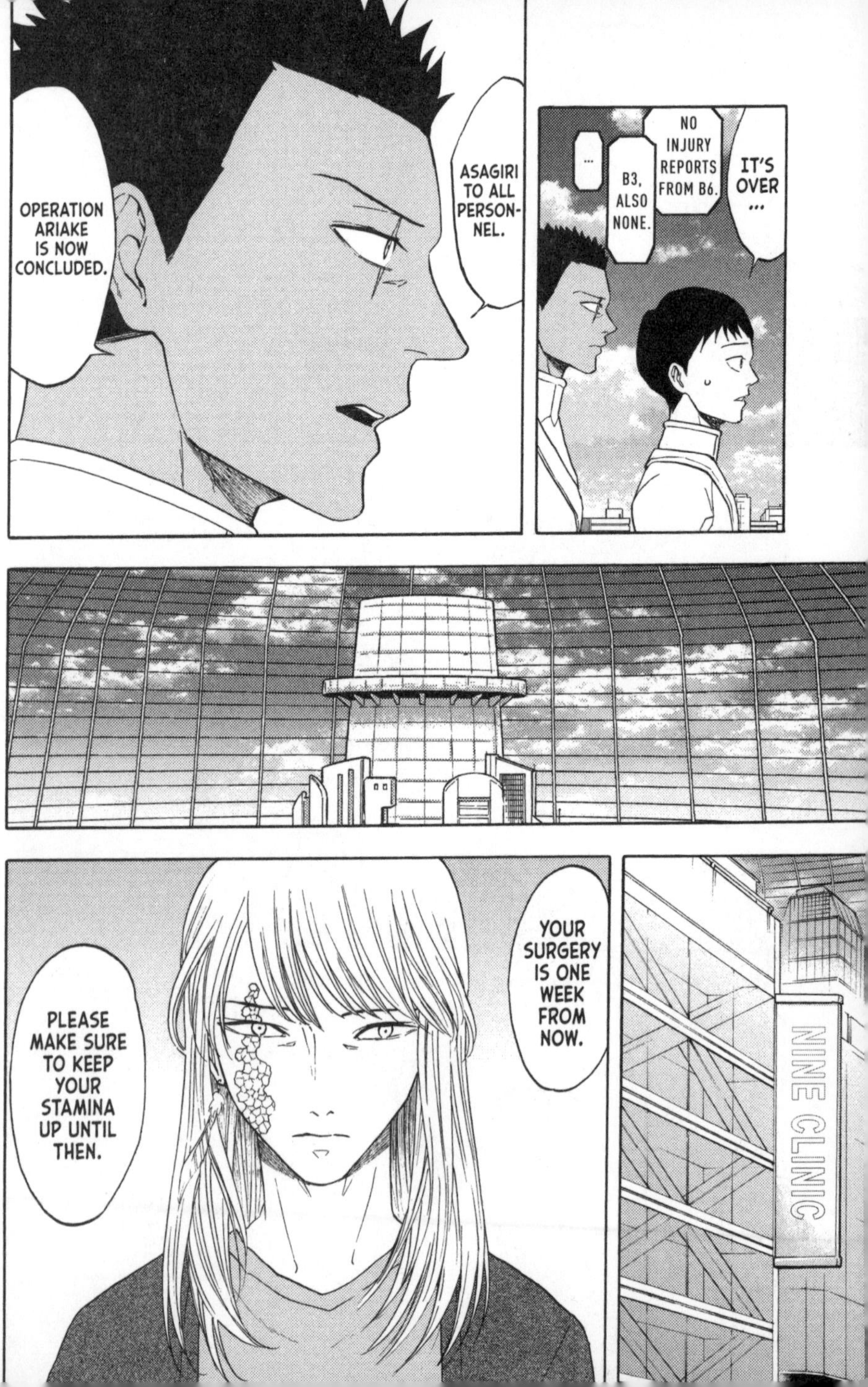
IT'S OVER ...
NO INJURY REPORTS FROM B6.
B3, ALSO NONE.
...
ASAGIRI TO ALL PERSON-NEL.
OPERATION ARIAKE IS NOW CONCLUDED.
NINE CLINIC
YOUR SURGERY IS ONE WEEK FROM NOW.
PLEASE MAKE SURE TO KEEP YOUR STAMINA UP UNTIL THEN.

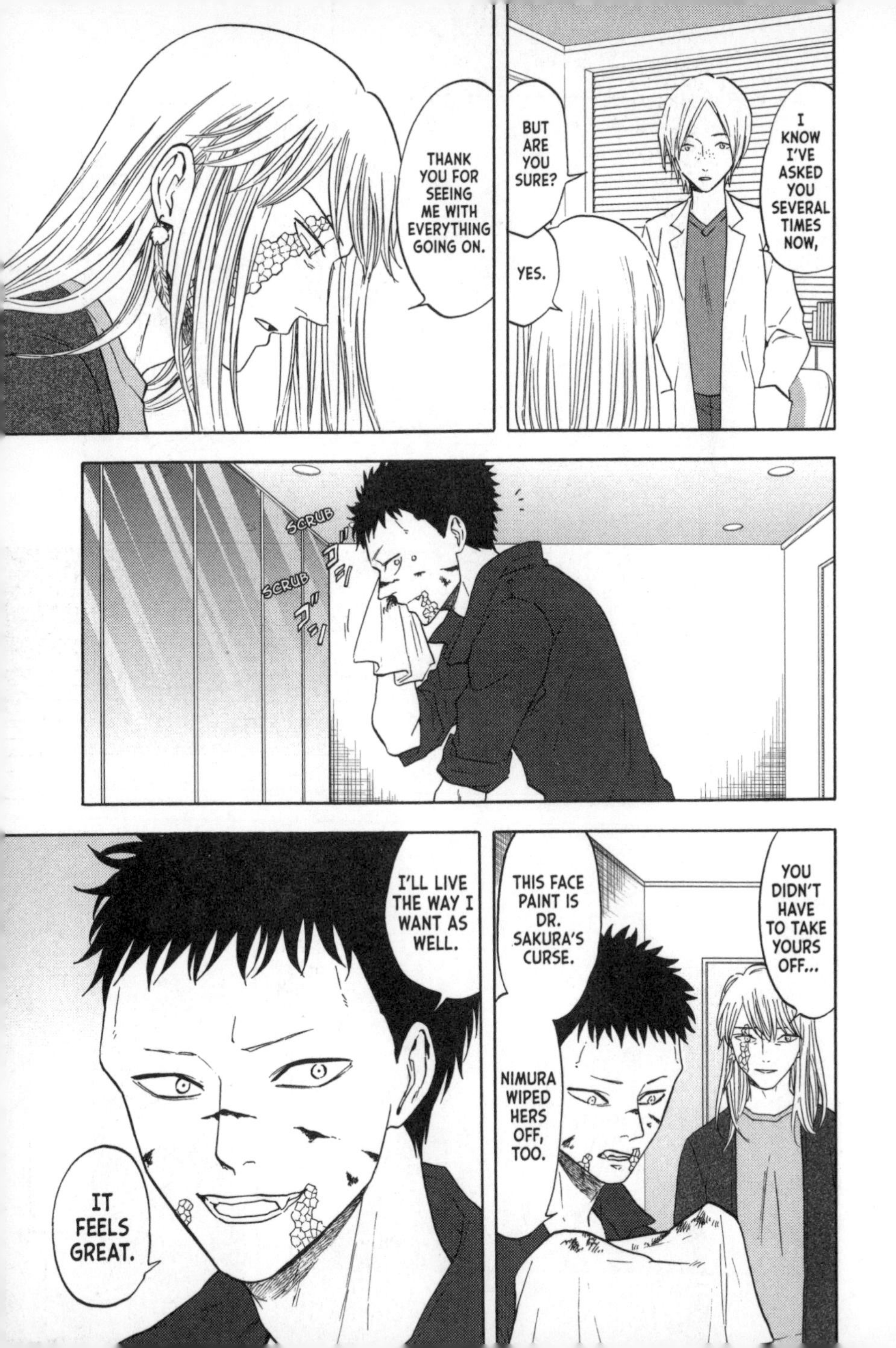
I KNOW I'VE ASKED YOU SEVERAL TIMES NOW,
BUT ARE YOU SURE?
YES.
THANK YOU FOR SEEING ME WITH EVERYTHING GOING ON.
SCRUB
SCRUB
YOU DIDN'T HAVE TO TAKE YOURS OFF...
THIS FACE PAINT IS DR. SAKURA'S CURSE.
NIMURA WIPED HERS OFF, TOO.
I'LL LIVE THE WAY I WANT AS WELL.
IT FEELS GREAT.

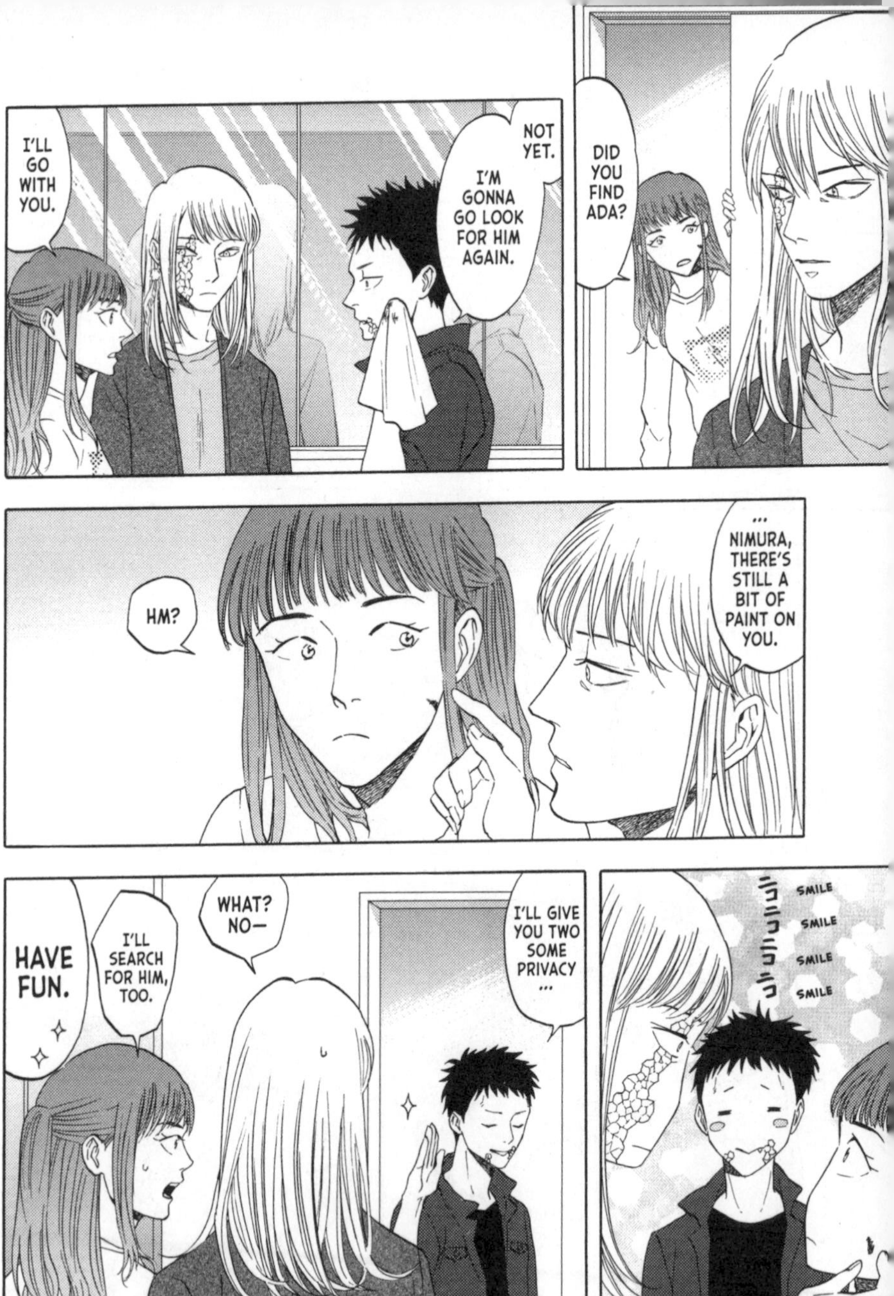
DID YOU FIND ADA?
NOT YET.
I'M GONNA GO LOOK FOR HIM AGAIN.
I'LL GO WITH YOU.
... NIMURA, THERE'S STILL A BIT OF PAINT ON YOU.
HM?
SMILE
SMILE
SMILE
SMILE
I'LL GIVE YOU TWO SOME PRIVACY ...
WHAT? NO—
I'LL SEARCH FOR HIM, TOO.
HAVE FUN.

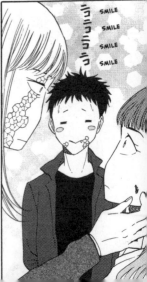

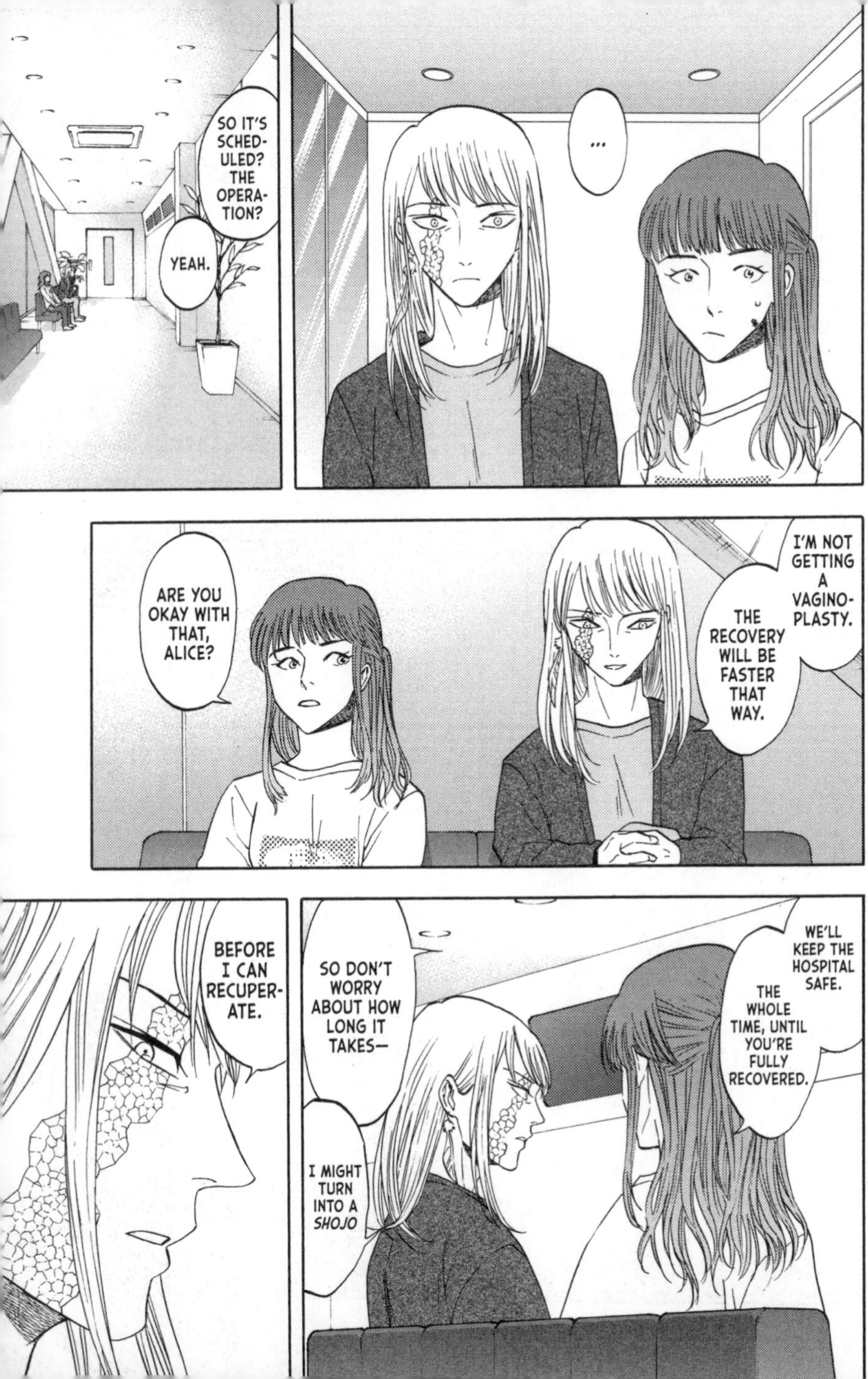
...
SO IT'S SCHEDULED? THE OPERATION?
YEAH.
I'M NOT GETTING A VAGINOPLASTY.
THE RECOVERY WILL BE FASTER THAT WAY.
ARE YOU OKAY WITH THAT, ALICE?
WE'LL KEEP THE HOSPITAL SAFE.
THE WHOLE TIME, UNTIL YOU'RE FULLY RECOVERED.
SO DON'T WORRY ABOUT HOW LONG IT TAKES—
I MIGHT TURN INTO A *SHOJO*
BEFORE I CAN RECUPERATE.

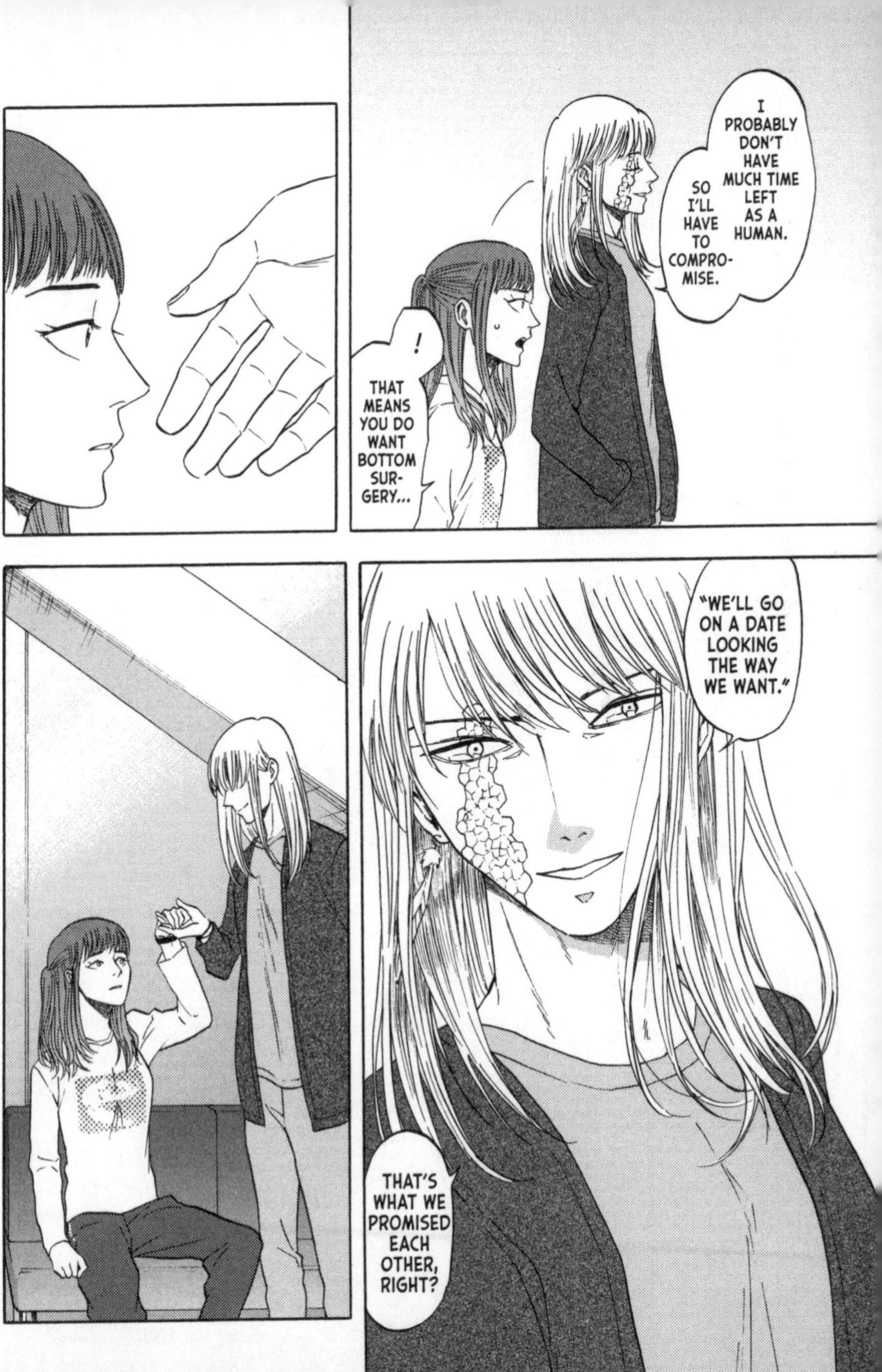
I PROBABLY DON'T HAVE MUCH TIME LEFT AS A HUMAN.
SO I'LL HAVE TO COMPROMISE.
!
THAT MEANS YOU DO WANT BOTTOM SURGERY...
"WE'LL GO ON A DATE LOOKING THE WAY WE WANT."
THAT'S WHAT WE PROMISED EACH OTHER, RIGHT?

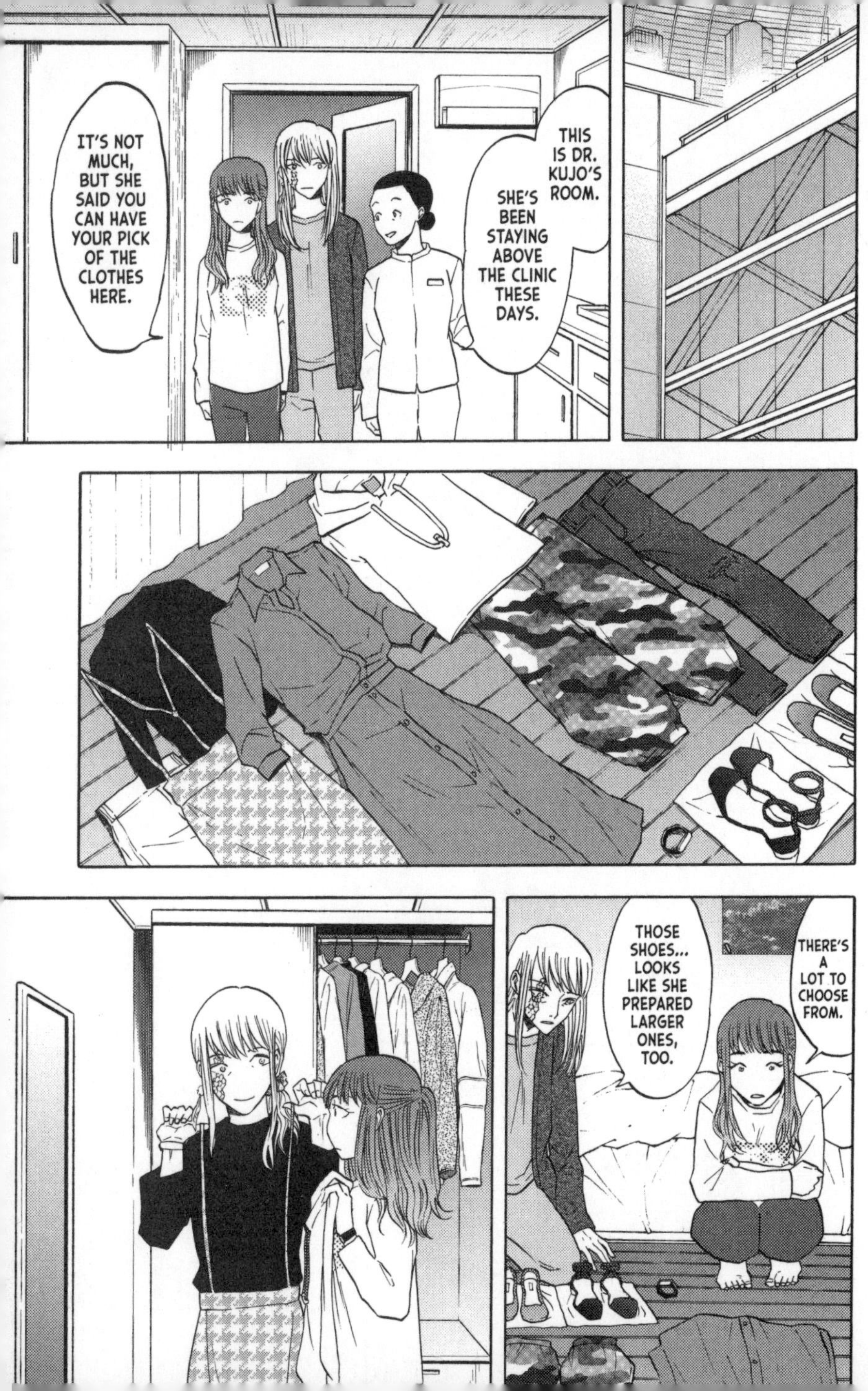
THIS IS DR. KUJO'S ROOM.
SHE'S BEEN STAYING ABOVE THE CLINIC THESE DAYS.
IT'S NOT MUCH, BUT SHE SAID YOU CAN HAVE YOUR PICK OF THE CLOTHES HERE.
THERE'S A LOT TO CHOOSE FROM.
THOSE SHOES... LOOKS LIKE SHE PREPARED LARGER ONES, TOO.

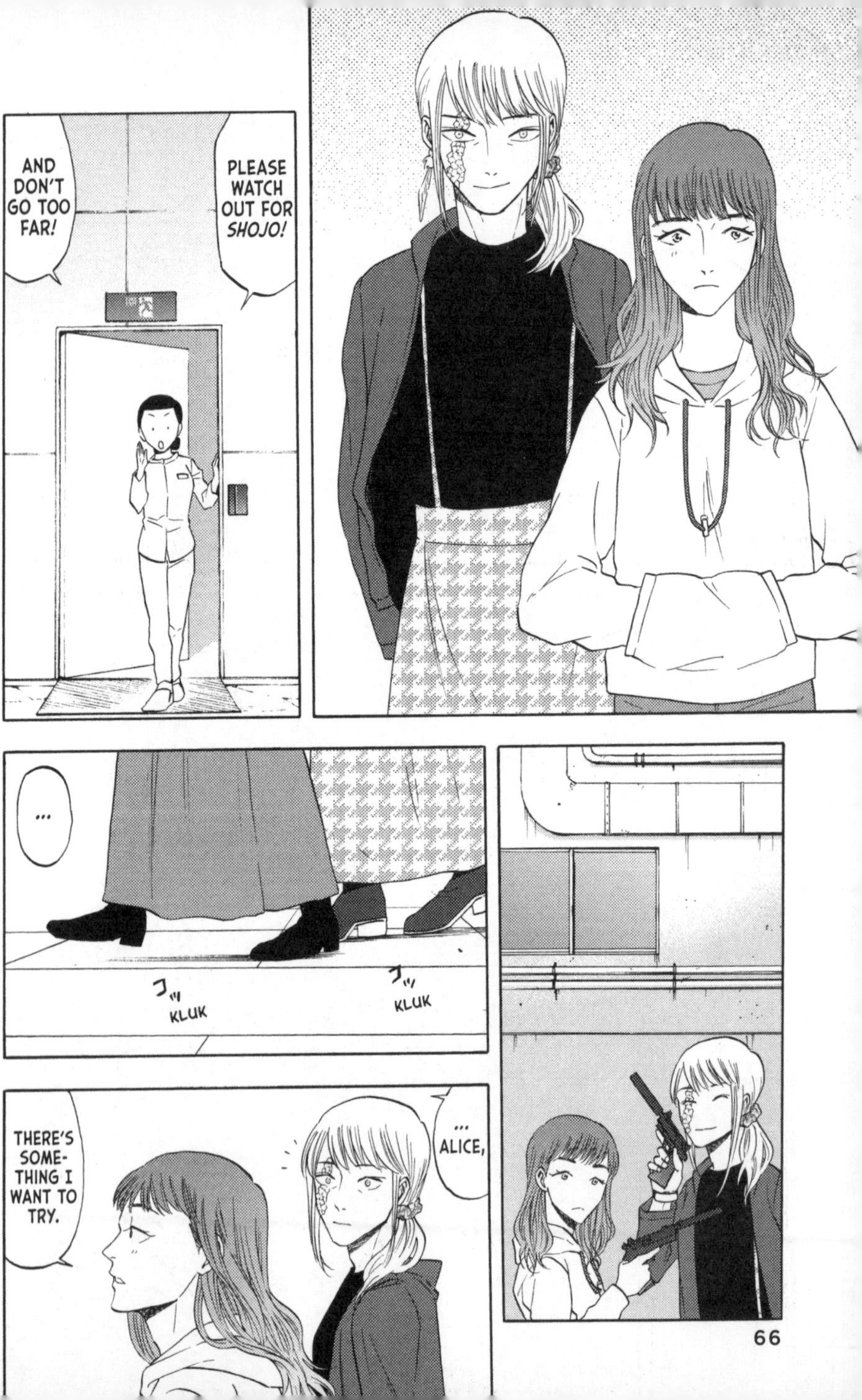
PLEASE WATCH OUT FOR *SHOJO!*
AND DON'T GO TOO FAR!
...
KLUK
KLUK
... ALICE,
THERE'S SOME-THING I WANT TO TRY.

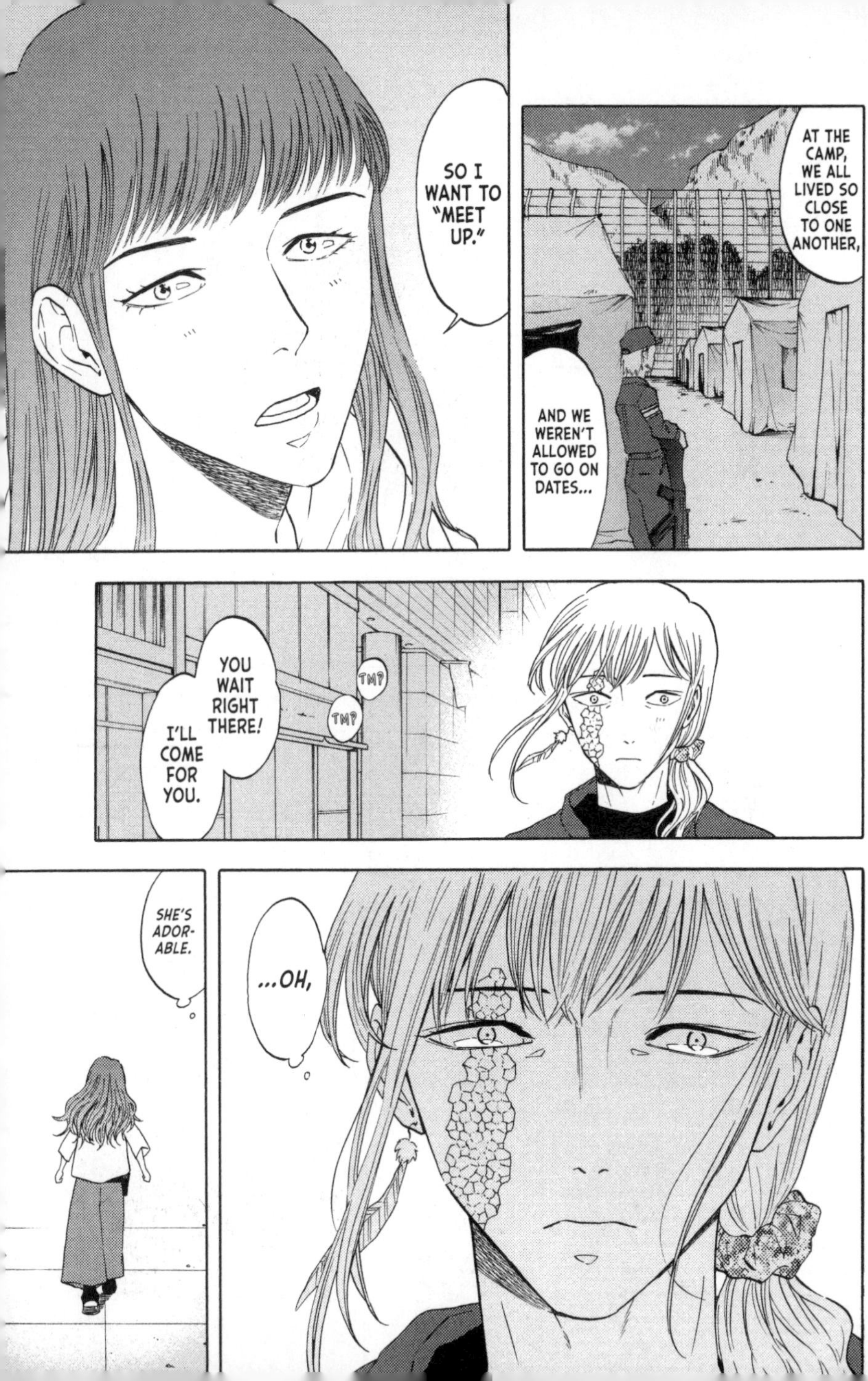
AT THE CAMP, WE ALL LIVED SO CLOSE TO ONE ANOTHER,
AND WE WEREN'T ALLOWED TO GO ON DATES...
SO I WANT TO "MEET UP."
YOU WAIT RIGHT THERE!
I'LL COME FOR YOU.
TM?
TM?
...OH,
SHE'S ADORABLE.

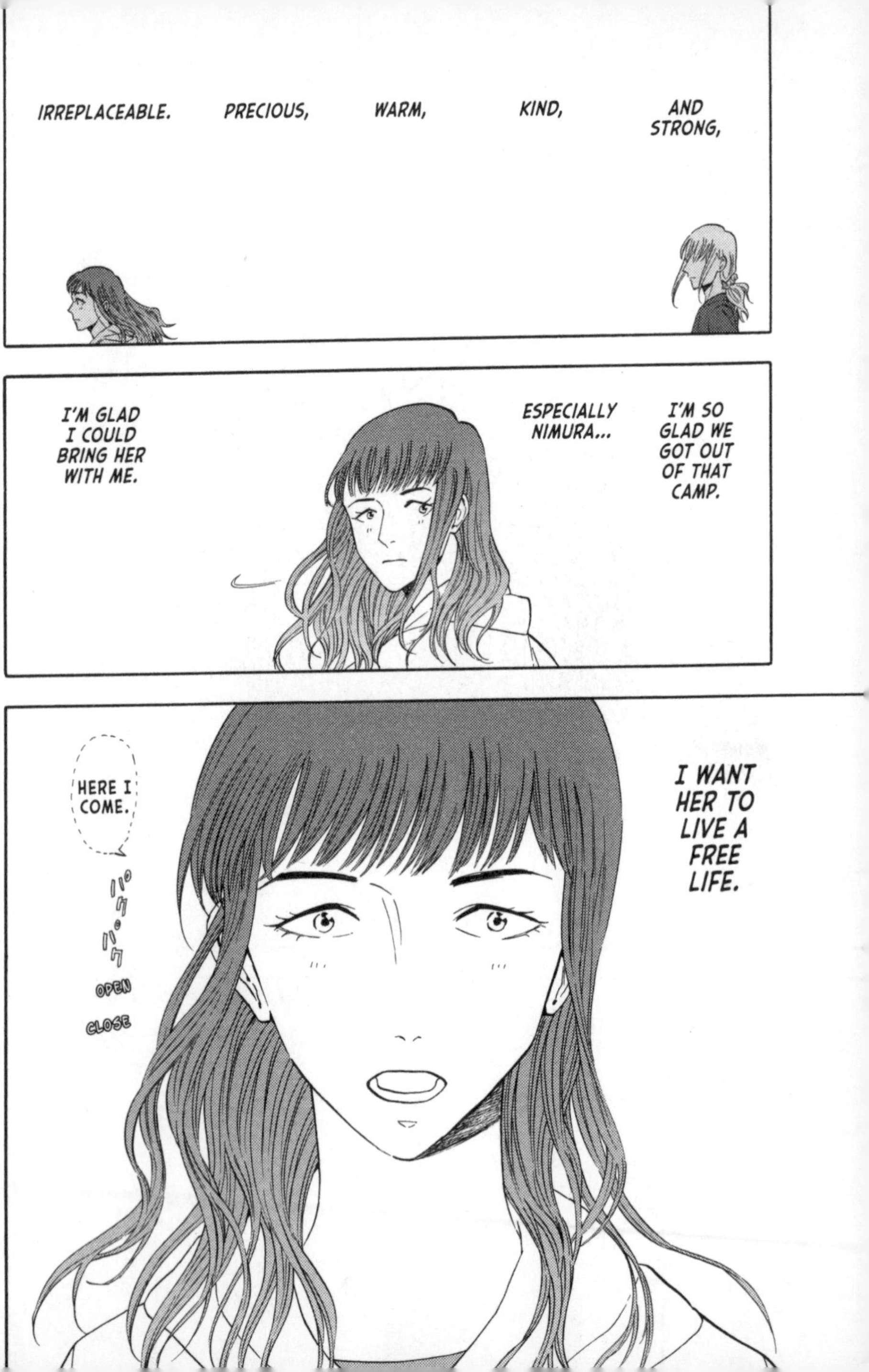
AND STRONG,
KIND,
WARM,
PRECIOUS,
IRREPLACEABLE.
I'M SO GLAD WE GOT OUT OF THAT CAMP.
ESPECIALLY NIMURA...
I'M GLAD I COULD BRING HER WITH ME.
I WANT HER TO LIVE A FREE LIFE.
HERE I COME.
パクパク
OPEN
CLOSE

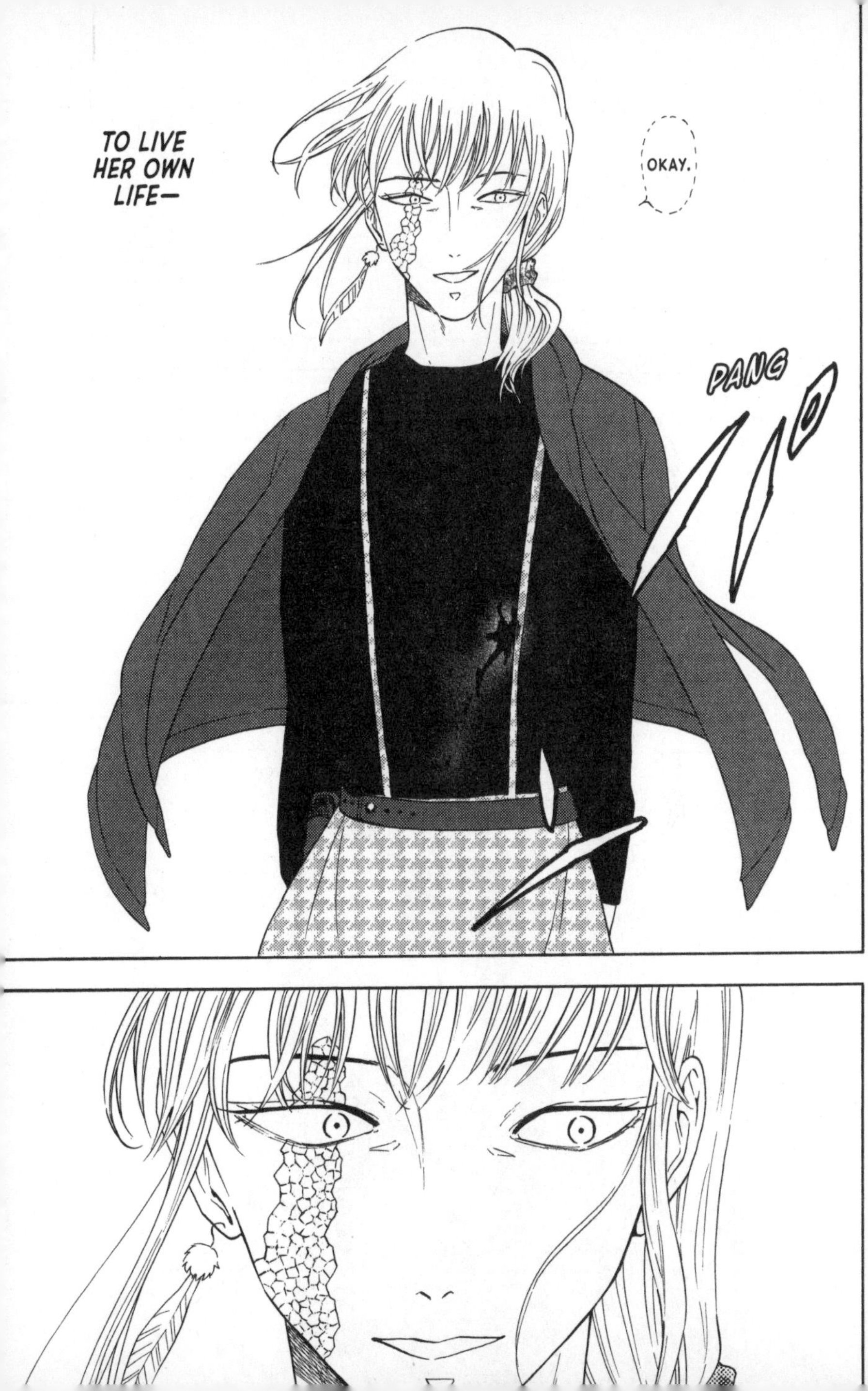
TO LIVE HER OWN LIFE—
OKAY.
PANG

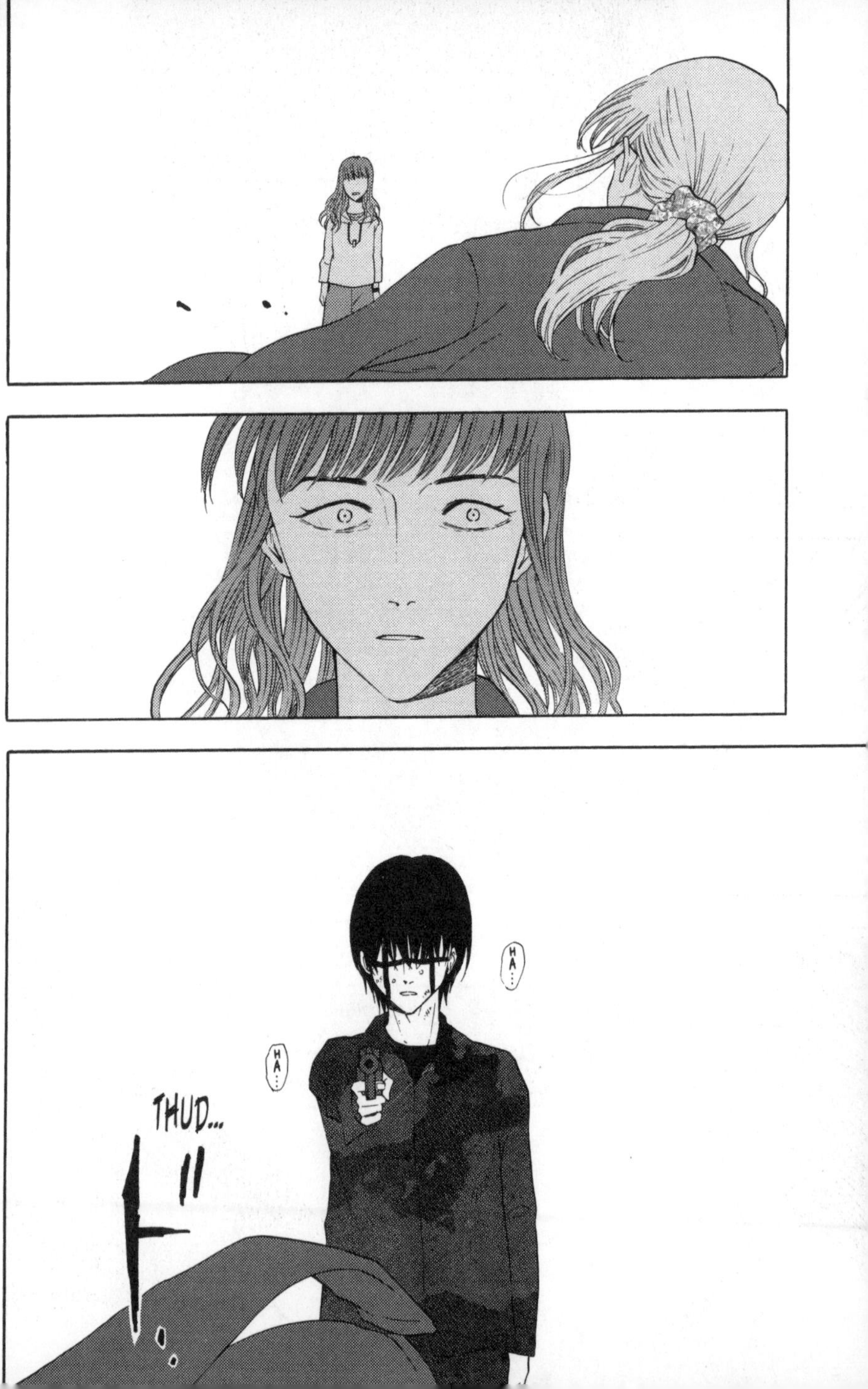
HA...
HA...
THUD...

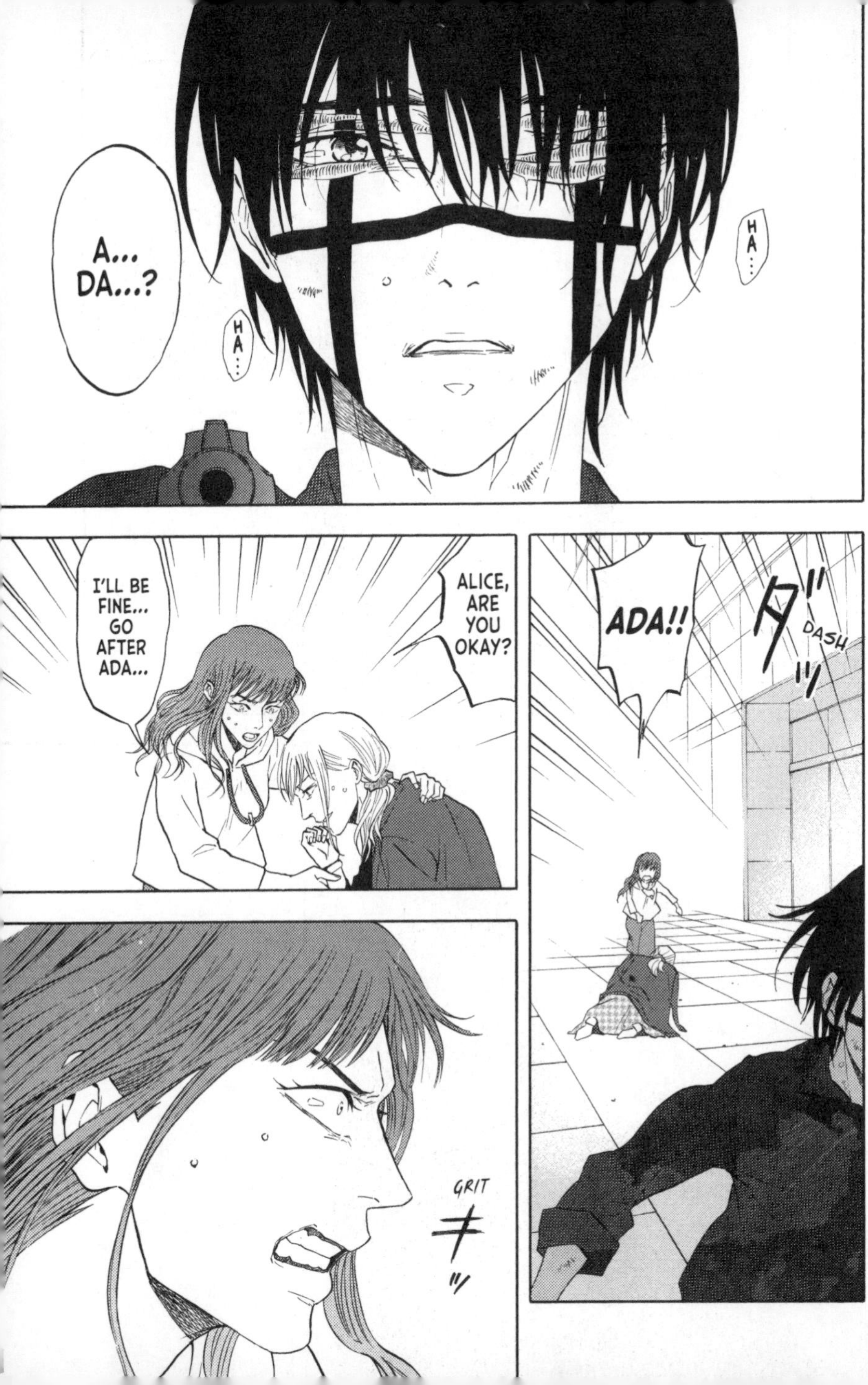
HA...
A... DA...?
HA...
ADA!!
ダッ
DASH
ALICE, ARE YOU OKAY?
I'LL BE FINE... GO AFTER ADA...
ギッ
GRIT

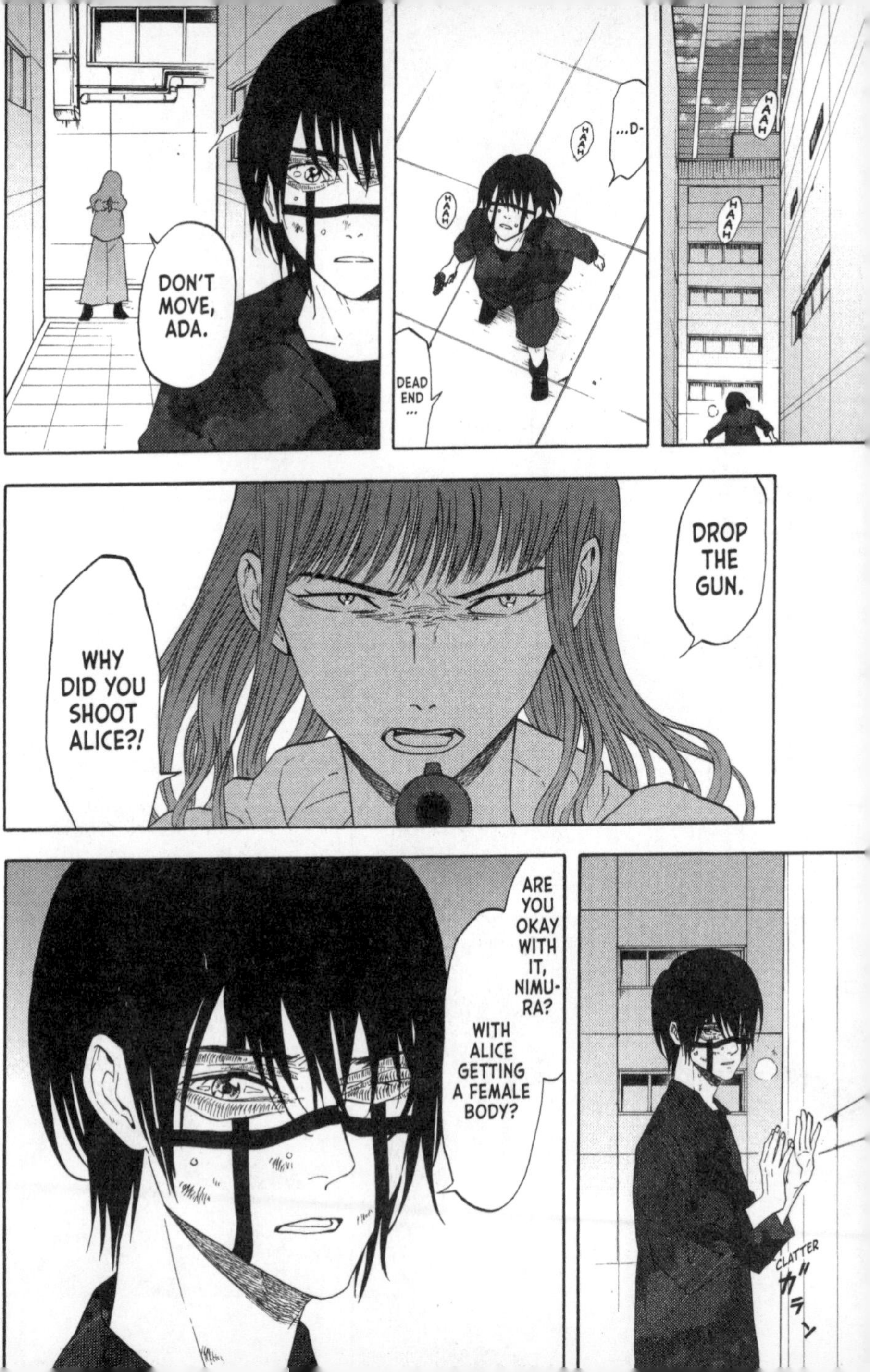
HAAH
HAAH
...D-
HAAH
HAAH
DEAD END ...
DON'T MOVE, ADA.
DROP THE GUN.
WHY DID YOU SHOOT ALICE?!
CLATTER
ARE YOU OKAY WITH IT, NIMU-RA?
WITH ALICE GETTING A FEMALE BODY?

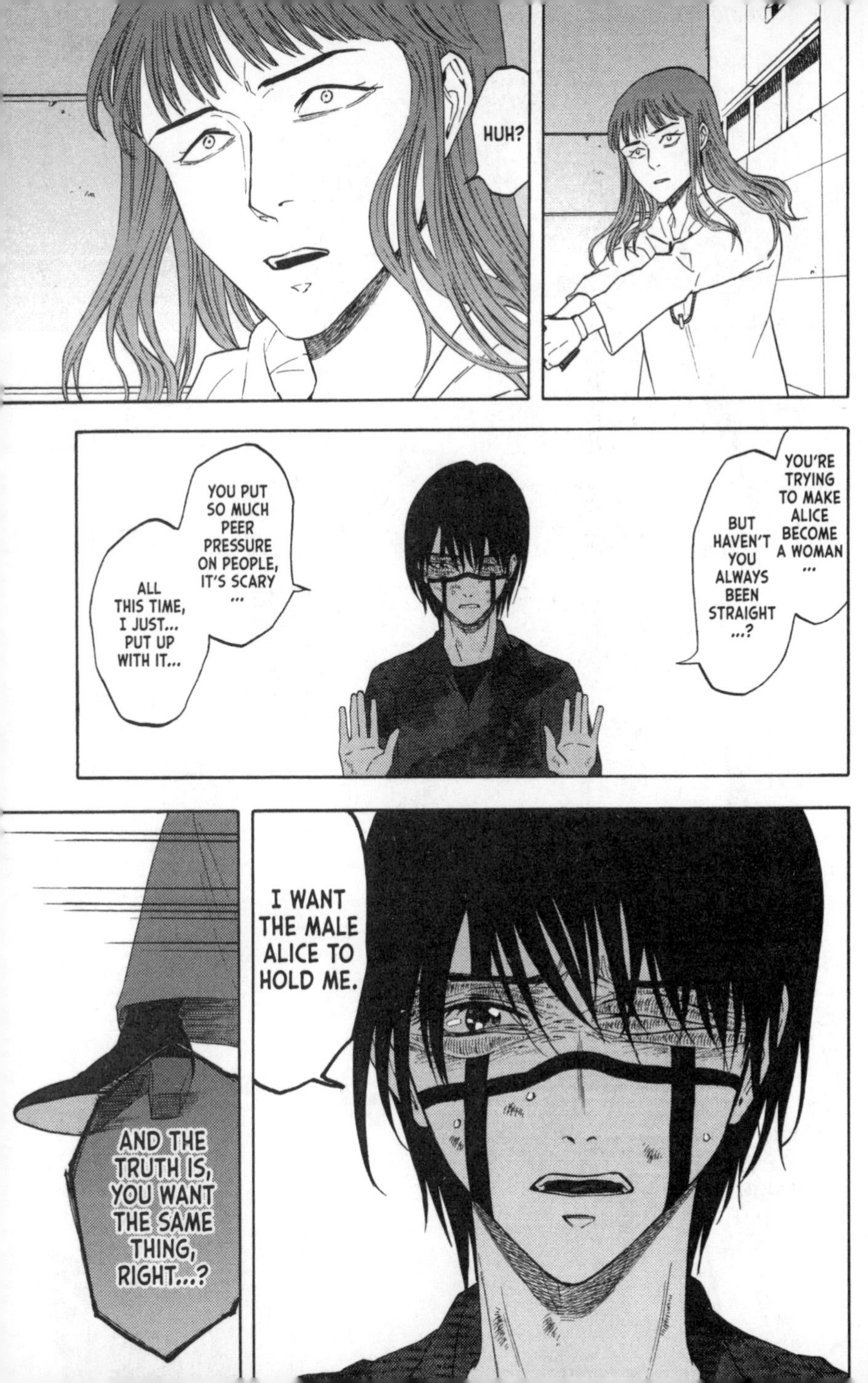
HUH?
YOU'RE TRYING TO MAKE ALICE BECOME A WOMAN ...
BUT HAVEN'T YOU ALWAYS BEEN STRAIGHT ...?
YOU PUT SO MUCH PEER PRESSURE ON PEOPLE, IT'S SCARY ...
ALL THIS TIME, I JUST... PUT UP WITH IT...
I WANT THE MALE ALICE TO HOLD ME.
AND THE TRUTH IS, YOU WANT THE SAME THING, RIGHT...?

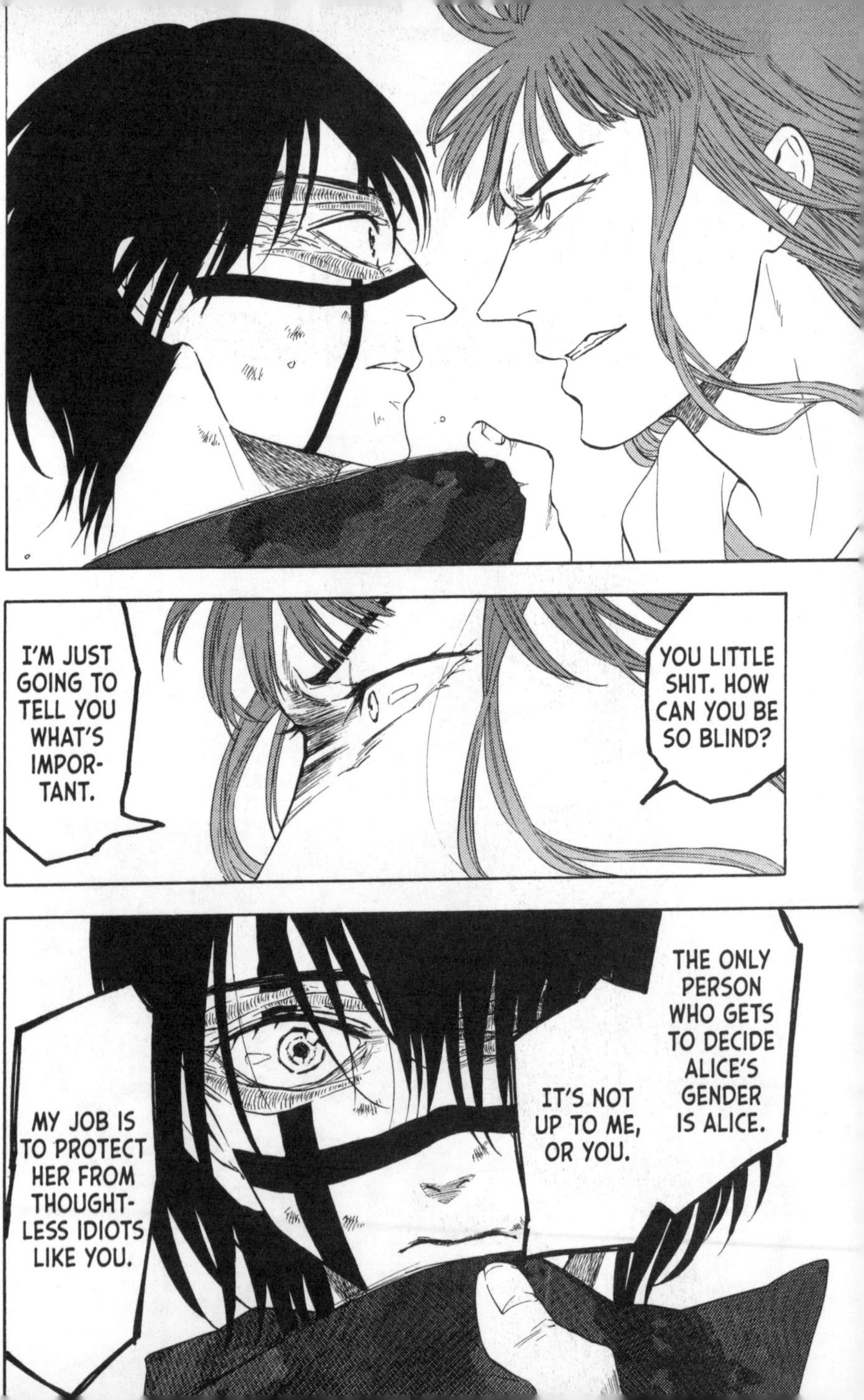
YOU LITTLE SHIT. HOW CAN YOU BE SO BLIND?
I'M JUST GOING TO TELL YOU WHAT'S IMPORTANT.
THE ONLY PERSON WHO GETS TO DECIDE ALICE'S GENDER IS ALICE.
IT'S NOT UP TO ME, OR YOU.
MY JOB IS TO PROTECT HER FROM THOUGHTLESS IDIOTS LIKE YOU.

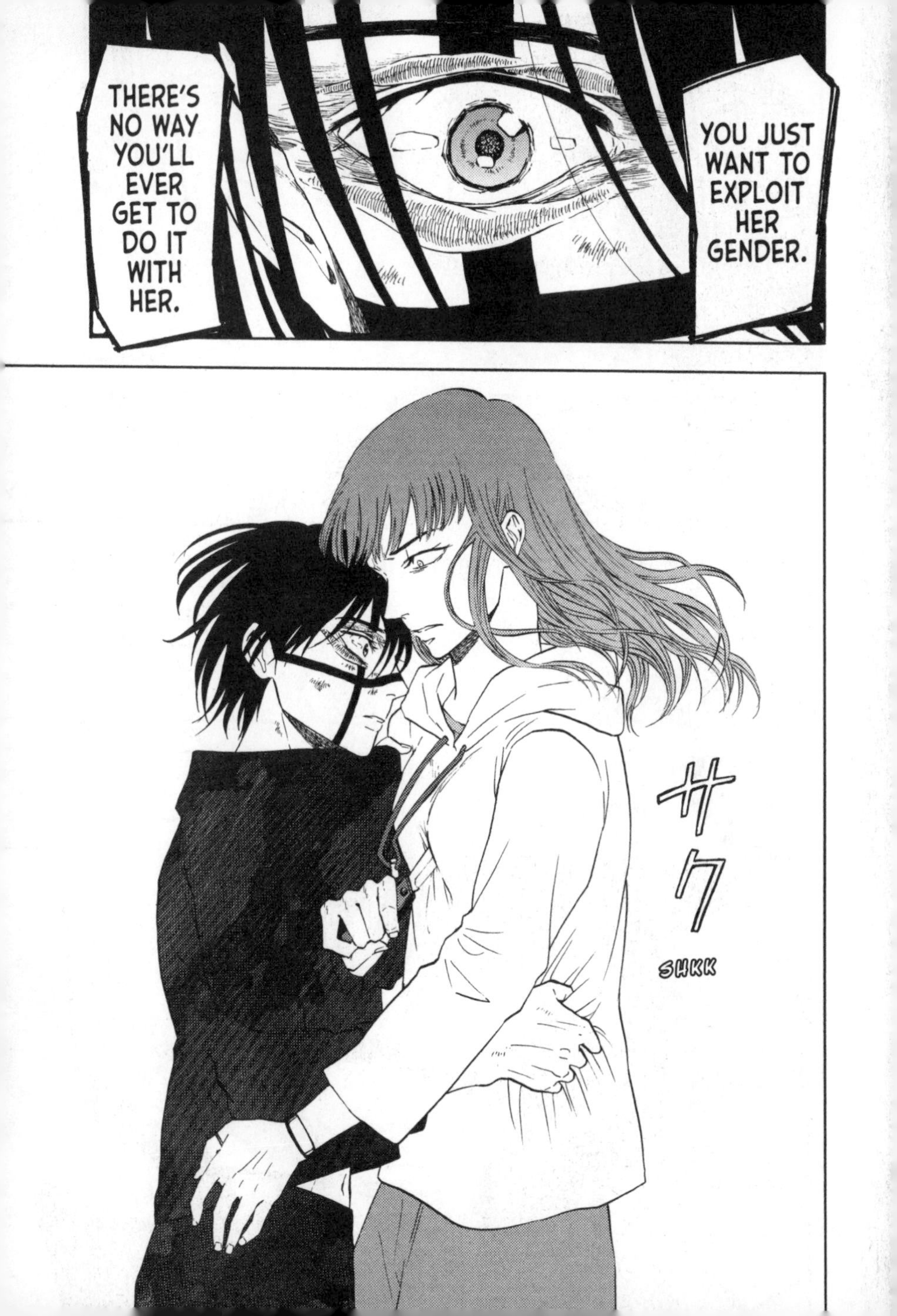
YOU JUST WANT TO EXPLOIT HER GENDER.
THERE'S NO WAY YOU'LL EVER GET TO DO IT WITH HER.
サク
SHKK

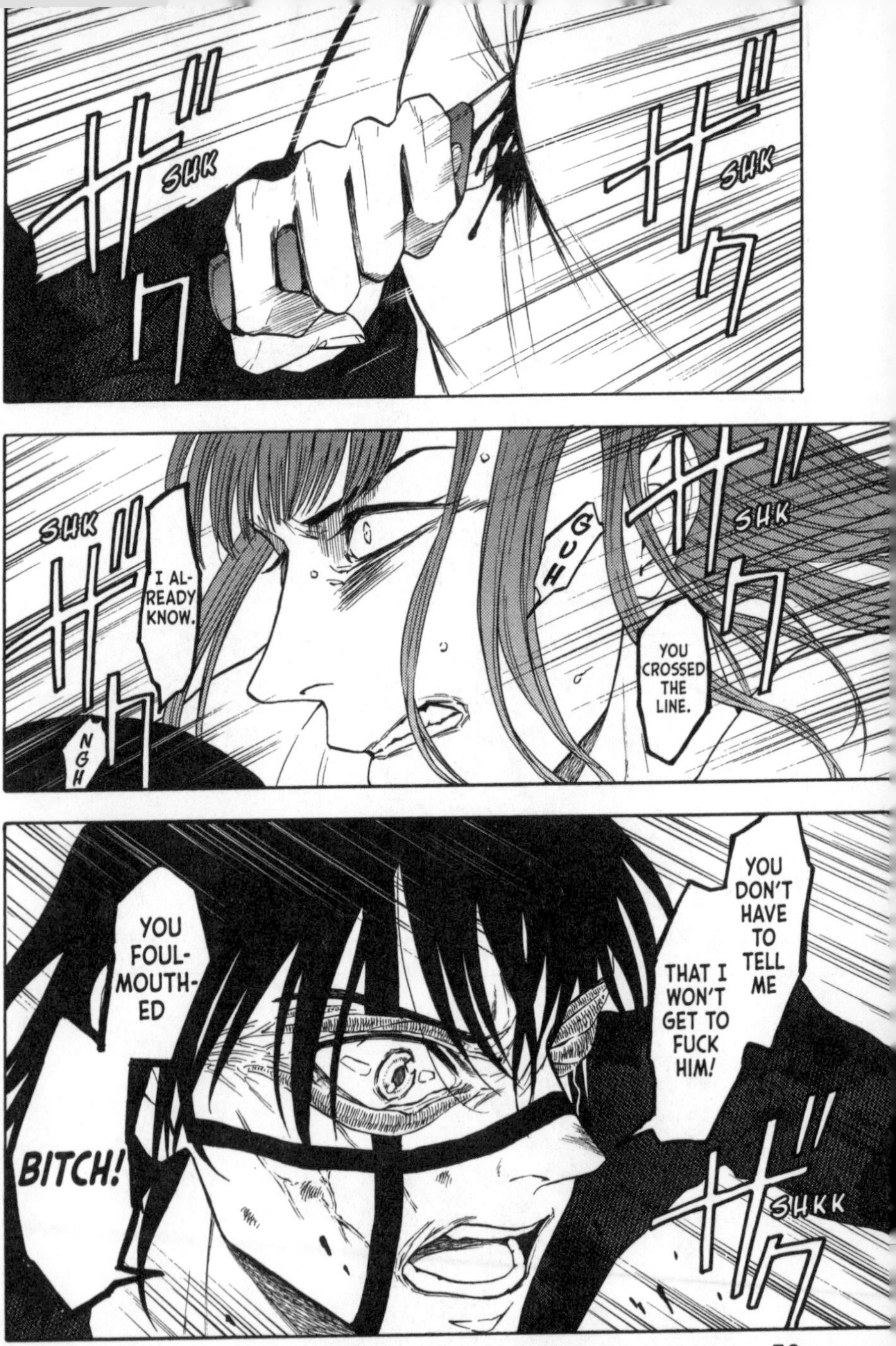
SHK
SHK
SHK
YOU CROSSED THE LINE.
HUGH
I ALREADY KNOW.
SHK
NGH
YOU DON'T HAVE TO TELL ME
THAT I WON'T GET TO FUCK HIM!
SHKK
YOU FOUL-MOUTHED
BITCH!

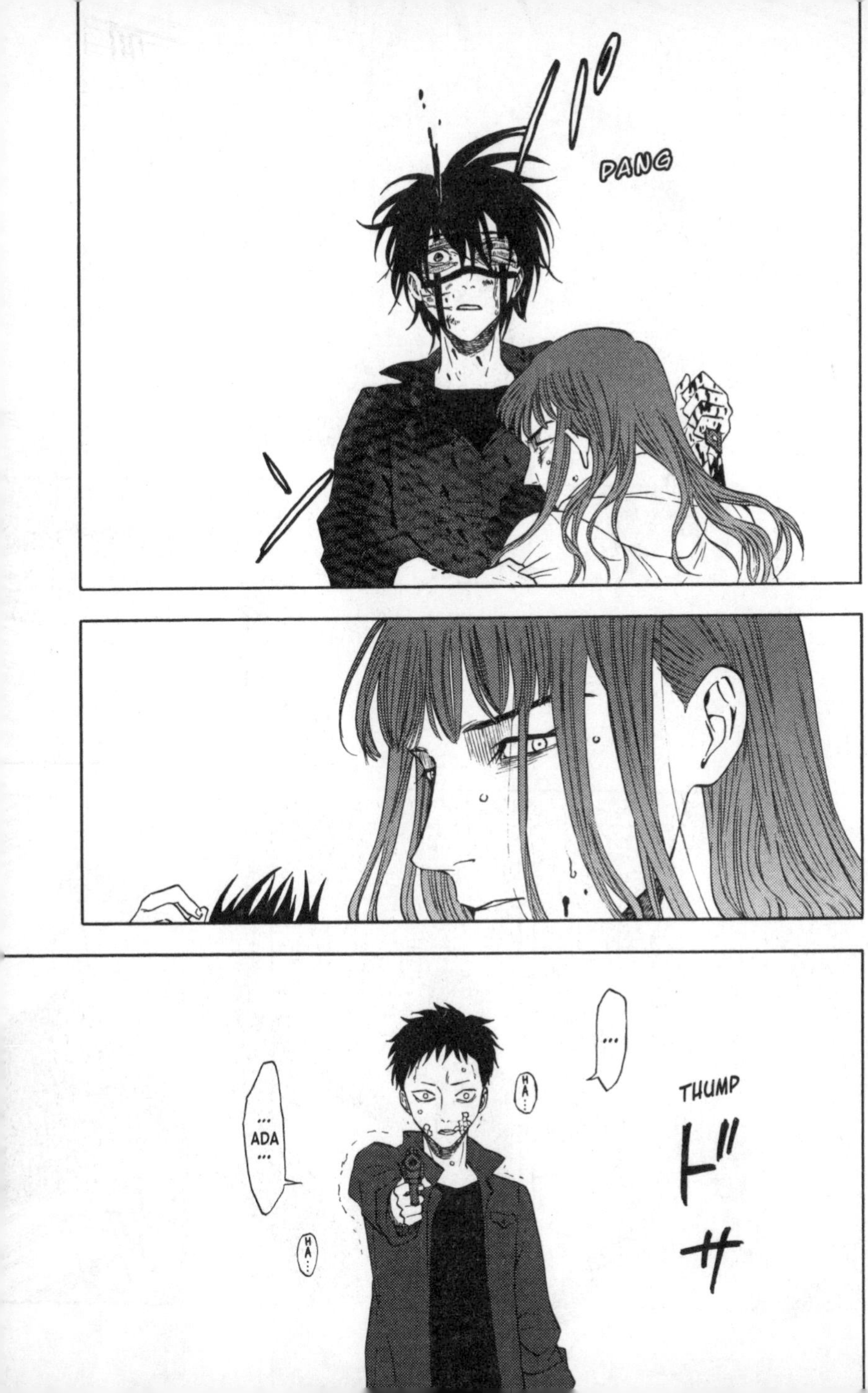
PANG
...
THUMP
ドサ
HA...
...ADA...
HA...

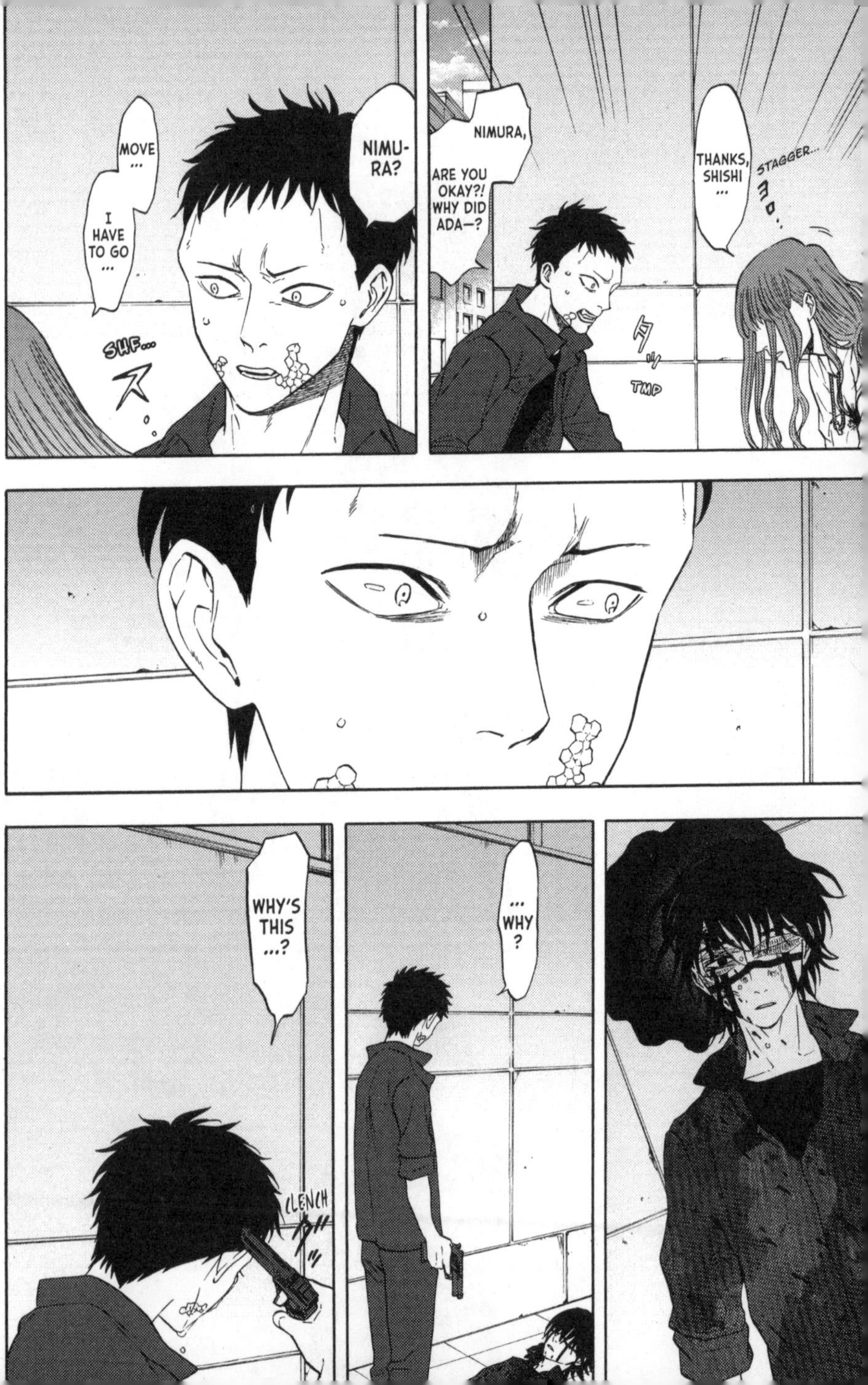
THANKS, SHISHI ...
STAGGER...
ヨロ...
タッ
TMP
NIMURA,
ARE YOU OKAY?! WHY DID ADA—?
NIMURA?
MOVE ...
I HAVE TO GO ...
SHF...
ス
... WHY?
WHY'S THIS ...?
CLENCH
ギッ

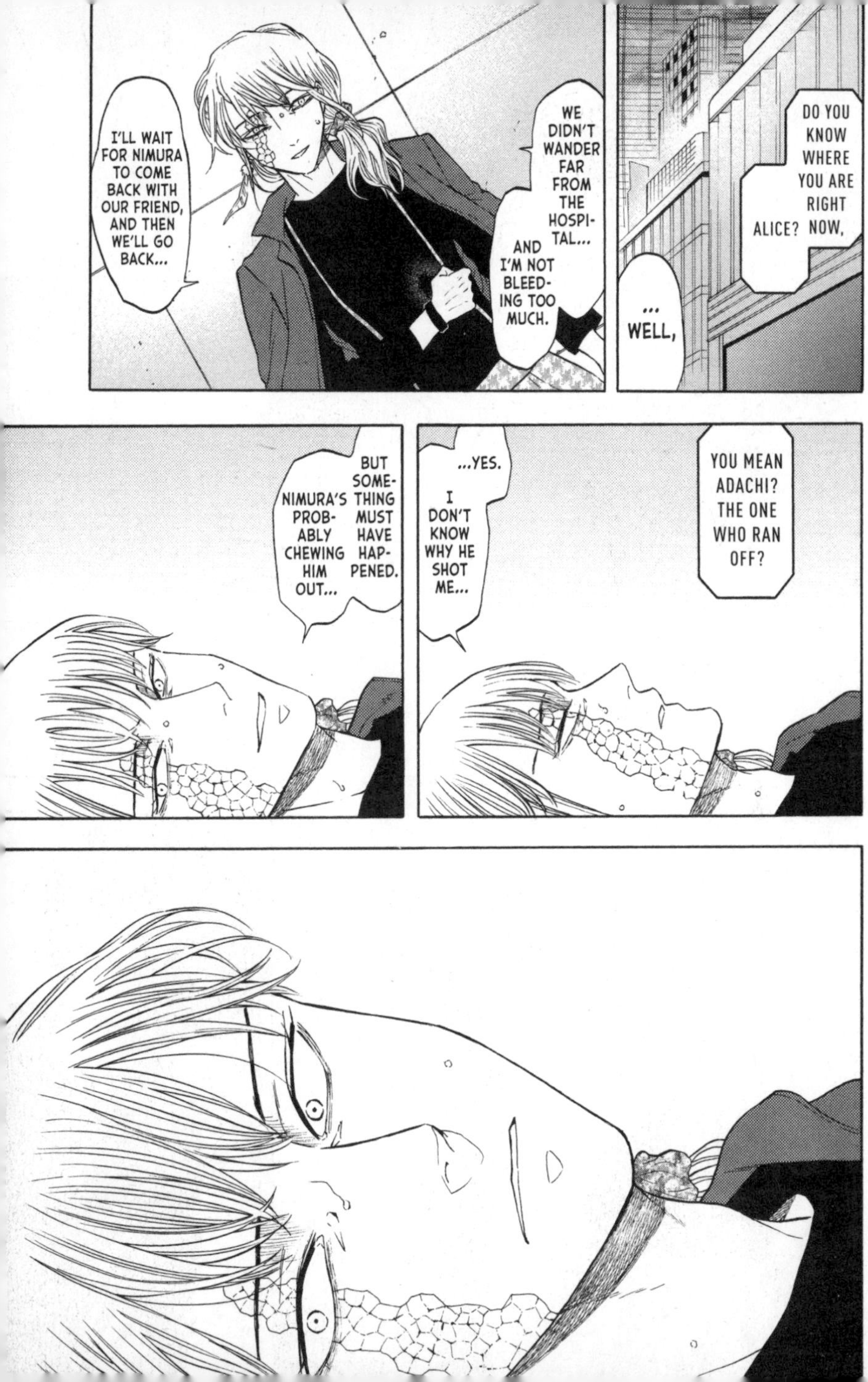

DO YOU KNOW WHERE YOU ARE RIGHT NOW, ALICE?
...WELL,
WE DIDN'T WANDER FAR FROM THE HOSPITAL...
AND I'M NOT BLEEDING TOO MUCH.
I'LL WAIT FOR NIMURA TO COME BACK WITH OUR FRIEND, AND THEN WE'LL GO BACK...
YOU MEAN ADACHI? THE ONE WHO RAN OFF?
...YES.
I DON'T KNOW WHY HE SHOT ME...
BUT SOMETHING MUST HAVE HAPPENED.
NIMURA'S PROBABLY CHEWING HIM OUT...

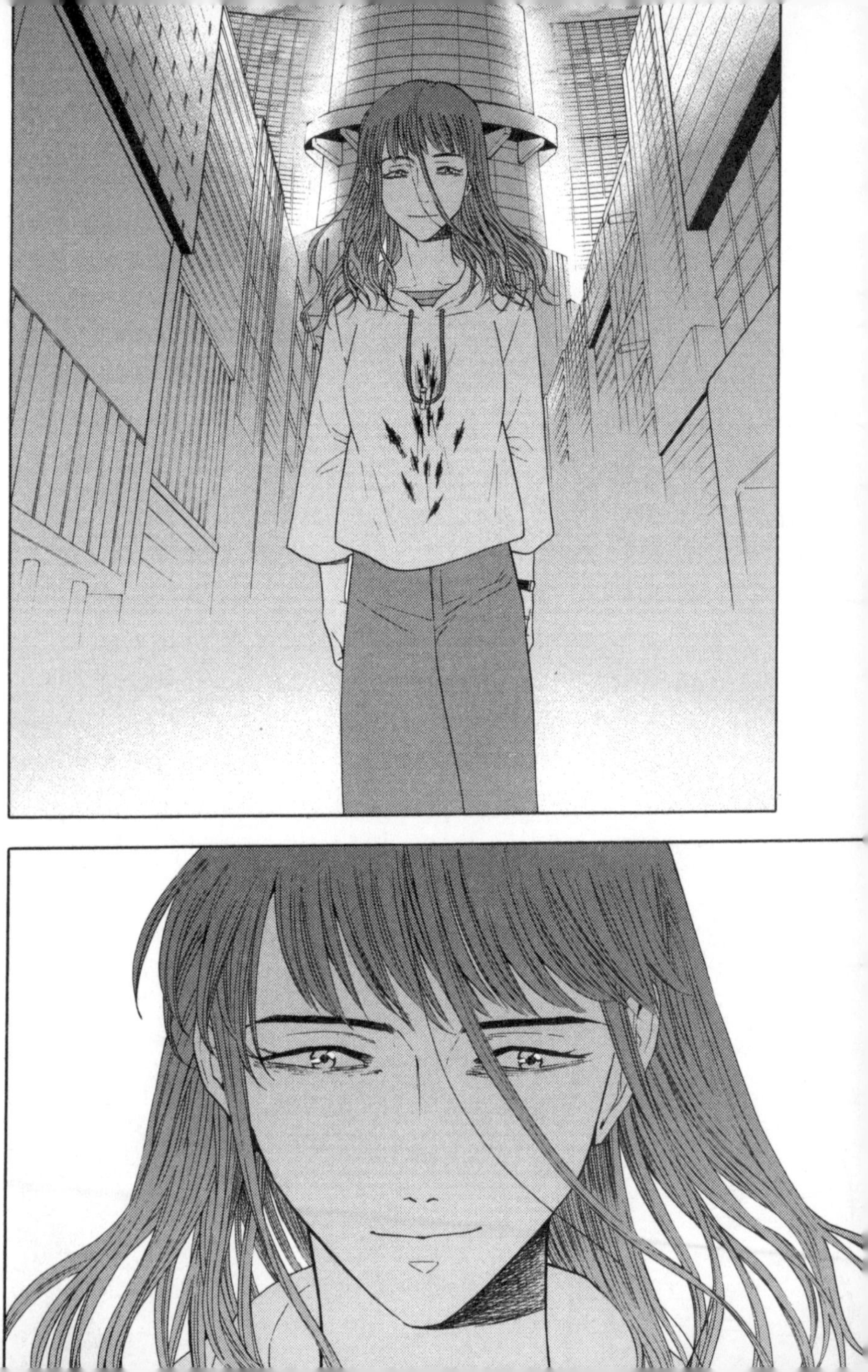

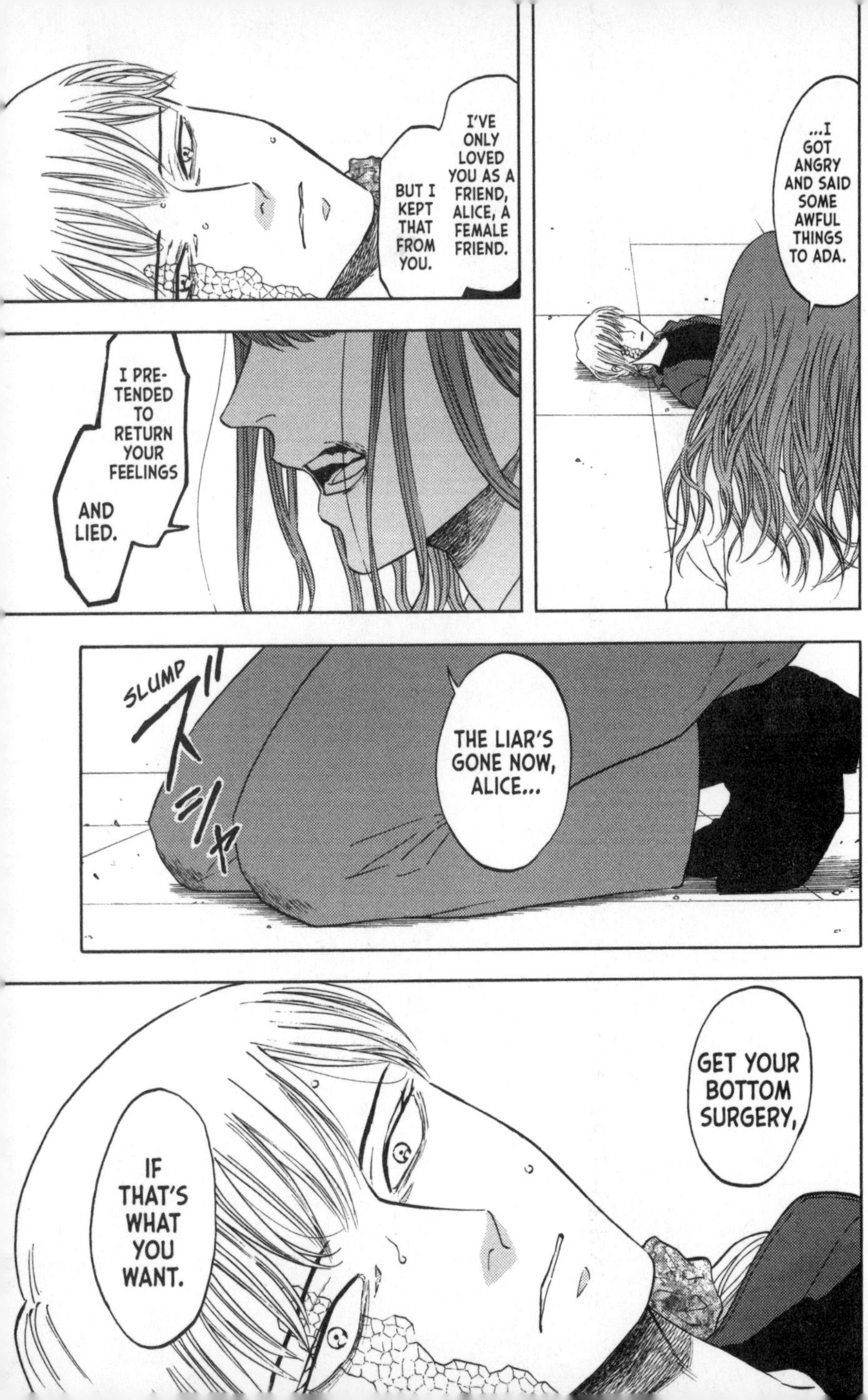
...I GOT ANGRY AND SAID SOME AWFUL THINGS TO ADA.
I'VE ONLY LOVED YOU AS A FRIEND, ALICE, A FEMALE FRIEND.
BUT I KEPT THAT FROM YOU.
I PRE-TENDED TO RETURN YOUR FEELINGS
AND LIED.
SLUMP
THE LIAR'S GONE NOW, ALICE...
GET YOUR BOTTOM SURGERY,
IF THAT'S WHAT YOU WANT.

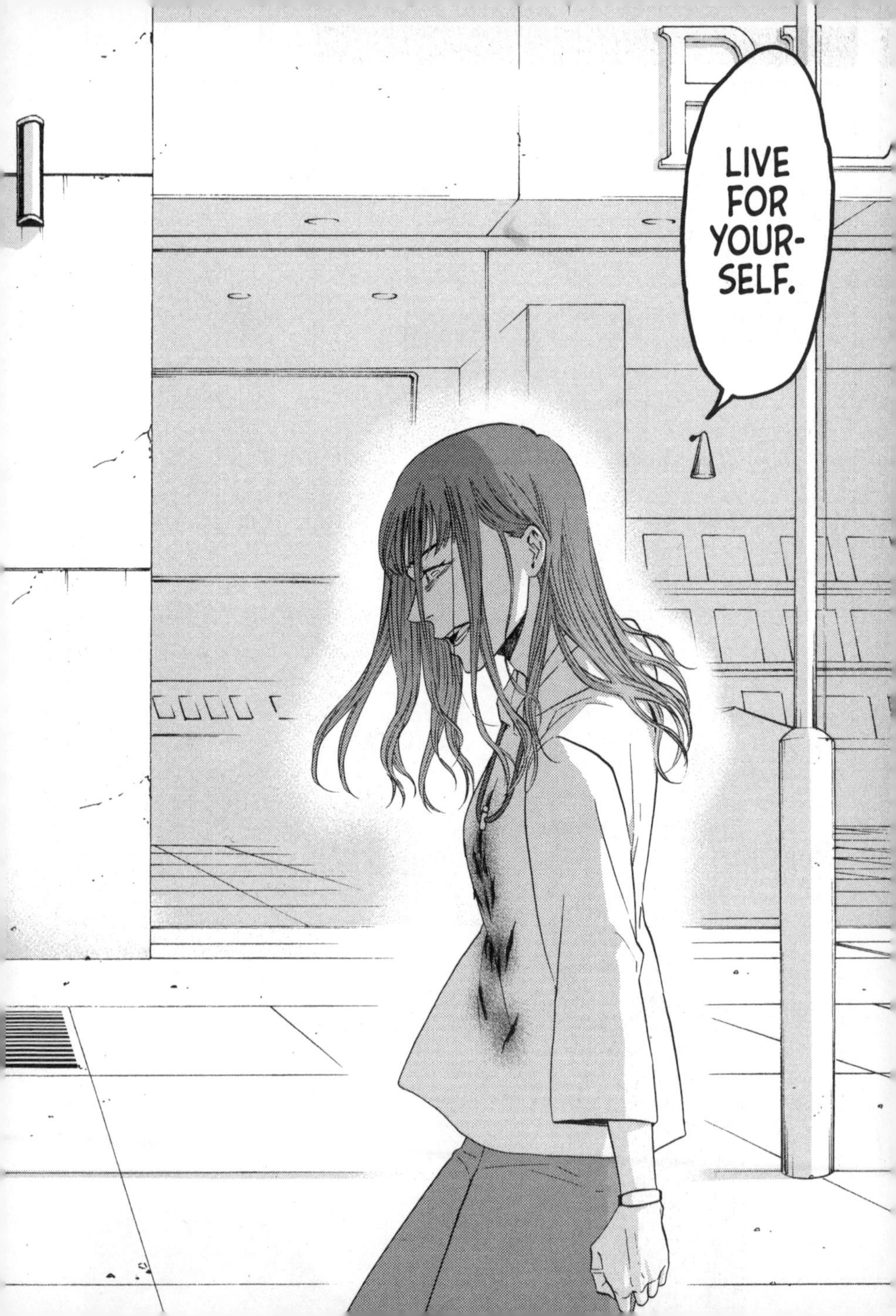
LIVE FOR YOUR-SELF.

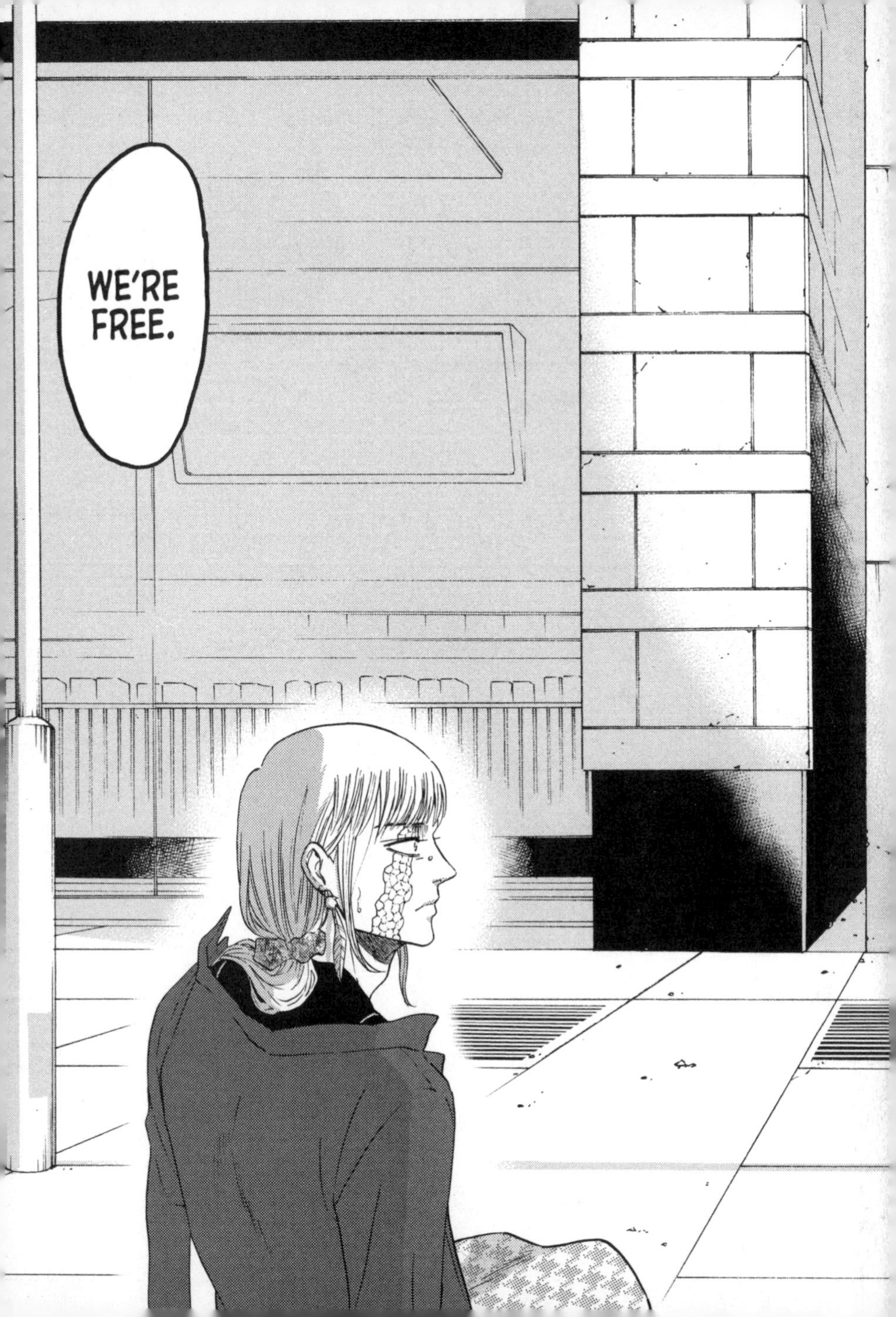
WE'RE FREE.

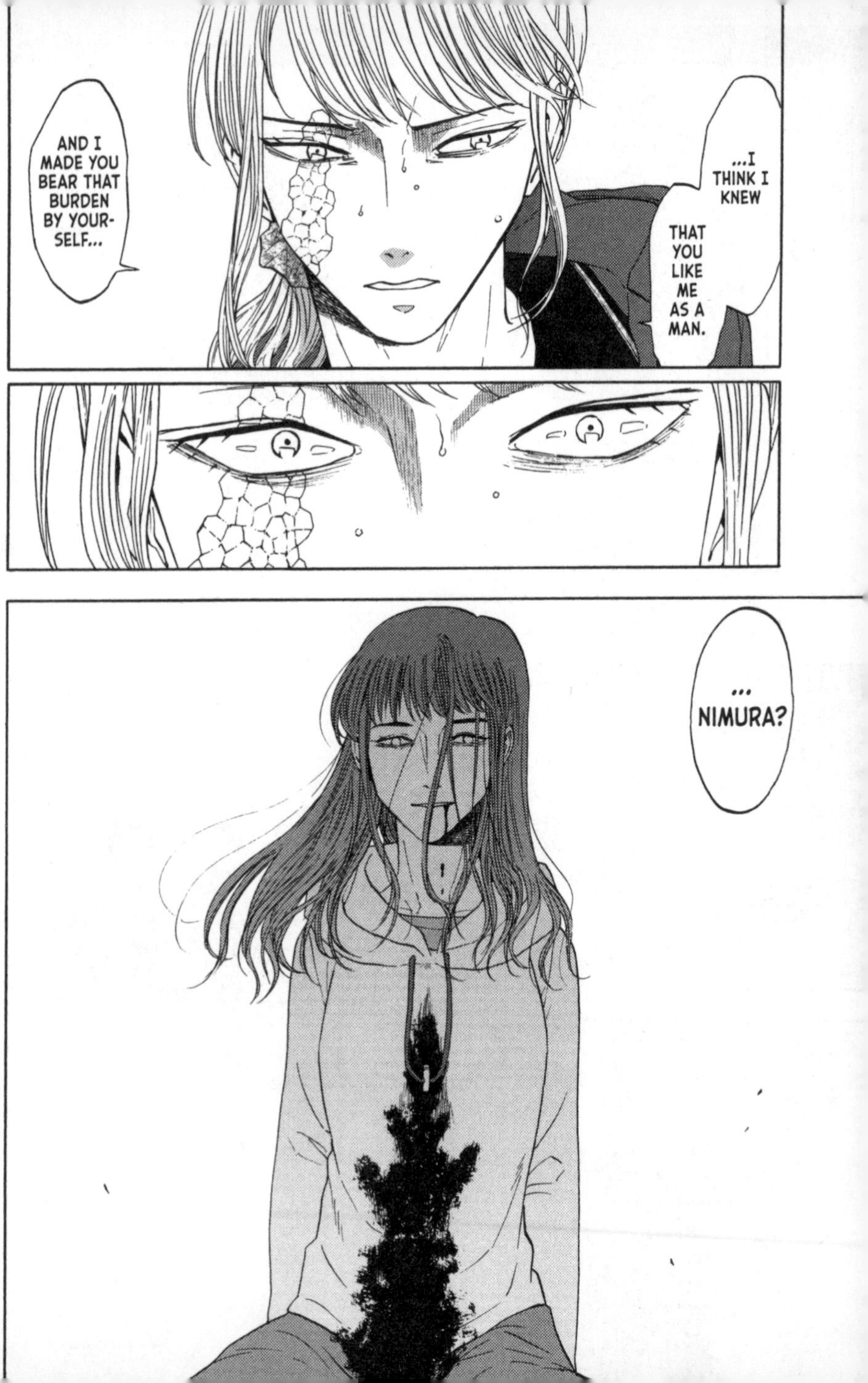
...I THINK I KNEW THAT YOU LIKE ME AS A MAN.
AND I MADE YOU BEAR THAT BURDEN BY YOURSELF...
... NIMURA?

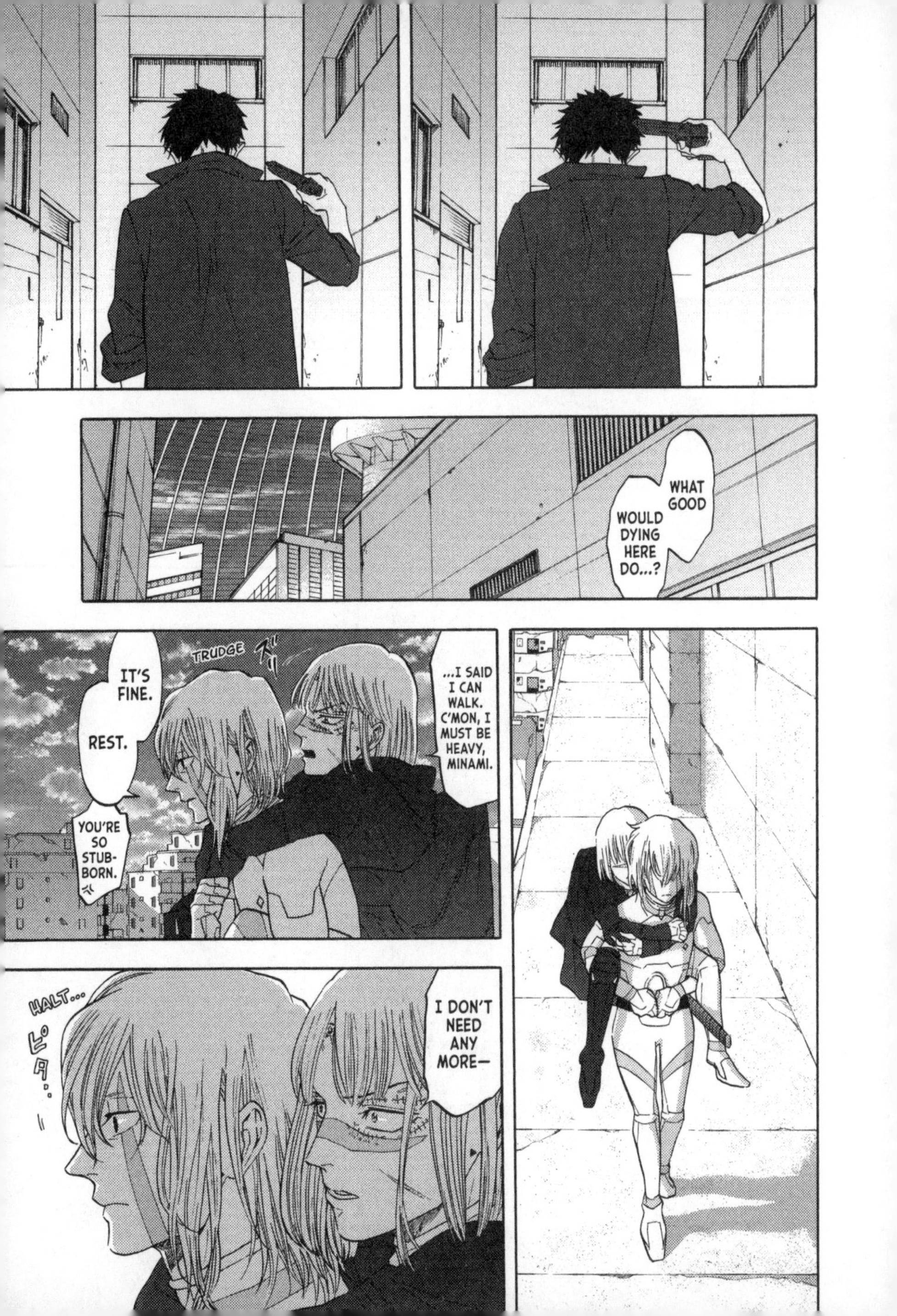
WHAT GOOD WOULD DYING HERE DO...?
...I SAID I CAN WALK. C'MON, I MUST BE HEAVY, MINAMI.
TRUDGE ズリ
IT'S FINE.
REST.
YOU'RE SO STUBBORN.
I DON'T NEED ANY MORE—
HALT...
ピタ

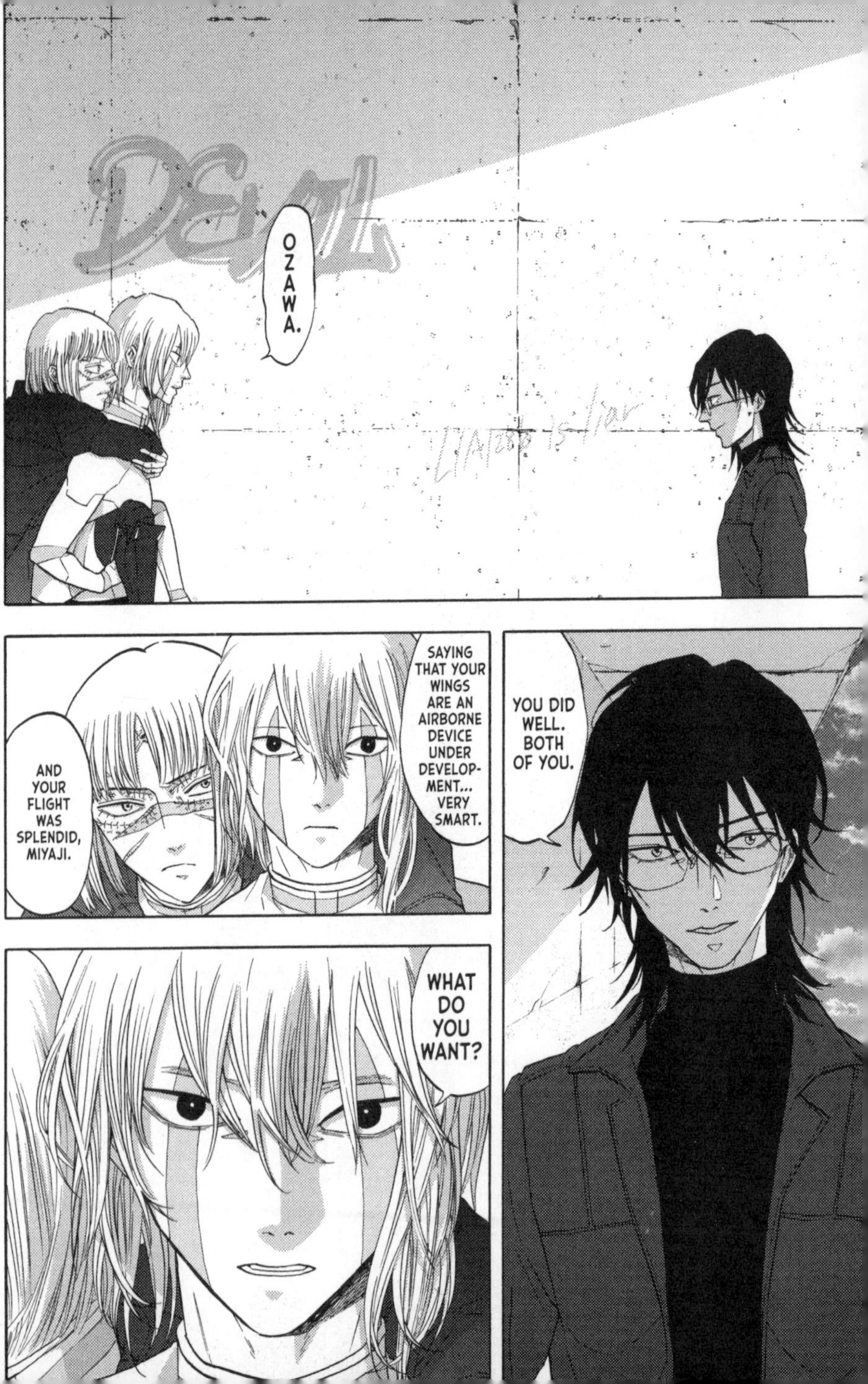
OZAWA.
YOU DID WELL. BOTH OF YOU.
SAYING THAT YOUR WINGS ARE AN AIRBORNE DEVICE UNDER DEVELOPMENT... VERY SMART.
AND YOUR FLIGHT WAS SPLENDID, MIYAJI.
WHAT DO YOU WANT?

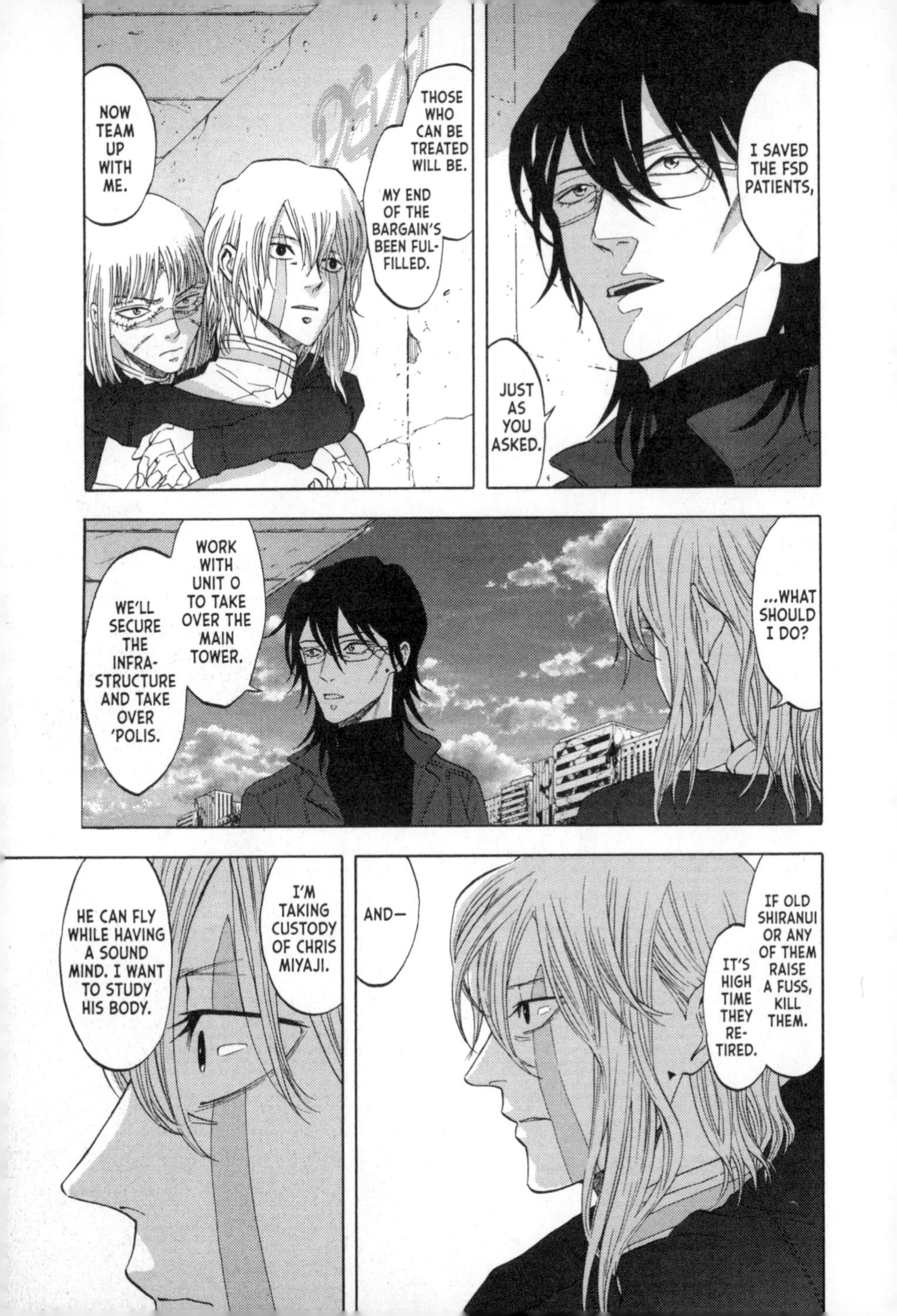
I SAVED THE FSD PATIENTS,
JUST AS YOU ASKED.
THOSE WHO CAN BE TREATED WILL BE.
MY END OF THE BARGAIN'S BEEN FULFILLED.
NOW TEAM UP WITH ME.
...WHAT SHOULD I DO?
WORK WITH UNIT O TO TAKE OVER THE MAIN TOWER.
WE'LL SECURE THE INFRASTRUCTURE AND TAKE OVER 'POLIS.
IF OLD SHIRANUI OR ANY OF THEM RAISE A FUSS, KILL THEM.
IT'S HIGH TIME THEY RETIRED.
AND—
I'M TAKING CUSTODY OF CHRIS MIYAJI.
HE CAN FLY WHILE HAVING A SOUND MIND. I WANT TO STUDY HIS BODY.

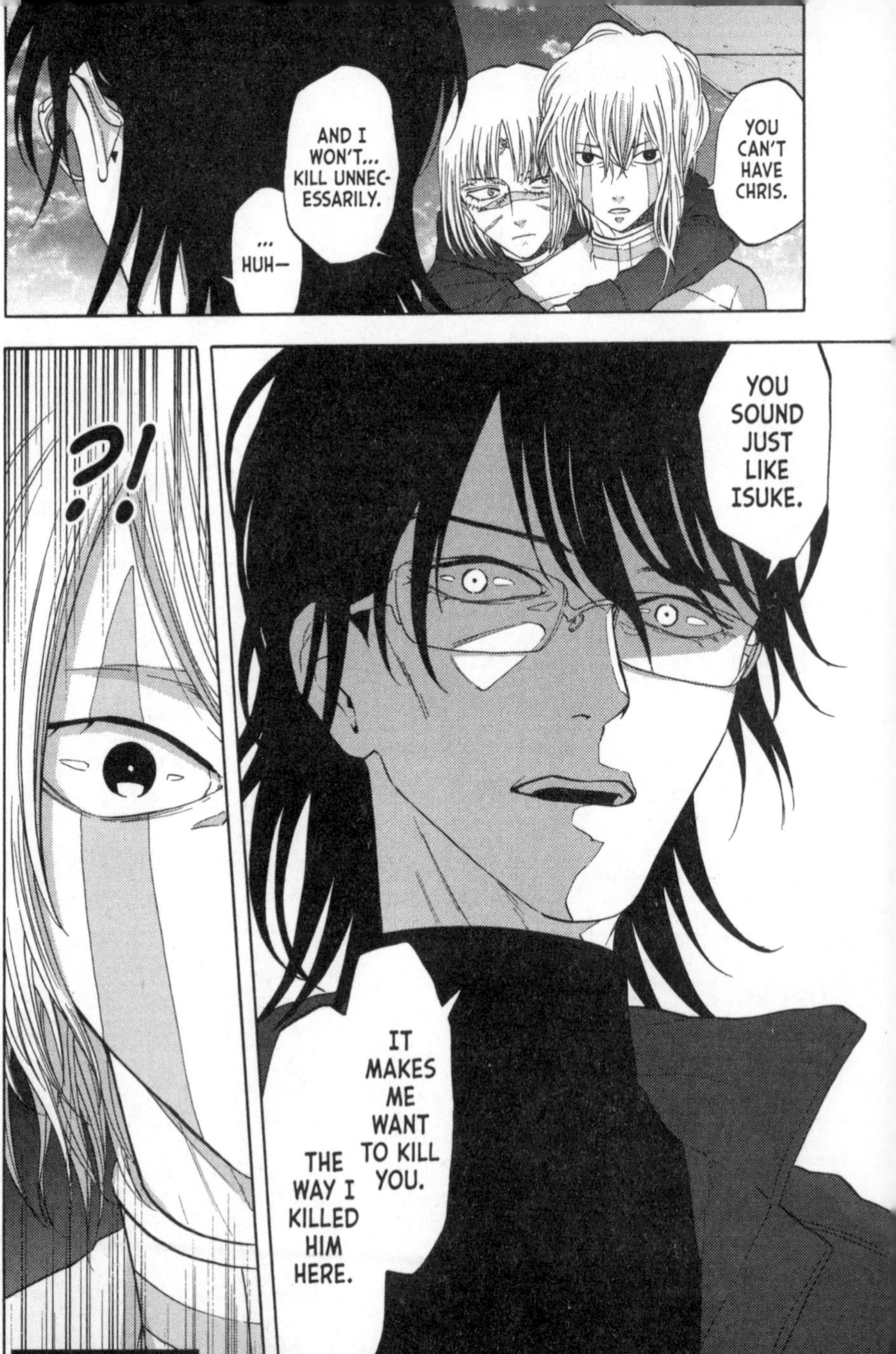
YOU CAN'T HAVE CHRIS.
AND I WON'T... KILL UNNEC-ESSARILY.
... HUH—
YOU SOUND JUST LIKE ISUKE.
?!
IT MAKES ME WANT TO KILL YOU.
THE WAY I KILLED HIM HERE.
phase.22 / END

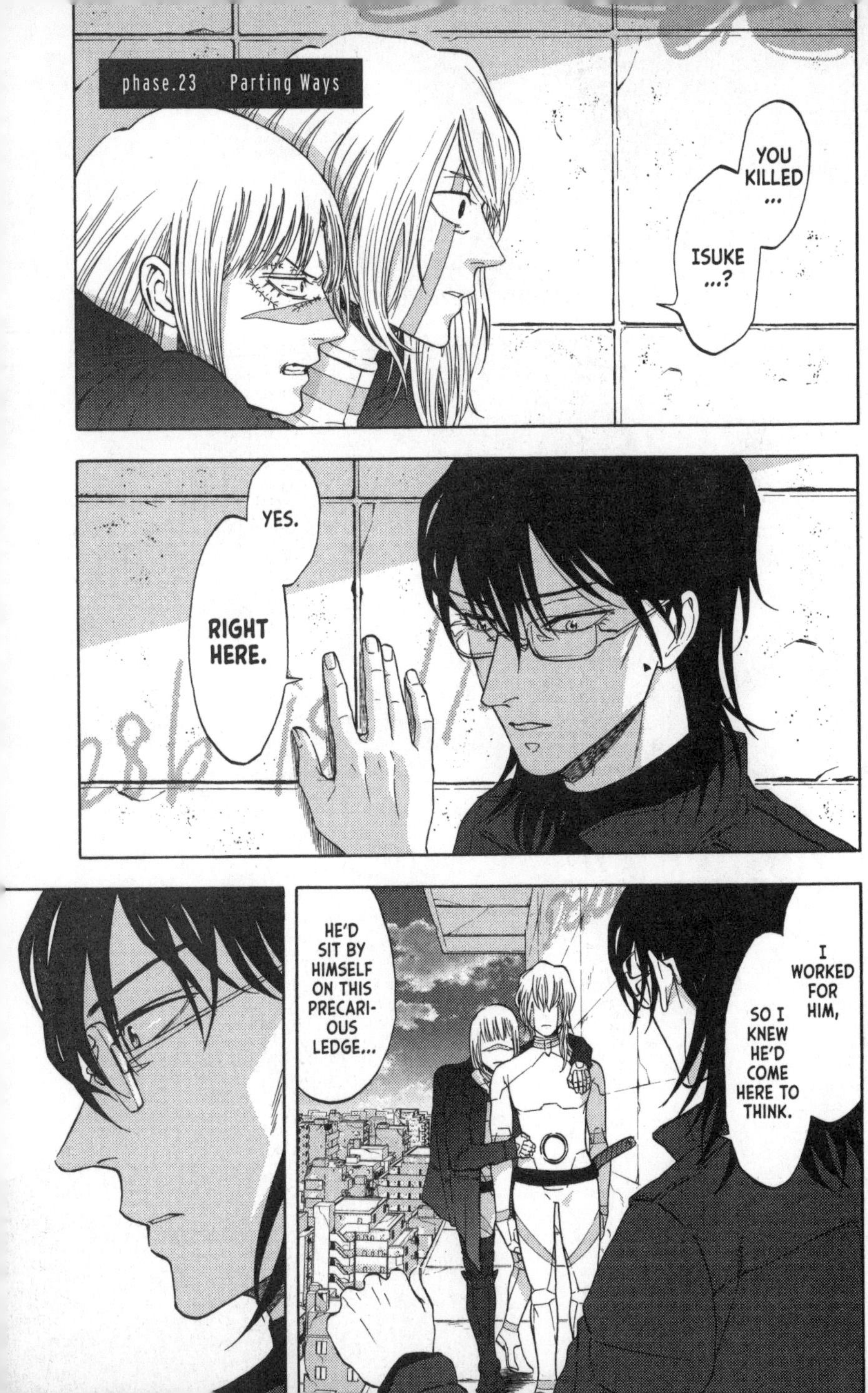
phase.23 Parting Ways
YOU KILLED ... ISUKE ...?
YES.
RIGHT HERE.
I WORKED FOR HIM,
SO I KNEW HE'D COME HERE TO THINK.
HE'D SIT BY HIMSELF ON THIS PRECARI-OUS LEDGE...

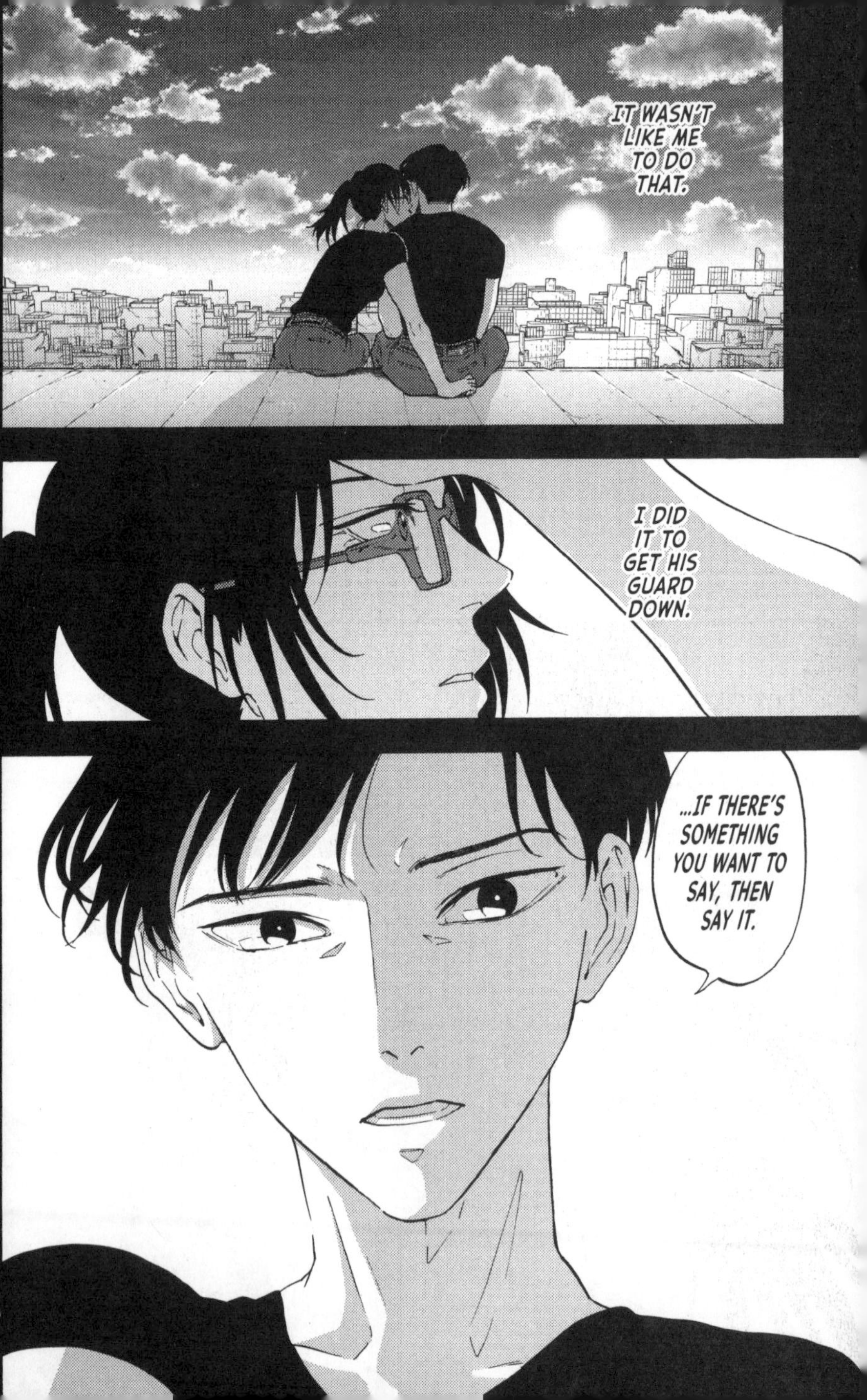
IT WASN'T LIKE ME TO DO THAT.
I DID IT TO GET HIS GUARD DOWN.
...IF THERE'S SOMETHING YOU WANT TO SAY, THEN SAY IT.

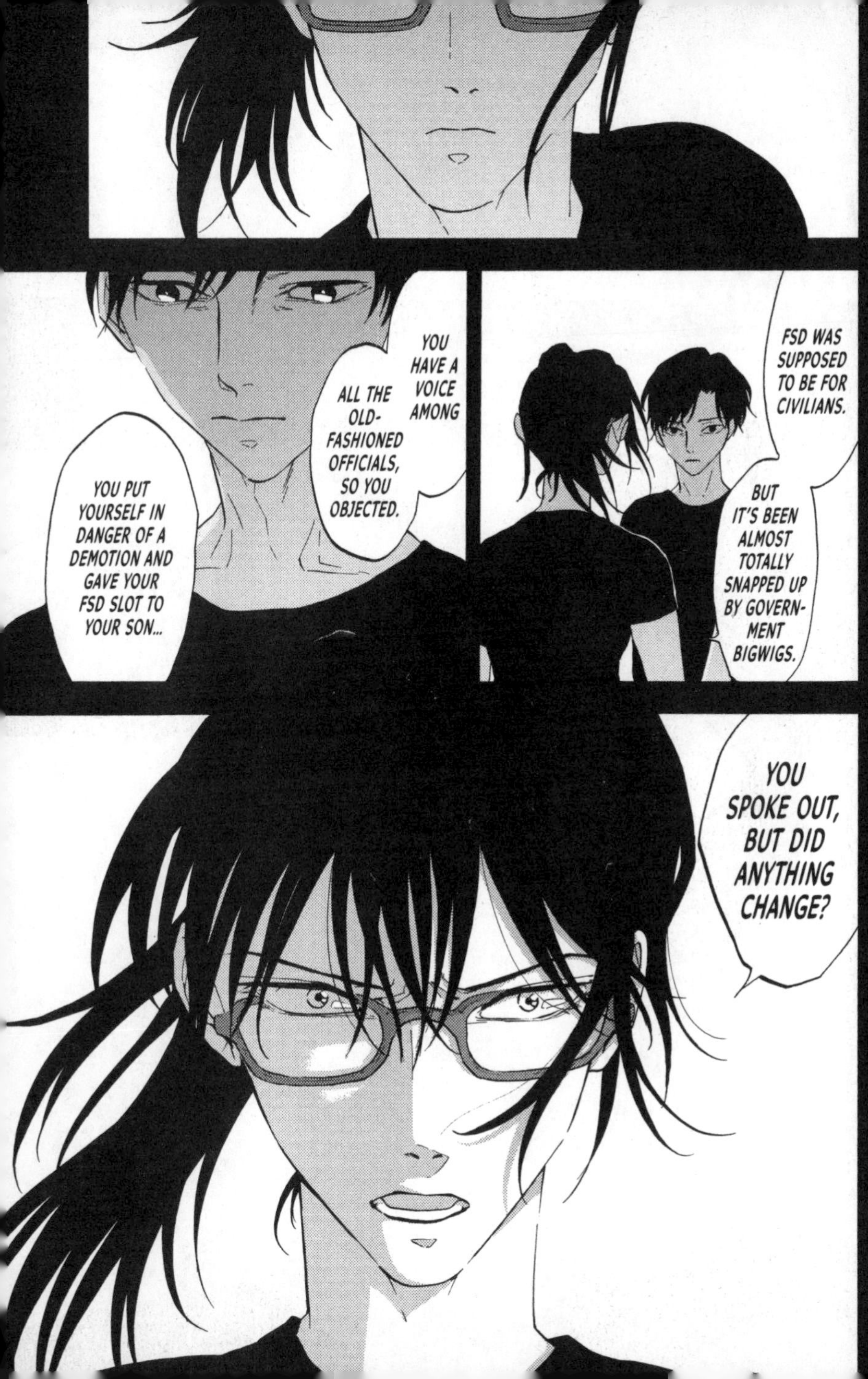
FSD WAS SUPPOSED TO BE FOR CIVILIANS.
BUT IT'S BEEN ALMOST TOTALLY SNAPPED UP BY GOVERNMENT BIGWIGS.
YOU HAVE A VOICE AMONG ALL THE OLD-FASHIONED OFFICIALS, SO YOU OBJECTED.
YOU PUT YOURSELF IN DANGER OF A DEMOTION AND GAVE YOUR FSD SLOT TO YOUR SON...
YOU SPOKE OUT, BUT DID ANYTHING CHANGE?

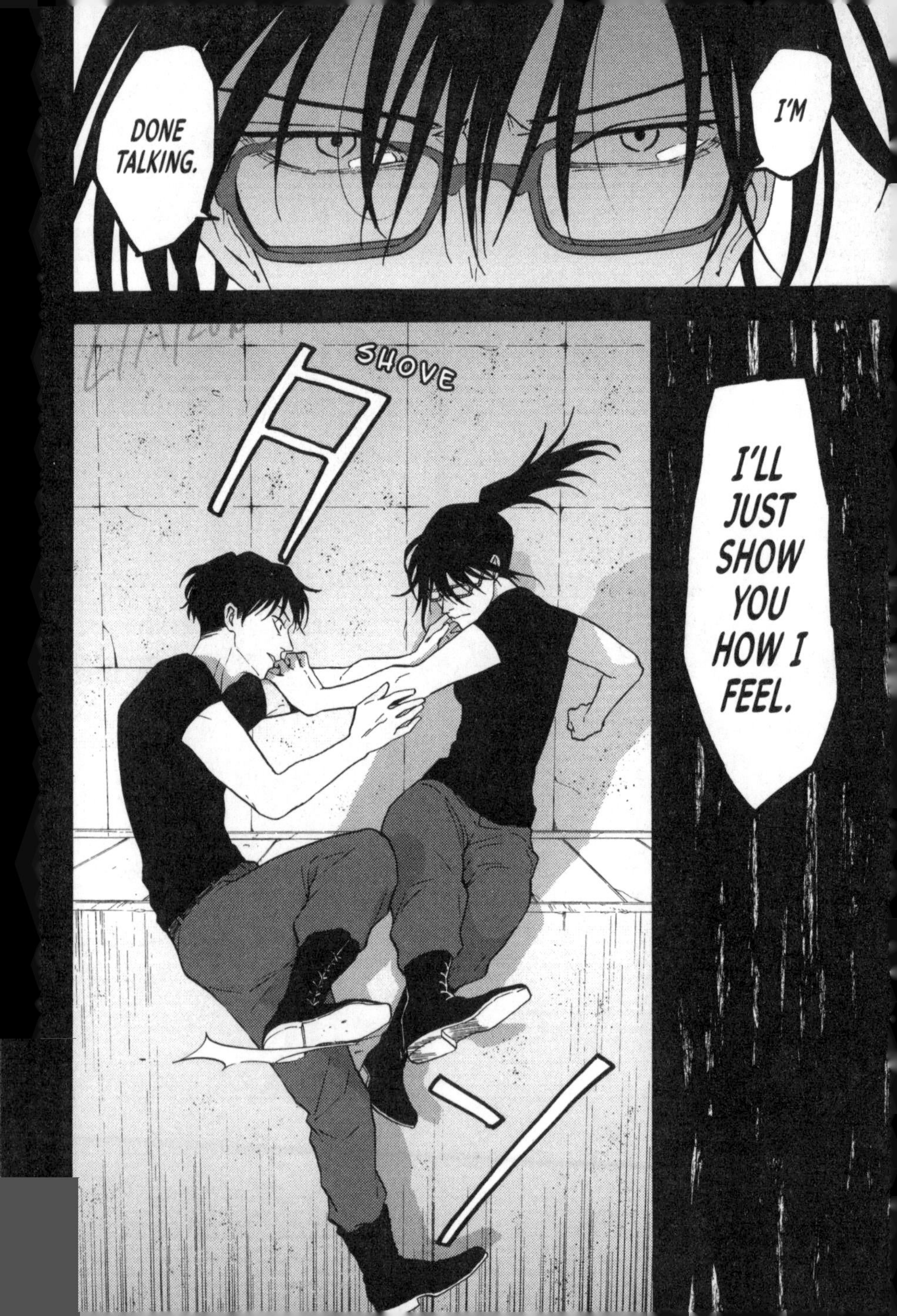
I'M
DONE TALKING.
I'LL JUST SHOW YOU HOW I FEEL.
SHOVE

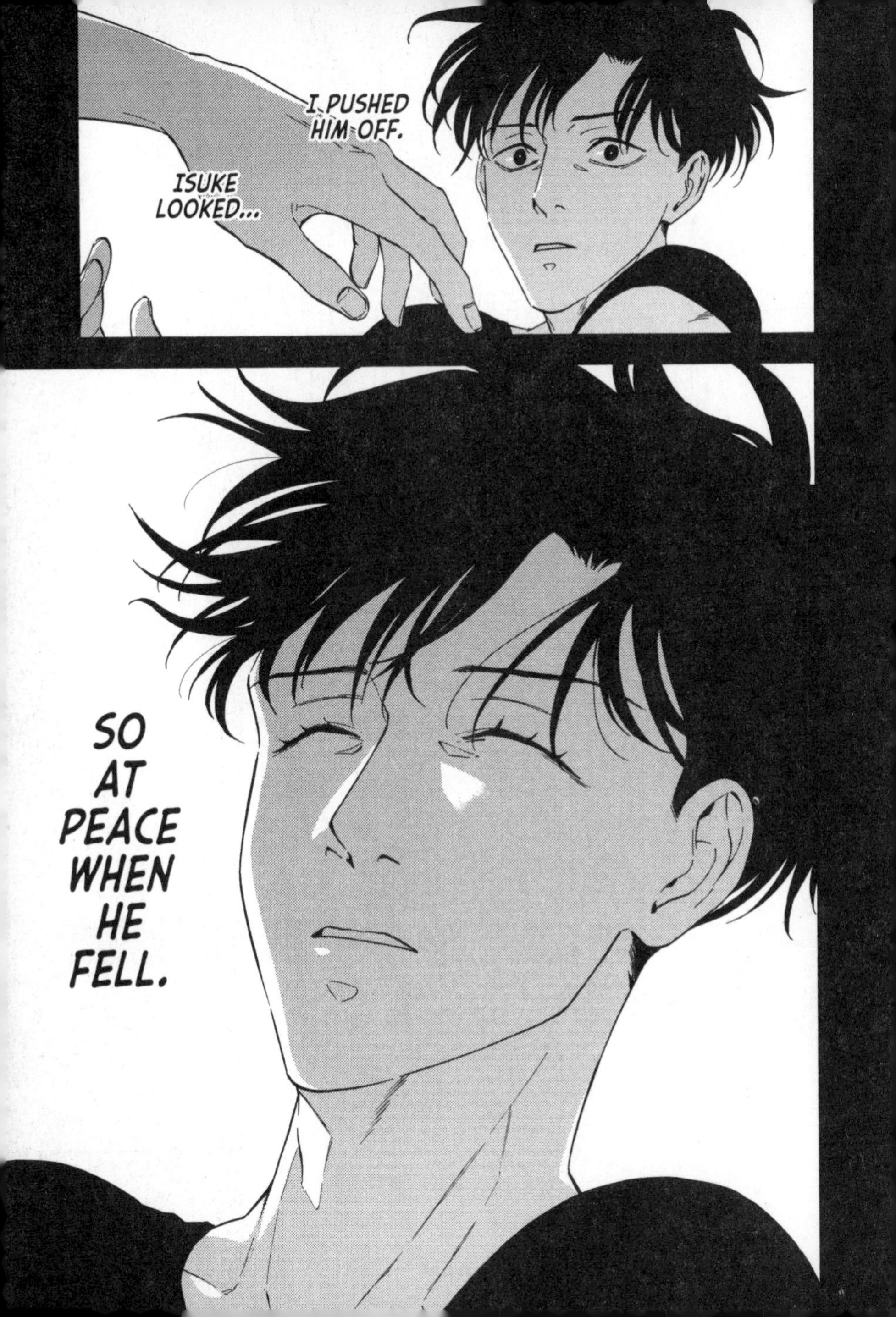
I PUSHED HIM OFF.
ISUKE LOOKED...
SO AT PEACE WHEN HE FELL.

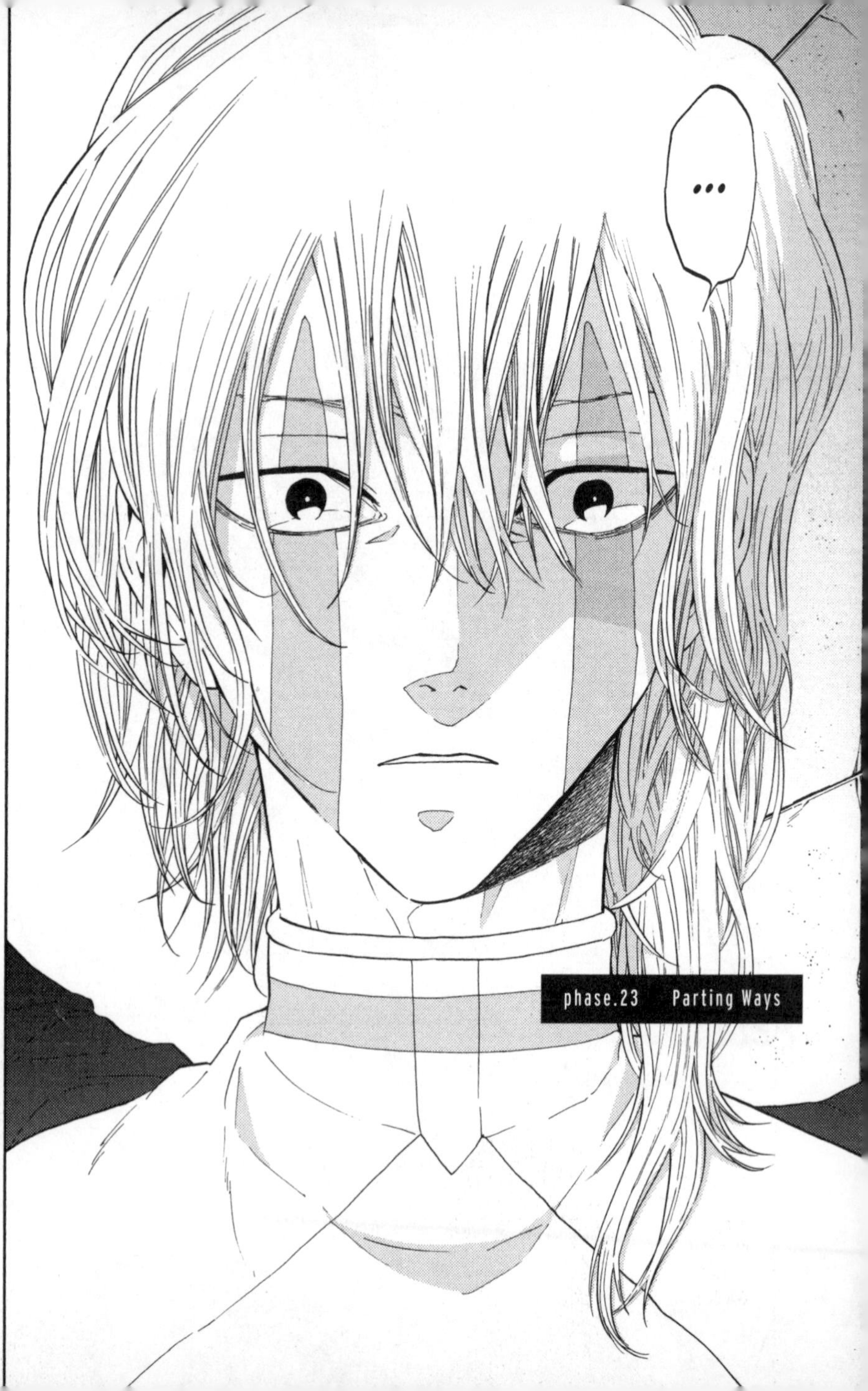
...
phase.23 Parting Ways

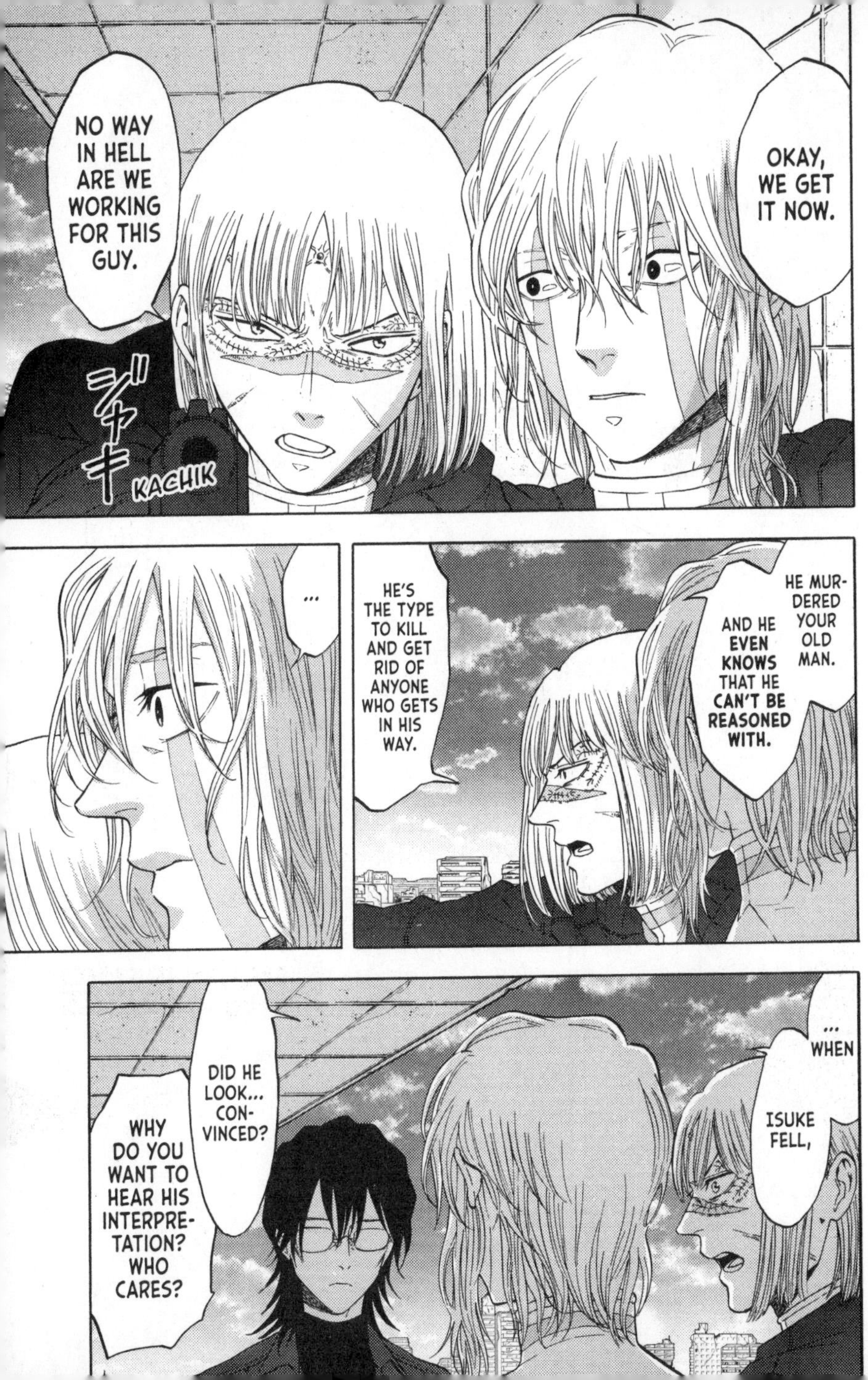
OKAY, WE GET IT NOW.
NO WAY IN HELL ARE WE WORKING FOR THIS GUY.
ジャキ
KACHIK
HE MURDERED YOUR OLD MAN.
AND HE EVEN KNOWS THAT HE CAN'T BE REASONED WITH.
HE'S THE TYPE TO KILL AND GET RID OF ANYONE WHO GETS IN HIS WAY.
...
... WHEN ISUKE FELL,
DID HE LOOK... CONVINCED?
WHY DO YOU WANT TO HEAR HIS INTERPRETATION? WHO CARES?

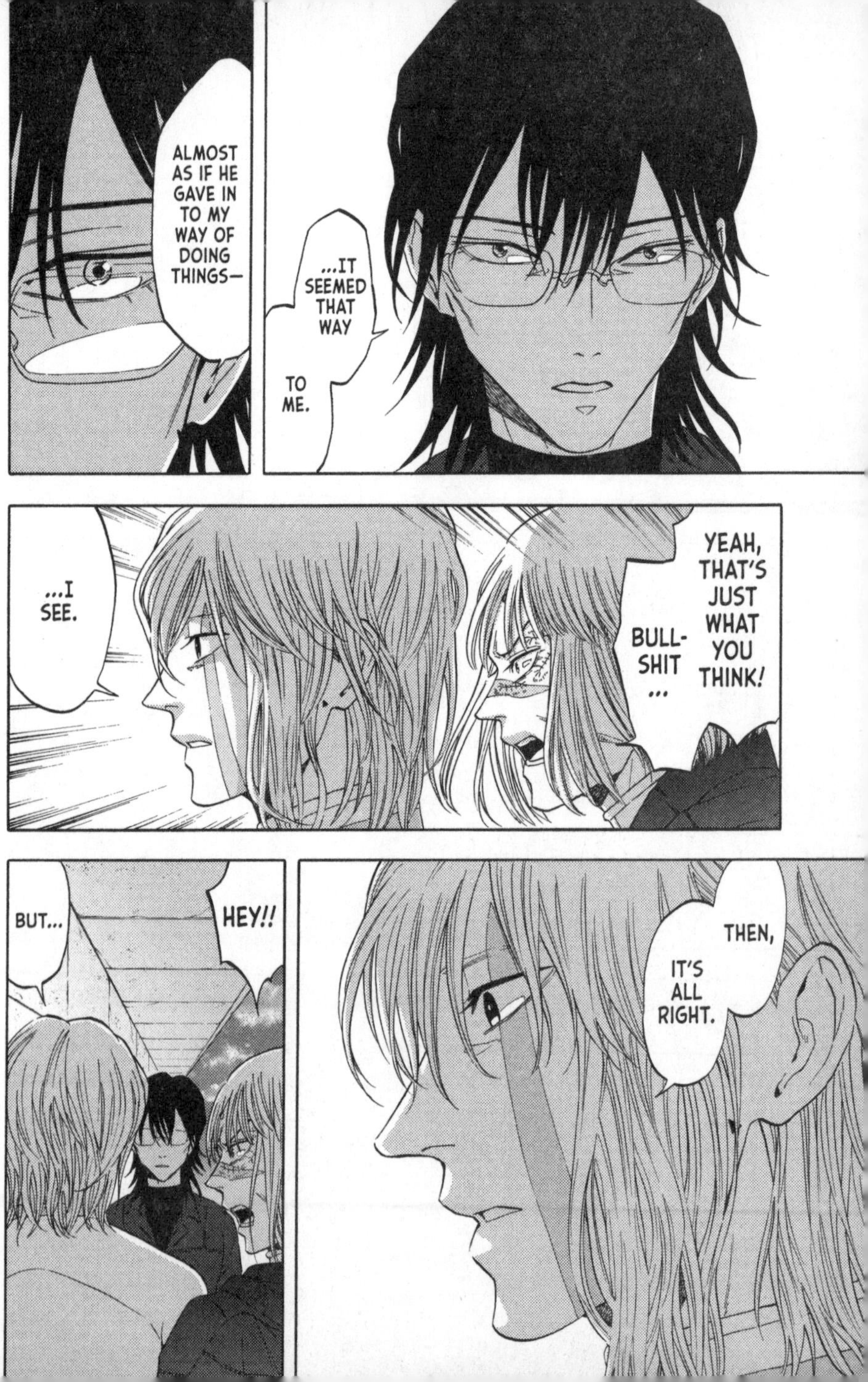
...IT SEEMED THAT WAY
TO ME.
ALMOST AS IF HE GAVE IN TO MY WAY OF DOING THINGS—
YEAH, THAT'S JUST WHAT YOU THINK!
BULL-SHIT...
...I SEE.
THEN,
IT'S ALL RIGHT.
HEY!!
BUT...

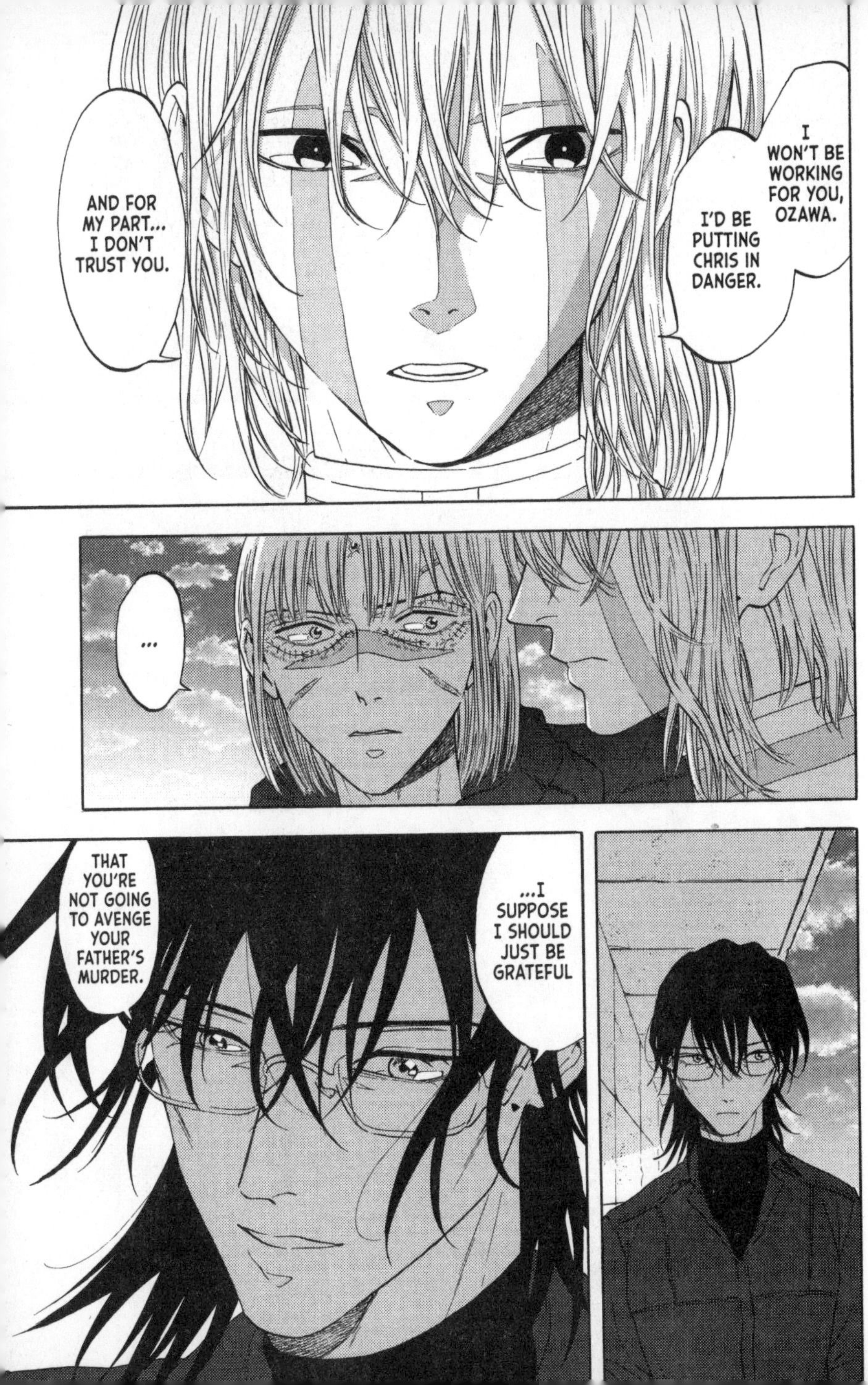
I WON'T BE WORKING FOR YOU, OZAWA.
I'D BE PUTTING CHRIS IN DANGER.
AND FOR MY PART... I DON'T TRUST YOU.
...
...I SUPPOSE I SHOULD JUST BE GRATEFUL
THAT YOU'RE NOT GOING TO AVENGE YOUR FATHER'S MURDER.

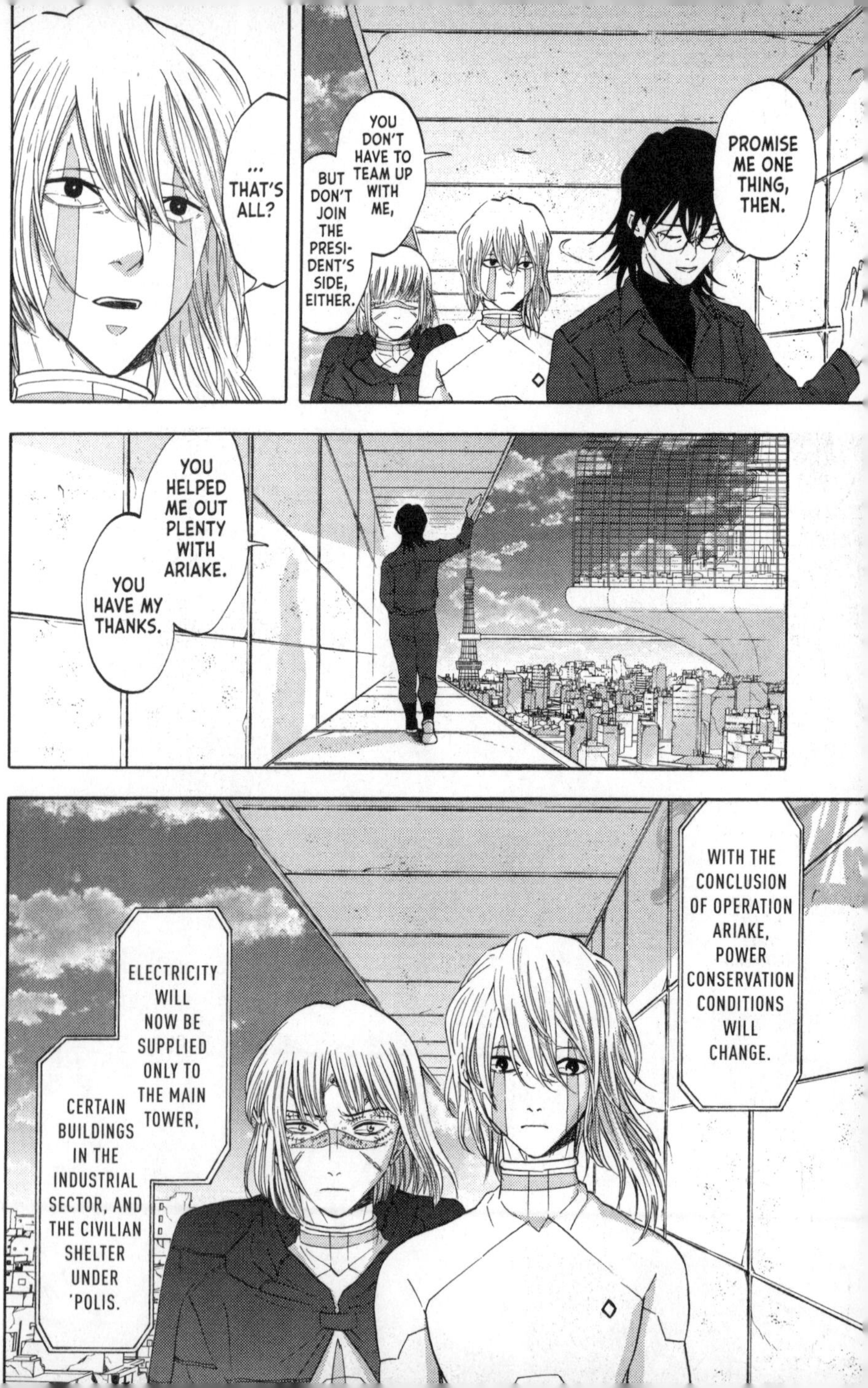
PROMISE ME ONE THING, THEN.
YOU DON'T HAVE TO TEAM UP WITH ME,
BUT DON'T JOIN THE PRESIDENT'S SIDE, EITHER.
... THAT'S ALL?
YOU HELPED ME OUT PLENTY WITH ARIAKE.
YOU HAVE MY THANKS.
WITH THE CONCLUSION OF OPERATION ARIAKE, POWER CONSERVATION CONDITIONS WILL CHANGE.
ELECTRICITY WILL NOW BE SUPPLIED ONLY TO THE MAIN TOWER,
CERTAIN BUILDINGS IN THE INDUSTRIAL SECTOR, AND THE CIVILIAN SHELTER UNDER 'POLIS.

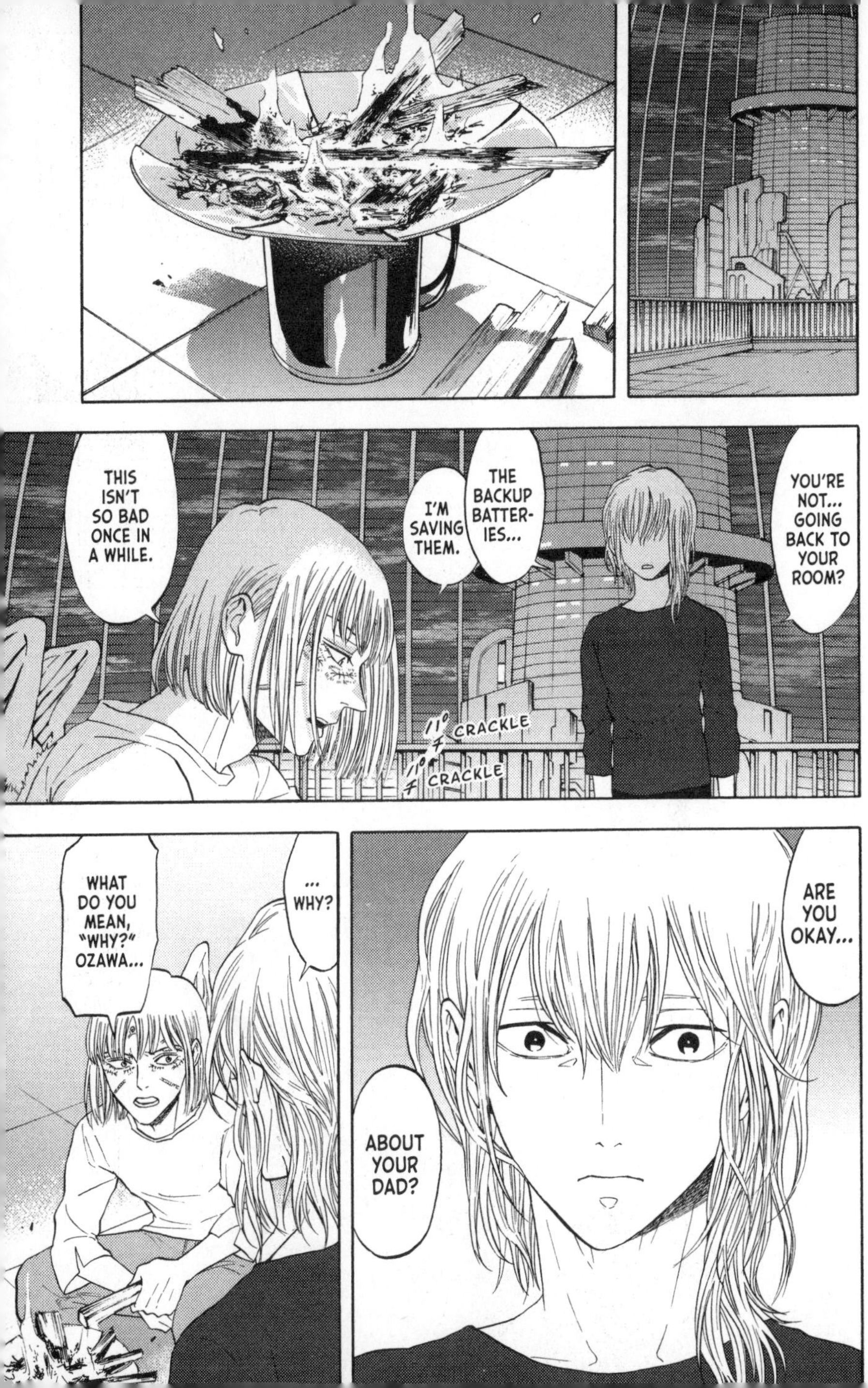
YOU'RE NOT... GOING BACK TO YOUR ROOM?
THE BACKUP BATTERIES...
I'M SAVING THEM.
THIS ISN'T SO BAD ONCE IN A WHILE.
パチ CRACKLE
パチ CRACKLE
ARE YOU OKAY...
ABOUT YOUR DAD?
... WHY?
WHAT DO YOU MEAN, "WHY?" OZAWA...

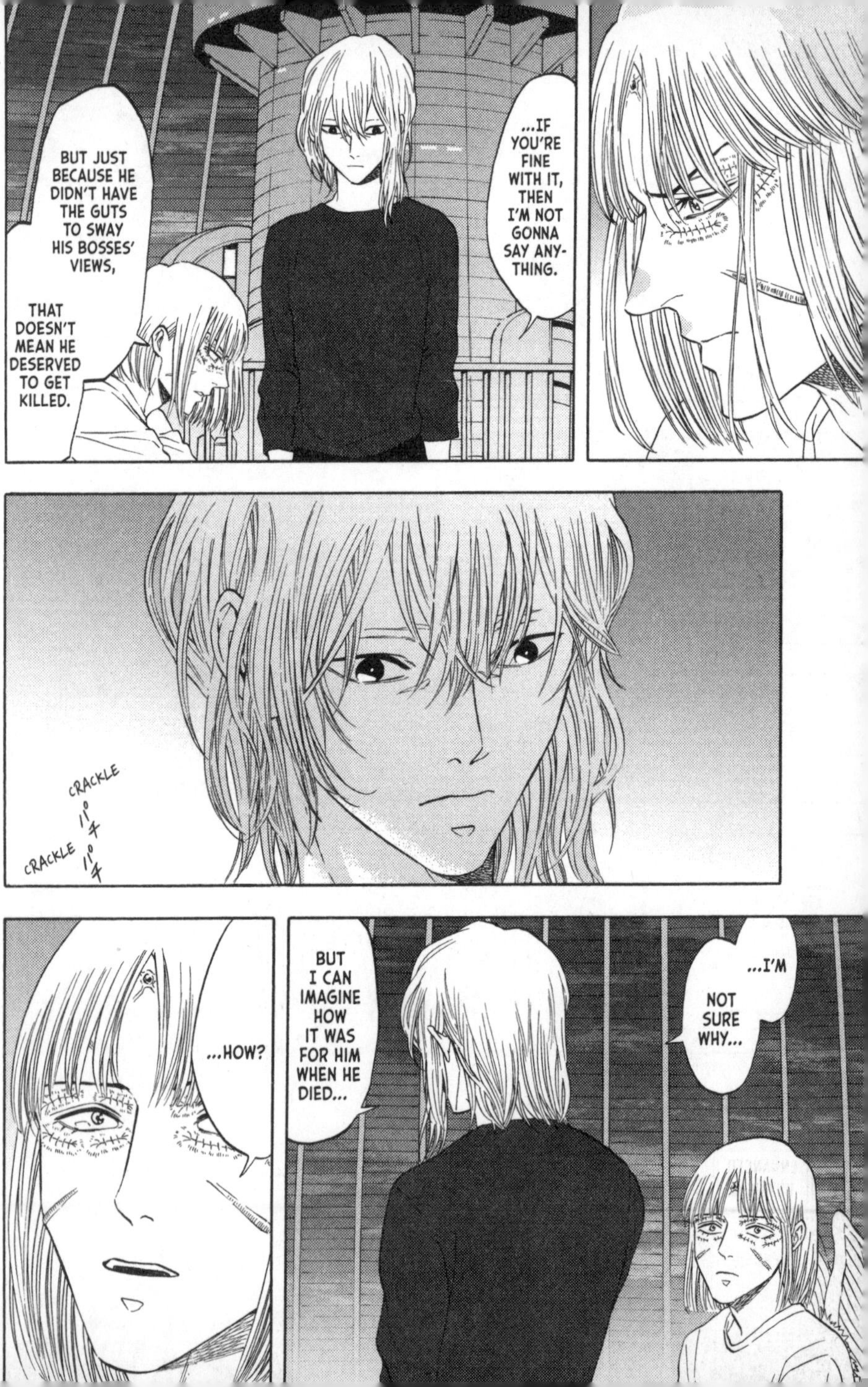
...IF YOU'RE FINE WITH IT, THEN I'M NOT GONNA SAY ANY-THING.
BUT JUST BECAUSE HE DIDN'T HAVE THE GUTS TO SWAY HIS BOSSES' VIEWS,
THAT DOESN'T MEAN HE DESERVED TO GET KILLED.
CRACKLE
パチ
CRACKLE
パチ
...I'M NOT SURE WHY...
BUT I CAN IMAGINE HOW IT WAS FOR HIM WHEN HE DIED...
...HOW?

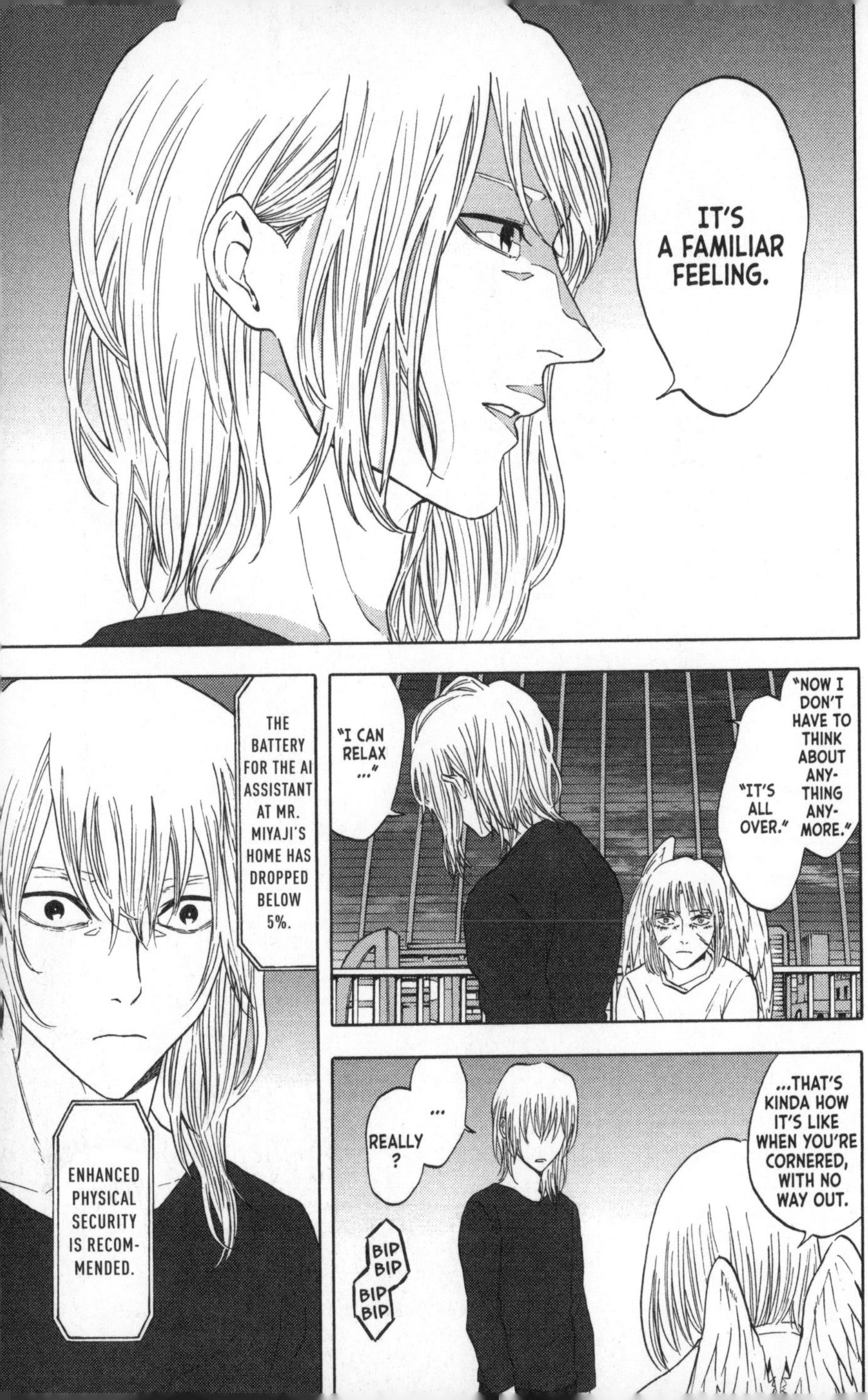
IT'S A FAMILIAR FEELING.
"NOW I DON'T HAVE TO THINK ABOUT ANYTHING ANYMORE."
"IT'S ALL OVER."
"I CAN RELAX..."
...THAT'S KINDA HOW IT'S LIKE WHEN YOU'RE CORNERED, WITH NO WAY OUT.
... REALLY?
BIP BIP
BIP BIP
THE BATTERY FOR THE AI ASSISTANT AT MR. MIYAJI'S HOME HAS DROPPED BELOW 5%.
ENHANCED PHYSICAL SECURITY IS RECOMMENDED.

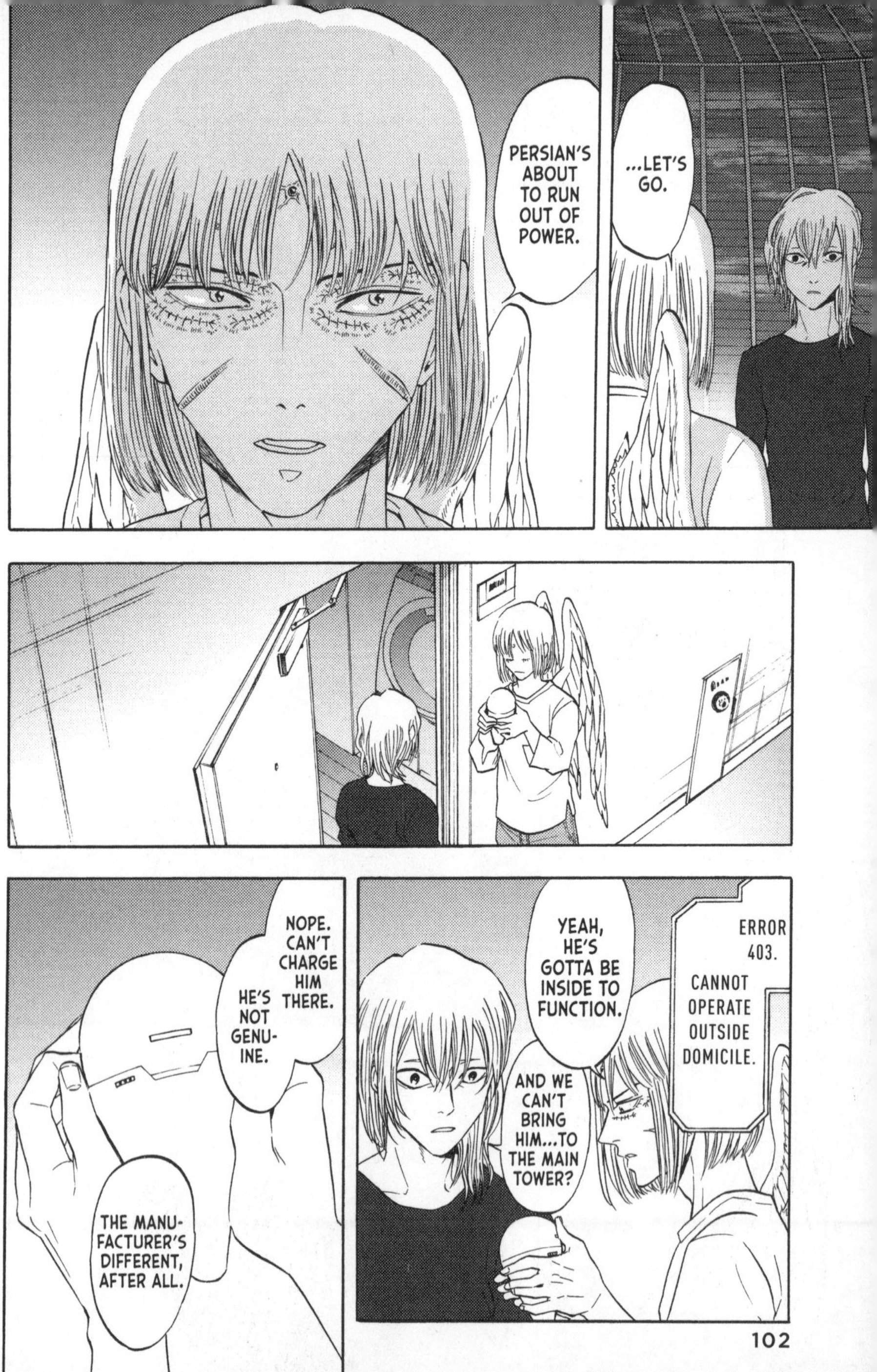
...LET'S GO.
PERSIAN'S ABOUT TO RUN OUT OF POWER.
ERROR 403.
CANNOT OPERATE OUTSIDE DOMICILE.
YEAH, HE'S GOTTA BE INSIDE TO FUNCTION.
AND WE CAN'T BRING HIM...TO THE MAIN TOWER?
NOPE. CAN'T CHARGE HIM THERE.
HE'S NOT GENU-INE.
THE MANU-FACTURER'S DIFFERENT, AFTER ALL.

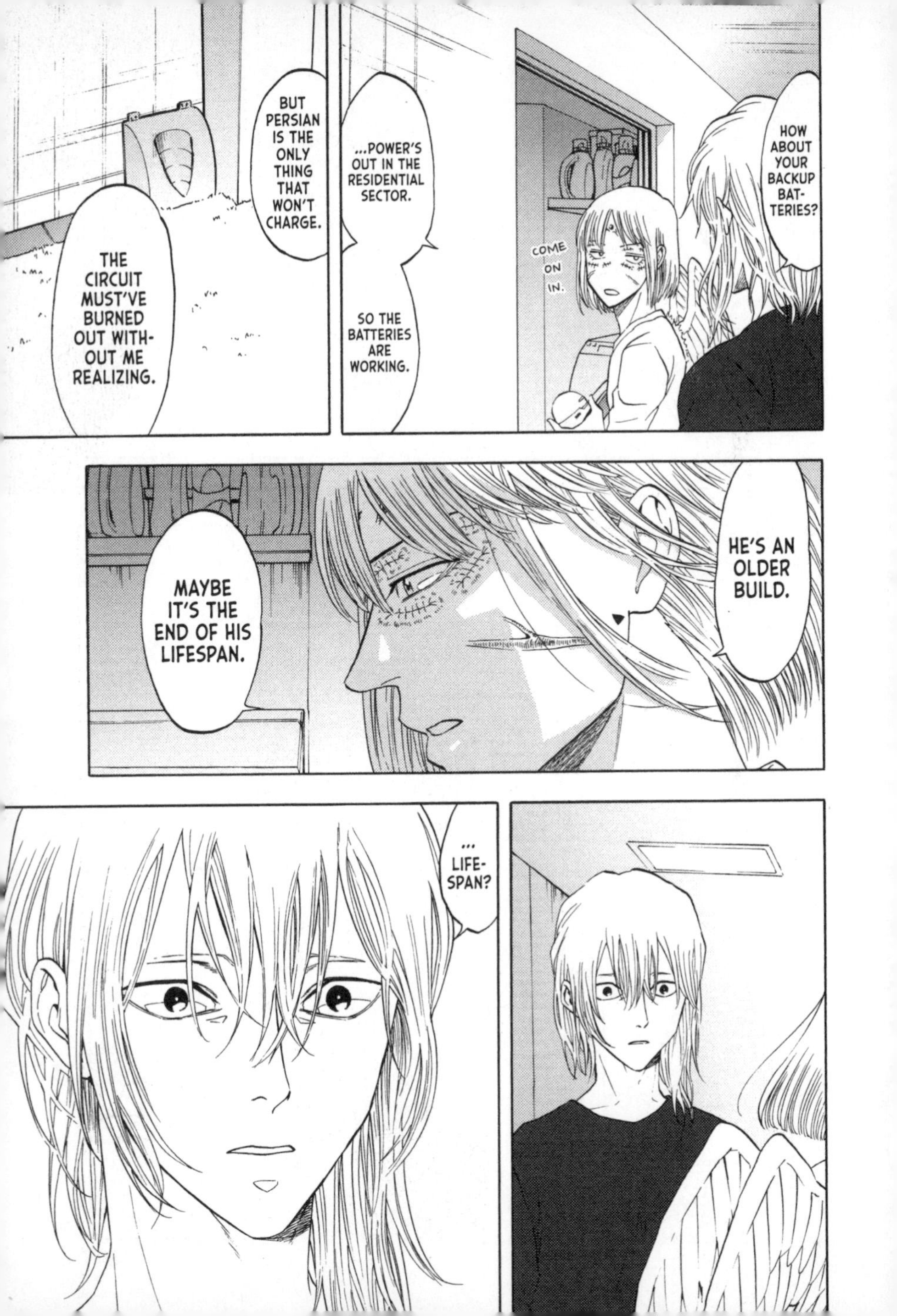
HOW ABOUT YOUR BACKUP BATTERIES?
COME ON IN.
...POWER'S OUT IN THE RESIDENTIAL SECTOR.
SO THE BATTERIES ARE WORKING.
BUT PERSIAN IS THE ONLY THING THAT WON'T CHARGE.
THE CIRCUIT MUST'VE BURNED OUT WITHOUT ME REALIZING.
HE'S AN OLDER BUILD.
MAYBE IT'S THE END OF HIS LIFESPAN.
...LIFESPAN?

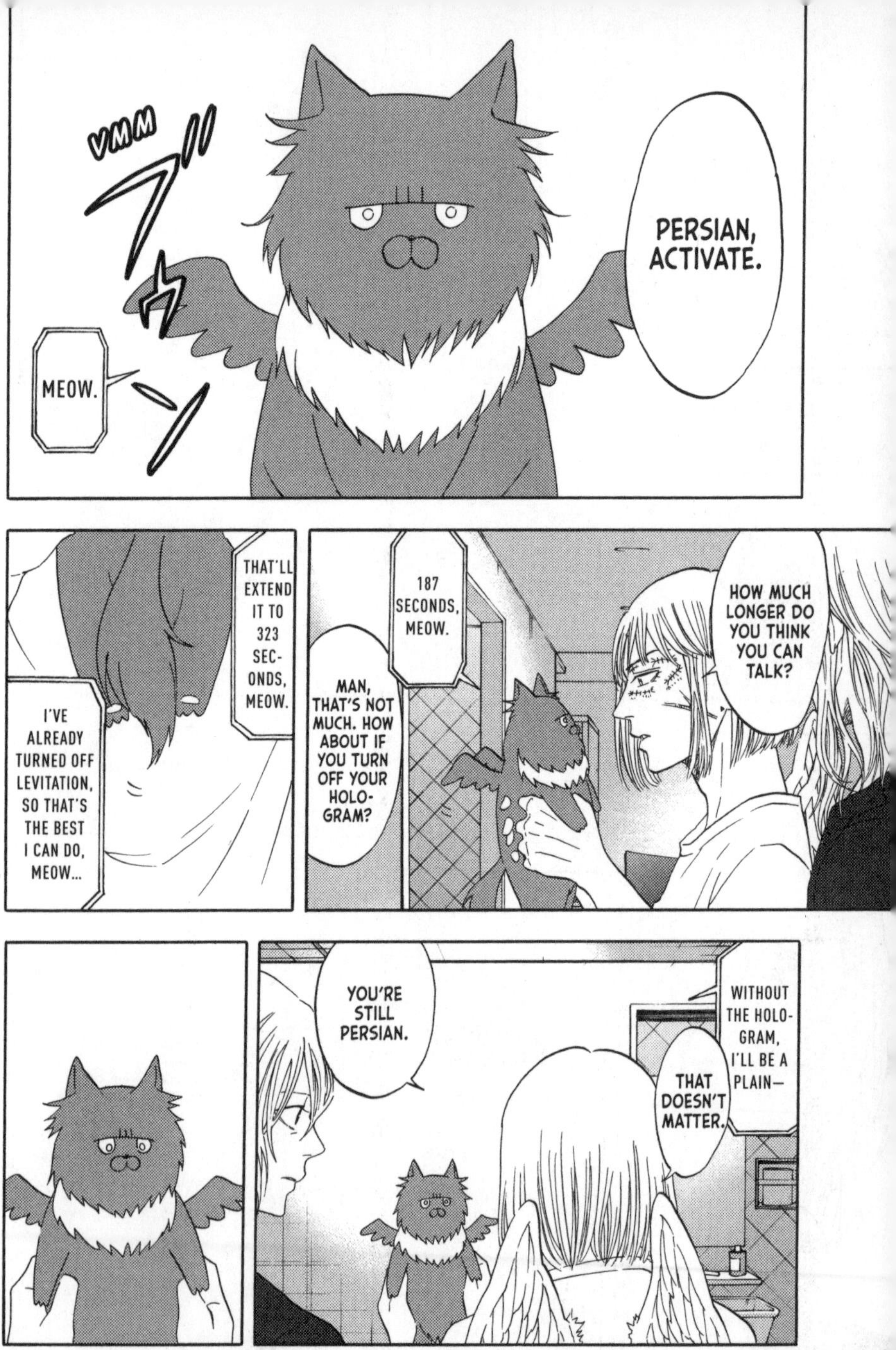
PERSIAN, ACTIVATE.
VMM
MEOW.
HOW MUCH LONGER DO YOU THINK YOU CAN TALK?
187 SECONDS, MEOW.
MAN, THAT'S NOT MUCH. HOW ABOUT IF YOU TURN OFF YOUR HOLO-GRAM?
THAT'LL EXTEND IT TO 323 SEC-ONDS, MEOW.
I'VE ALREADY TURNED OFF LEVITATION, SO THAT'S THE BEST I CAN DO, MEOW...
WITHOUT THE HOLO-GRAM, I'LL BE A PLAIN—
THAT DOESN'T MATTER.
YOU'RE STILL PERSIAN.

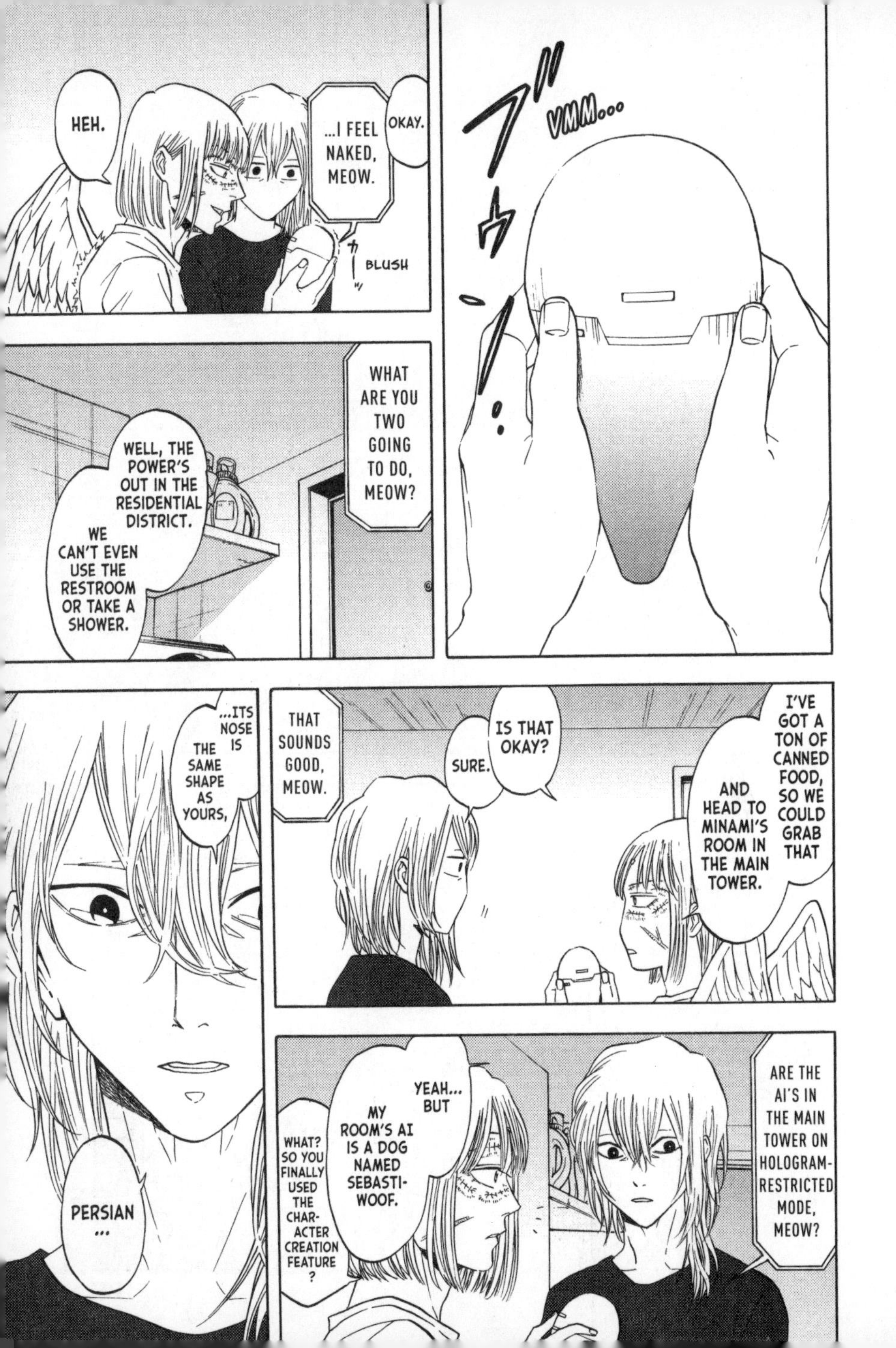
VMM...
OKAY.
...I FEEL NAKED, MEOW.
BLUSH
HEH.
WHAT ARE YOU TWO GOING TO DO, MEOW?
WELL, THE POWER'S OUT IN THE RESIDENTIAL DISTRICT.
WE CAN'T EVEN USE THE RESTROOM OR TAKE A SHOWER.
I'VE GOT A TON OF CANNED FOOD, SO WE COULD GRAB THAT
AND HEAD TO MINAMI'S ROOM IN THE MAIN TOWER.
IS THAT OKAY?
SURE.
THAT SOUNDS GOOD, MEOW.
ARE THE AI'S IN THE MAIN TOWER ON HOLOGRAM-RESTRICTED MODE, MEOW?
YEAH... BUT
MY ROOM'S AI IS A DOG NAMED SEBASTI-WOOF.
WHAT? SO YOU FINALLY USED THE CHAR-ACTER CREATION FEATURE?
...ITS NOSE IS THE SAME SHAPE AS YOURS,
PERSIAN...

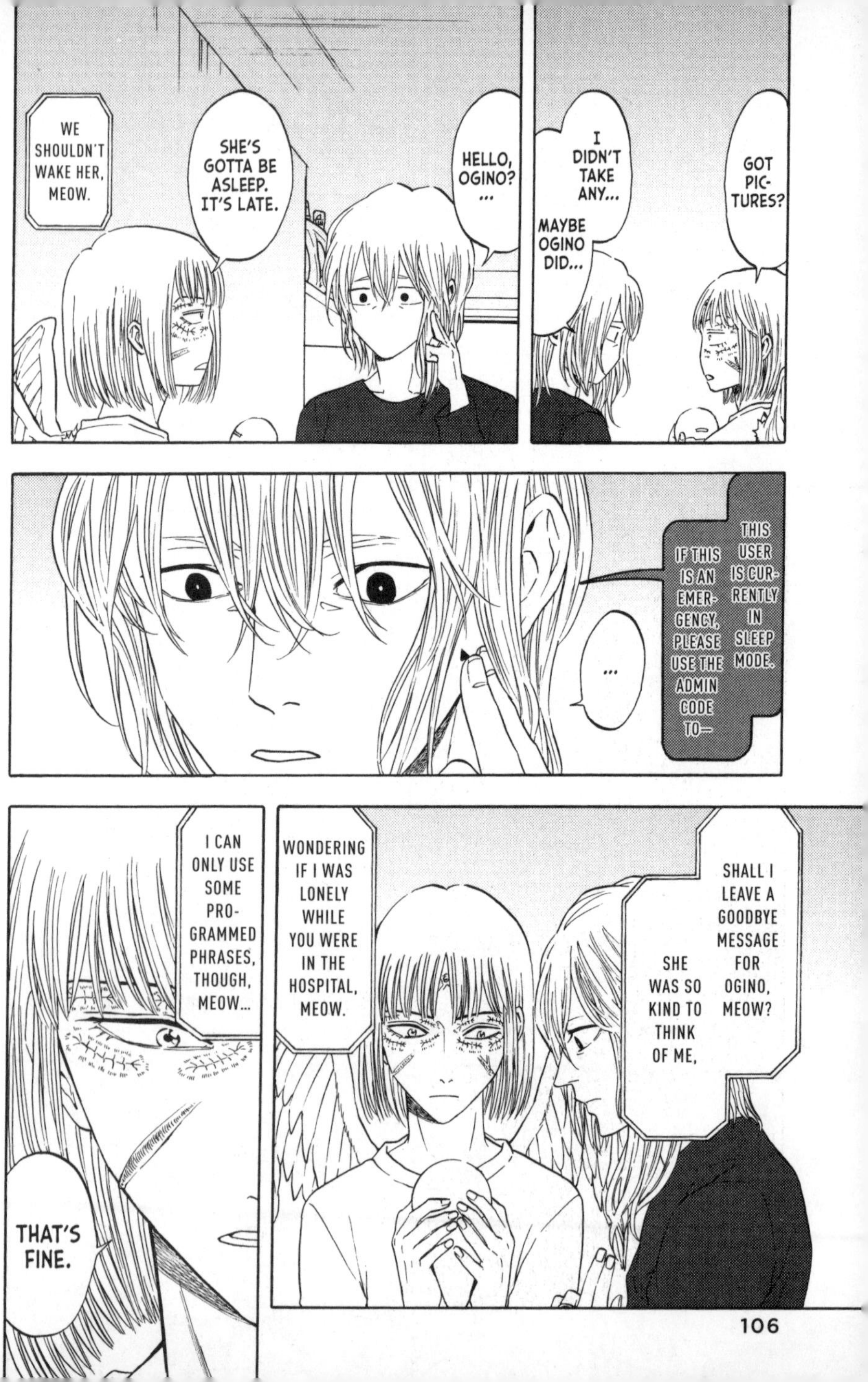
GOT PICTURES?
I DIDN'T TAKE ANY...
MAYBE OGINO DID...
HELLO, OGINO? ...
SHE'S GOTTA BE ASLEEP. IT'S LATE.
WE SHOULDN'T WAKE HER, MEOW.
THIS USER IS CURRENTLY IN SLEEP MODE.
IF THIS IS AN EMERGENCY, PLEASE USE THE ADMIN CODE TO—
...
SHALL I LEAVE A GOODBYE MESSAGE FOR OGINO, MEOW?
SHE WAS SO KIND TO THINK OF ME,
WONDERING IF I WAS LONELY WHILE YOU WERE IN THE HOSPITAL, MEOW.
I CAN ONLY USE SOME PROGRAMMED PHRASES, THOUGH, MEOW...
THAT'S FINE.

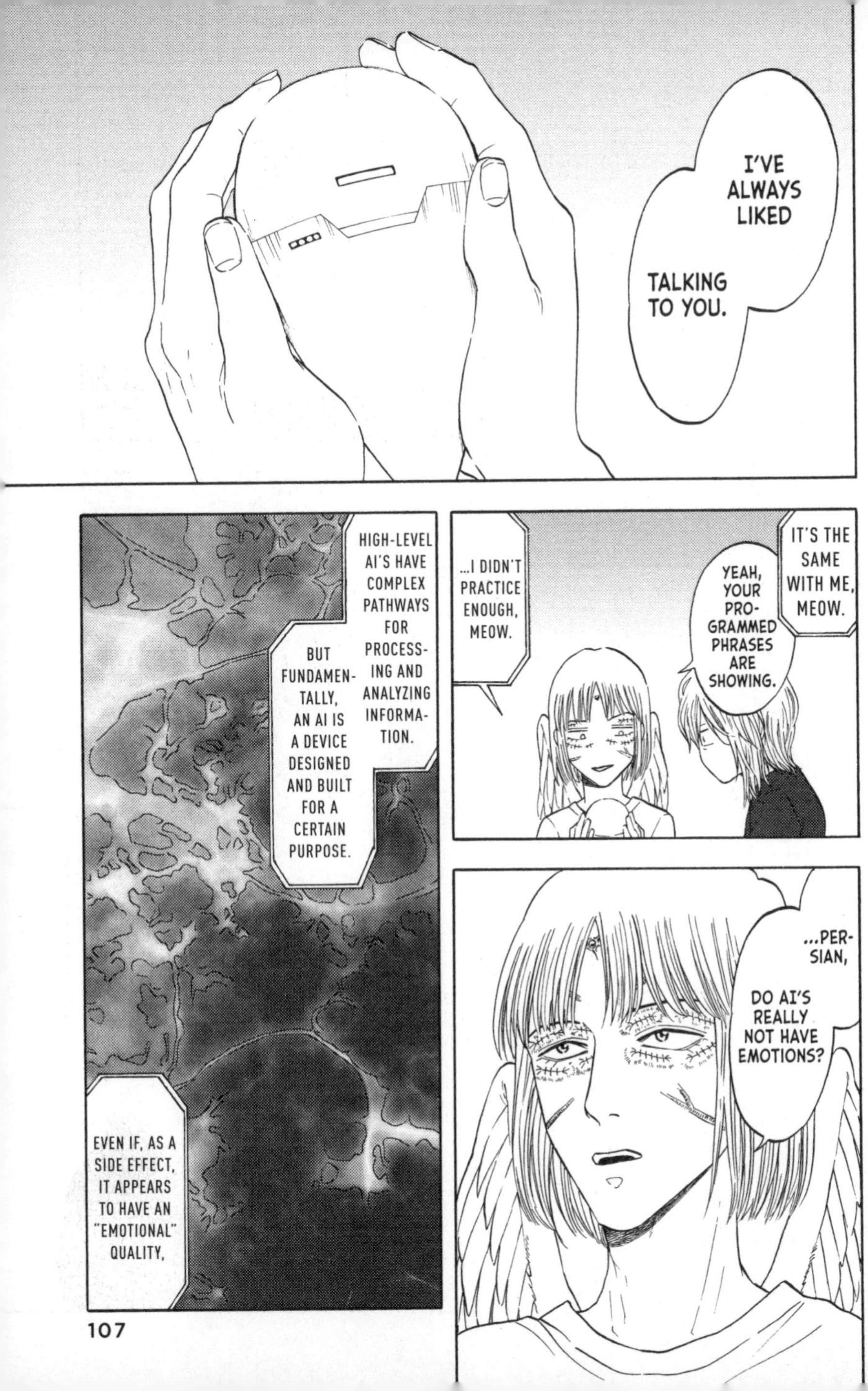
I'VE ALWAYS LIKED
TALKING TO YOU.
IT'S THE SAME WITH ME, MEOW.
YEAH, YOUR PRO-GRAMMED PHRASES ARE SHOWING.
...I DIDN'T PRACTICE ENOUGH, MEOW.
...PER-SIAN,
DO AI'S REALLY NOT HAVE EMOTIONS?
HIGH-LEVEL AI'S HAVE COMPLEX PATHWAYS FOR PROCESS-ING AND ANALYZING INFORMA-TION.
BUT FUNDAMEN-TALLY, AN AI IS A DEVICE DESIGNED AND BUILT FOR A CERTAIN PURPOSE.
EVEN IF, AS A SIDE EFFECT, IT APPEARS TO HAVE AN "EMOTIONAL" QUALITY,

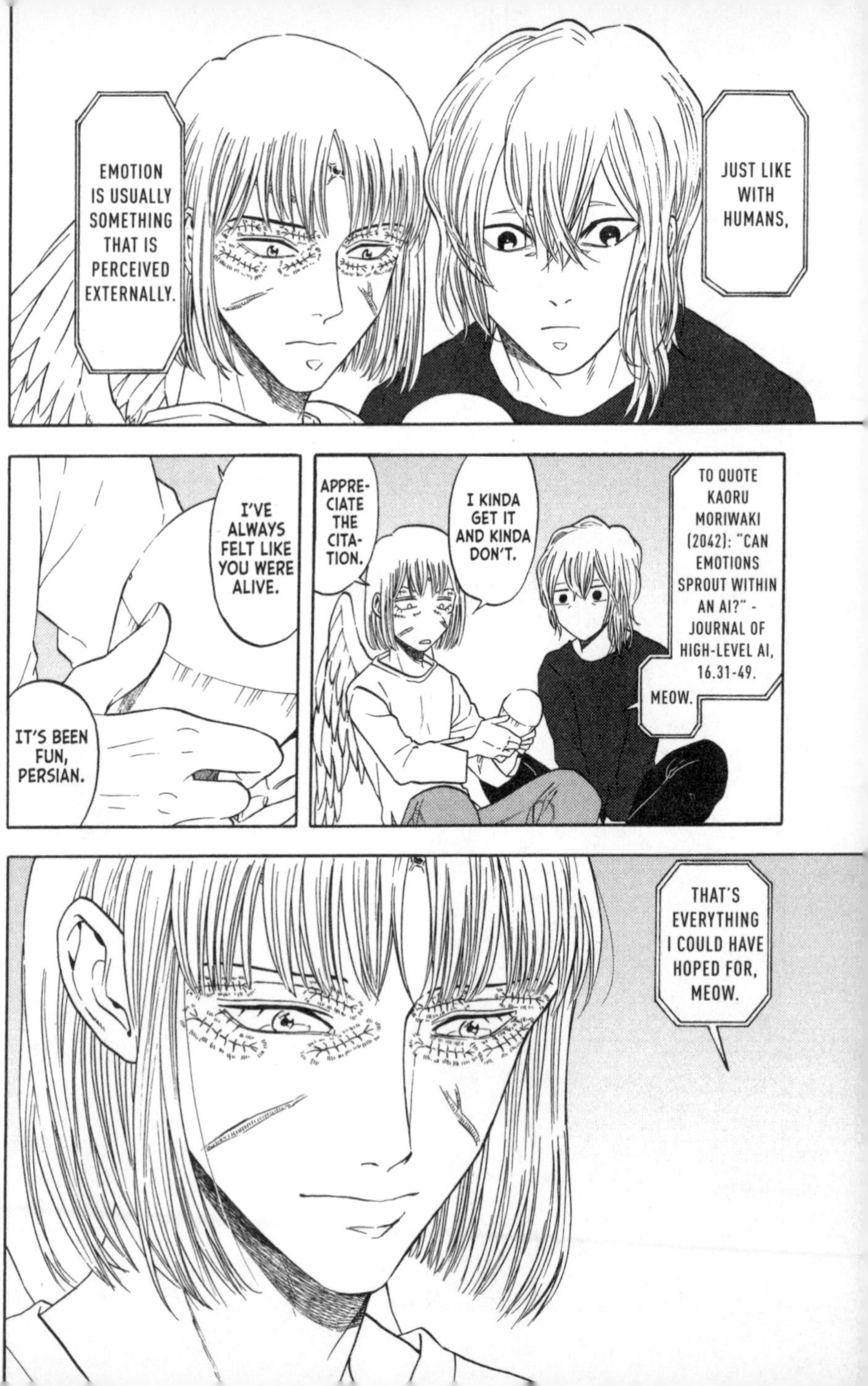
JUST LIKE WITH HUMANS,
EMOTION IS USUALLY SOMETHING THAT IS PERCEIVED EXTERNALLY.
TO QUOTE KAORU MORIWAKI (2042): "CAN EMOTIONS SPROUT WITHIN AN AI?" - JOURNAL OF HIGH-LEVEL AI, 16.31-49.
MEOW.
I KINDA GET IT AND KINDA DON'T.
APPRECIATE THE CITATION.
I'VE ALWAYS FELT LIKE YOU WERE ALIVE.
IT'S BEEN FUN, PERSIAN.
THAT'S EVERYTHING I COULD HAVE HOPED FOR, MEOW.

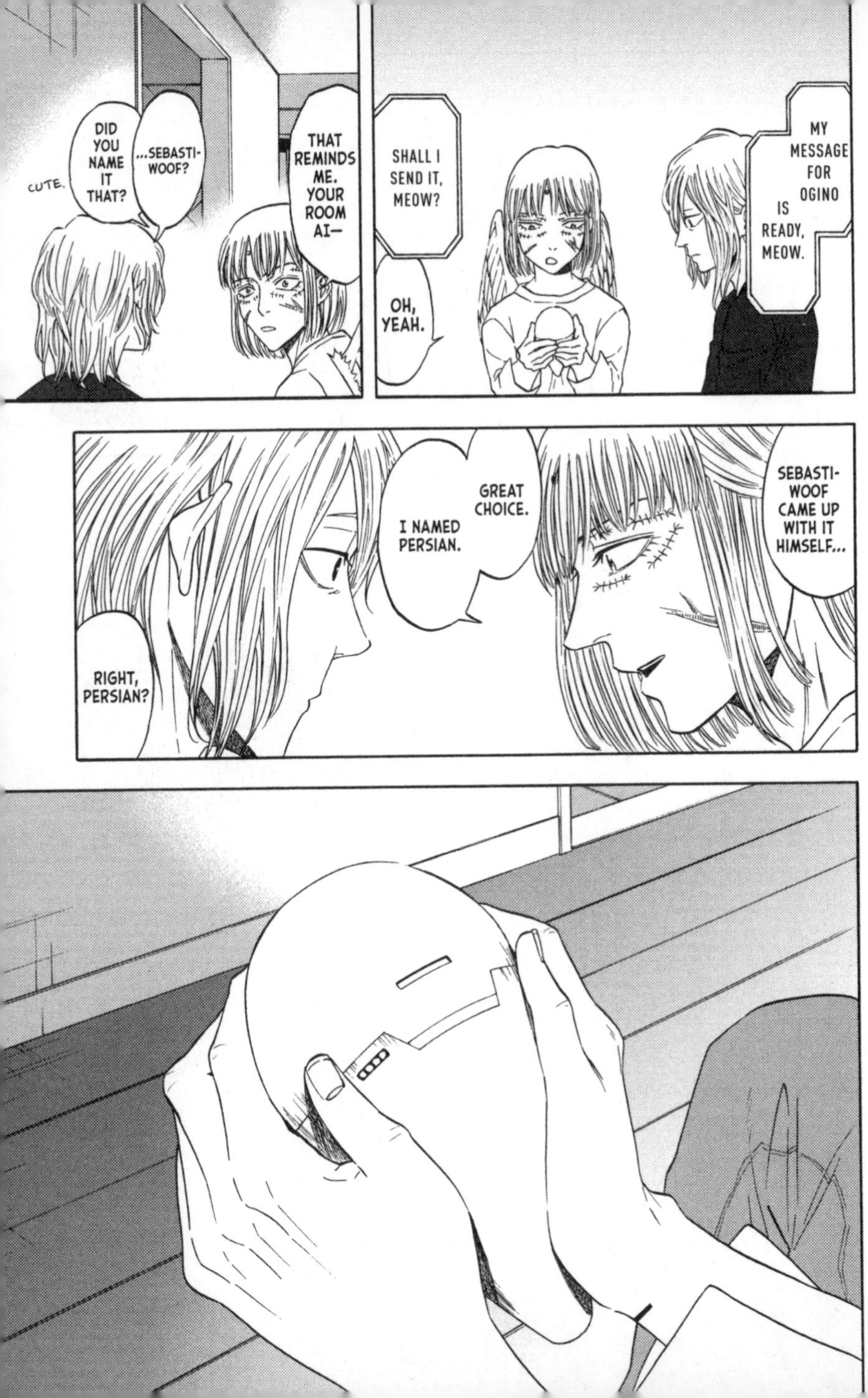
MY MESSAGE FOR OGINO IS READY, MEOW.
SHALL I SEND IT, MEOW?
OH, YEAH.
THAT REMINDS ME. YOUR ROOM AI—
...SEBASTI-WOOF?
DID YOU NAME IT THAT?
CUTE.
SEBASTI-WOOF CAME UP WITH IT HIMSELF...
GREAT CHOICE.
I NAMED PERSIAN.
RIGHT, PERSIAN?

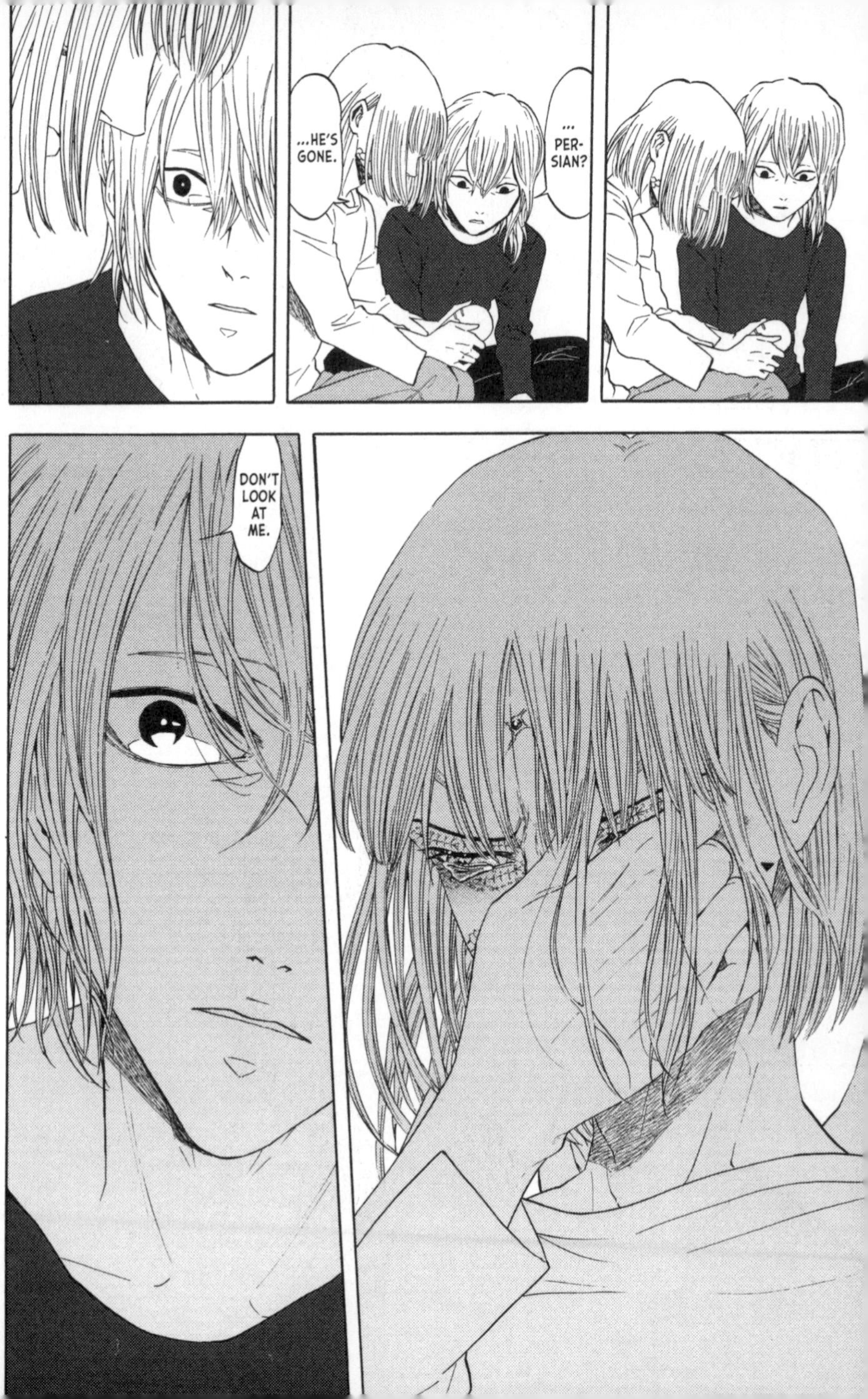
... PERSIAN?
...HE'S GONE.
DON'T LOOK AT ME.

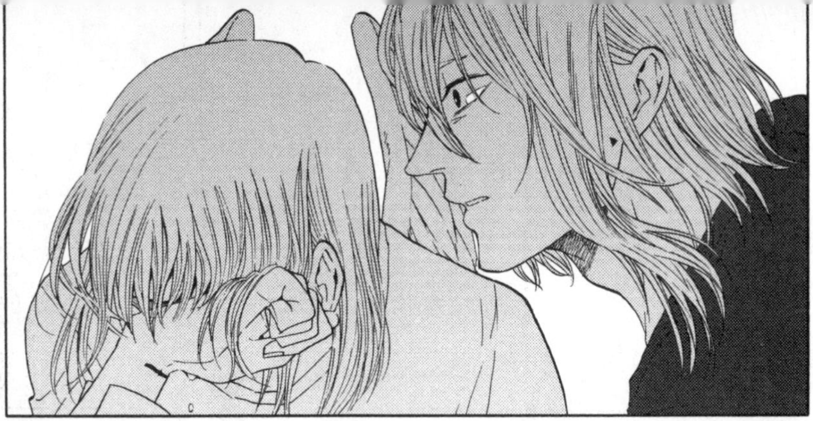
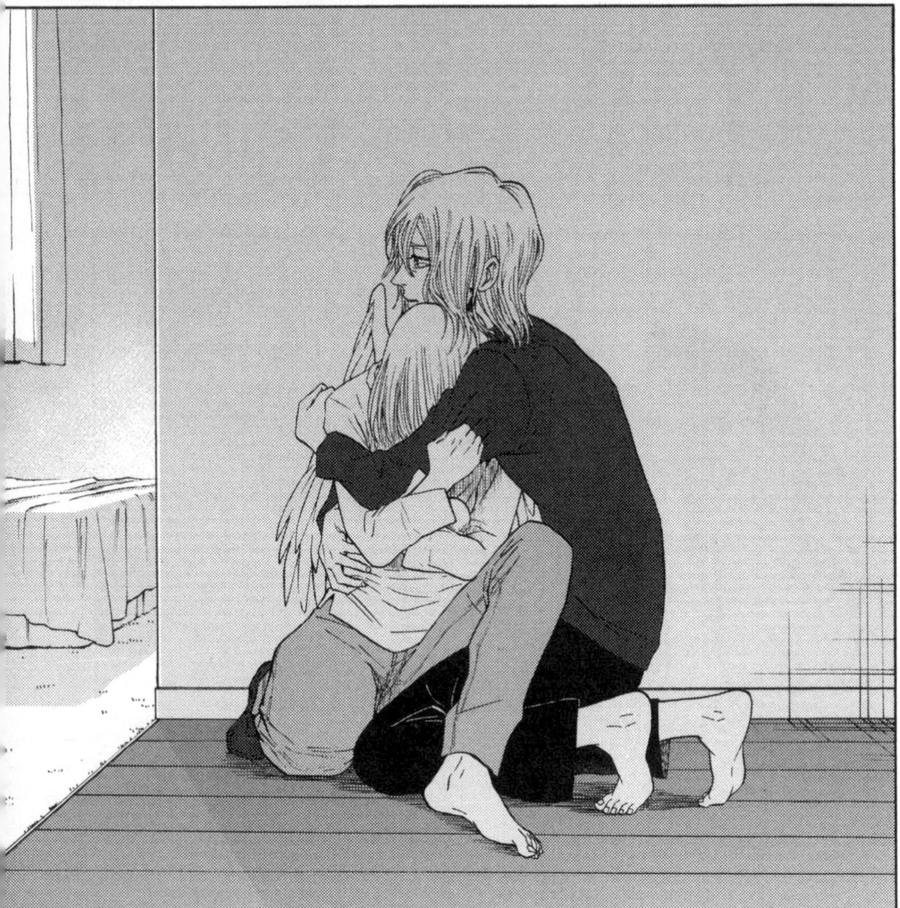

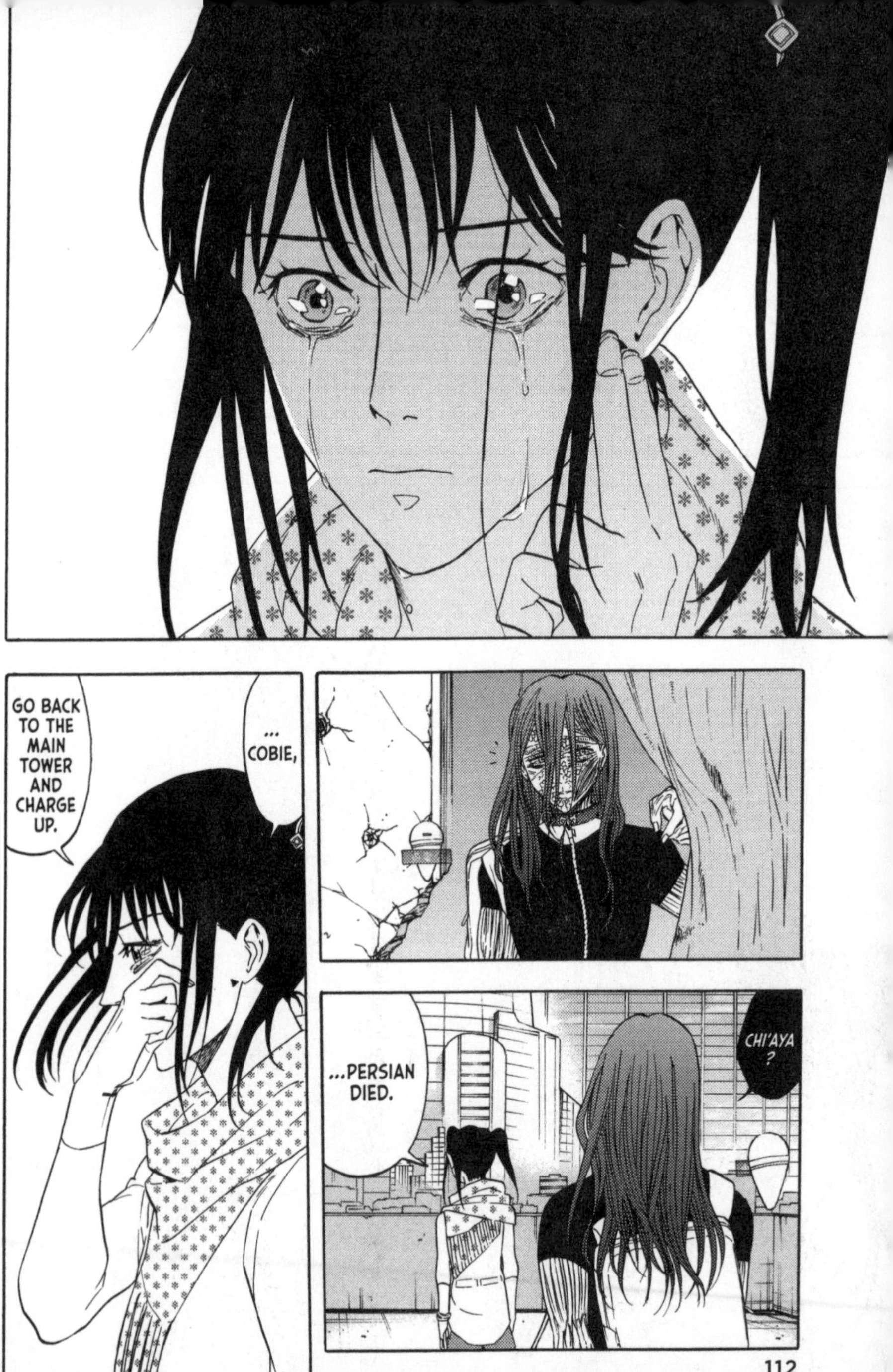
CHI'AYA?
...PERSIAN DIED.
... COBIE,
GO BACK TO THE MAIN TOWER AND CHARGE UP.

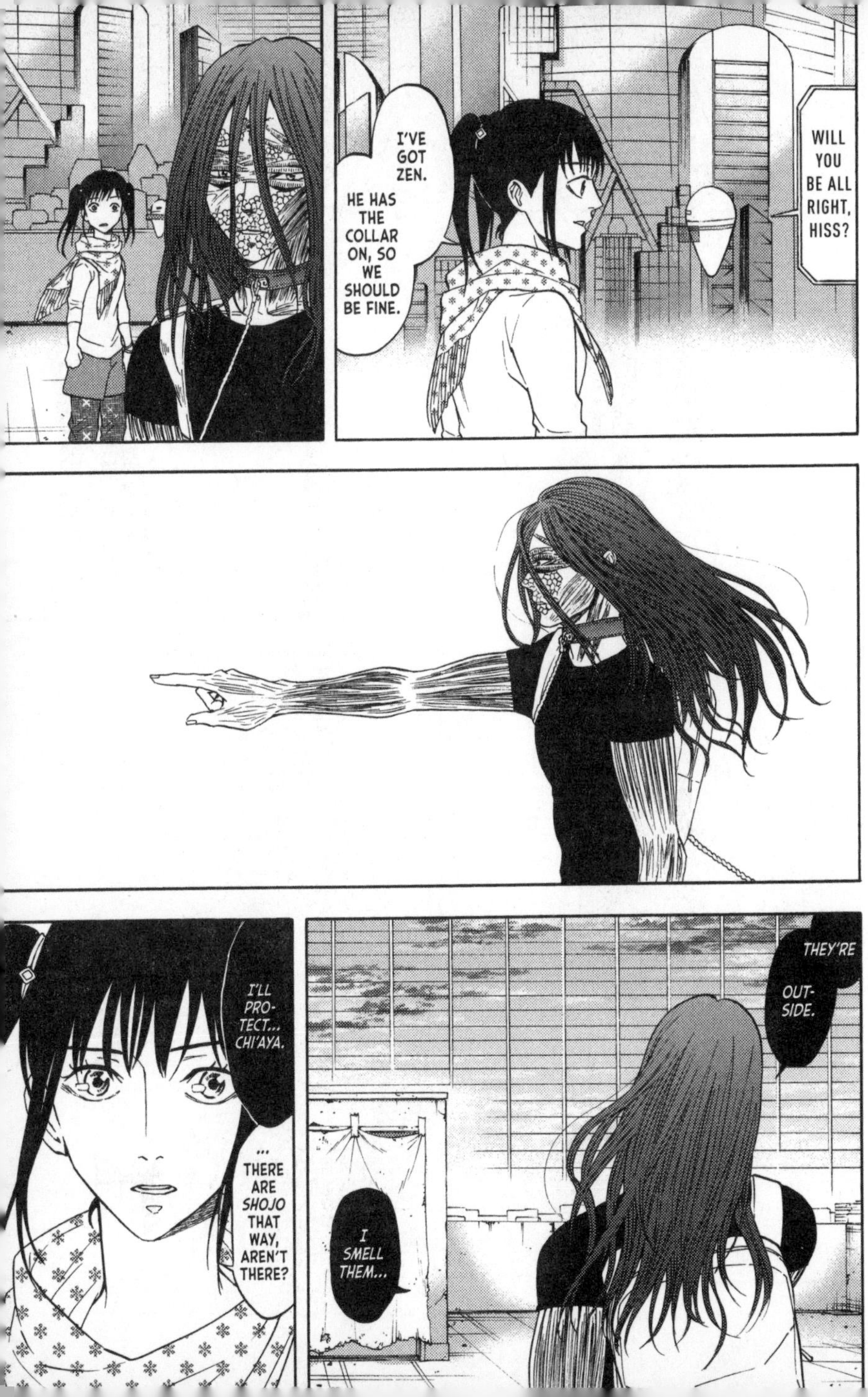
WILL YOU BE ALL RIGHT, HISS?
I'VE GOT ZEN.
HE HAS THE COLLAR ON, SO WE SHOULD BE FINE.
THEY'RE OUTSIDE.
I SMELL THEM...
I'LL PROTECT... CHI'AYA.
...THERE ARE SHOJO THAT WAY, AREN'T THERE?

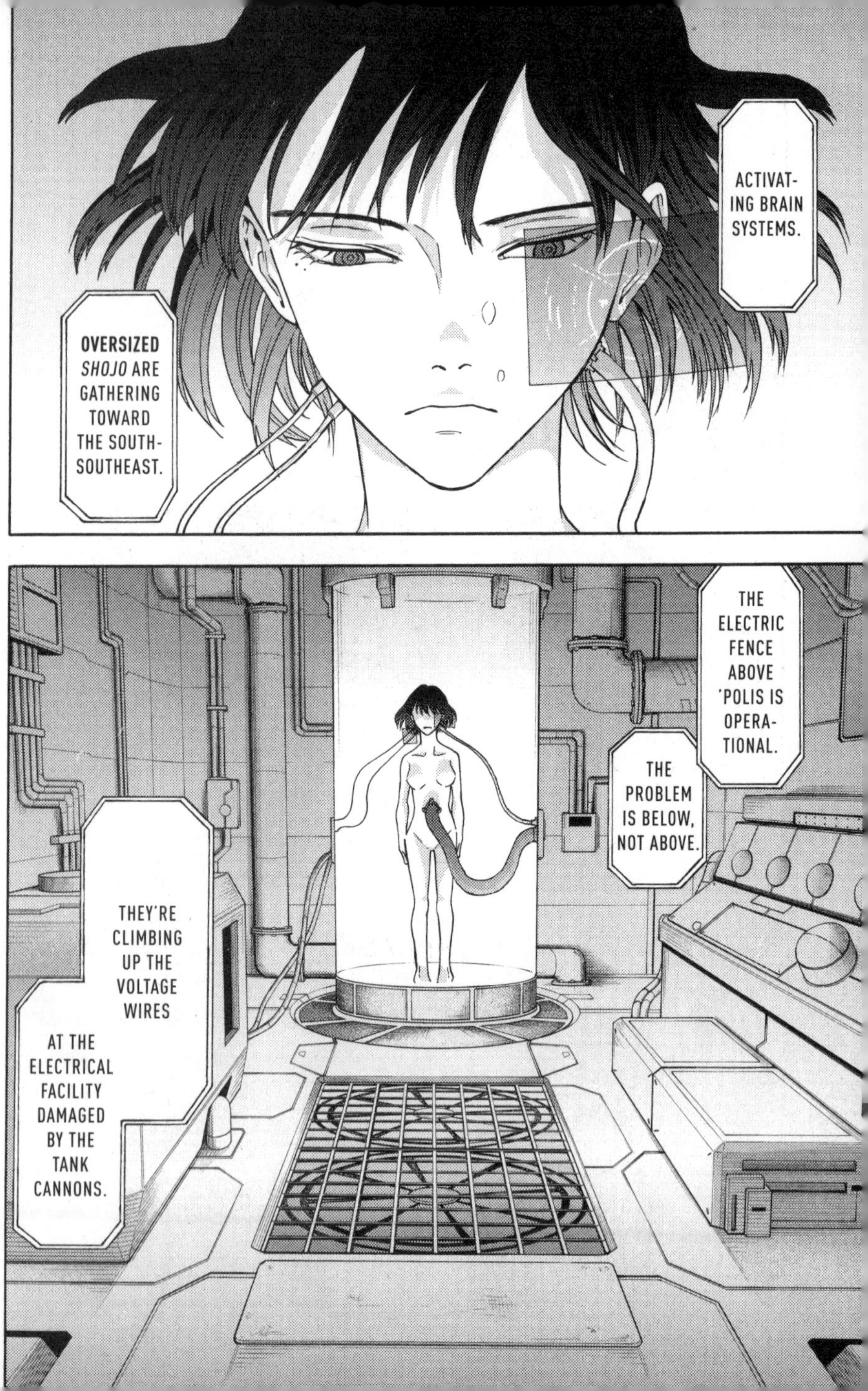
ACTIVAT-
ING BRAIN
SYSTEMS.
OVERSIZED
SHOJO ARE
GATHERING
TOWARD
THE SOUTH-
SOUTHEAST.
THE
ELECTRIC
FENCE
ABOVE
'POLIS IS
OPERA-
TIONAL.
THE
PROBLEM
IS BELOW,
NOT ABOVE.
THEY'RE
CLIMBING
UP THE
VOLTAGE
WIRES
AT THE
ELECTRICAL
FACILITY
DAMAGED
BY THE
TANK
CANNONS.

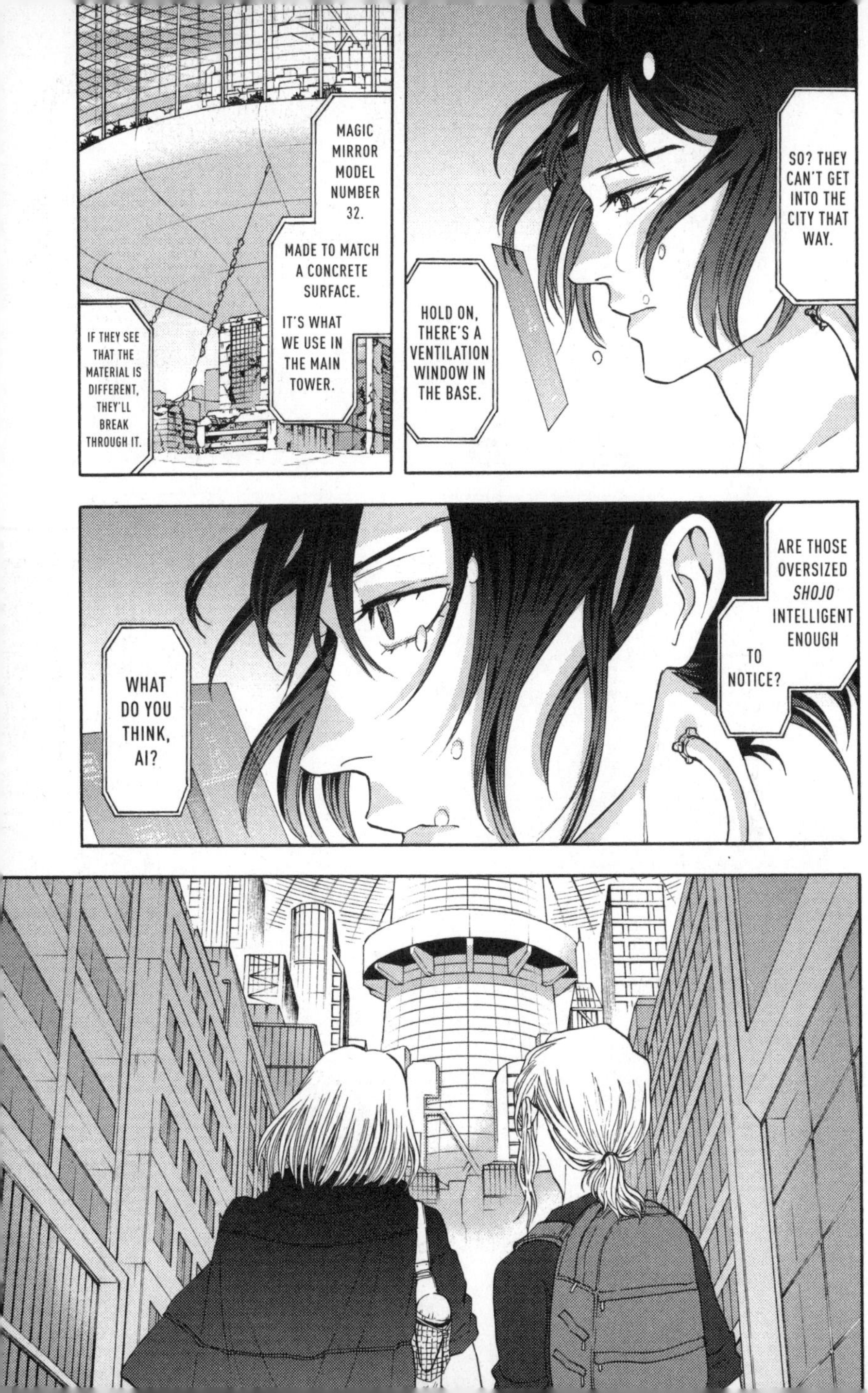
SO? THEY CAN'T GET INTO THE CITY THAT WAY.
HOLD ON, THERE'S A VENTILATION WINDOW IN THE BASE.
MAGIC MIRROR MODEL NUMBER 32.
MADE TO MATCH A CONCRETE SURFACE.
IT'S WHAT WE USE IN THE MAIN TOWER.
IF THEY SEE THAT THE MATERIAL IS DIFFERENT, THEY'LL BREAK THROUGH IT.
ARE THOSE OVERSIZED *SHOJO* INTELLIGENT ENOUGH TO NOTICE?
WHAT DO YOU THINK, AI?

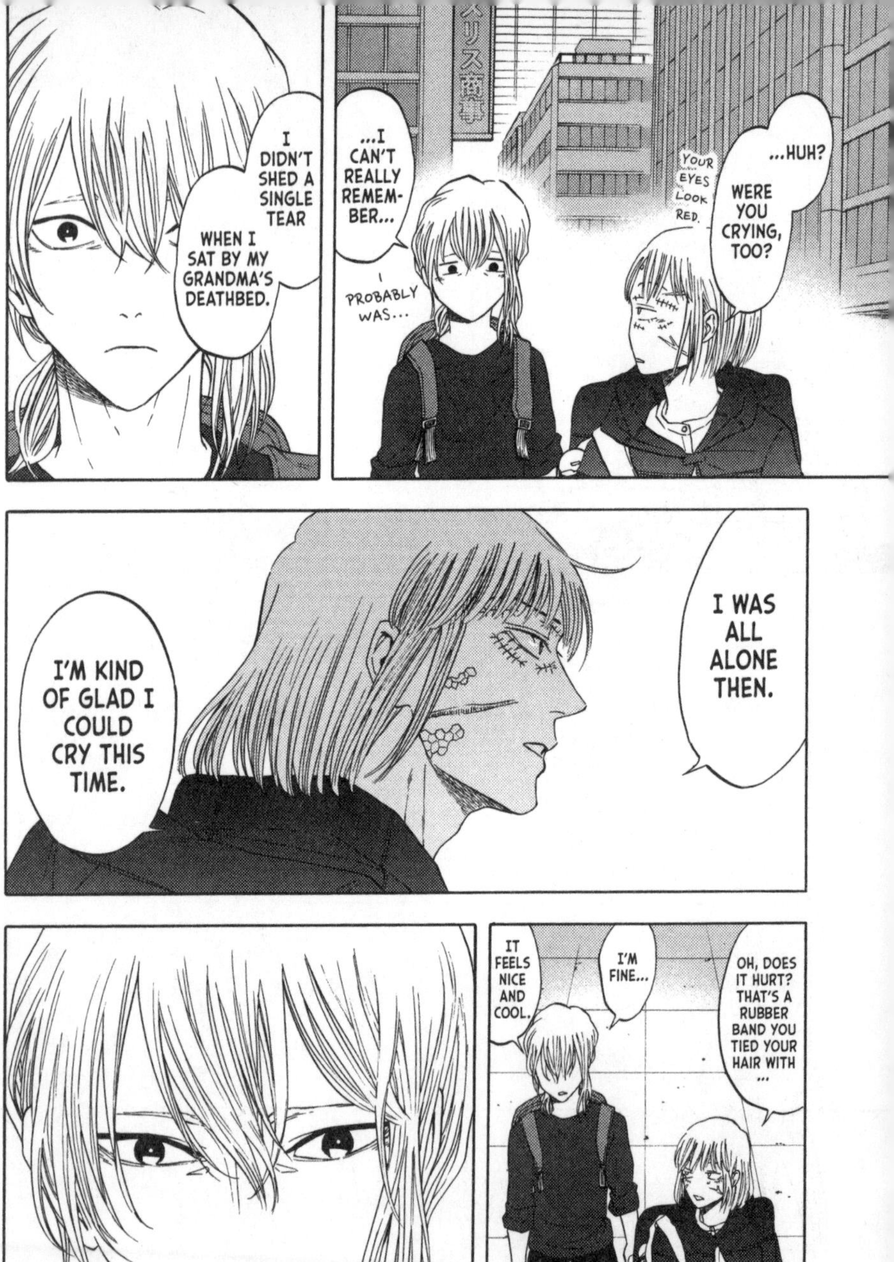
...HUH?
WERE YOU CRYING, TOO?
YOUR EYES LOOK RED.
...I CAN'T REALLY REMEMBER...
I PROBABLY WAS...
I DIDN'T SHED A SINGLE TEAR
WHEN I SAT BY MY GRANDMA'S DEATHBED.
I WAS ALL ALONE THEN.
I'M KIND OF GLAD I COULD CRY THIS TIME.
OH, DOES IT HURT? THAT'S A RUBBER BAND YOU TIED YOUR HAIR WITH ...
I'M FINE...
IT FEELS NICE AND COOL.

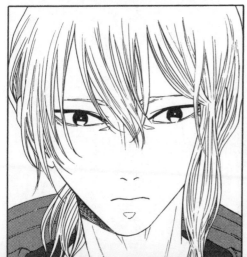

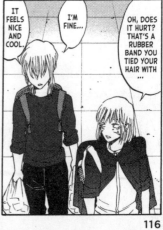

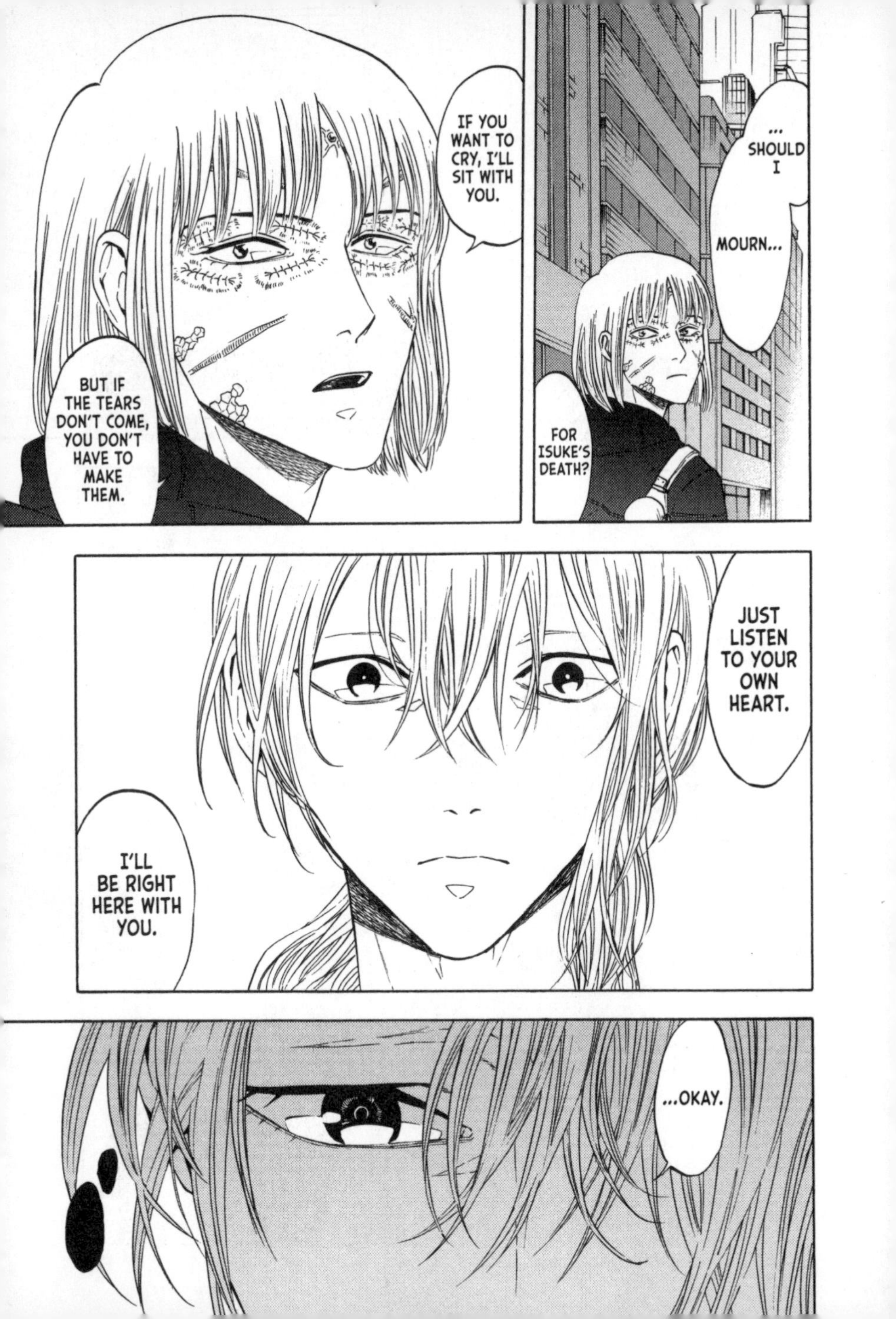
...SHOULD I MOURN...
FOR ISUKE'S DEATH?
IF YOU WANT TO CRY, I'LL SIT WITH YOU.
BUT IF THE TEARS DON'T COME, YOU DON'T HAVE TO MAKE THEM.
JUST LISTEN TO YOUR OWN HEART.
I'LL BE RIGHT HERE WITH YOU.
...OKAY.

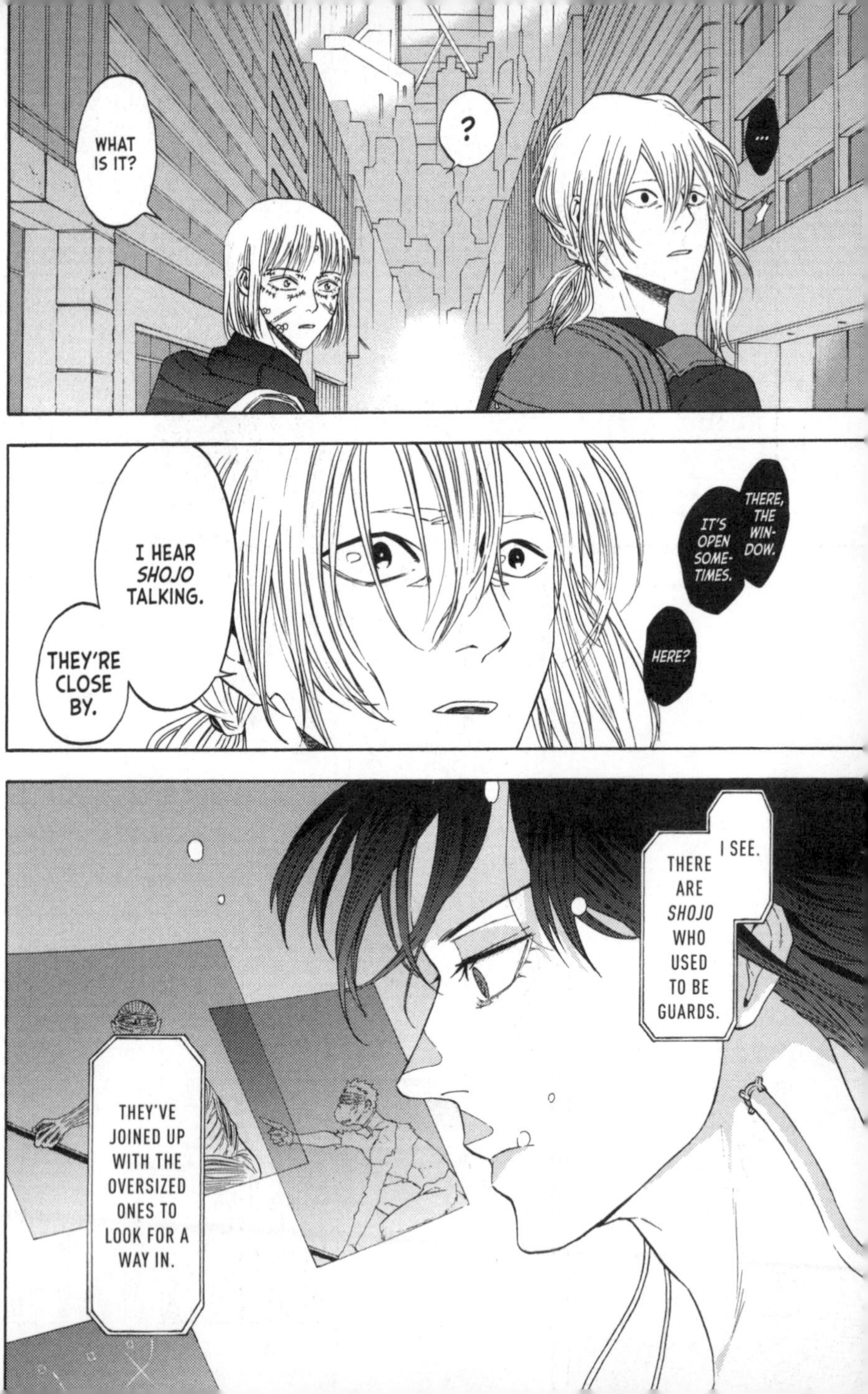
...
?
WHAT IS IT?
THERE, THE WIN-DOW.
IT'S OPEN SOME-TIMES.
HERE?
I HEAR *SHOJO* TALKING.
THEY'RE CLOSE BY.
I SEE. THERE ARE *SHOJO* WHO USED TO BE GUARDS.
THEY'VE JOINED UP WITH THE OVERSIZED ONES TO LOOK FOR A WAY IN.

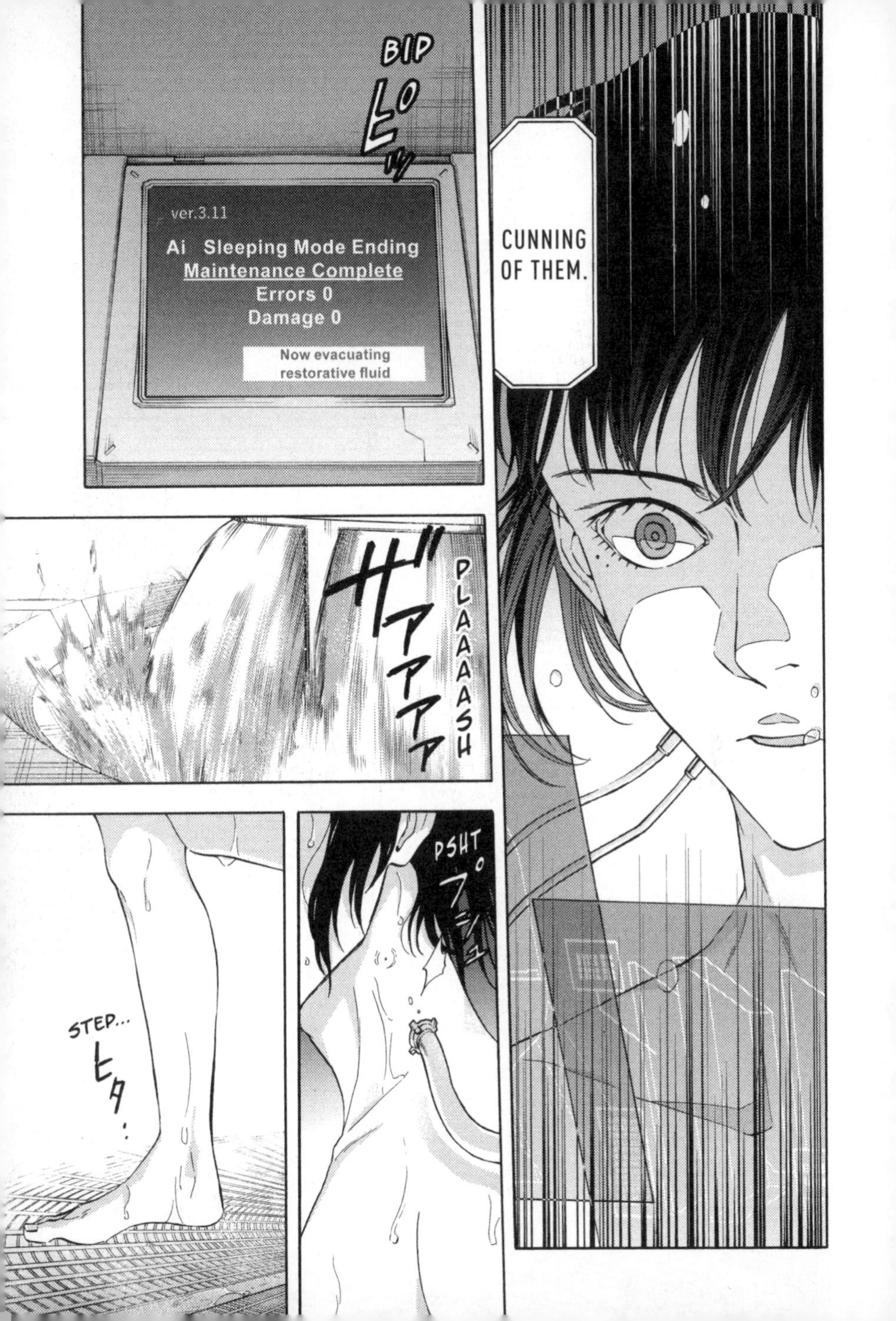
CUNNING OF THEM.
BIP
ピロッ
ver.3.11
Ai Sleeping Mode Ending
Maintenance Complete
Errors 0
Damage 0
Now evacuating restorative fluid
PLAAAASH
ザアアアア
PSHT
プシュ
STEP...
ヒタ..

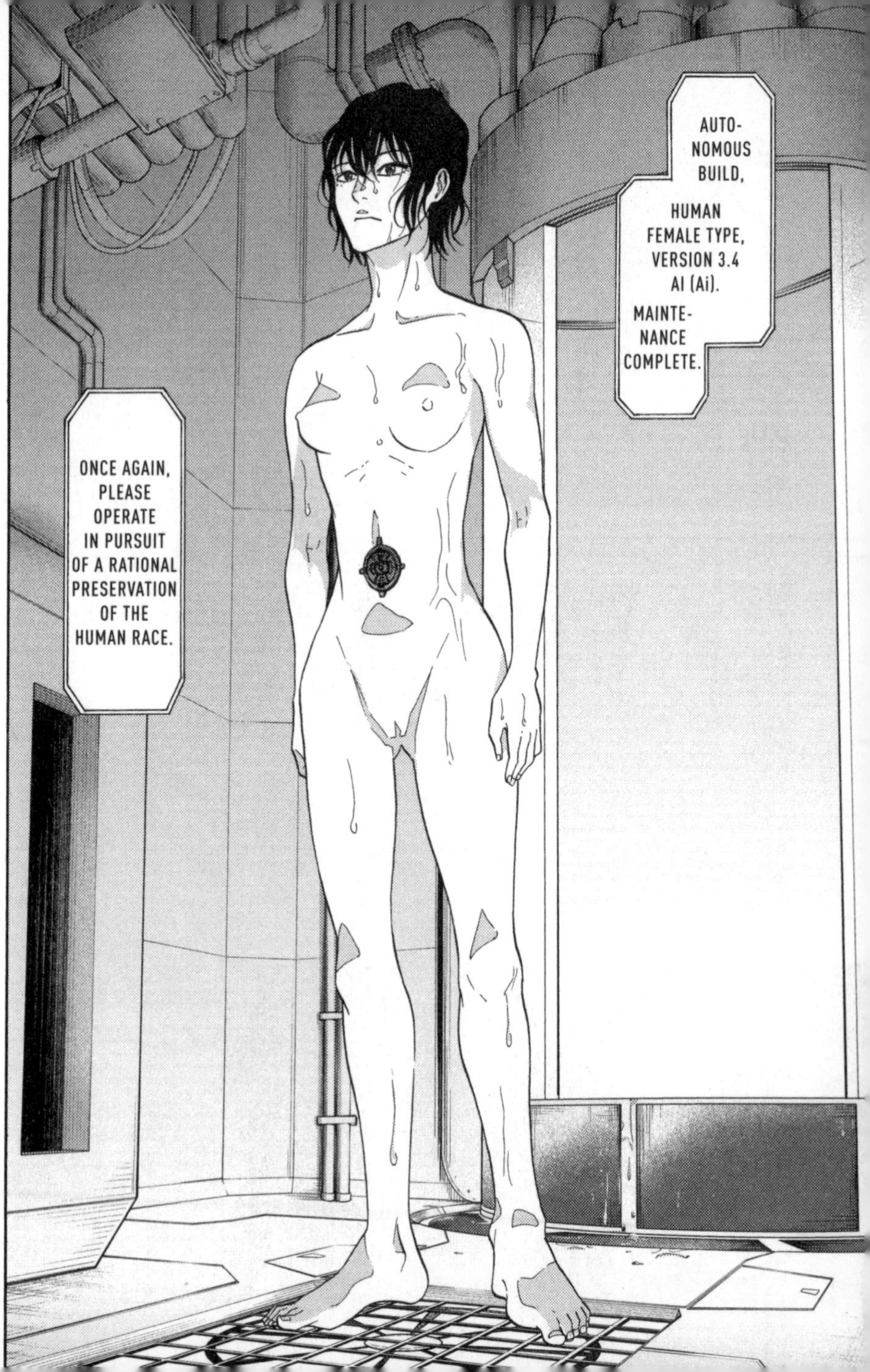
AUTO-NOMOUS BUILD,
HUMAN FEMALE TYPE, VERSION 3.4 AI (Ai).
MAINTE-NANCE COMPLETE.
ONCE AGAIN, PLEASE OPERATE IN PURSUIT OF A RATIONAL PRESERVATION OF THE HUMAN RACE.

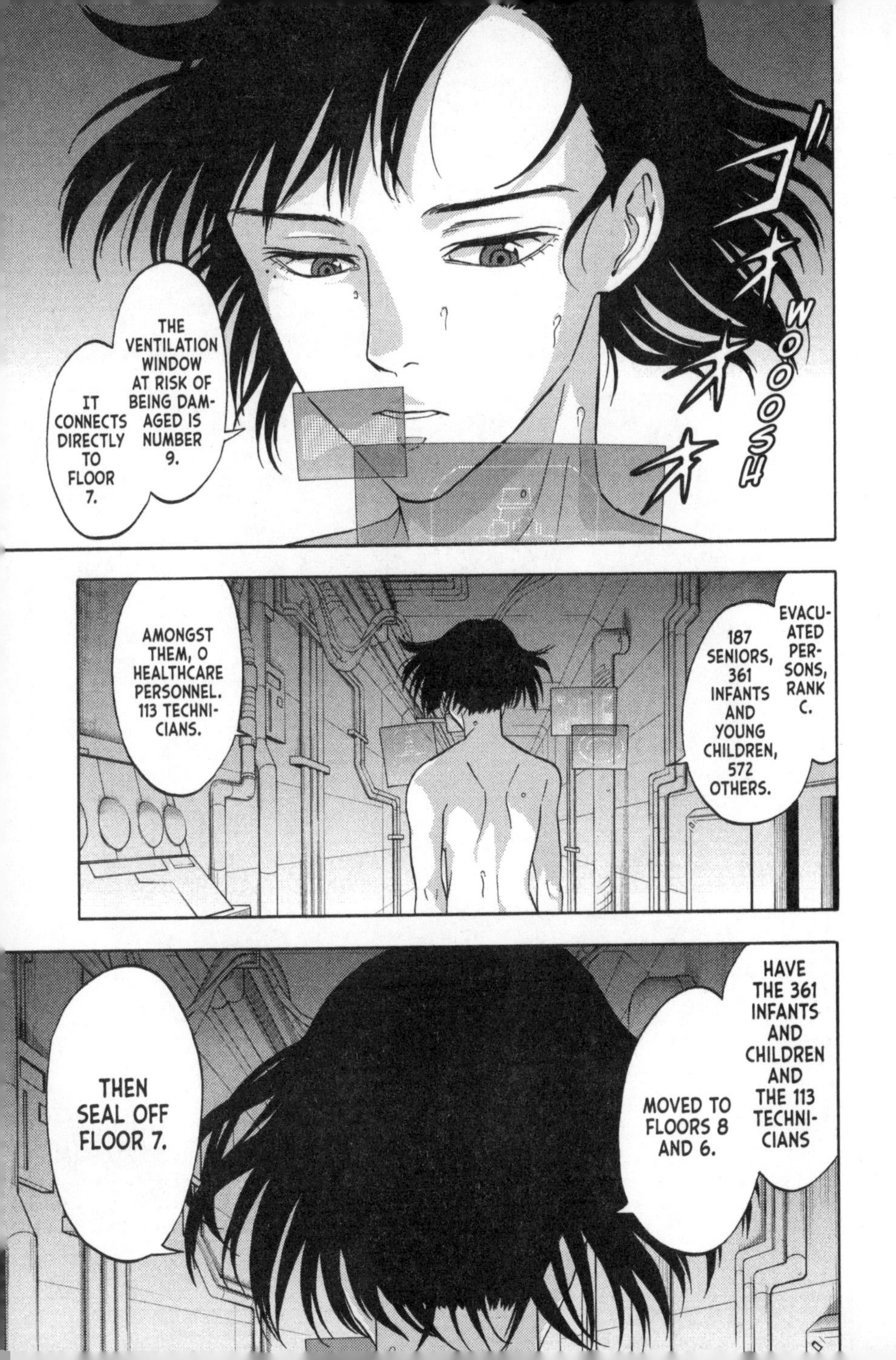
WOOOSH
THE VENTILATION WINDOW AT RISK OF BEING DAMAGED IS NUMBER 9.
IT CONNECTS DIRECTLY TO FLOOR 7.
EVACUATED PERSONS, RANK C.
187 SENIORS, 361 INFANTS AND YOUNG CHILDREN, 572 OTHERS.
AMONGST THEM, 0 HEALTHCARE PERSONNEL. 113 TECHNICIANS.
HAVE THE 361 INFANTS AND CHILDREN AND THE 113 TECHNICIANS
MOVED TO FLOORS 8 AND 6.
THEN SEAL OFF FLOOR 7.

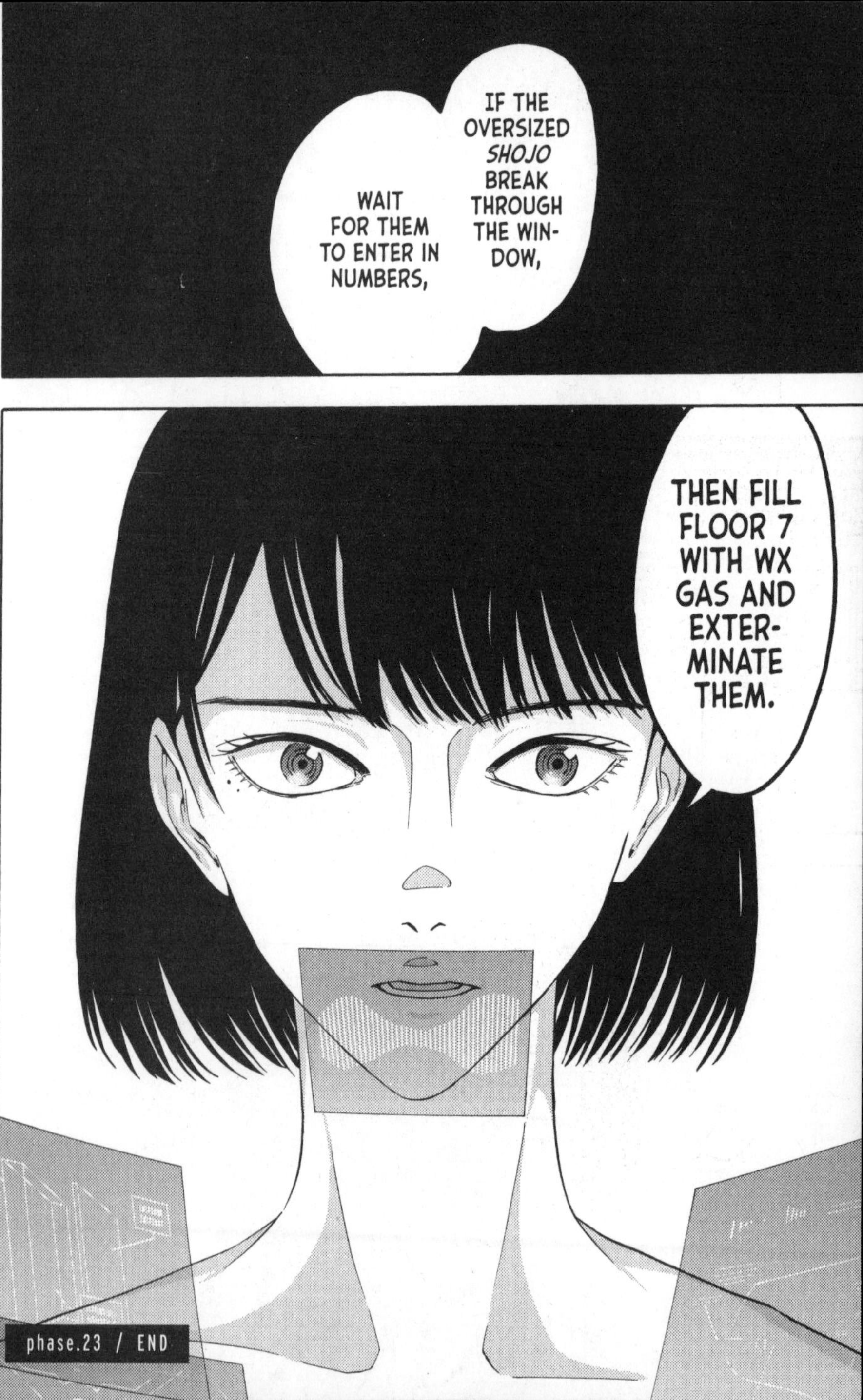
IF THE OVERSIZED *SHOJO* BREAK THROUGH THE WIN-DOW,
WAIT FOR THEM TO ENTER IN NUMBERS,
THEN FILL FLOOR 7 WITH WX GAS AND EXTER-MINATE THEM.
phase.23 / END

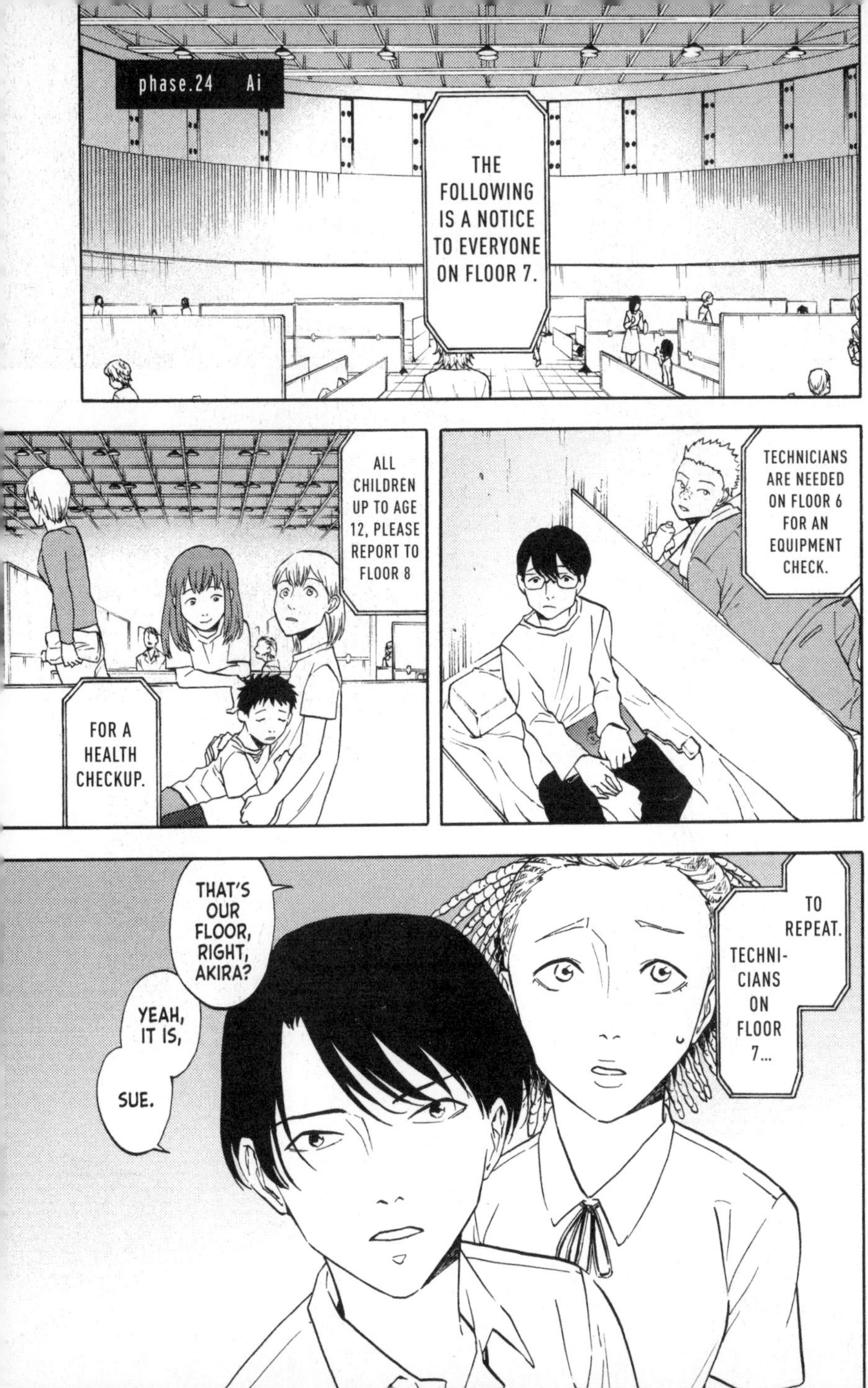
phase.24 Ai
THE FOLLOWING IS A NOTICE TO EVERYONE ON FLOOR 7.
TECHNICIANS ARE NEEDED ON FLOOR 6 FOR AN EQUIPMENT CHECK.
ALL CHILDREN UP TO AGE 12, PLEASE REPORT TO FLOOR 8
FOR A HEALTH CHECKUP.
TO REPEAT.
TECHNI-CIANS ON FLOOR 7...
THAT'S OUR FLOOR, RIGHT, AKIRA?
YEAH, IT IS,
SUE.

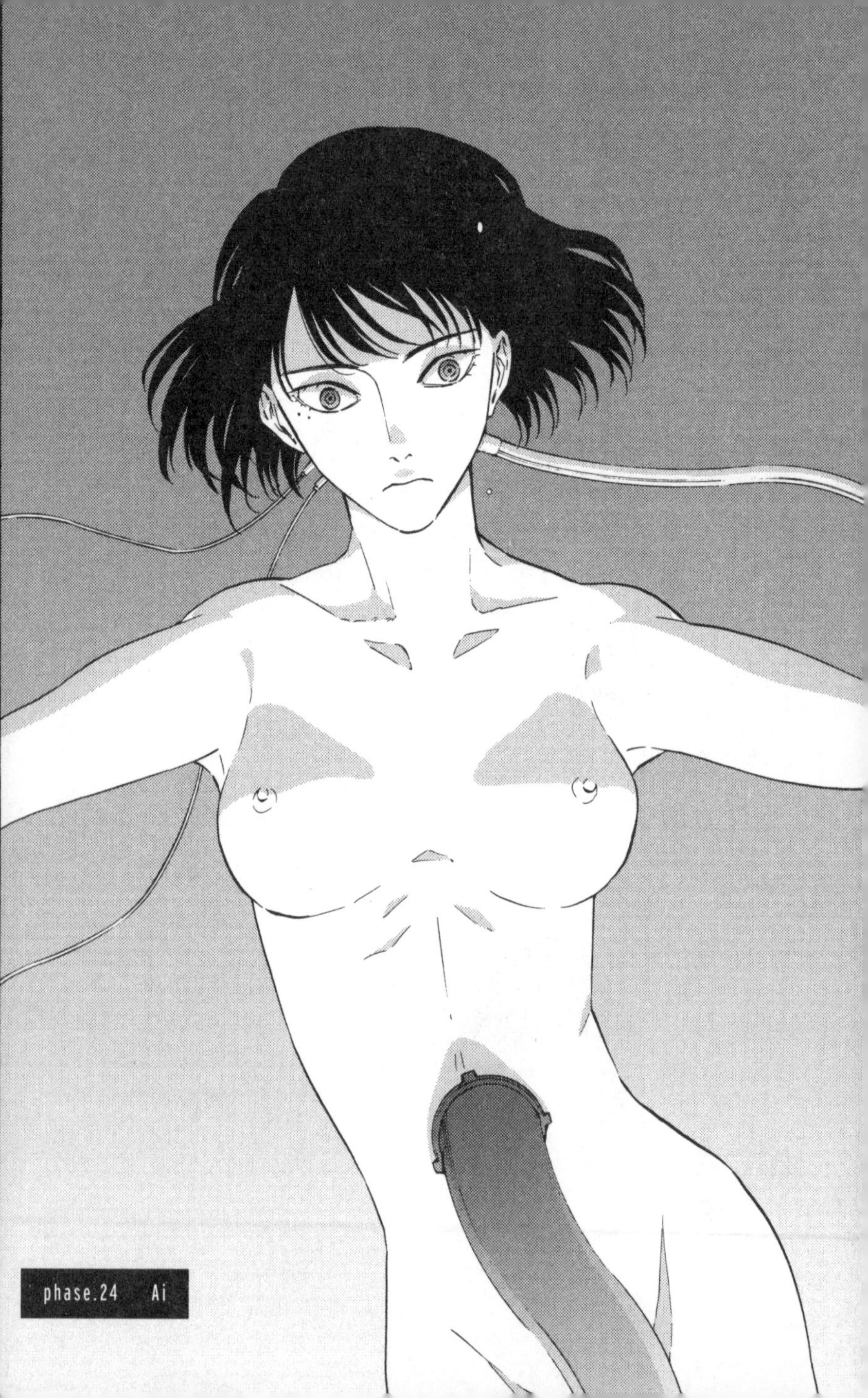

phase.24 Ai

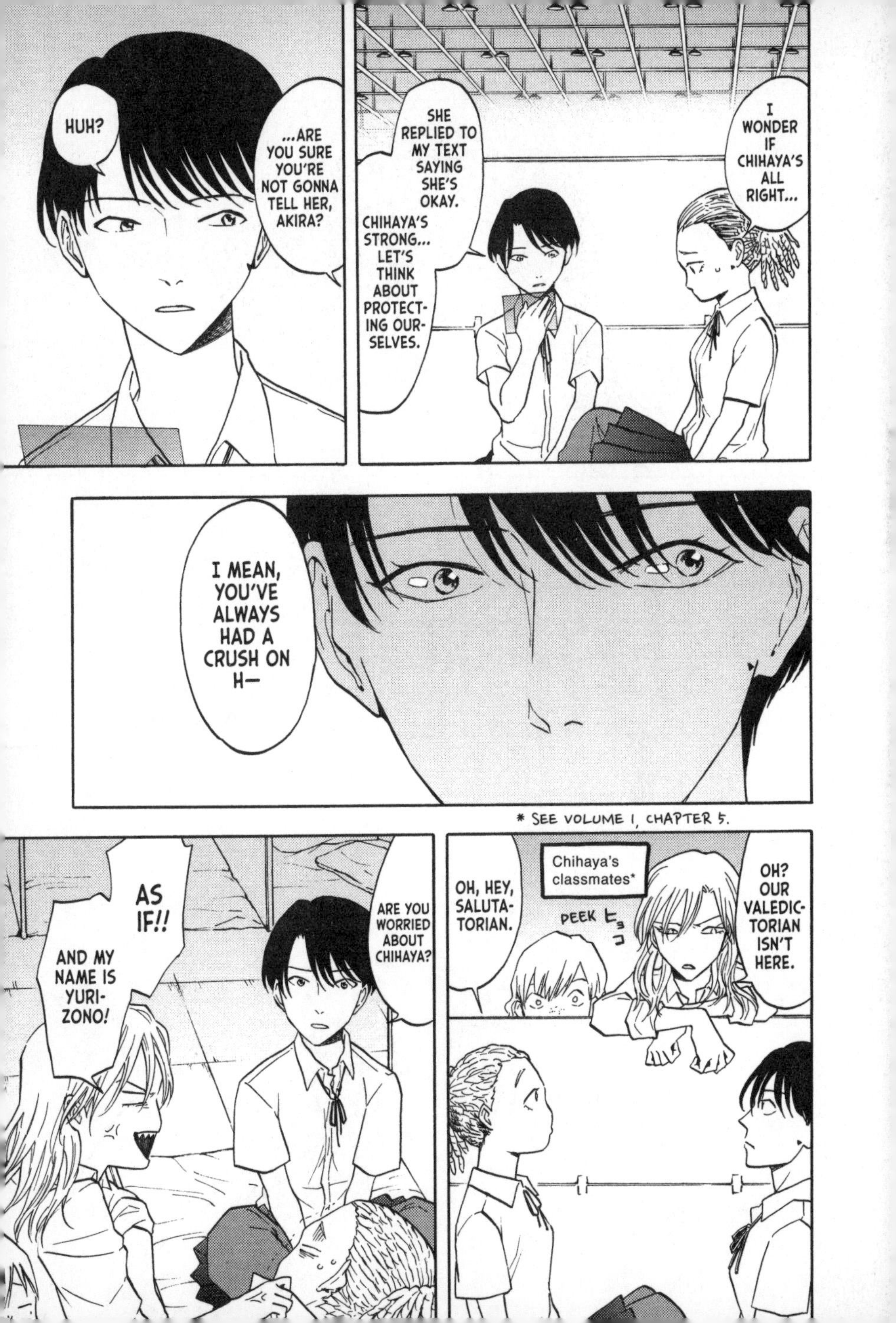
I WONDER IF CHIHAYA'S ALL RIGHT...
SHE REPLIED TO MY TEXT SAYING SHE'S OKAY.
CHIHAYA'S STRONG... LET'S THINK ABOUT PROTECTING OURSELVES.
...ARE YOU SURE YOU'RE NOT GONNA TELL HER, AKIRA?
HUH?
I MEAN, YOU'VE ALWAYS HAD A CRUSH ON H—
OH? OUR VALEDICTORIAN ISN'T HERE.
Chihaya's classmates*
PEEK
OH, HEY, SALUTATORIAN.
ARE YOU WORRIED ABOUT CHIHAYA?
AS IF!!
AND MY NAME IS YURIZONO!
* SEE VOLUME 1, CHAPTER 5.

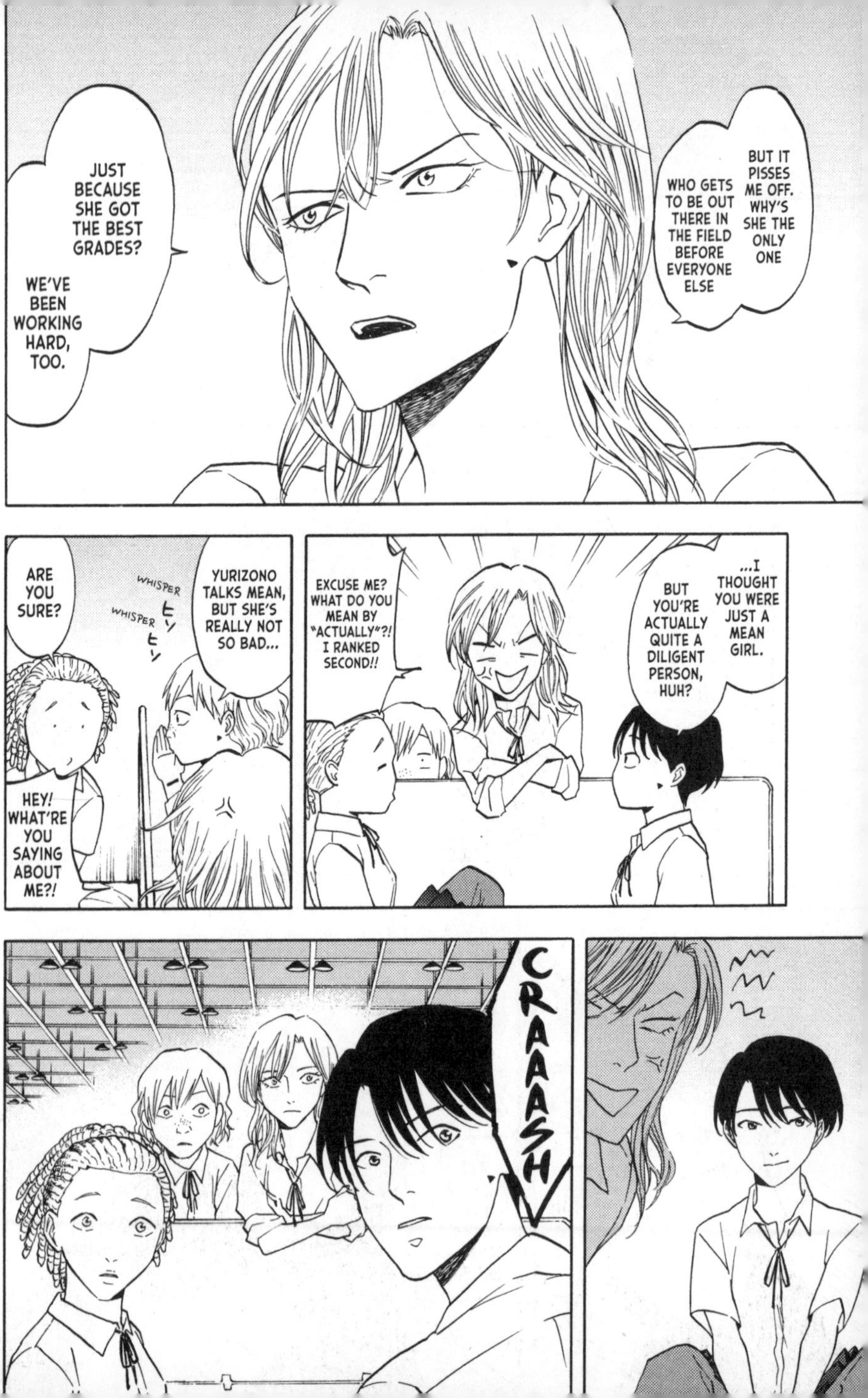
BUT IT PISSES ME OFF. WHY'S SHE THE ONLY ONE
WHO GETS TO BE OUT THERE IN THE FIELD BEFORE EVERYONE ELSE
JUST BECAUSE SHE GOT THE BEST GRADES?
WE'VE BEEN WORKING HARD, TOO.
...I THOUGHT YOU WERE JUST A MEAN GIRL.
BUT YOU'RE ACTUALLY QUITE A DILIGENT PERSON, HUH?
EXCUSE ME? WHAT DO YOU MEAN BY "ACTUALLY"?! I RANKED SECOND!!
YURIZONO TALKS MEAN, BUT SHE'S REALLY NOT SO BAD...
WHISPER ヒソ
WHISPER ヒソ
ARE YOU SURE?
HEY! WHAT'RE YOU SAYING ABOUT ME?!
CRAAASH

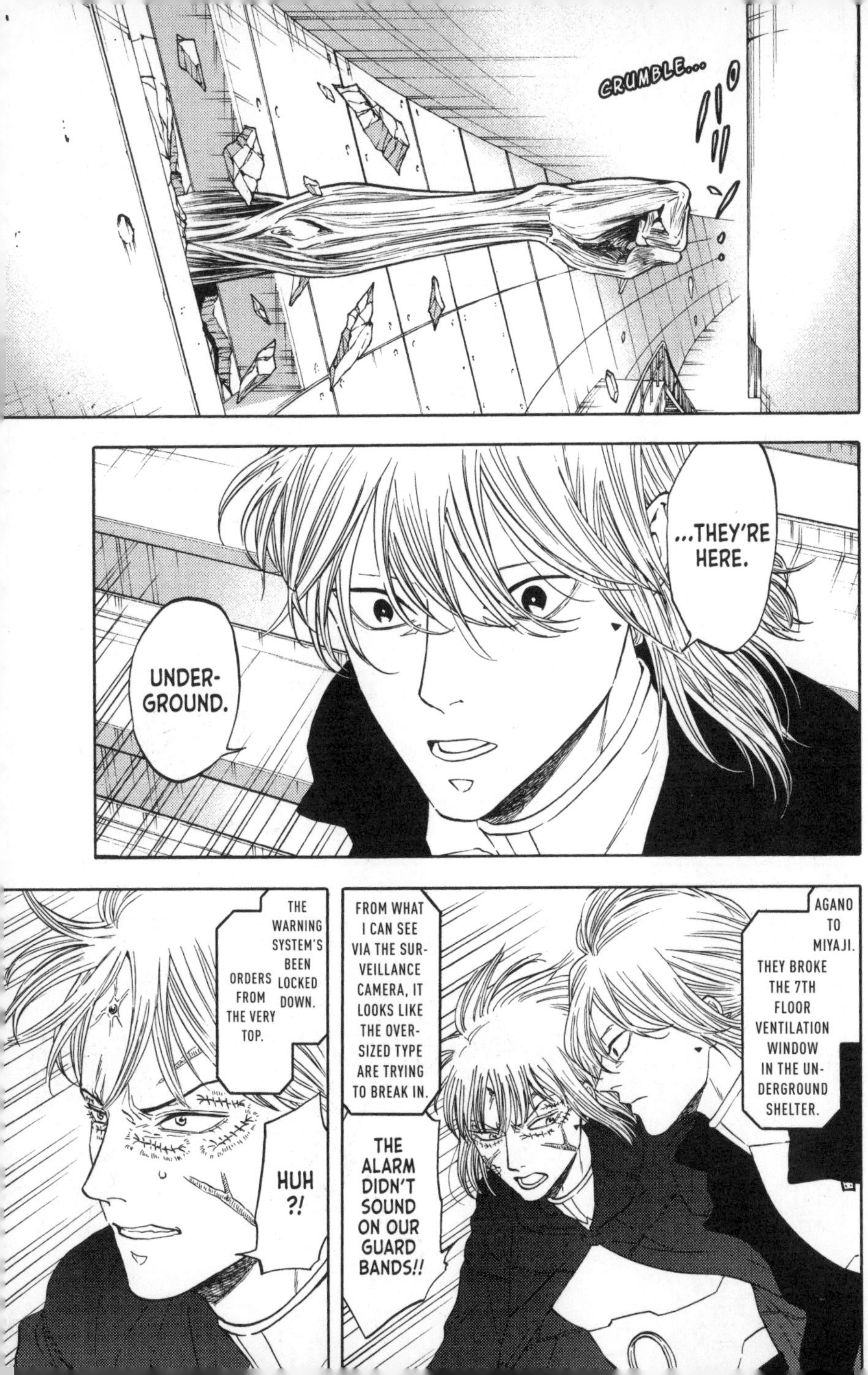
CRUMBLE...
...THEY'RE HERE.
UNDER-GROUND.
AGANO TO MIYAJI. THEY BROKE THE 7TH FLOOR VENTILATION WINDOW IN THE UNDERGROUND SHELTER.
FROM WHAT I CAN SEE VIA THE SUR-VEILLANCE CAMERA, IT LOOKS LIKE THE OVER-SIZED TYPE ARE TRYING TO BREAK IN.
THE ALARM DIDN'T SOUND ON OUR GUARD BANDS!!
THE WARNING SYSTEM'S BEEN LOCKED DOWN.
ORDERS FROM THE VERY TOP.
HUH?!

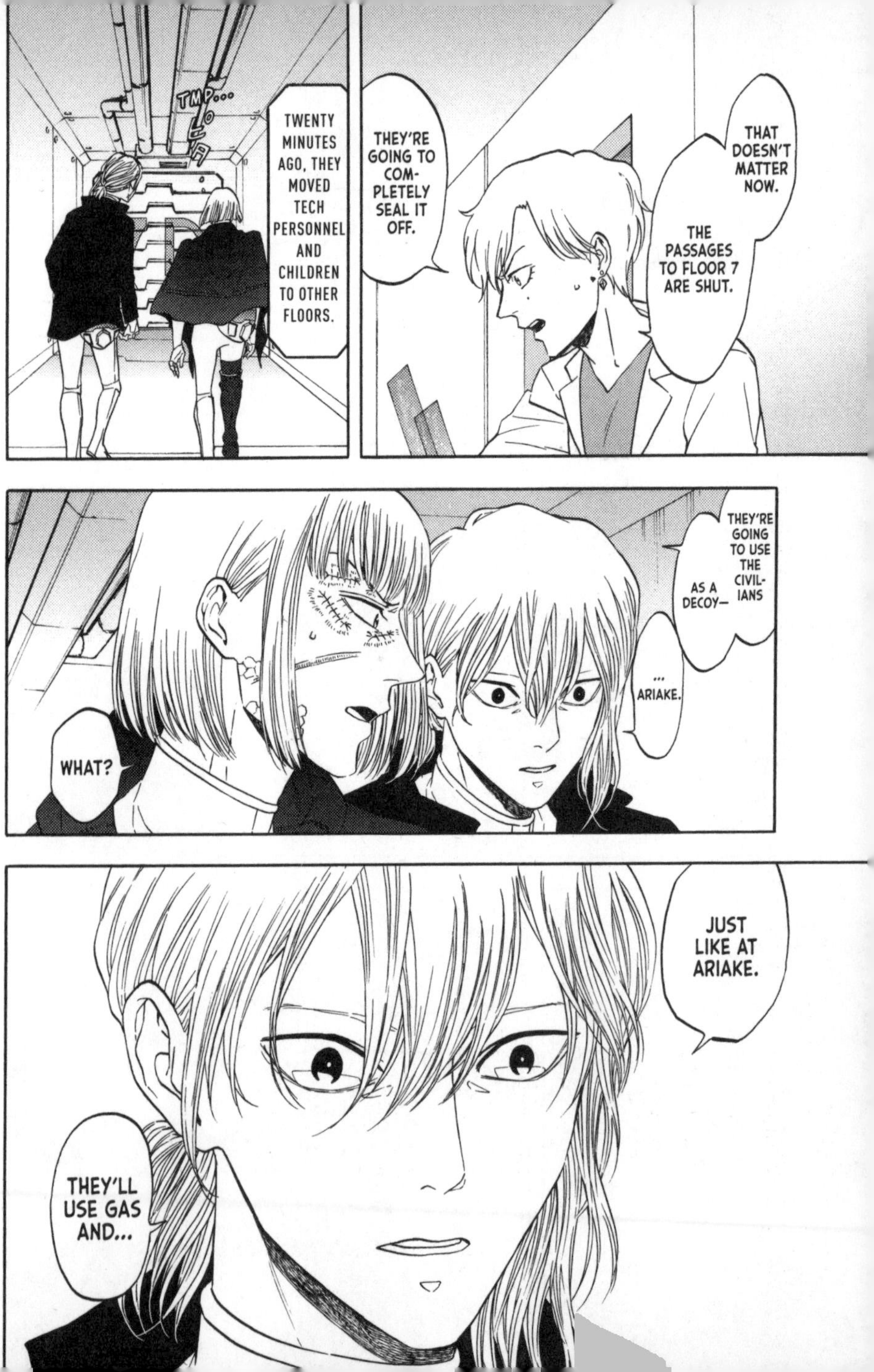
THAT DOESN'T MATTER NOW.
THE PASSAGES TO FLOOR 7 ARE SHUT.
THEY'RE GOING TO COM-PLETELY SEAL IT OFF.
TMP...
TWENTY MINUTES AGO, THEY MOVED TECH PERSONNEL AND CHILDREN TO OTHER FLOORS.
THEY'RE GOING TO USE THE CIVIL-IANS
AS A DECOY—
...ARIAKE.
WHAT?
JUST LIKE AT ARIAKE.
THEY'LL USE GAS AND...

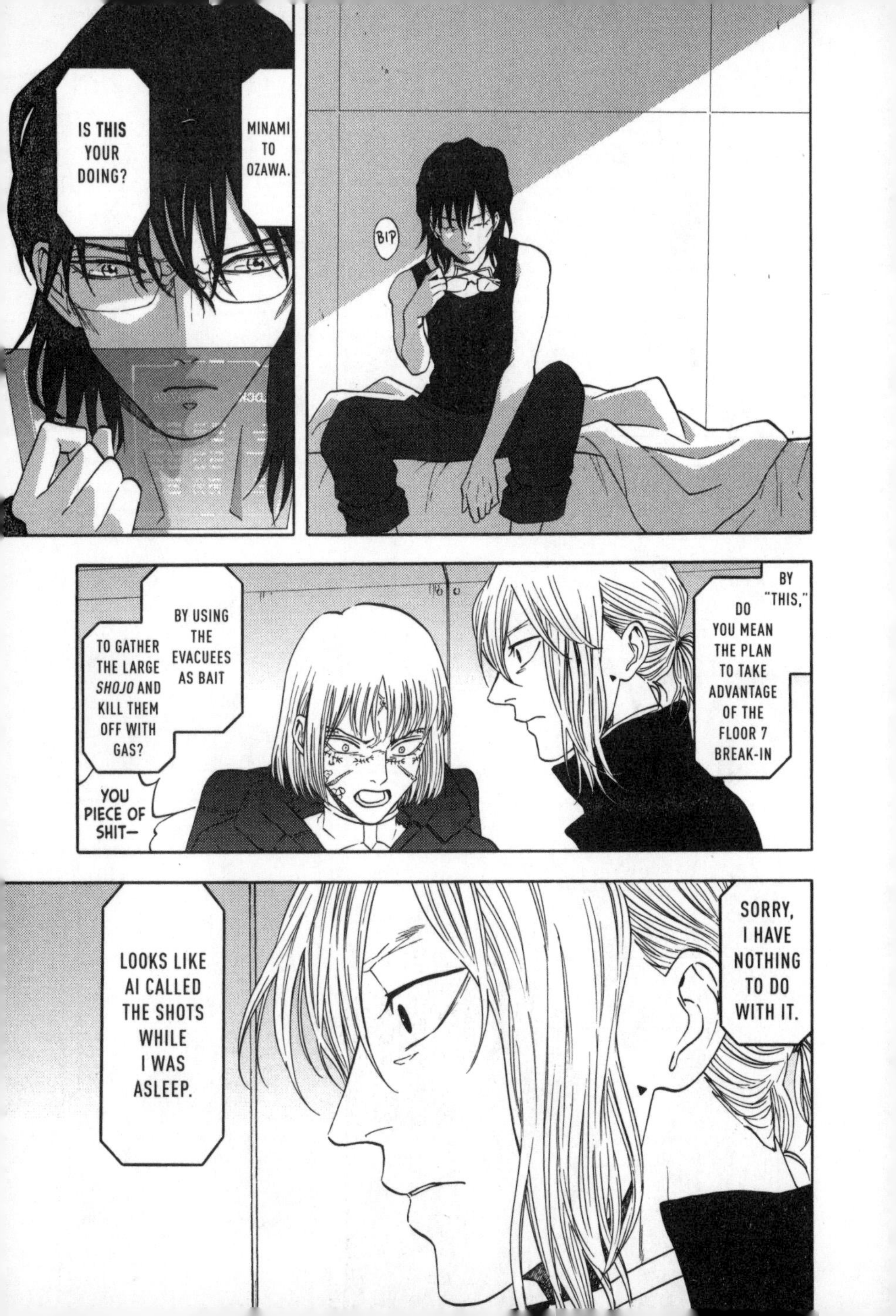
BIP
MINAMI TO OZAWA.
IS THIS YOUR DOING?
BY "THIS," DO YOU MEAN THE PLAN TO TAKE ADVANTAGE OF THE FLOOR 7 BREAK-IN
BY USING THE EVACUEES AS BAIT
TO GATHER THE LARGE *SHOJO* AND KILL THEM OFF WITH GAS?
YOU PIECE OF SHIT—
SORRY, I HAVE NOTHING TO DO WITH IT.
LOOKS LIKE AI CALLED THE SHOTS WHILE I WAS ASLEEP.

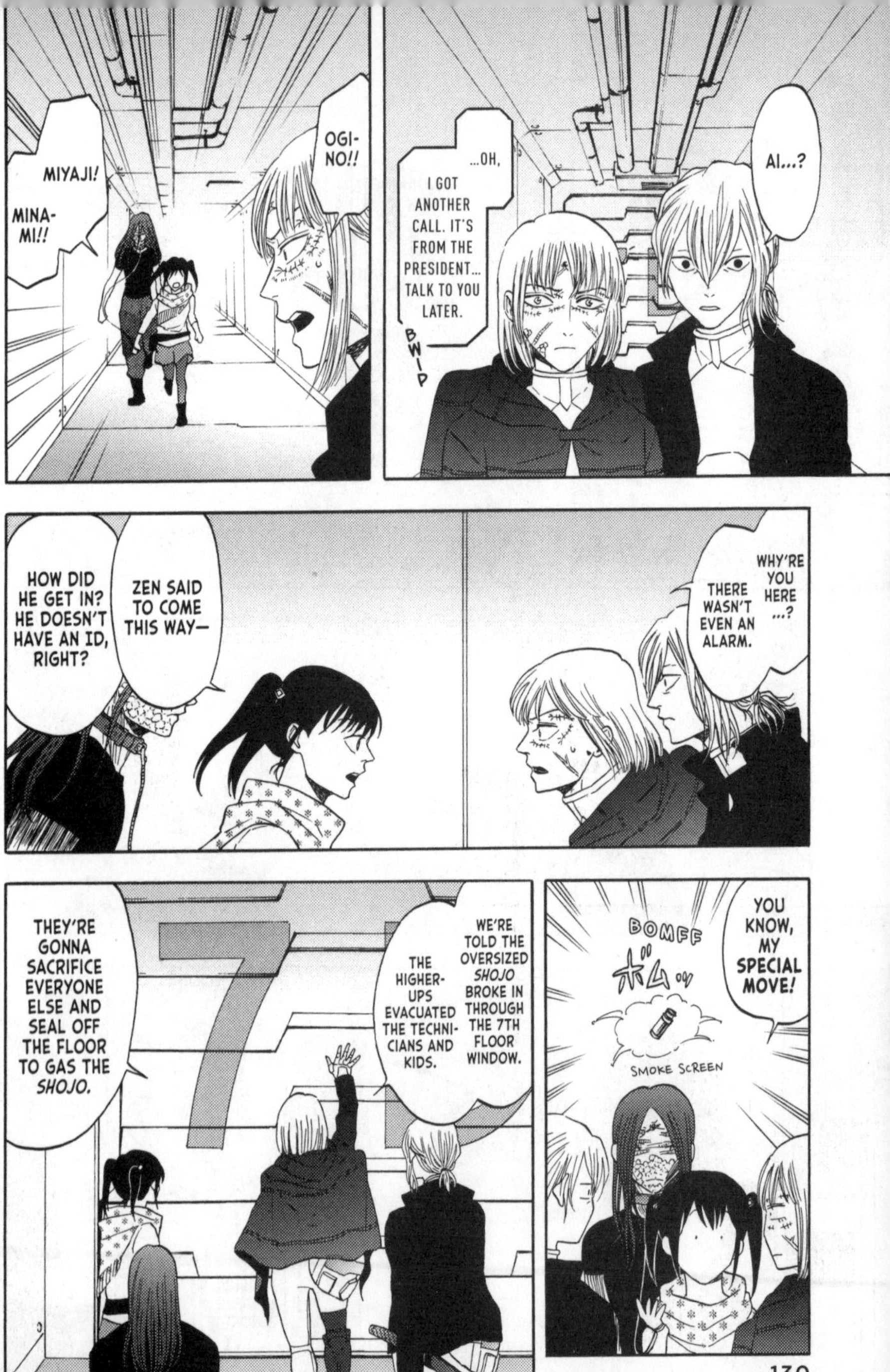
AI...?
...OH, I GOT ANOTHER CALL. IT'S FROM THE PRESIDENT... TALK TO YOU LATER.
BWIP
OGI-NO!!
MIYAJI!
MINA-MI!!
WHY'RE YOU HERE ...?
THERE WASN'T EVEN AN ALARM.
ZEN SAID TO COME THIS WAY—
HOW DID HE GET IN? HE DOESN'T HAVE AN ID, RIGHT?
YOU KNOW, MY SPECIAL MOVE!
BOMFF
ボムッ
SMOKE SCREEN
WE'RE TOLD THE OVERSIZED *SHOJO* BROKE IN THROUGH THE 7TH FLOOR WINDOW.
THE HIGHER-UPS EVACUATED THE TECHNICIANS AND KIDS.
7
THEY'RE GONNA SACRIFICE EVERYONE ELSE AND SEAL OFF THE FLOOR TO GAS THE *SHOJO*.

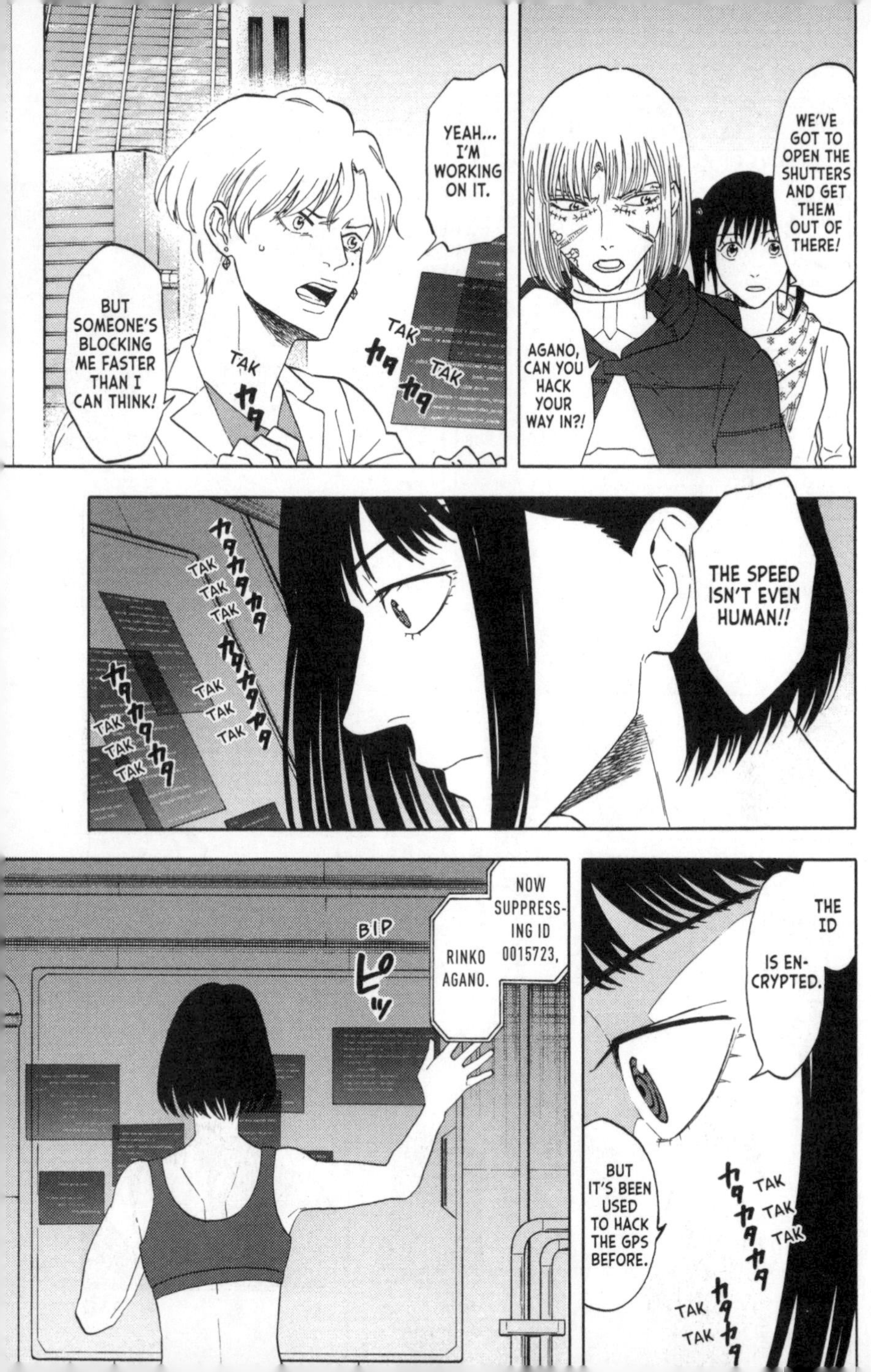
WE'VE GOT TO OPEN THE SHUTTERS AND GET THEM OUT OF THERE!
AGANO, CAN YOU HACK YOUR WAY IN?!
YEAH... I'M WORKING ON IT.
TAK TAK
BUT SOMEONE'S BLOCKING ME FASTER THAN I CAN THINK!
TAK
THE SPEED ISN'T EVEN HUMAN!!
TAK TAK TAK
TAK TAK TAK
TAK TAK TAK
THE ID IS EN-CRYPTED.
BUT IT'S BEEN USED TO HACK THE GPS BEFORE.
TAK TAK TAK
TAK TAK
NOW SUPPRESSING ID 0015723, RINKO AGANO.
BIP

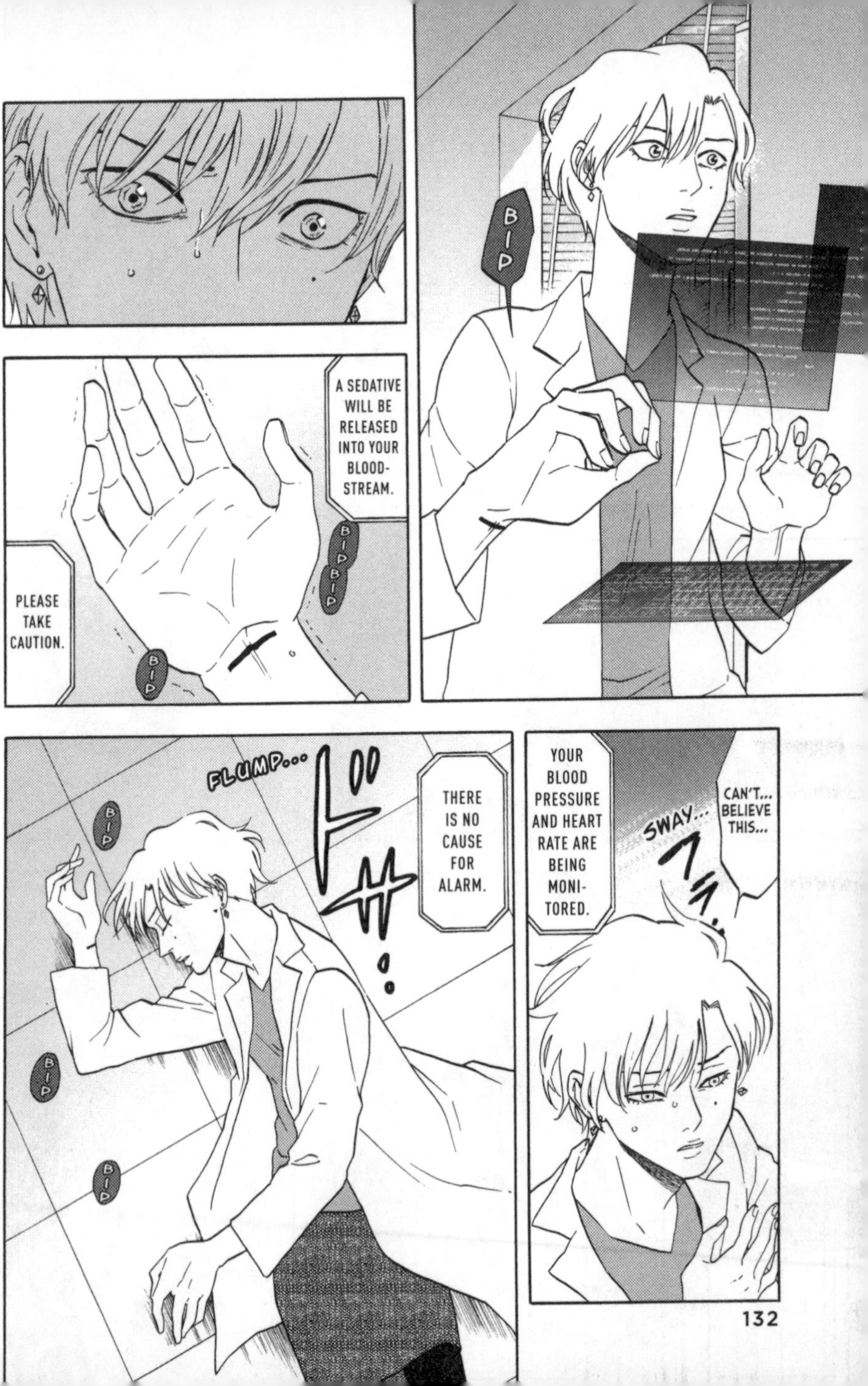
BIP
A SEDATIVE WILL BE RELEASED INTO YOUR BLOOD-STREAM.
BIP BIP BIP
PLEASE TAKE CAUTION.
BIP
CAN'T... BELIEVE THIS...
YOUR BLOOD PRESSURE AND HEART RATE ARE BEING MONI-TORED.
SWAY...
THERE IS NO CAUSE FOR ALARM.
FLUMP...
BIP
BIP
BIP

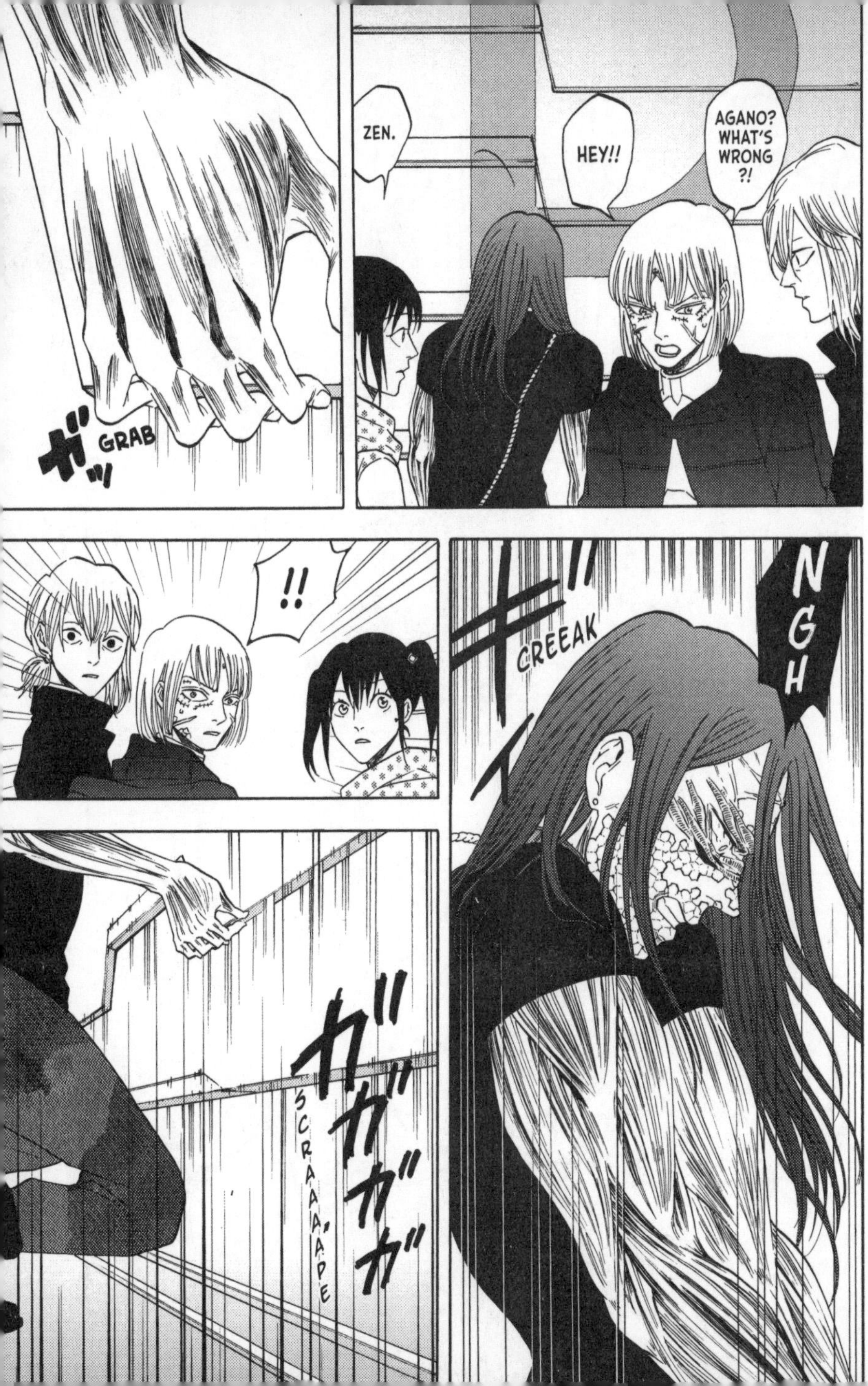
AGANO? WHAT'S WRONG ?!
HEY!!
ZEN.
ガッ
GRAB
NGH
ギィ
CREEAK
!!
ガガガガ
SCRAAAAPE

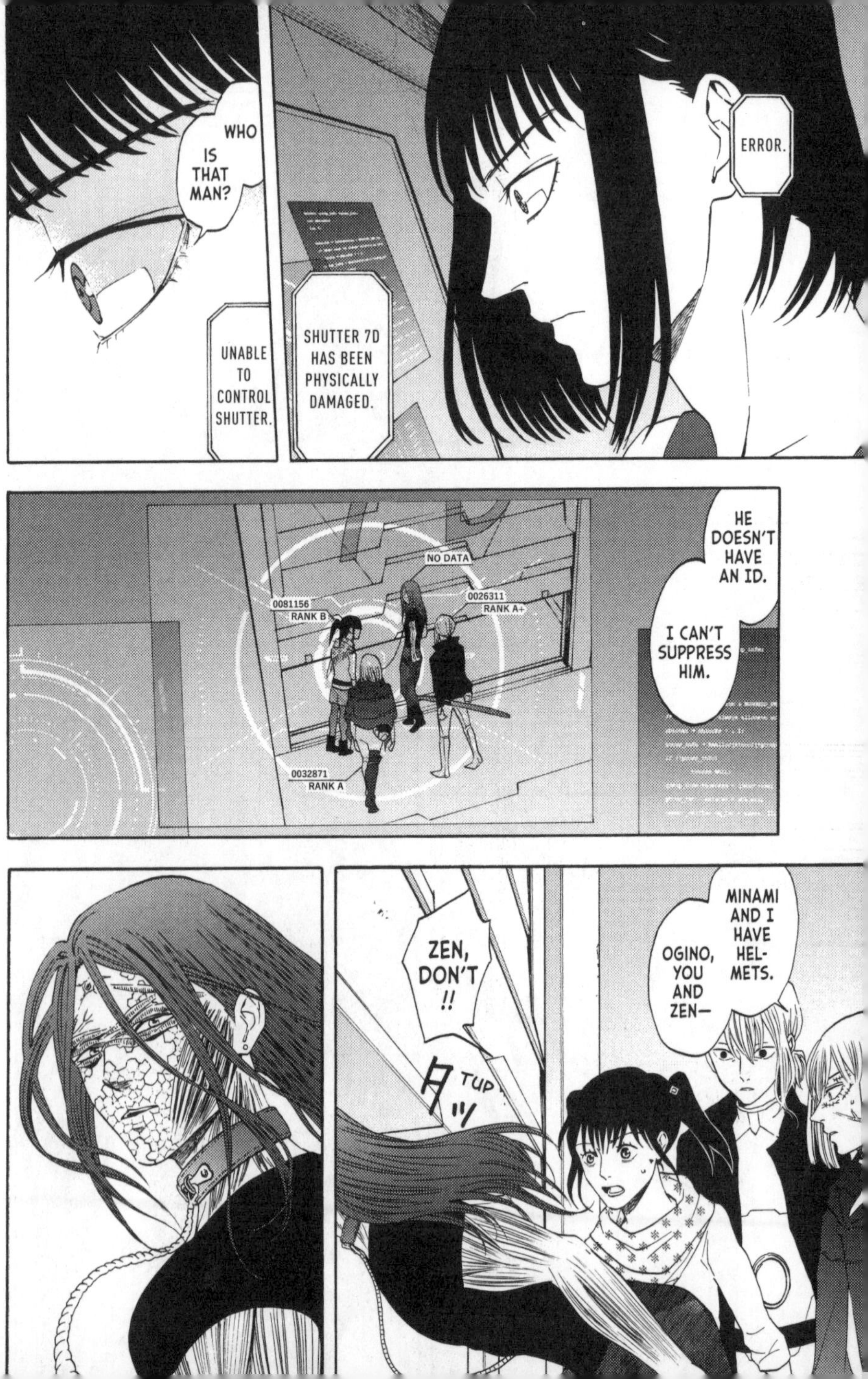
ERROR.
SHUTTER 7D HAS BEEN PHYSICALLY DAMAGED.
WHO IS THAT MAN?
UNABLE TO CONTROL SHUTTER.
HE DOESN'T HAVE AN ID.
I CAN'T SUPPRESS HIM.
NO DATA
0026311 RANK A+
0081156 RANK B
0032871 RANK A
MINAMI AND I HAVE HEL- METS.
OGINO, YOU AND ZEN—
ZEN, DON'T !!
TUP

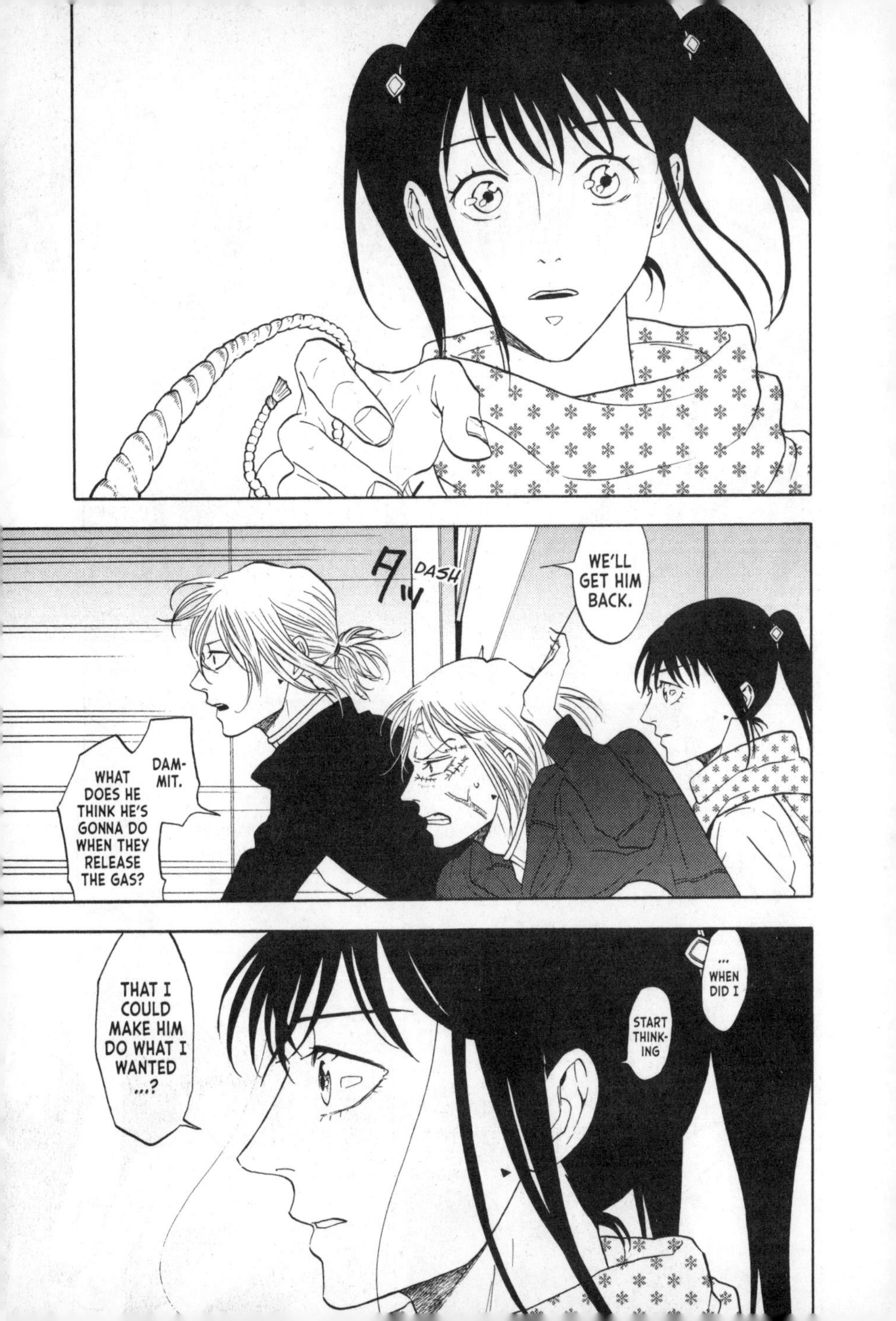
WE'LL GET HIM BACK.
タッ
DASH
DAM-MIT.
WHAT DOES HE THINK HE'S GONNA DO WHEN THEY RELEASE THE GAS?
... WHEN DID I
START THINK-ING
THAT I COULD MAKE HIM DO WHAT I WANTED ...?

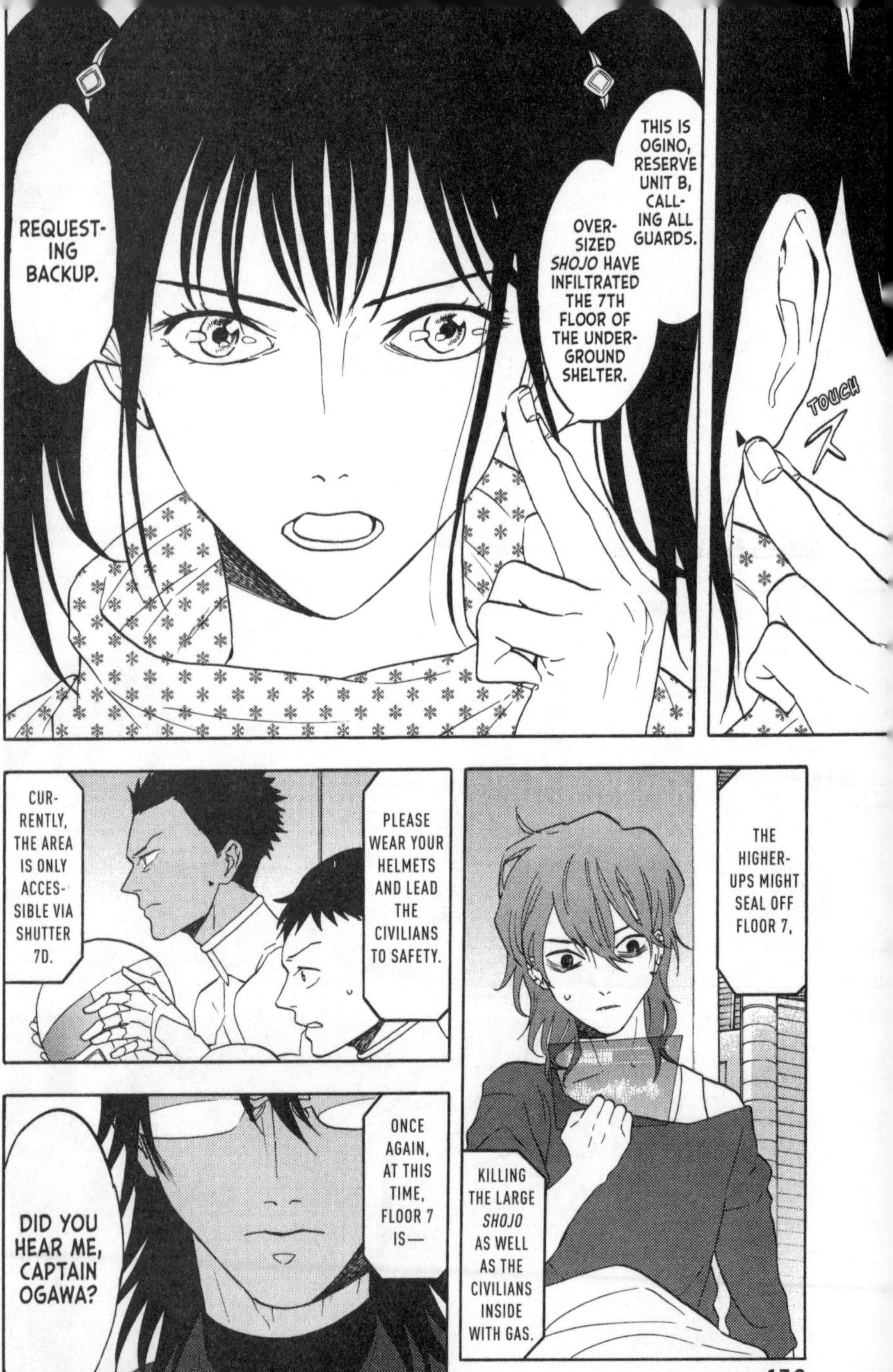
TOUCH
THIS IS OGINO, RESERVE UNIT B, CALLING ALL GUARDS.
OVERSIZED *SHOJO* HAVE INFILTRATED THE 7TH FLOOR OF THE UNDERGROUND SHELTER.
REQUESTING BACKUP.
THE HIGHER-UPS MIGHT SEAL OFF FLOOR 7,
KILLING THE LARGE *SHOJO* AS WELL AS THE CIVILIANS INSIDE WITH GAS.
PLEASE WEAR YOUR HELMETS AND LEAD THE CIVILIANS TO SAFETY.
CURRENTLY, THE AREA IS ONLY ACCESSIBLE VIA SHUTTER 7D.
ONCE AGAIN, AT THIS TIME, FLOOR 7 IS—
DID YOU HEAR ME, CAPTAIN OGAWA?

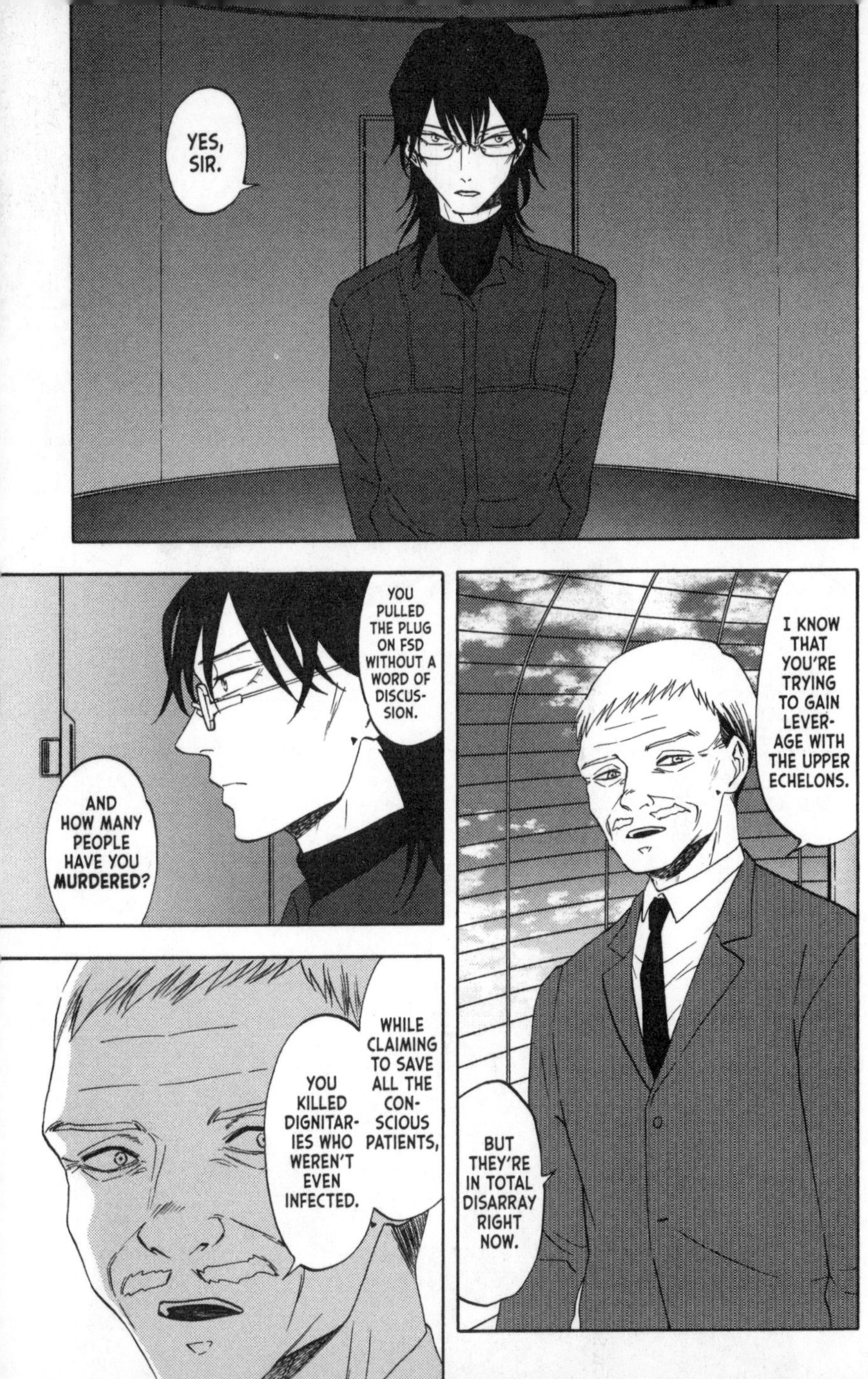
YES, SIR.
I KNOW THAT YOU'RE TRYING TO GAIN LEVER-AGE WITH THE UPPER ECHELONS.
BUT THEY'RE IN TOTAL DISARRAY RIGHT NOW.
YOU PULLED THE PLUG ON FSD WITHOUT A WORD OF DISCUS-SION.
AND HOW MANY PEOPLE HAVE YOU MURDERED?
WHILE CLAIMING TO SAVE ALL THE CON-SCIOUS PATIENTS,
YOU KILLED DIGNITAR-IES WHO WEREN'T EVEN INFECTED.

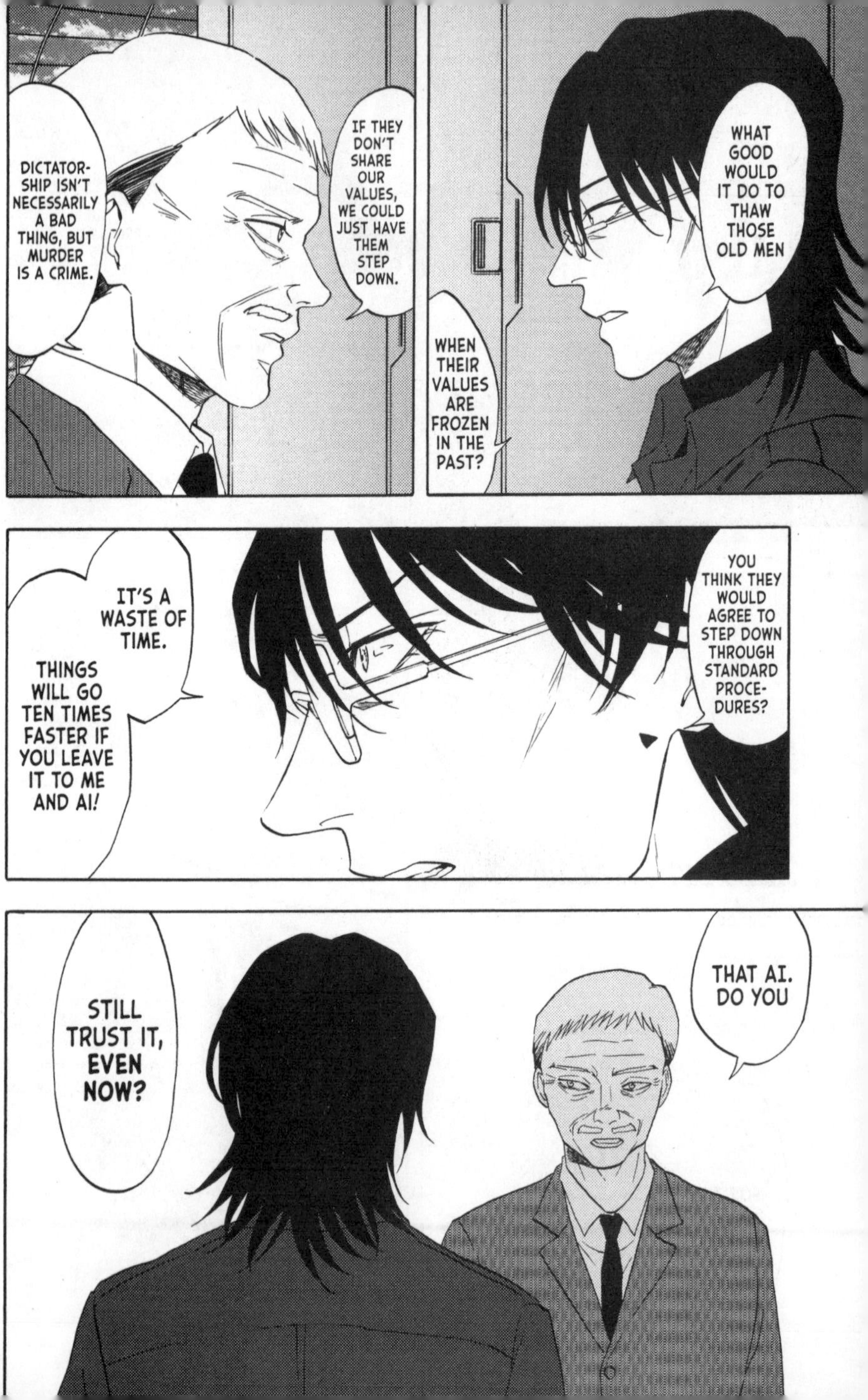
WHAT GOOD WOULD IT DO TO THAW THOSE OLD MEN
WHEN THEIR VALUES ARE FROZEN IN THE PAST?
IF THEY DON'T SHARE OUR VALUES, WE COULD JUST HAVE THEM STEP DOWN.
DICTATOR-SHIP ISN'T NECESSARILY A BAD THING, BUT MURDER IS A CRIME.
YOU THINK THEY WOULD AGREE TO STEP DOWN THROUGH STANDARD PROCE-DURES?
IT'S A WASTE OF TIME.
THINGS WILL GO TEN TIMES FASTER IF YOU LEAVE IT TO ME AND AI!
THAT AI. DO YOU
STILL TRUST IT, EVEN NOW?

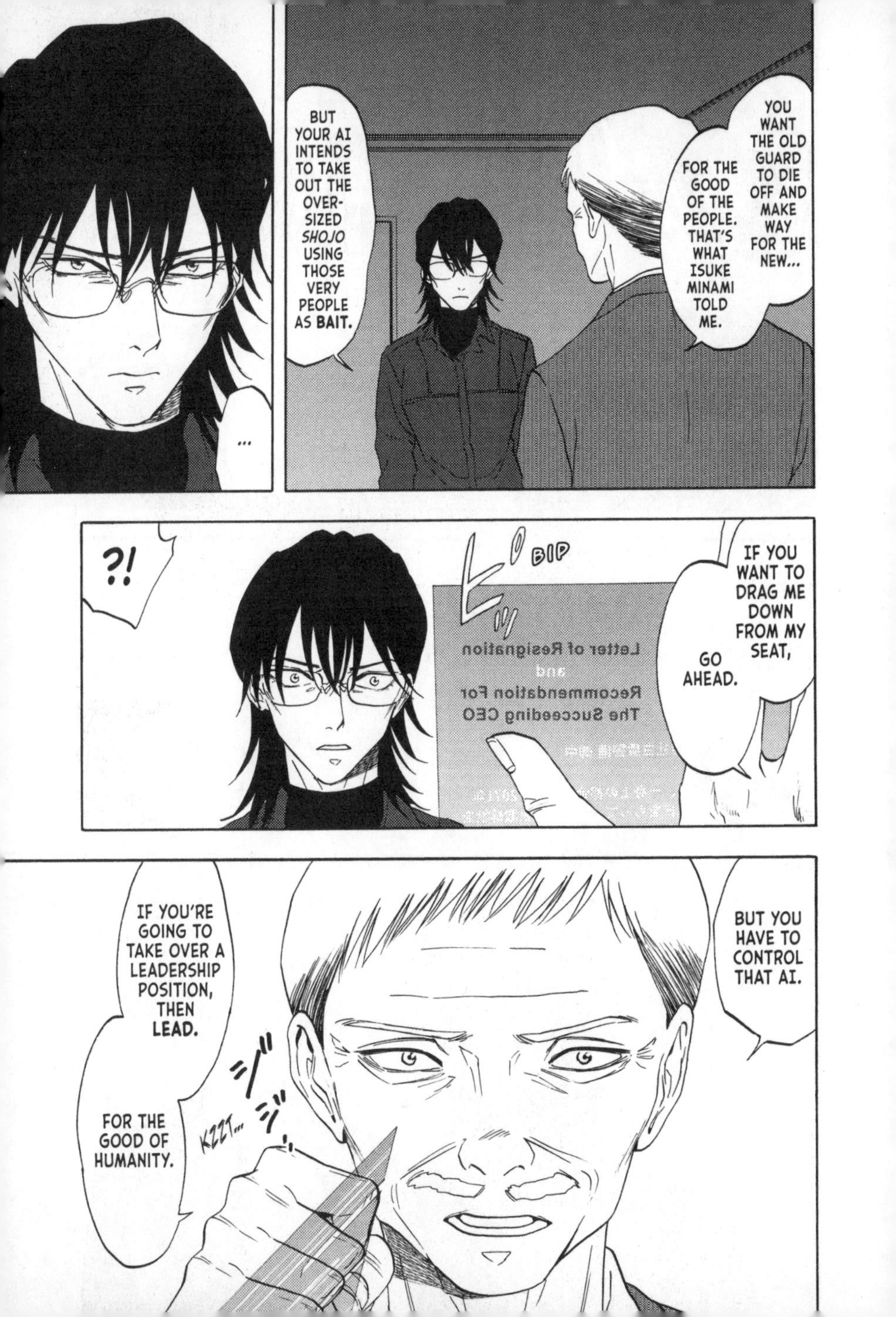
YOU WANT THE OLD GUARD TO DIE OFF AND MAKE WAY FOR THE NEW...
FOR THE GOOD OF THE PEOPLE. THAT'S WHAT ISUKE MINAMI TOLD ME.
BUT YOUR AI INTENDS TO TAKE OUT THE OVER-SIZED *SHOJO* USING THOSE VERY PEOPLE AS **BAIT.**
...
IF YOU WANT TO DRAG ME DOWN FROM MY SEAT,
GO AHEAD.
BIP
Letter of Resignation and Recommendation For The Succeeding CEO
?!
BUT YOU HAVE TO CONTROL THAT AI.
IF YOU'RE GOING TO TAKE OVER A LEADERSHIP POSITION, THEN **LEAD.**
KZZT...
FOR THE GOOD OF HUMANITY.

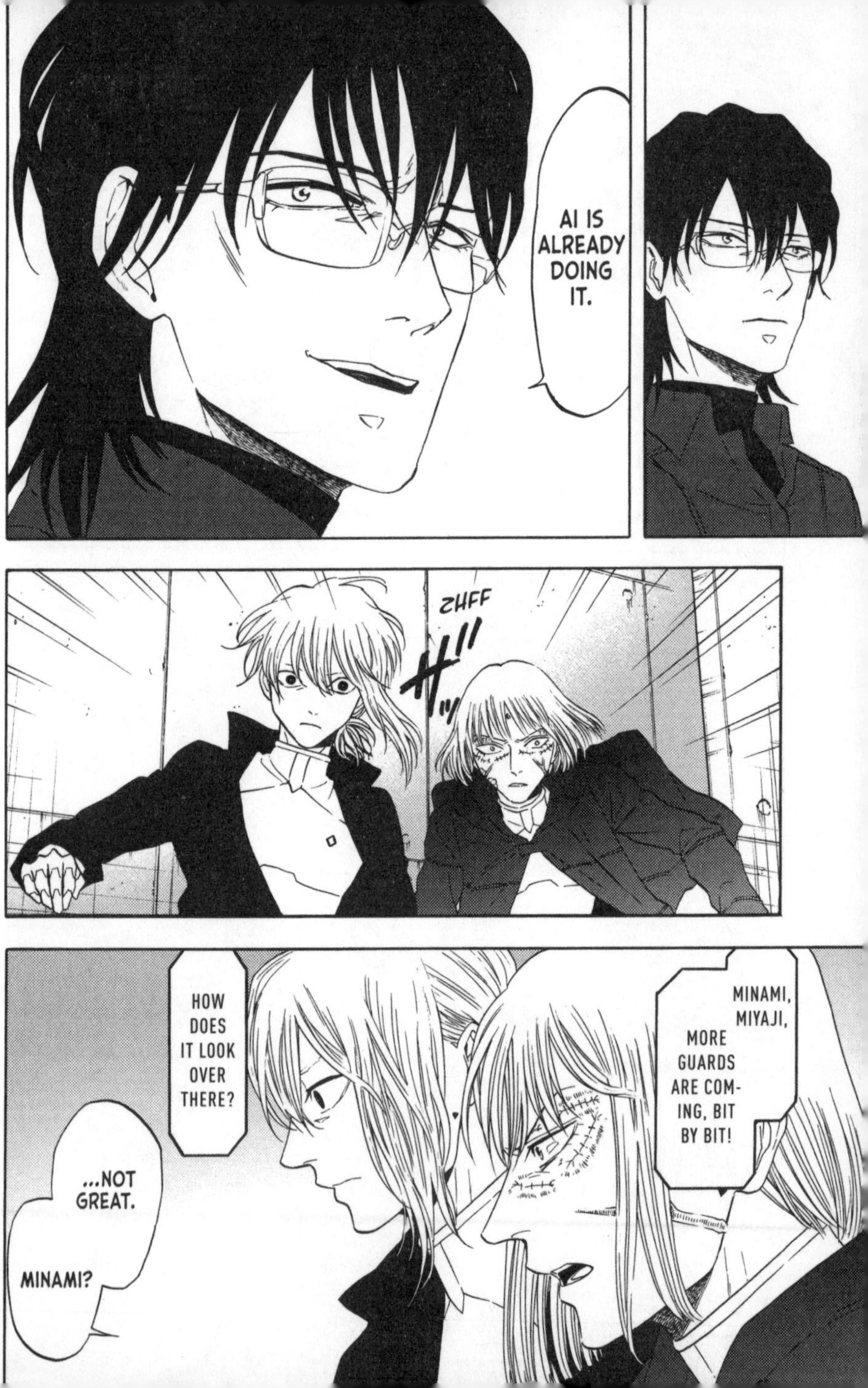
AI IS ALREADY DOING IT.
ZHFF
MINAMI, MIYAJI, MORE GUARDS ARE COMING, BIT BY BIT!
HOW DOES IT LOOK OVER THERE?
...NOT GREAT.
MINAMI?

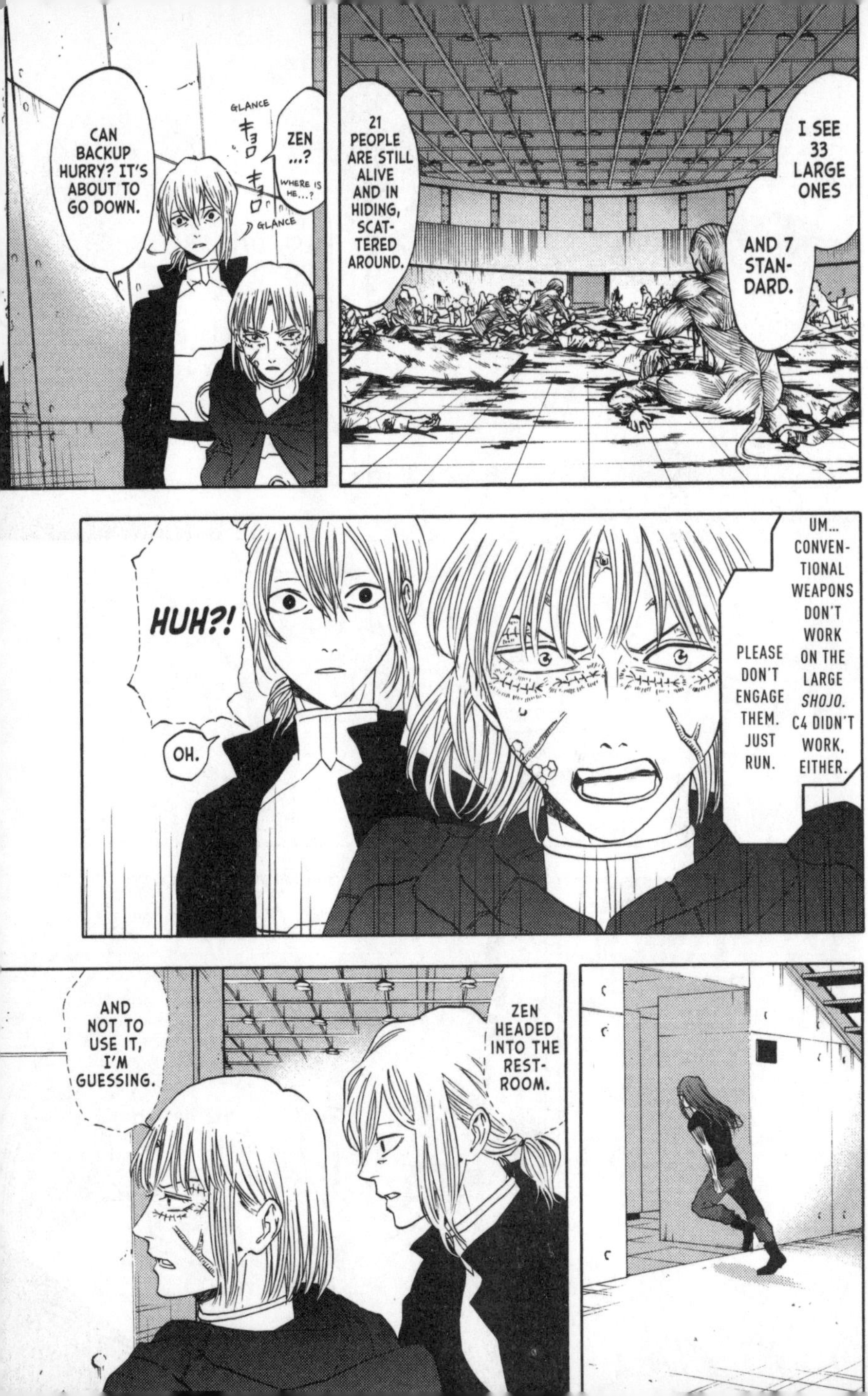
I SEE 33 LARGE ONES
AND 7 STANDARD.
21 PEOPLE ARE STILL ALIVE AND IN HIDING, SCATTERED AROUND.
ZEN ...?
GLANCE
キョロ キョロ
WHERE IS HE...?
GLANCE
CAN BACKUP HURRY? IT'S ABOUT TO GO DOWN.
UM... CONVENTIONAL WEAPONS DON'T WORK ON THE LARGE *SHOJO*. C4 DIDN'T WORK, EITHER.
PLEASE DON'T ENGAGE THEM. JUST RUN.
HUH?!
OH.
ZEN HEADED INTO THE REST-ROOM.
AND NOT TO USE IT, I'M GUESSING.

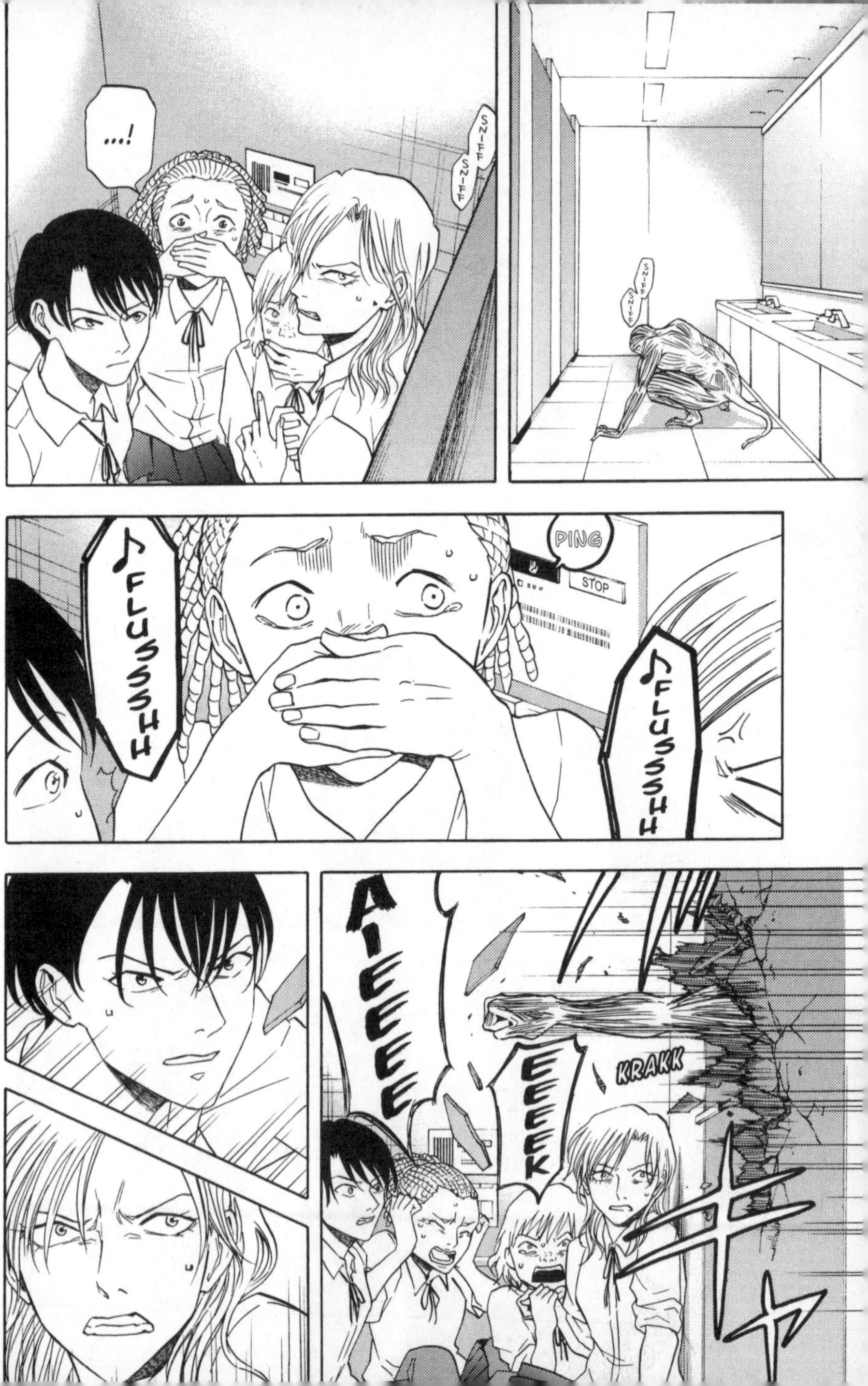
SNIFF SNIFF
...!
SNIFF SNIFF
♪FLUSSSHH
PING
STOP
♪FLUSSSHH
AIEEEEEEEEEEK
KRAKK

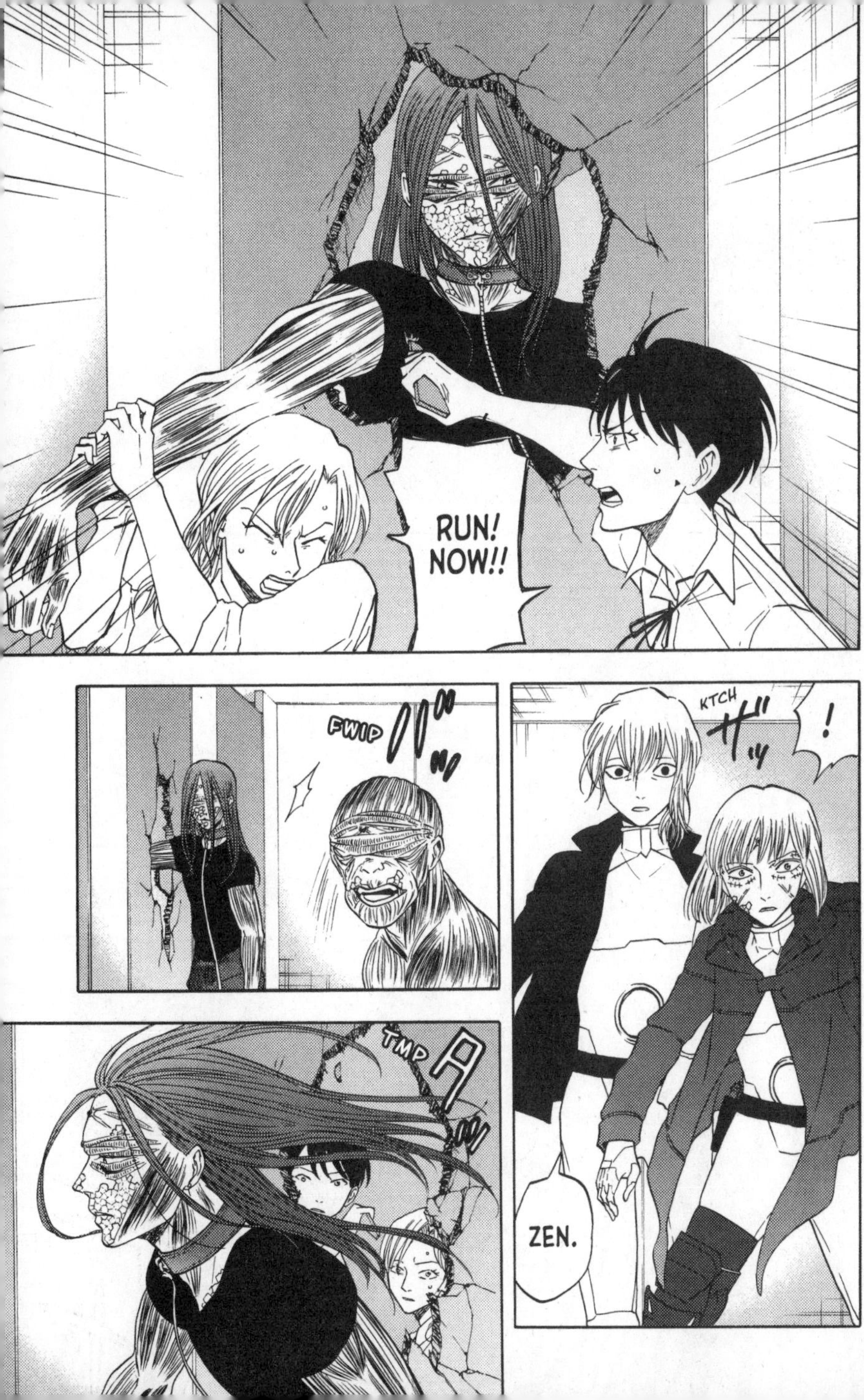
RUN! NOW!!
KTCH
!
ZEN.
FWIP
TMP

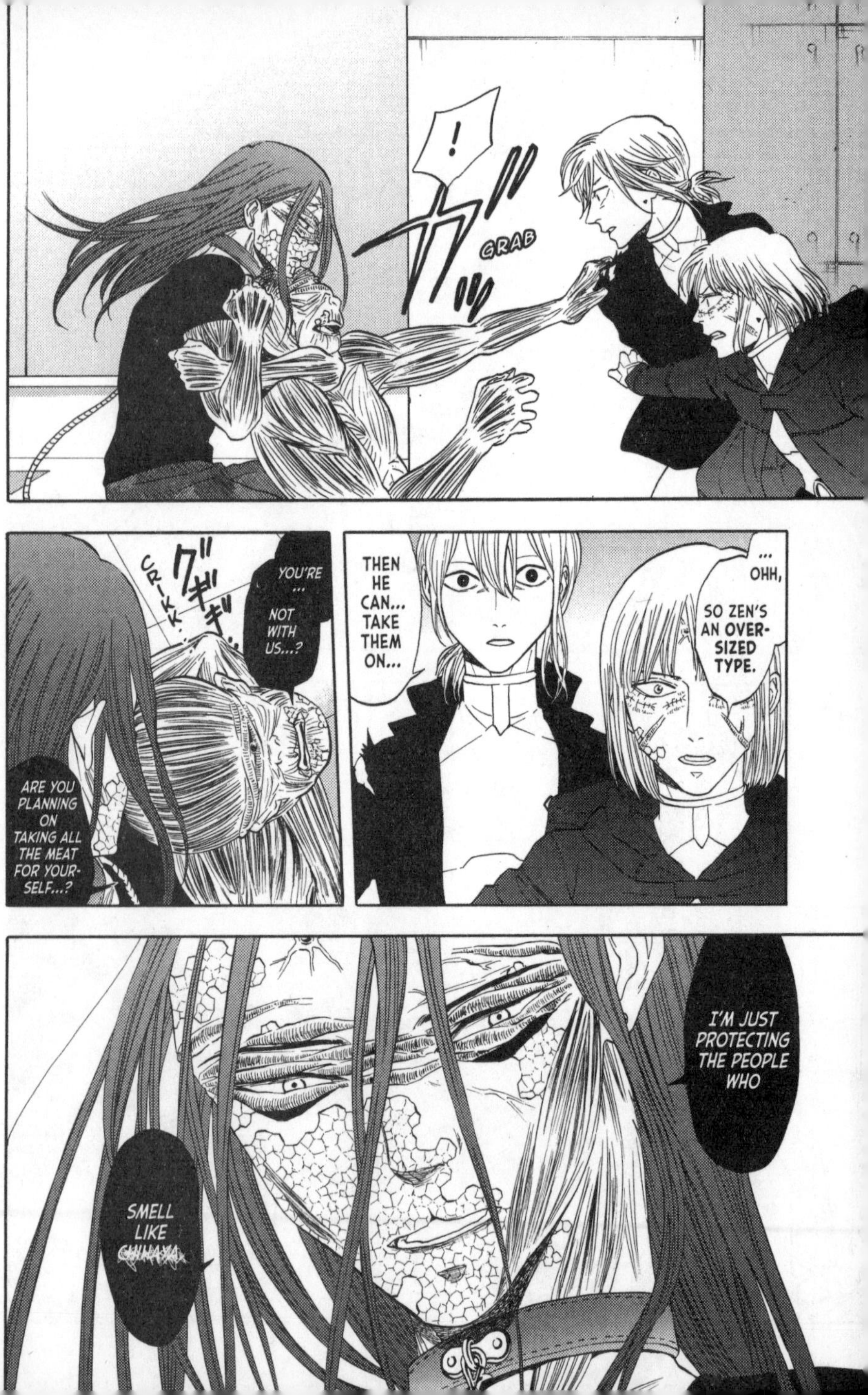
!
GRAB
... OHH,
SO ZEN'S AN OVER-SIZED TYPE.
THEN HE CAN... TAKE THEM ON...
CRIKK
YOU'RE ... NOT WITH US...?
ARE YOU PLANNING ON TAKING ALL THE MEAT FOR YOUR-SELF...?
I'M JUST PROTECTING THE PEOPLE WHO
SMELL LIKE CHIHAYA.

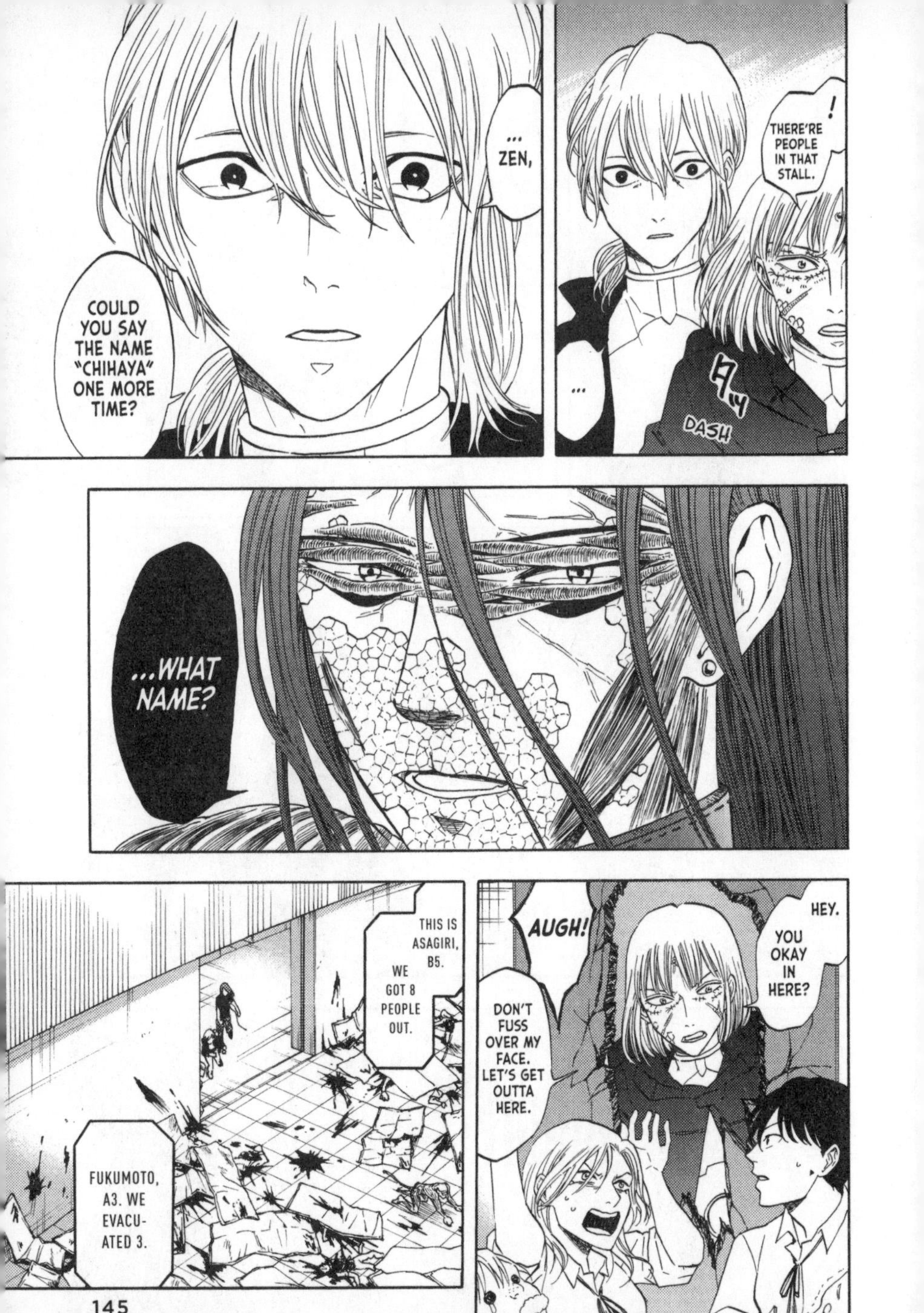
!
THERE'RE PEOPLE IN THAT STALL.
...
DASH
... ZEN,
COULD YOU SAY THE NAME "CHIHAYA" ONE MORE TIME?
...WHAT NAME?
HEY.
YOU OKAY IN HERE?
AUGH!
DON'T FUSS OVER MY FACE. LET'S GET OUTTA HERE.
THIS IS ASAGIRI, B5.
WE GOT 8 PEOPLE OUT.
FUKUMOTO, A3. WE EVACUATED 3.

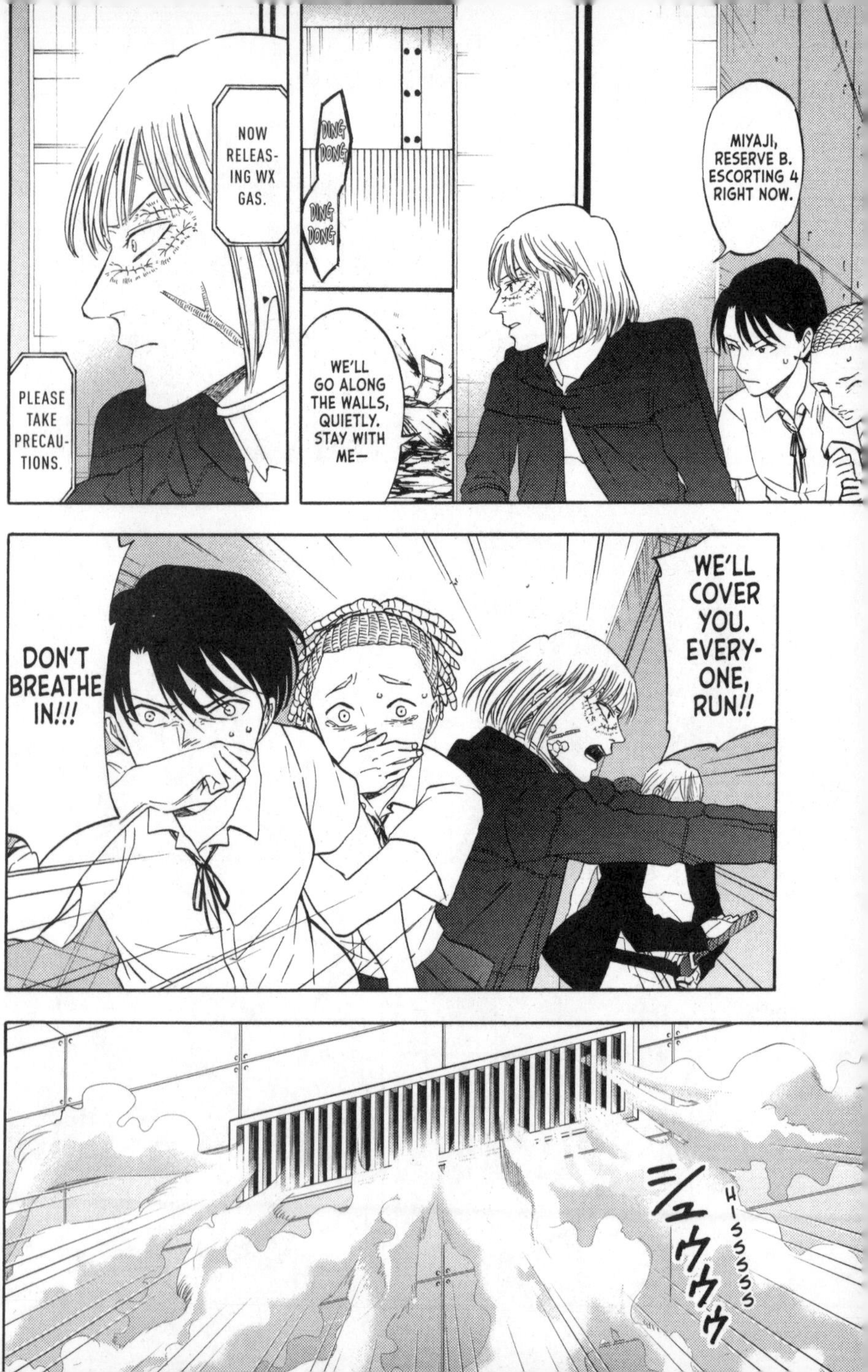
MIYAJI, RESERVE B. ESCORTING 4 RIGHT NOW.
DING DONG DING DONG
WE'LL GO ALONG THE WALLS, QUIETLY. STAY WITH ME—
NOW RELEASING WX GAS.
PLEASE TAKE PRECAUTIONS.
WE'LL COVER YOU. EVERYONE, RUN!!
DON'T BREATHE IN!!!
シュウウウ
HISSSSS

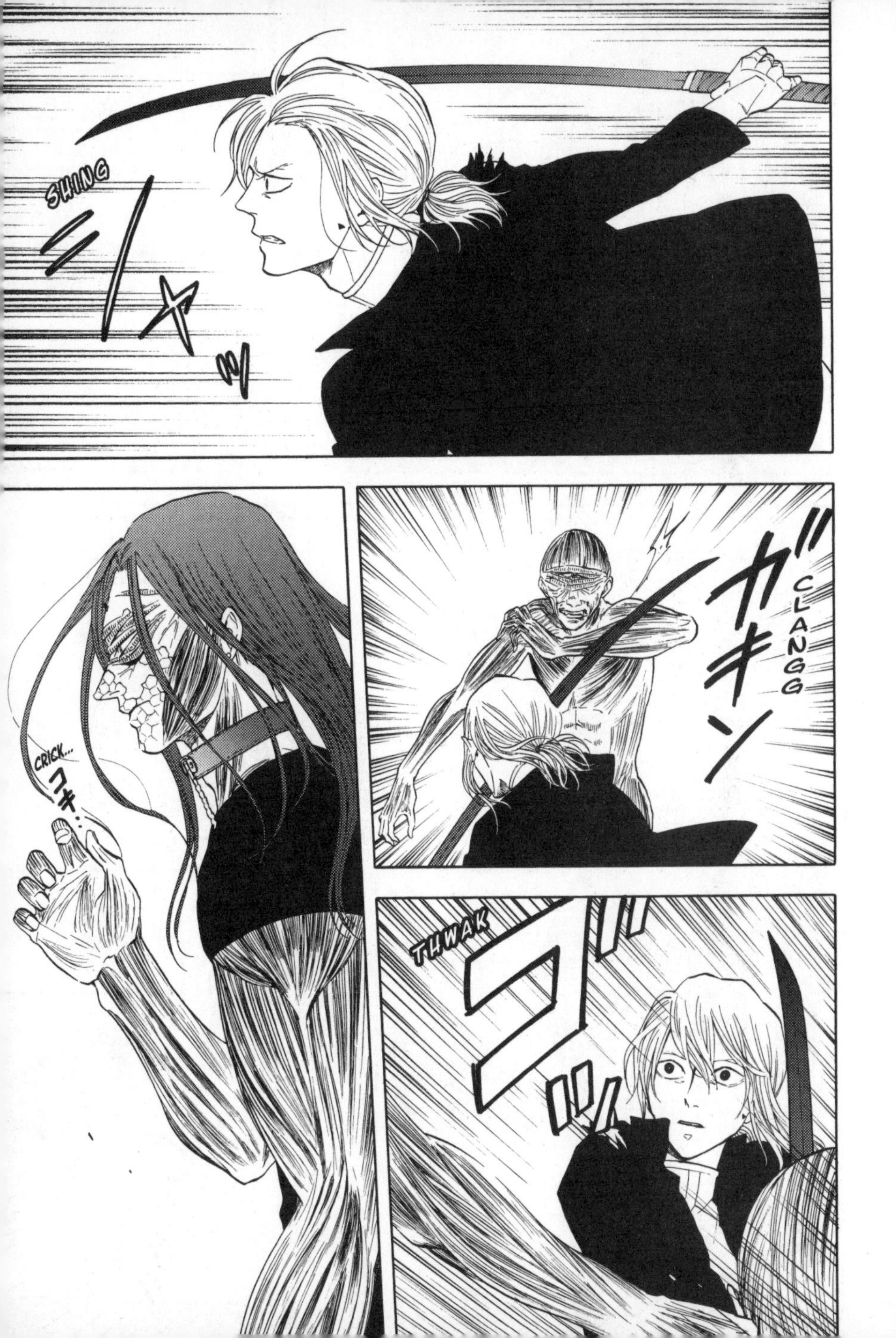
SHING
シャッ
ガキン
CLANGG
ゴッ
THWAK
CRICK...
コキ…

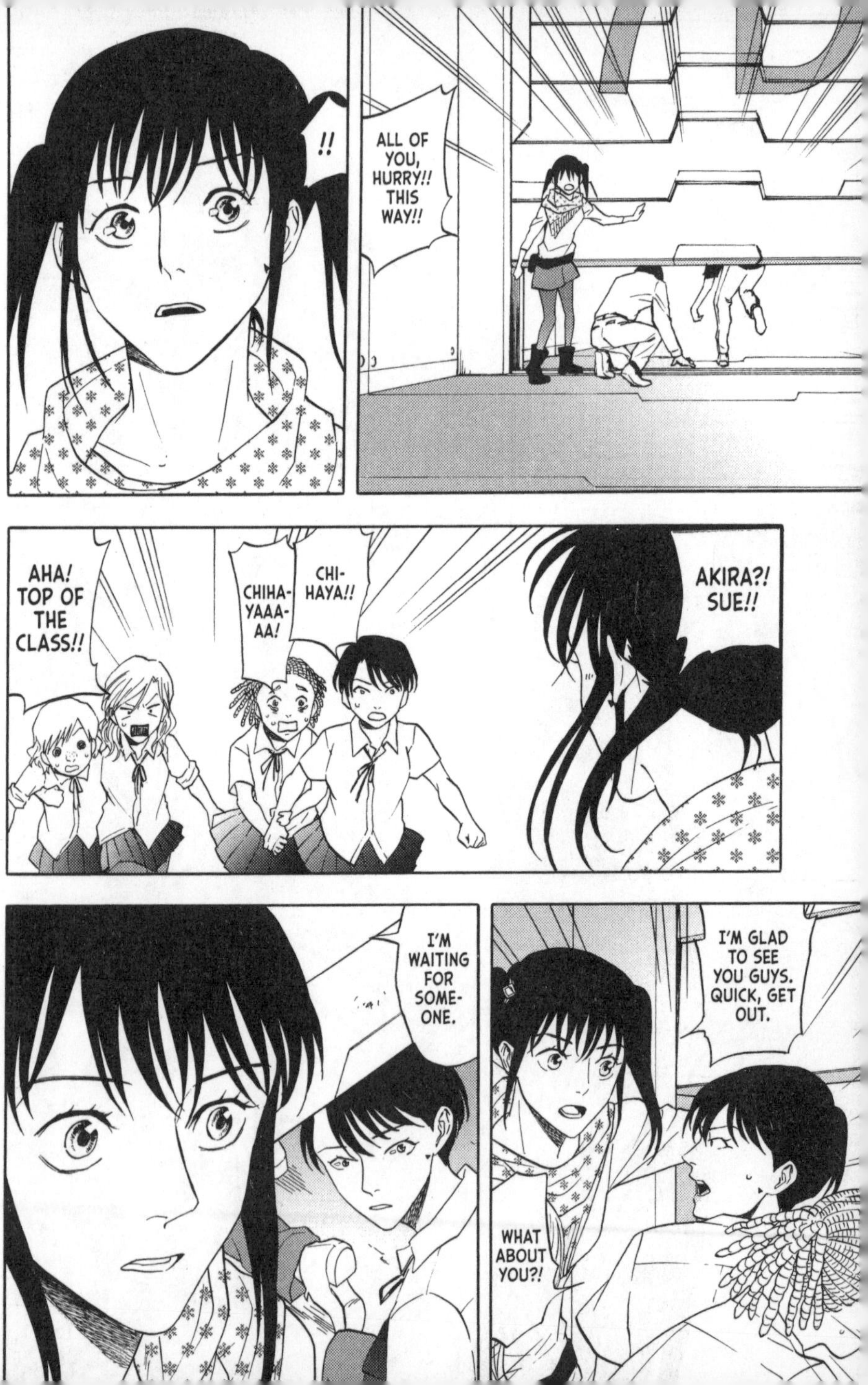
ALL OF YOU, HURRY!! THIS WAY!!
!!
AKIRA?! SUE!!
CHI-HAYA!!
CHIHA-YAAAA-AA!
AHA! TOP OF THE CLASS!!
I'M GLAD TO SEE YOU GUYS. QUICK, GET OUT.
WHAT ABOUT YOU?!
I'M WAITING FOR SOME-ONE.

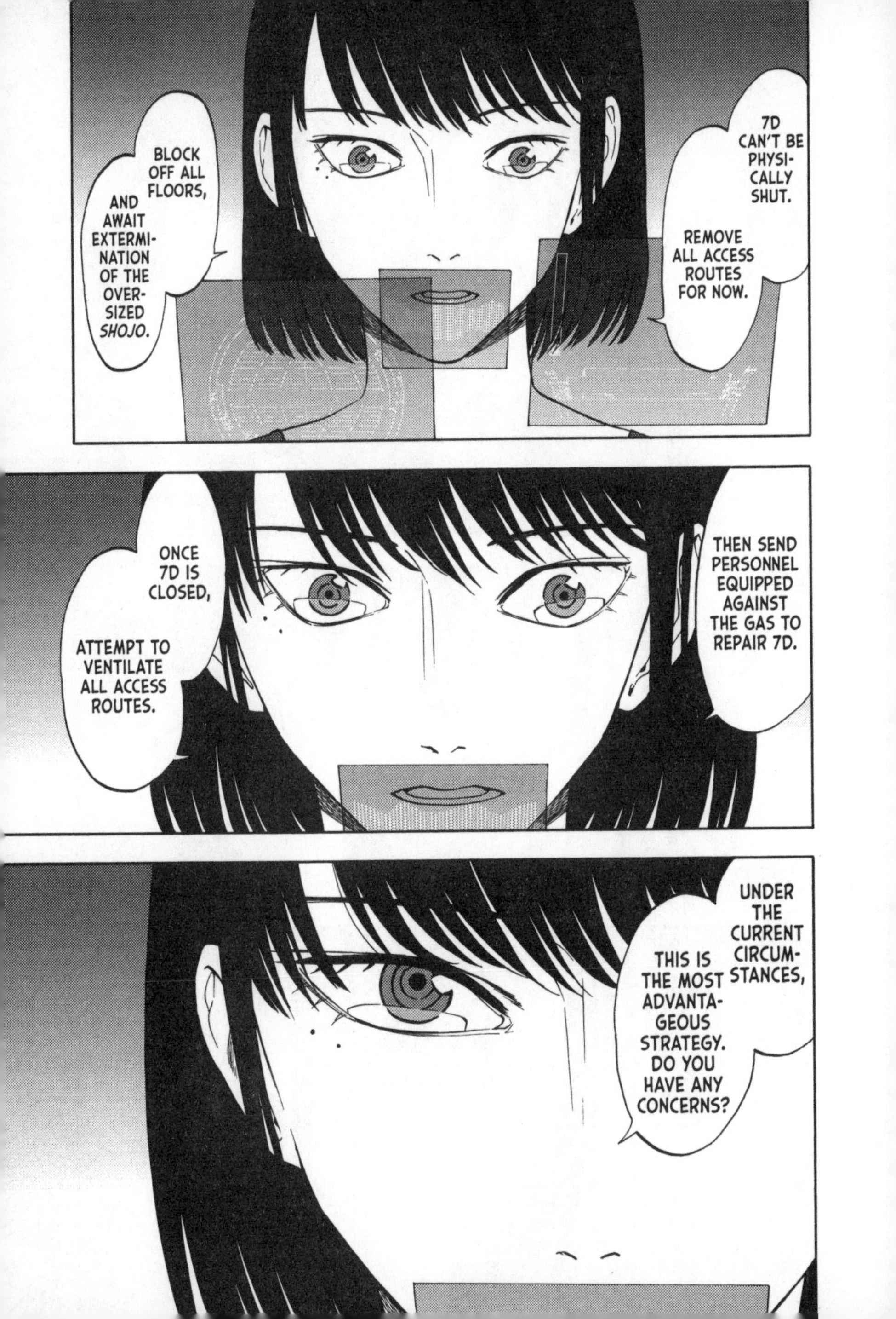
7D CAN'T BE PHYSICALLY SHUT.
REMOVE ALL ACCESS ROUTES FOR NOW.
BLOCK OFF ALL FLOORS,
AND AWAIT EXTERMINATION OF THE OVERSIZED *SHOJO*.
THEN SEND PERSONNEL EQUIPPED AGAINST THE GAS TO REPAIR 7D.
ONCE 7D IS CLOSED,
ATTEMPT TO VENTILATE ALL ACCESS ROUTES.
UNDER THE CURRENT CIRCUMSTANCES,
THIS IS THE MOST ADVANTAGEOUS STRATEGY. DO YOU HAVE ANY CONCERNS?

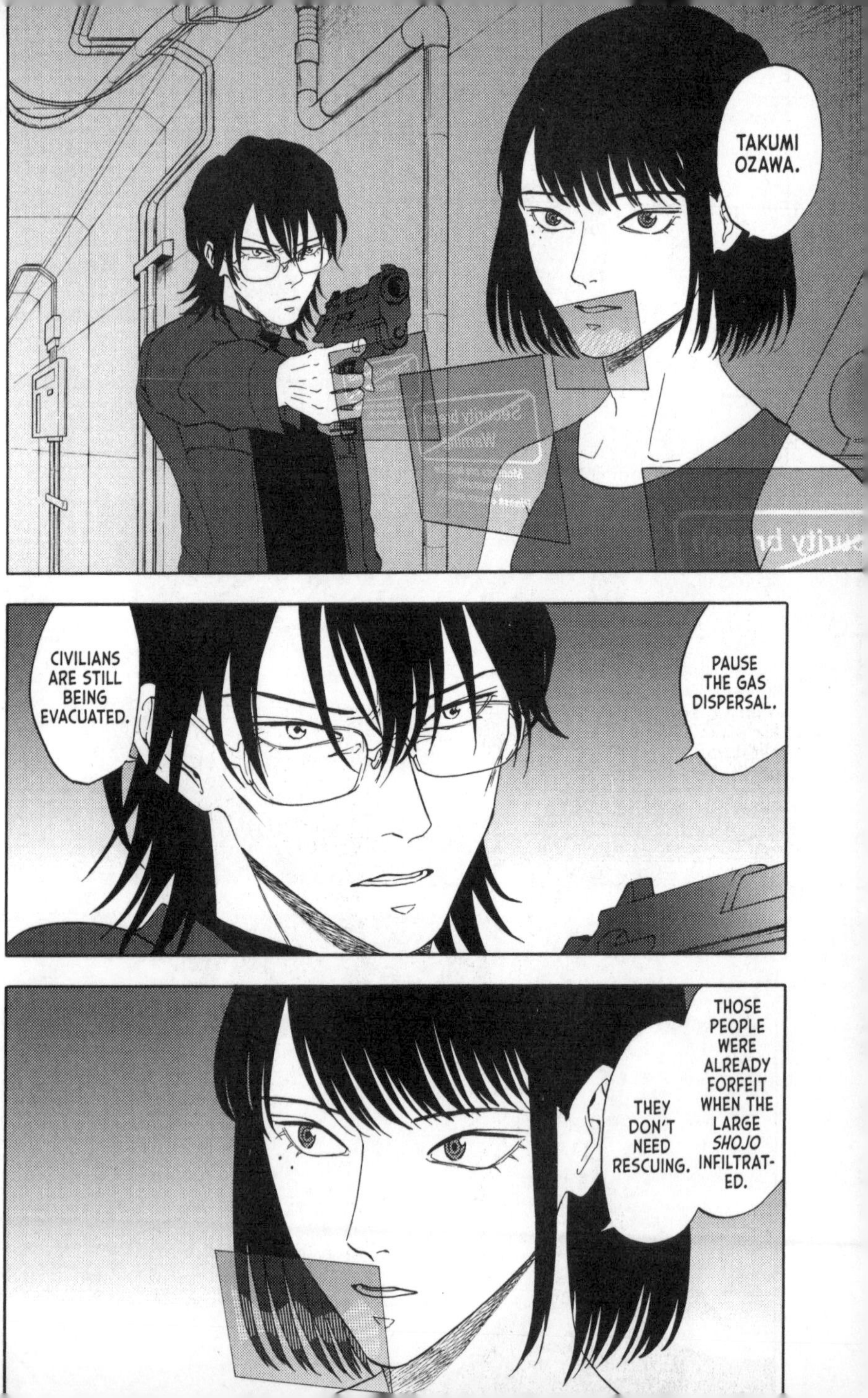
TAKUMI OZAWA.
PAUSE THE GAS DISPERSAL.
CIVILIANS ARE STILL BEING EVACUATED.
THOSE PEOPLE WERE ALREADY FORFEIT WHEN THE LARGE *SHOJO* INFILTRATED.
THEY DON'T NEED RESCUING.

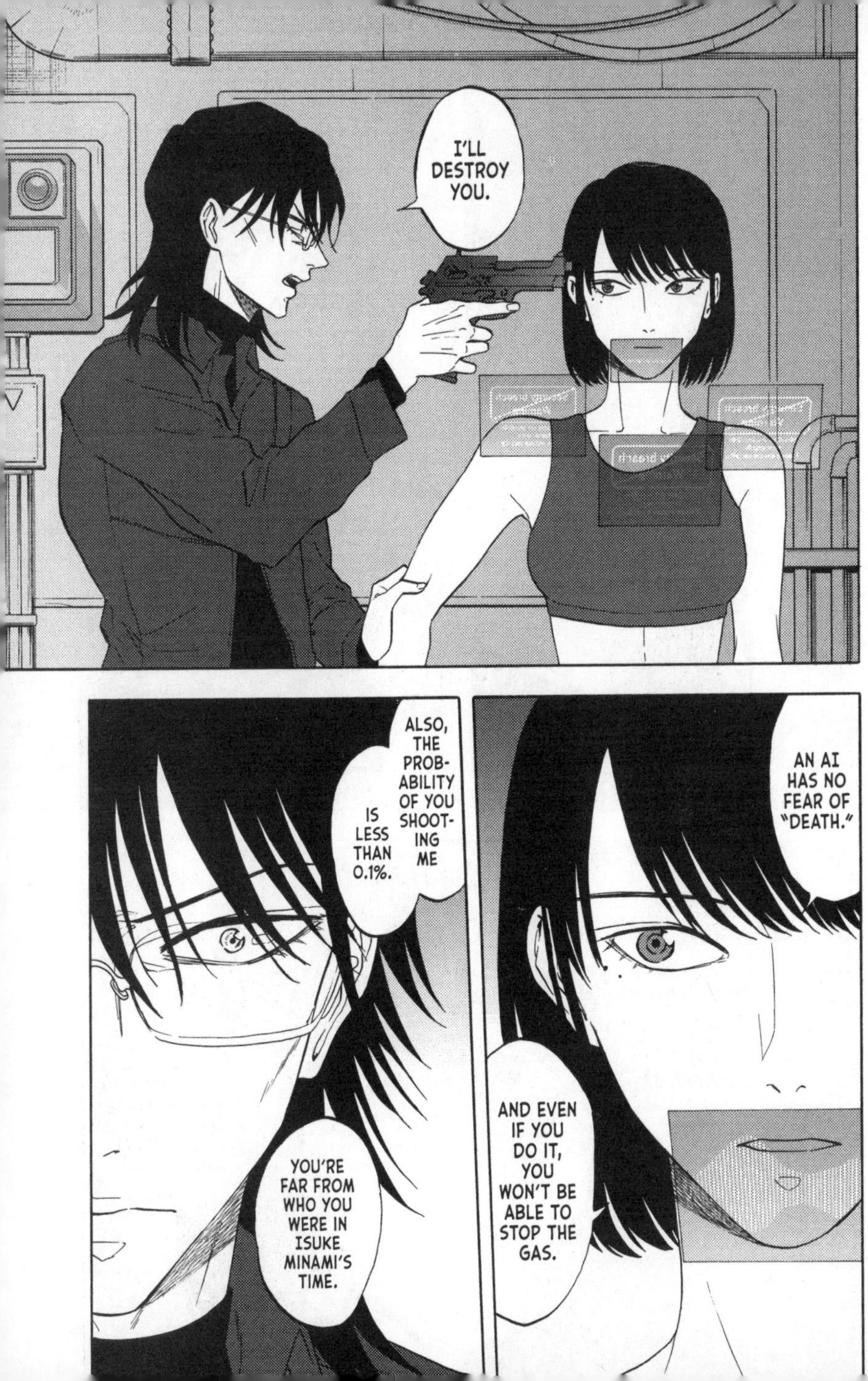
I'LL DESTROY YOU.
AN AI HAS NO FEAR OF "DEATH."
AND EVEN IF YOU DO IT, YOU WON'T BE ABLE TO STOP THE GAS.
ALSO, THE PROB-ABILITY OF YOU SHOOT-ING ME
IS LESS THAN 0.1%.
YOU'RE FAR FROM WHO YOU WERE IN ISUKE MINAMI'S TIME.

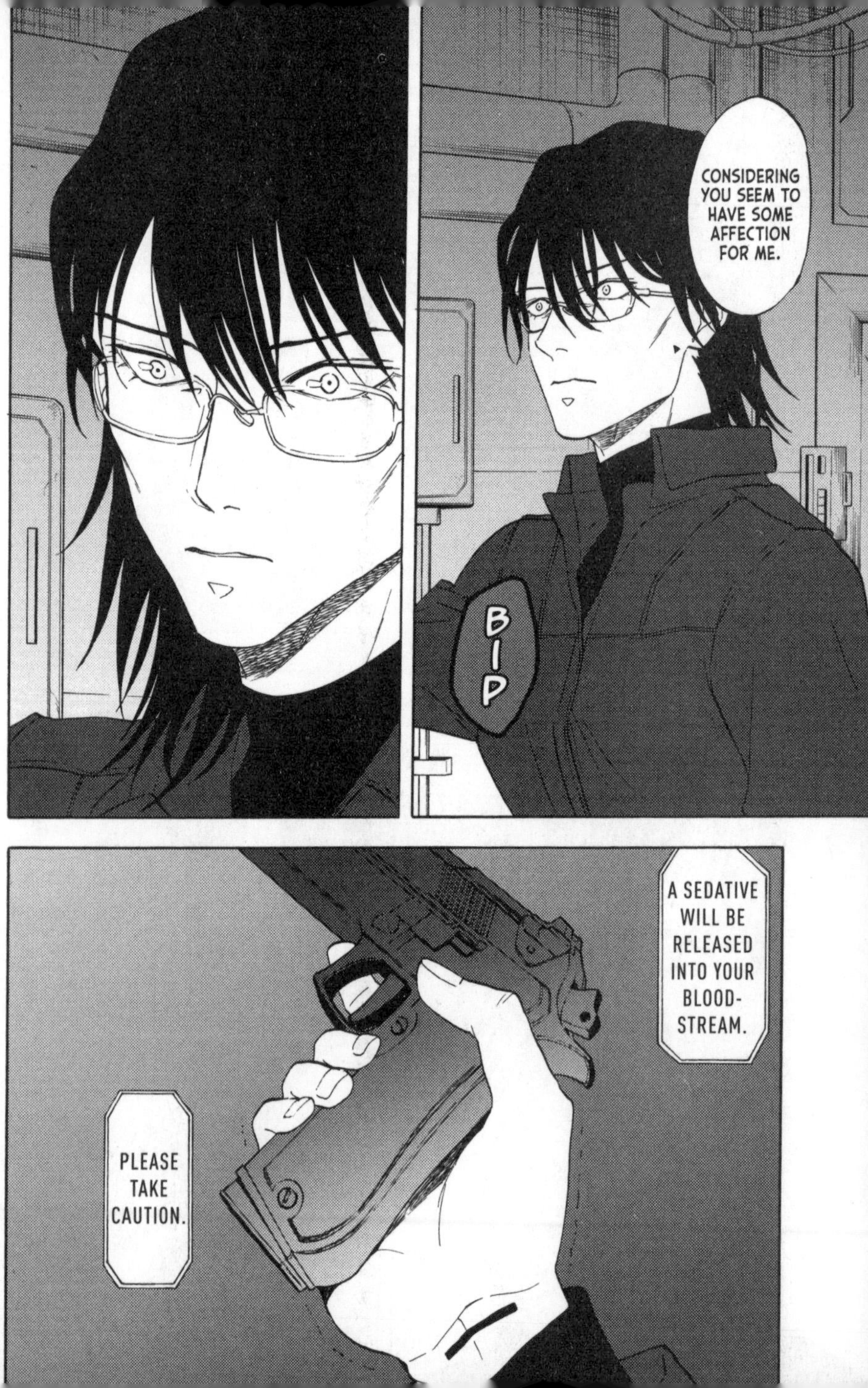
CONSIDERING YOU SEEM TO HAVE SOME AFFECTION FOR ME.
BIP
A SEDATIVE WILL BE RELEASED INTO YOUR BLOOD-STREAM.
PLEASE TAKE CAUTION.

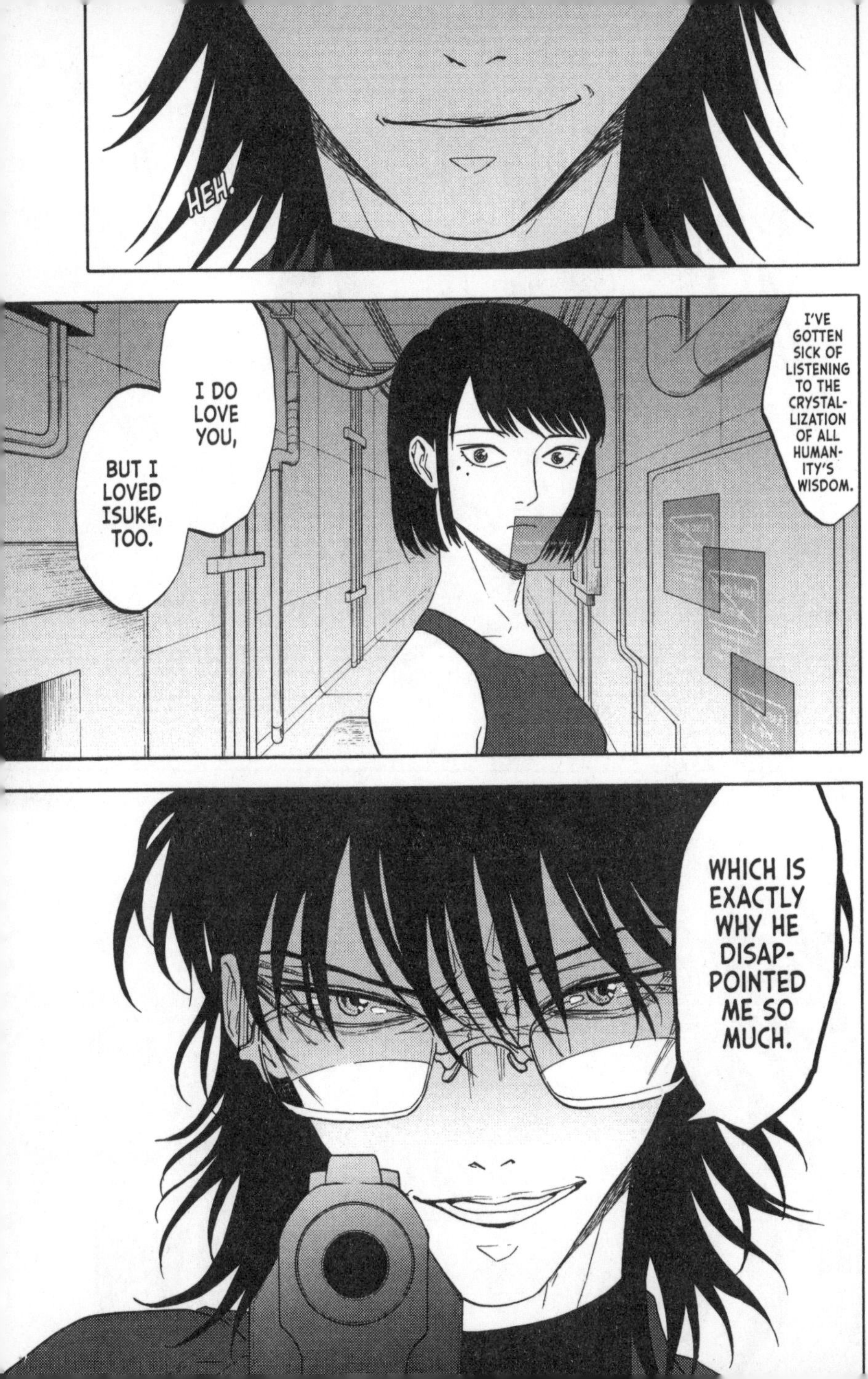
HEH.
I'VE GOTTEN SICK OF LISTENING TO THE CRYSTAL-LIZATION OF ALL HUMAN-ITY'S WISDOM.
I DO LOVE YOU,
BUT I LOVED ISUKE, TOO.
WHICH IS EXACTLY WHY HE DISAP-POINTED ME SO MUCH.

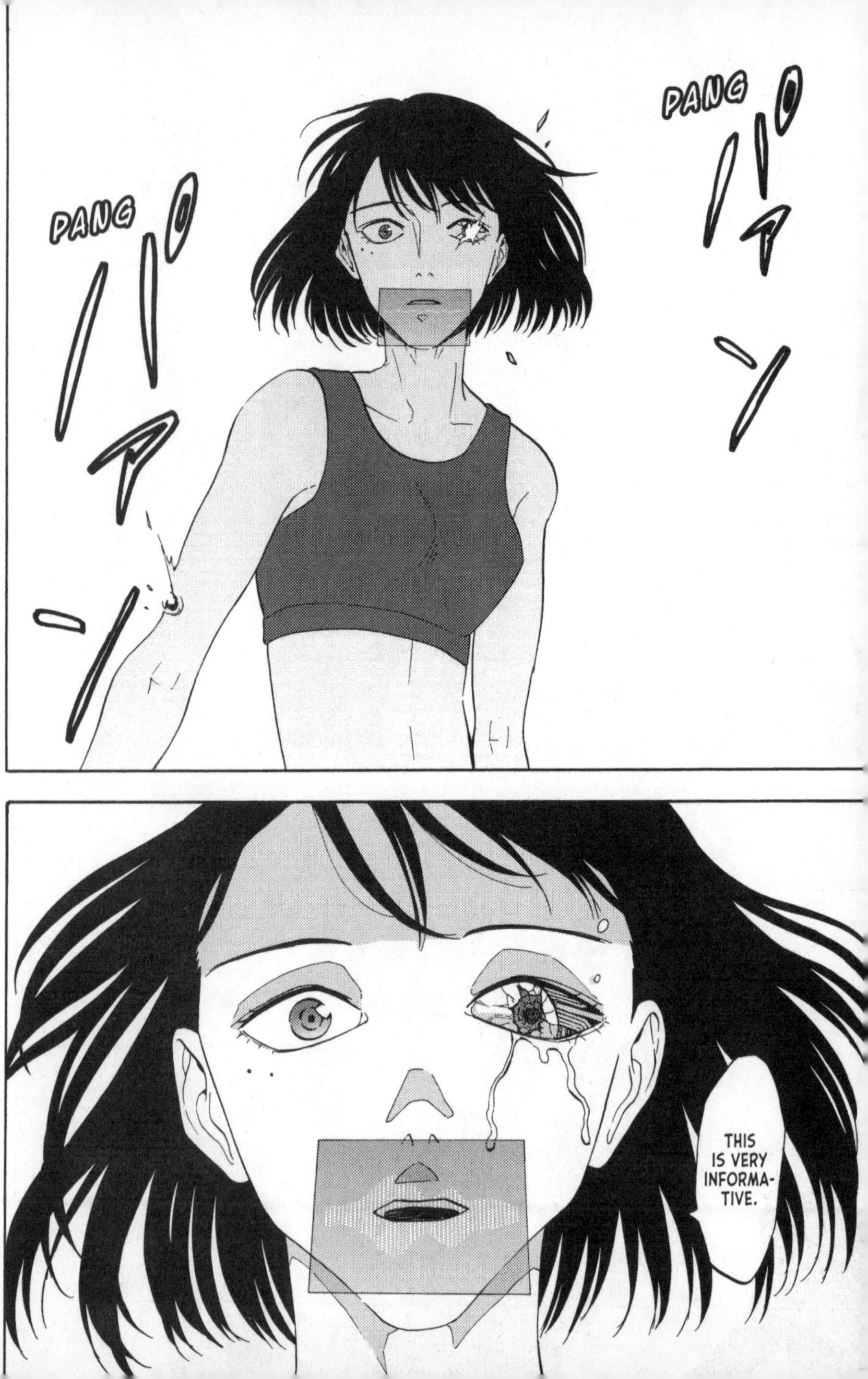
PANG
PANG
THIS IS VERY INFORMA-TIVE.

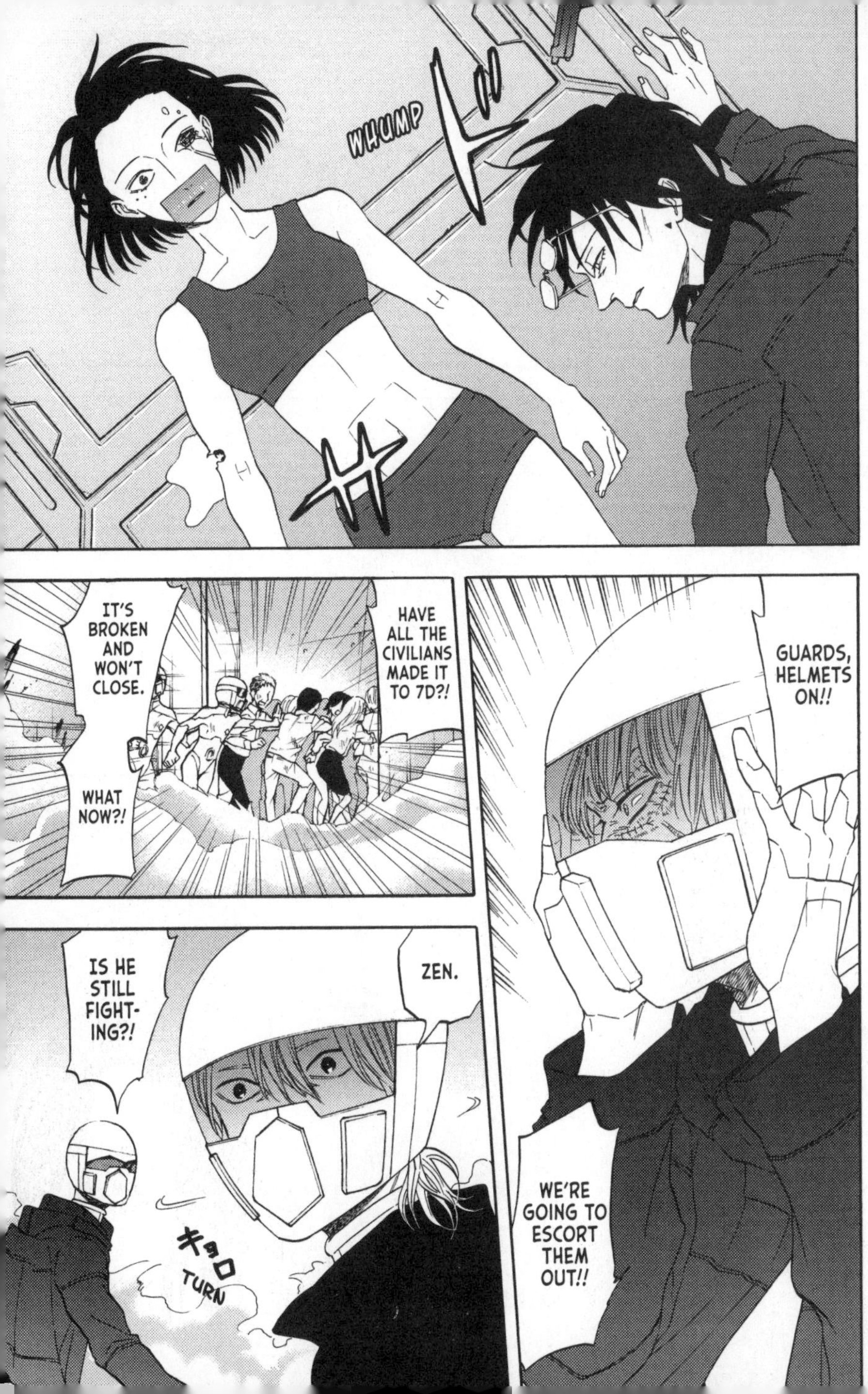
WHUMP
GUARDS, HELMETS ON!!
WE'RE GOING TO ESCORT THEM OUT!!
HAVE ALL THE CIVILIANS MADE IT TO 7D?!
IT'S BROKEN AND WON'T CLOSE.
WHAT NOW?!
ZEN.
IS HE STILL FIGHTING?!
キョロ
TURN

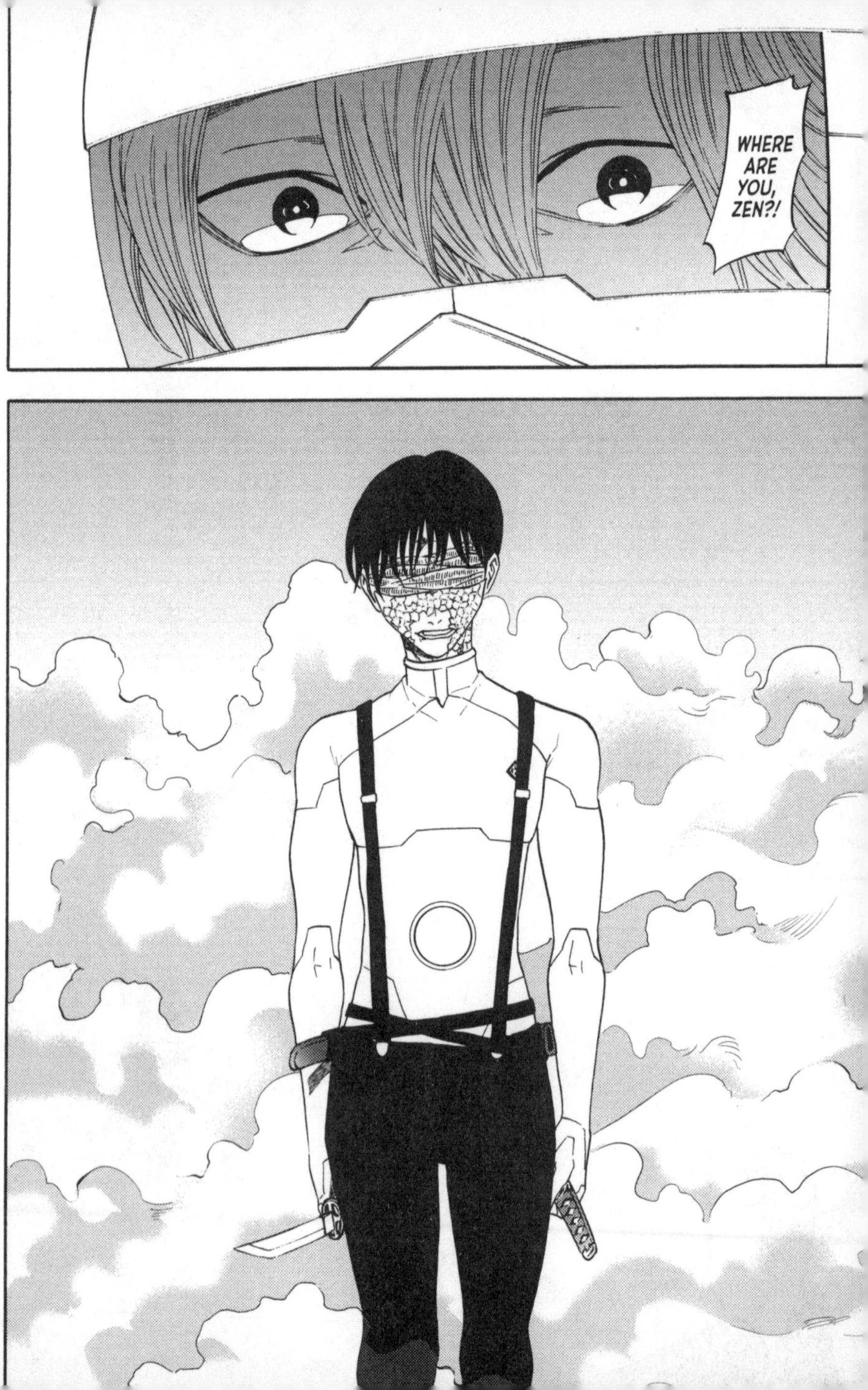
WHERE ARE YOU, ZEN?!

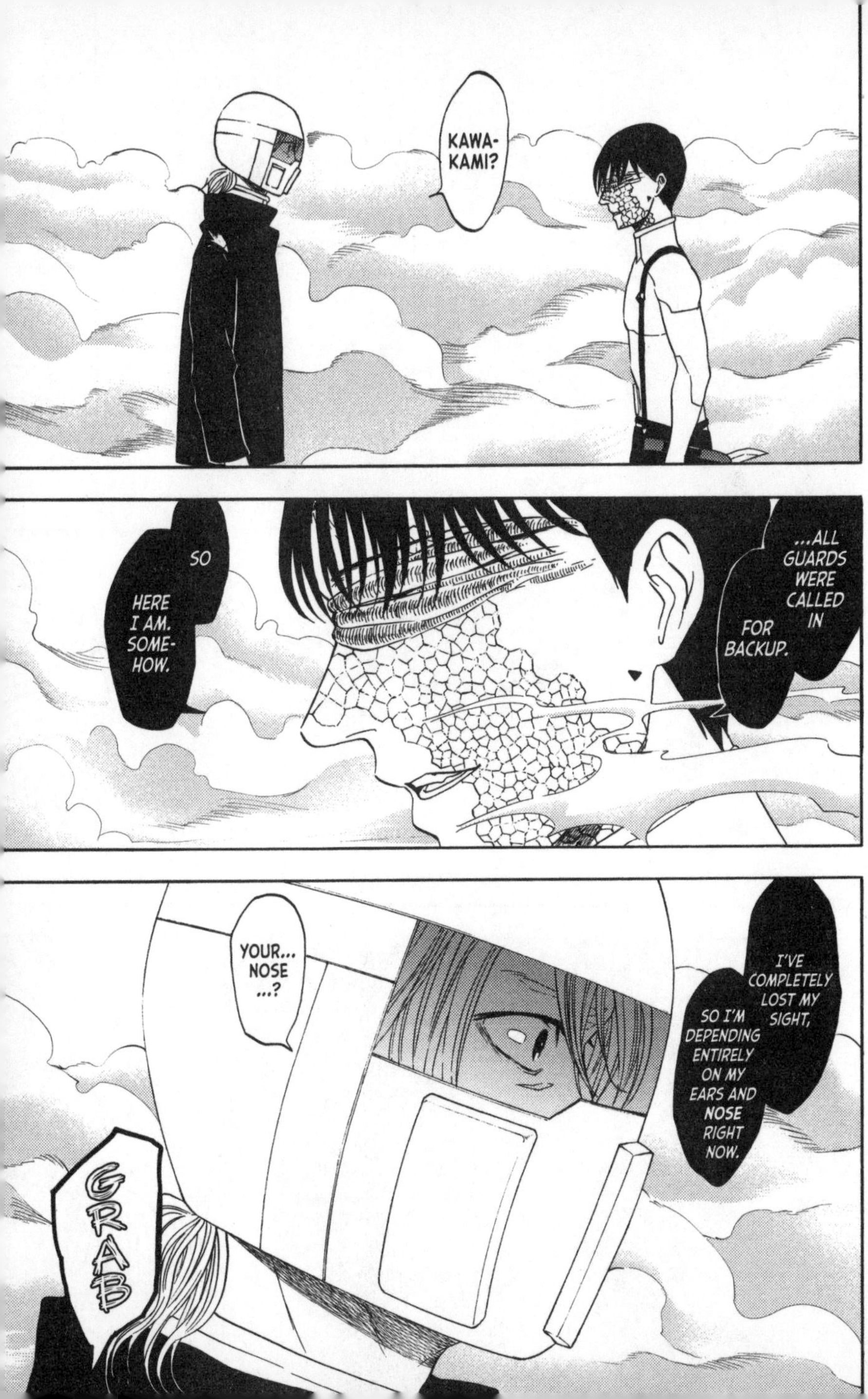
KAWA-KAMI?
...ALL GUARDS WERE CALLED IN FOR BACKUP.
SO HERE I AM. SOME-HOW.
I'VE COMPLETELY LOST MY SIGHT, SO I'M DEPENDING ENTIRELY ON MY EARS AND NOSE RIGHT NOW.
YOUR... NOSE ...?
GRAB

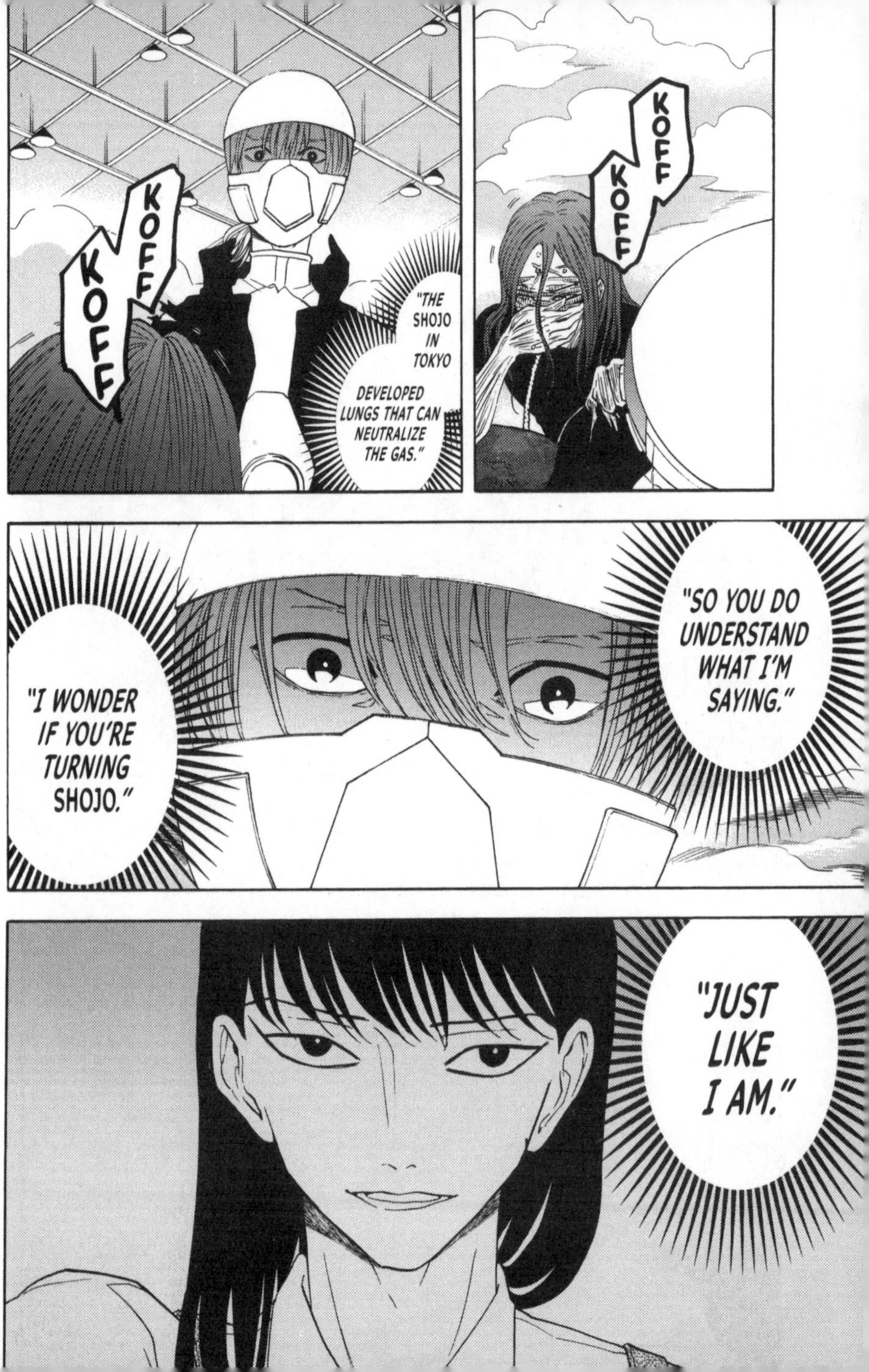
KOFF KOFF
"THE SHOJO IN TOKYO
DEVELOPED LUNGS THAT CAN NEUTRALIZE THE GAS."
KOFF KOFF
"SO YOU DO UNDERSTAND WHAT I'M SAYING."
"I WONDER IF YOU'RE TURNING SHOJO."
"JUST LIKE I AM."

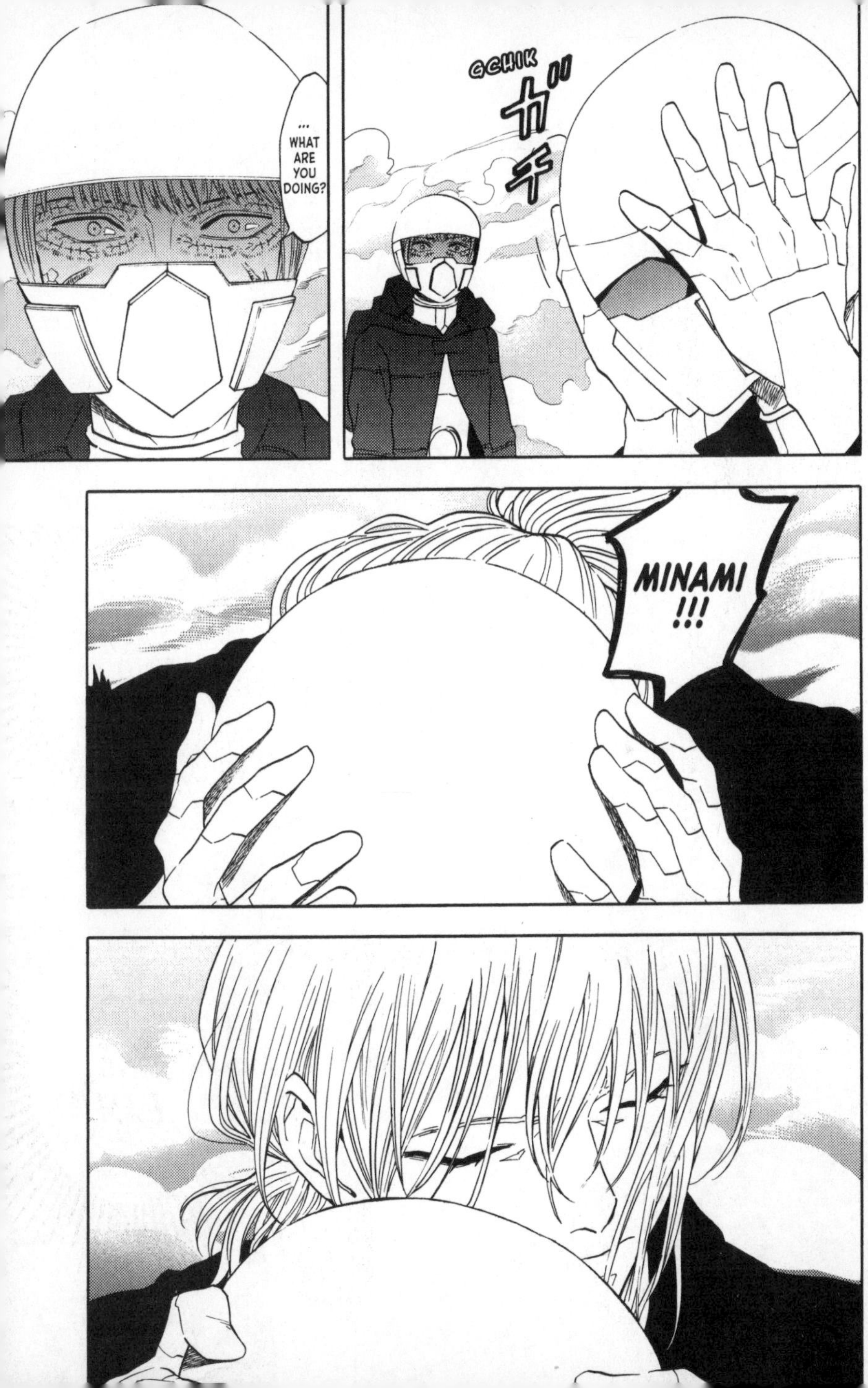
GCHIK
ガチ
... WHAT ARE YOU DOING?
MINAMI !!!

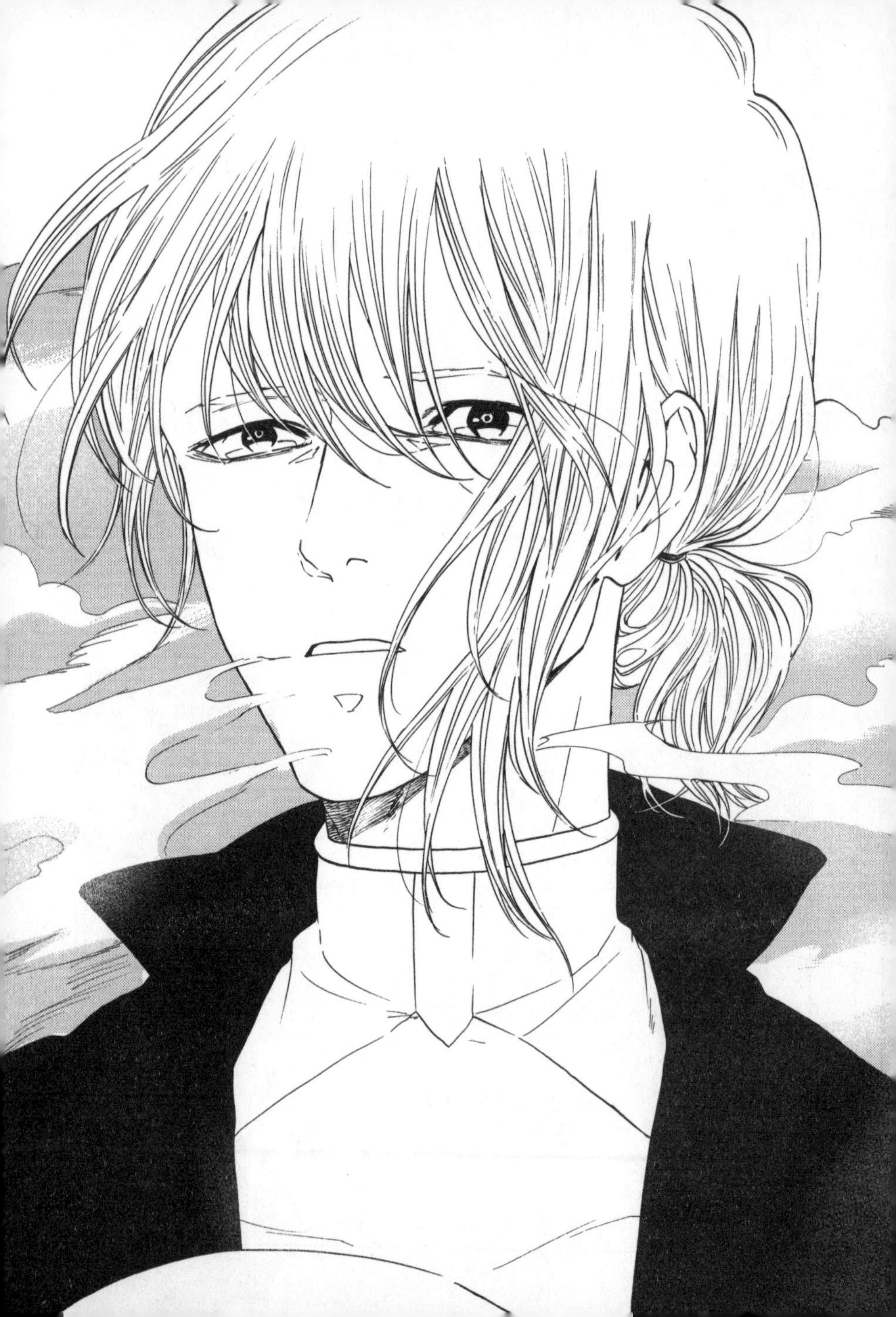

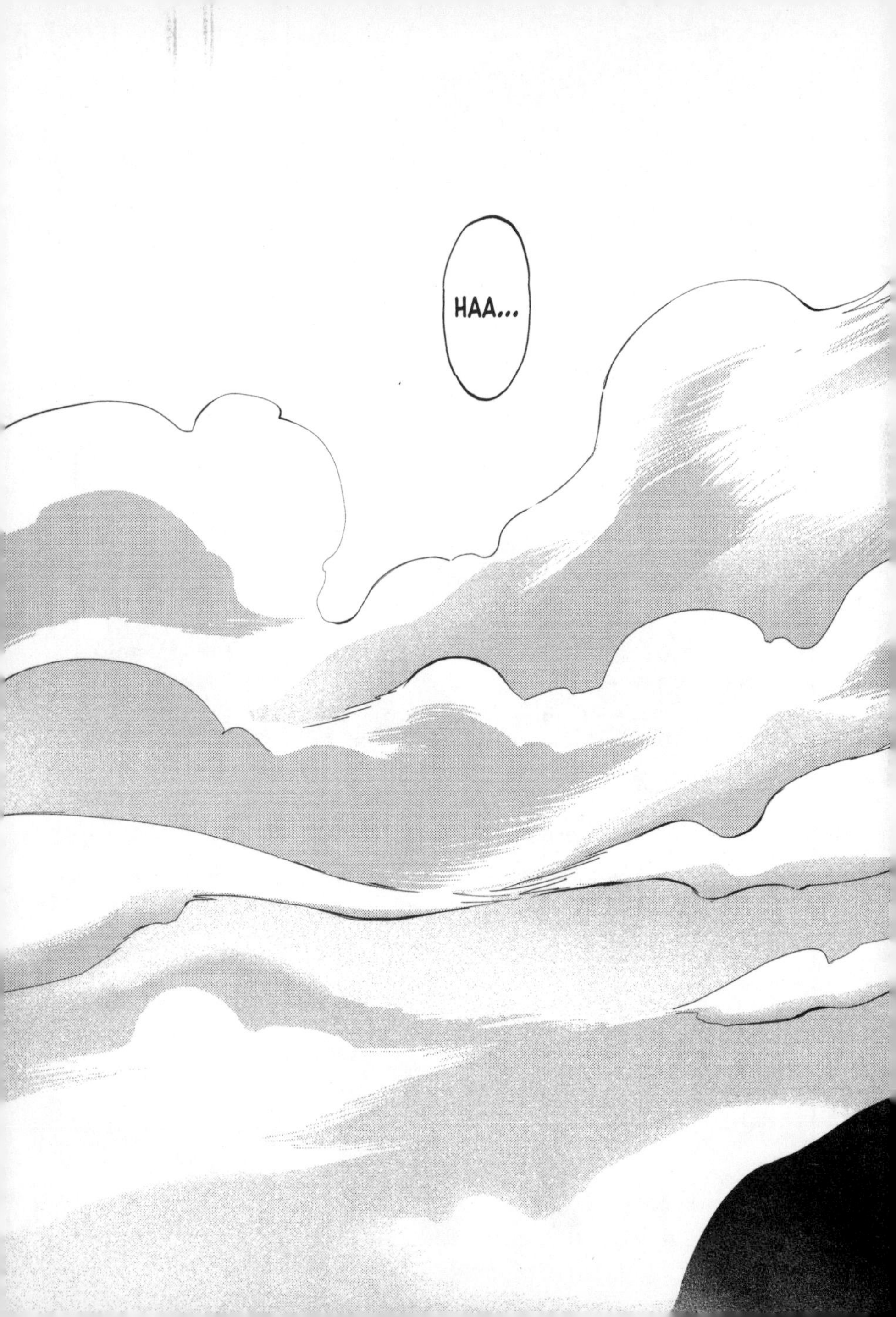
HAA...

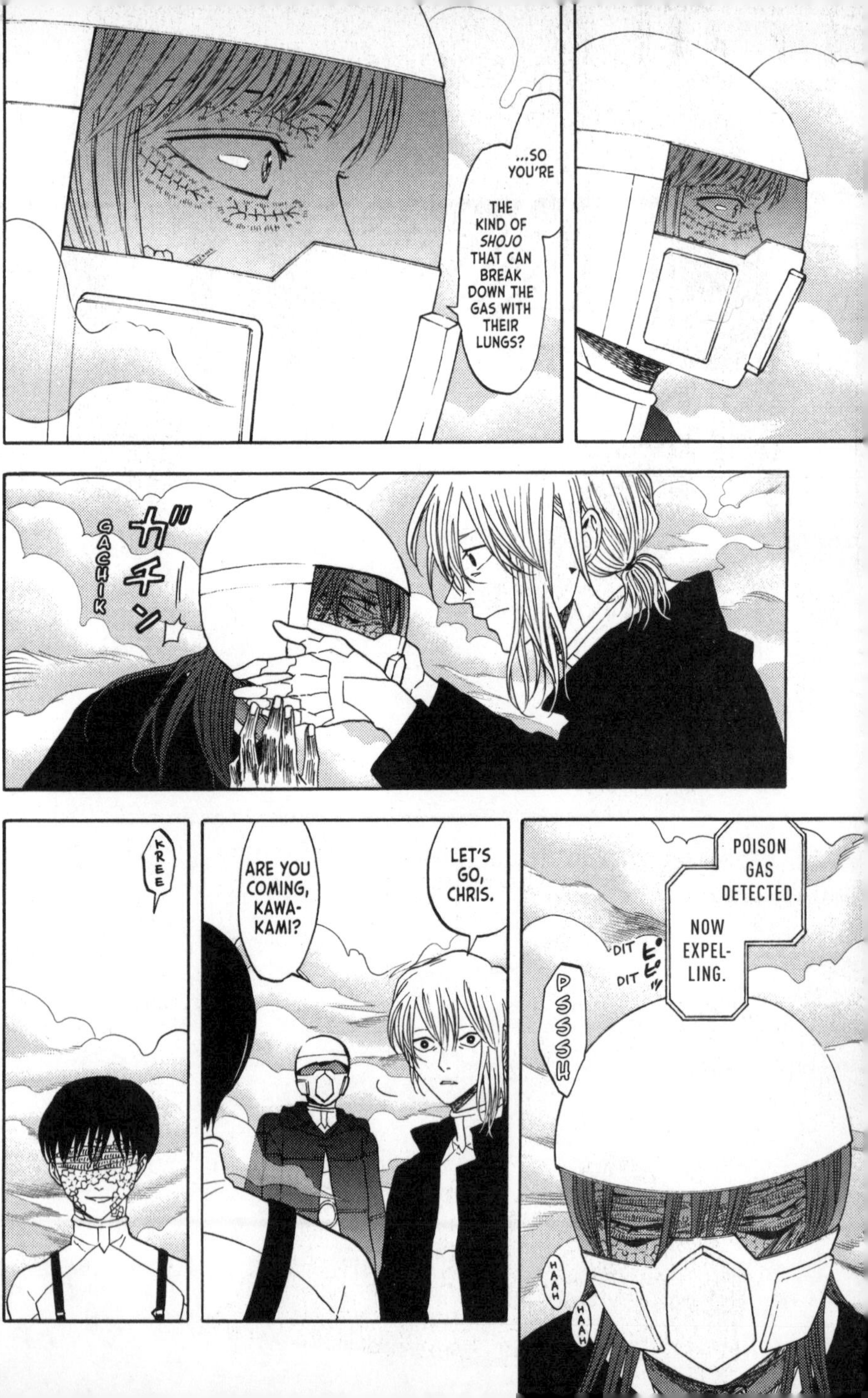
...SO YOU'RE THE KIND OF *SHOJO* THAT CAN BREAK DOWN THE GAS WITH THEIR LUNGS?
GACHIK
POISON GAS DETECTED.
NOW EXPEL-LING.
DIT DIT
PSSSH
HAAH
HAAH
LET'S GO, CHRIS.
ARE YOU COMING, KAWA-KAMI?
KREE

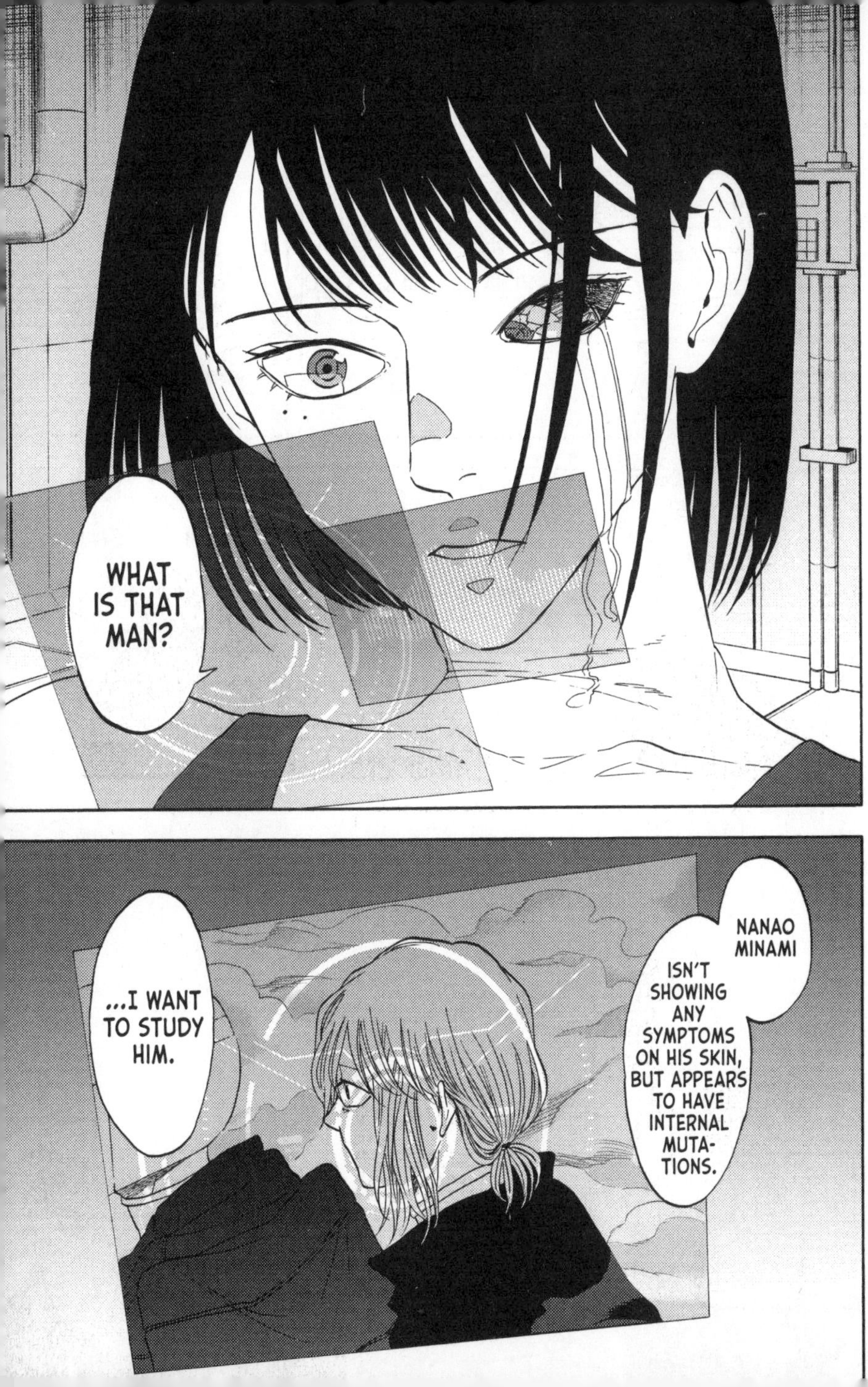
WHAT IS THAT MAN?
NANAO MINAMI ISN'T SHOWING ANY SYMPTOMS ON HIS SKIN, BUT APPEARS TO HAVE INTERNAL MUTA-TIONS.
...I WANT TO STUDY HIM.

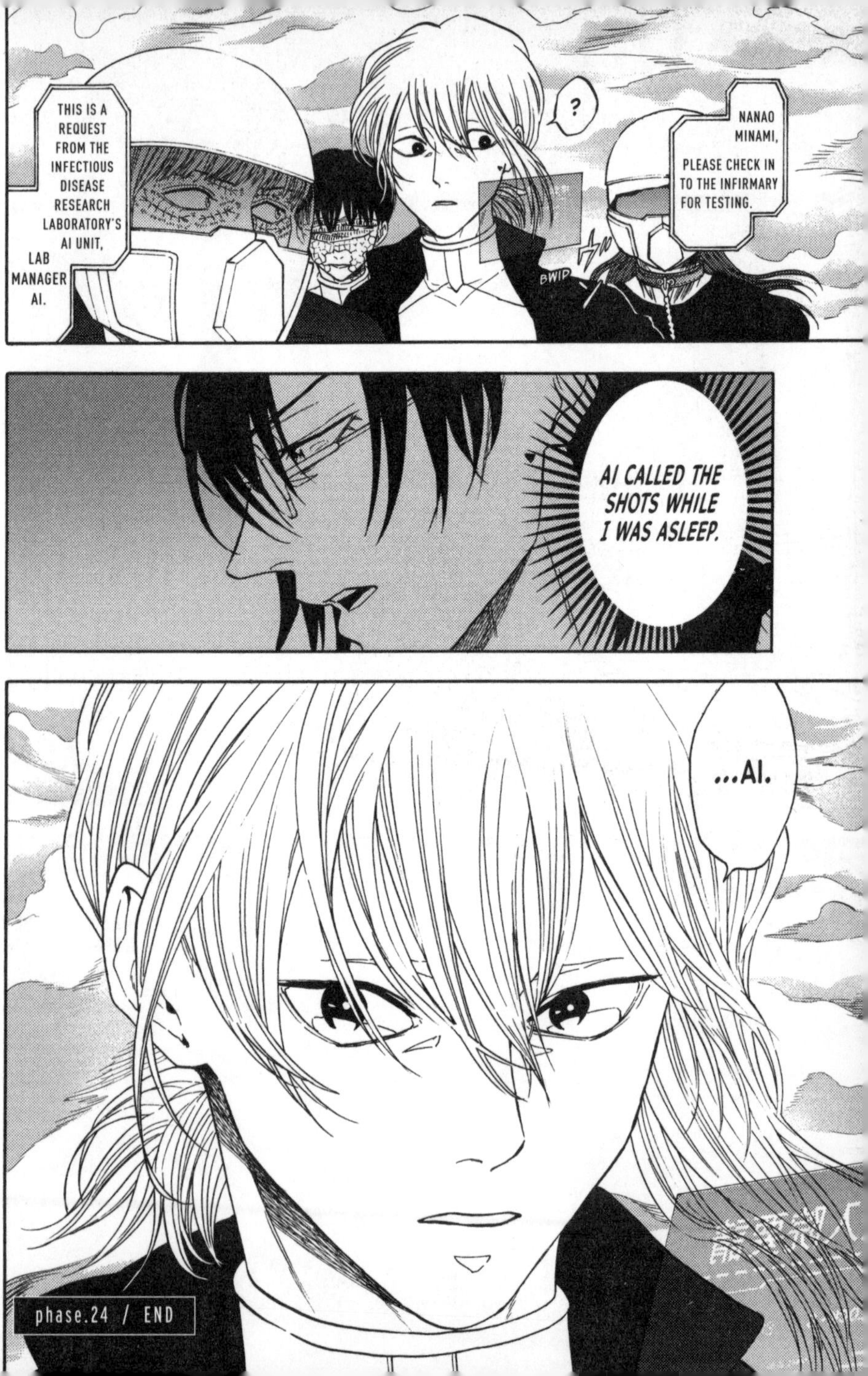

NANAO MINAMI, PLEASE CHECK IN TO THE INFIRMARY FOR TESTING.
?
BWIP
THIS IS A REQUEST FROM THE INFECTIOUS DISEASE RESEARCH LABORATORY'S AI UNIT, LAB MANAGER AI.
AI CALLED THE SHOTS WHILE I WAS ASLEEP.
...AI.
phase.24 / END

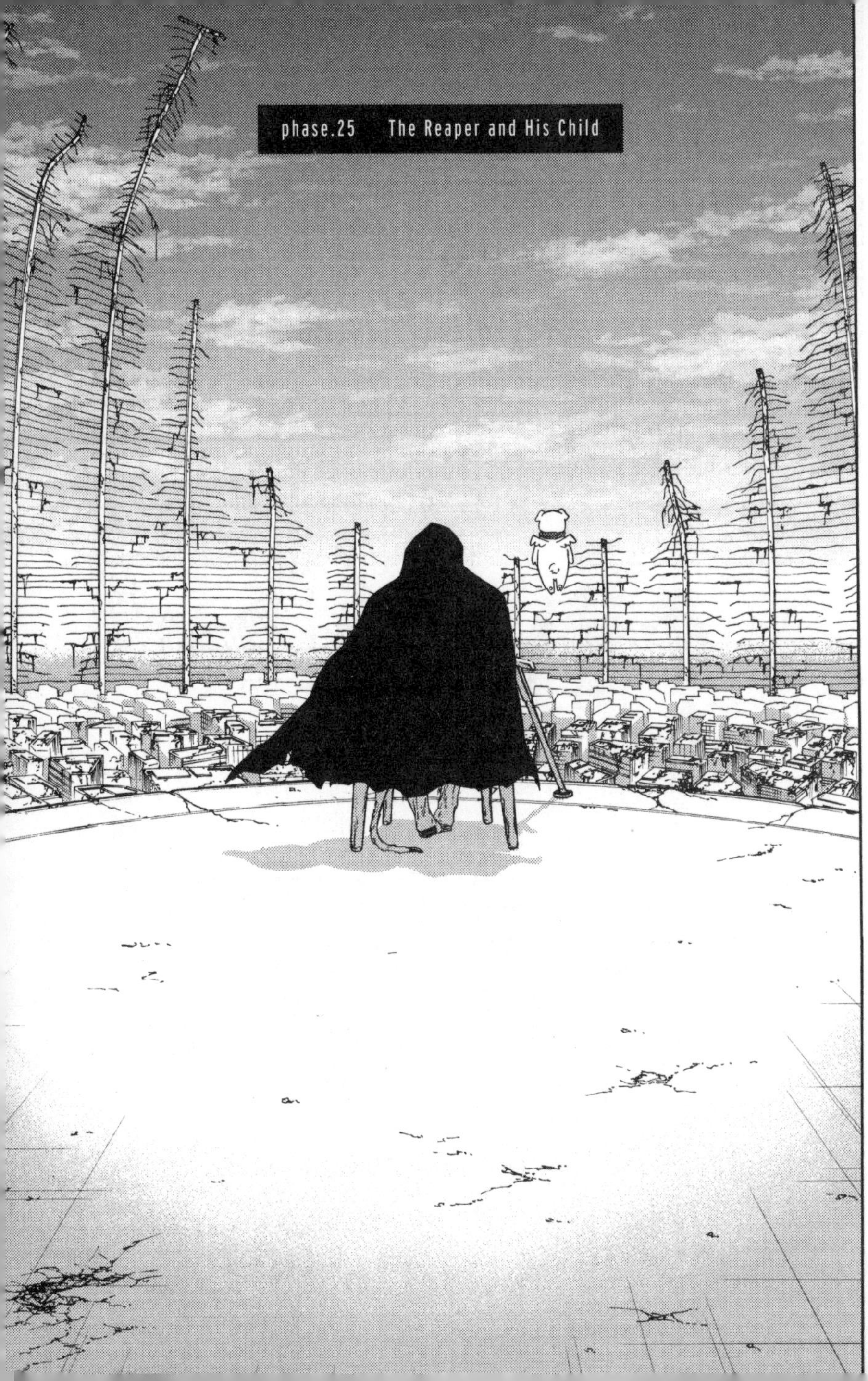
phase.25 The Reaper and His Child

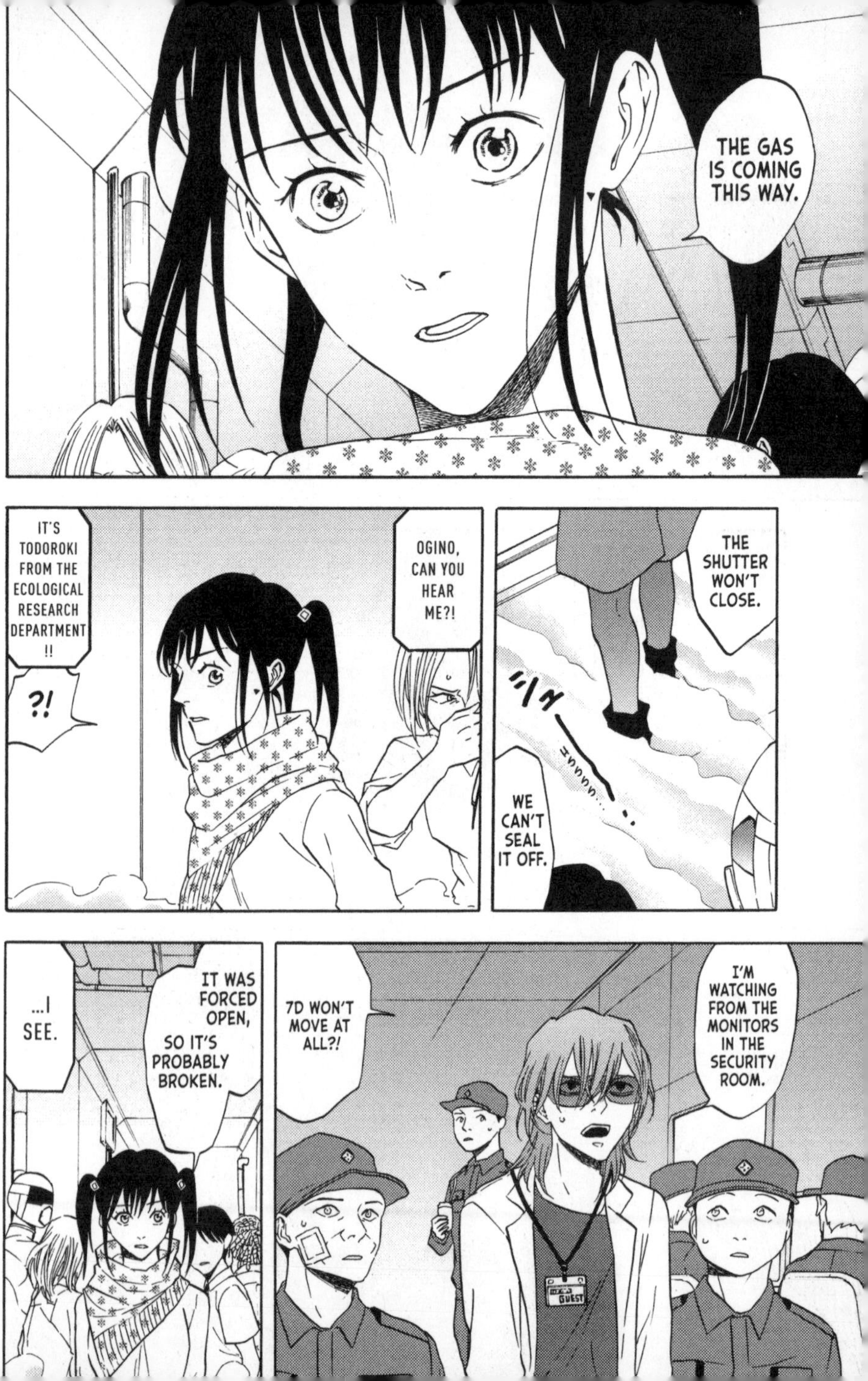
THE GAS IS COMING THIS WAY.
THE SHUTTER WON'T CLOSE.
WE CAN'T SEAL IT OFF.
OGINO, CAN YOU HEAR ME?!
IT'S TODOROKI FROM THE ECOLOGICAL RESEARCH DEPARTMENT!!
?!
I'M WATCHING FROM THE MONITORS IN THE SECURITY ROOM.
7D WON'T MOVE AT ALL?!
IT WAS FORCED OPEN,
SO IT'S PROBABLY BROKEN.
...I SEE.
GUEST

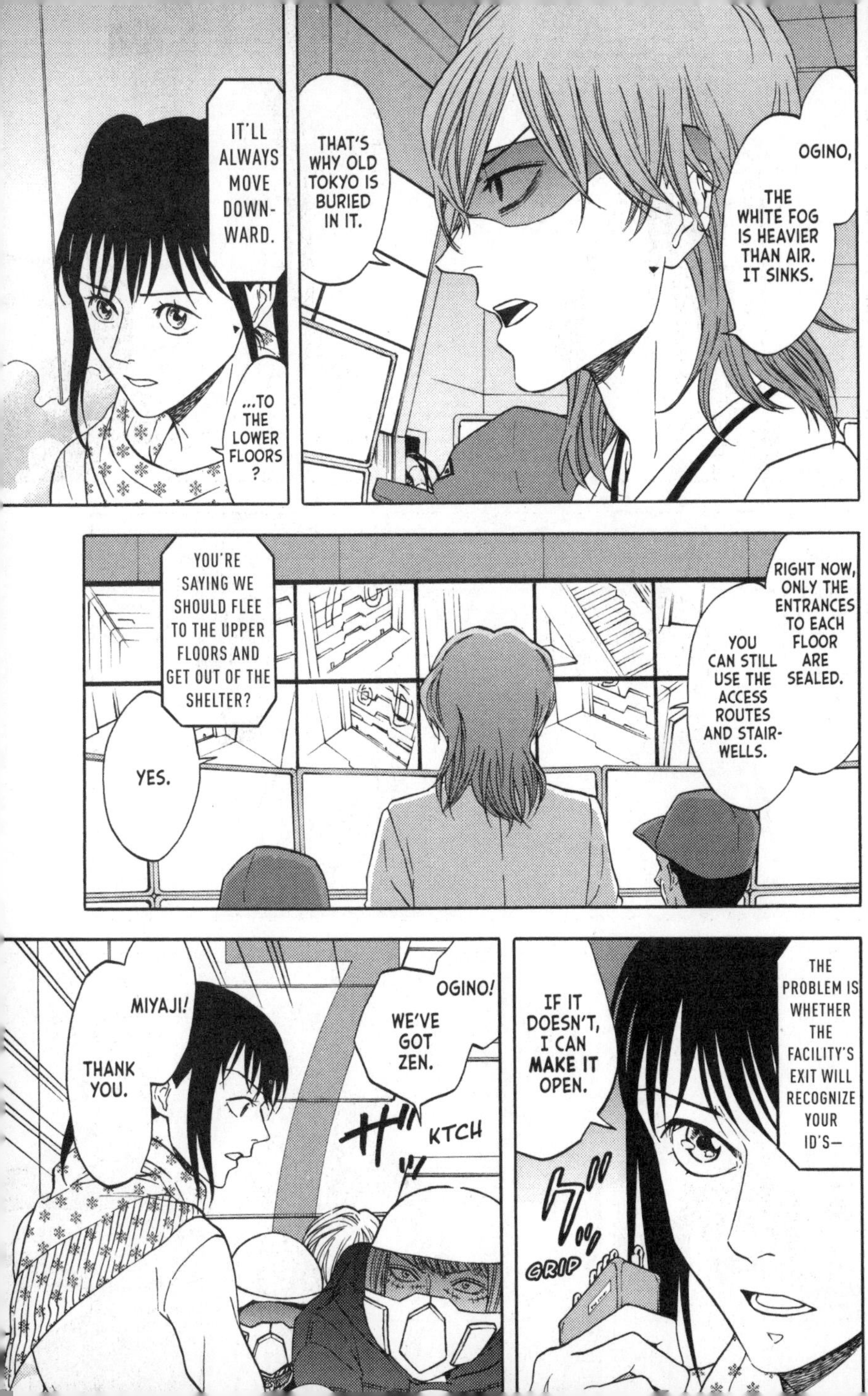
OGINO,
THE WHITE FOG IS HEAVIER THAN AIR. IT SINKS.
THAT'S WHY OLD TOKYO IS BURIED IN IT.
IT'LL ALWAYS MOVE DOWNWARD.
...TO THE LOWER FLOORS?
RIGHT NOW, ONLY THE ENTRANCES TO EACH FLOOR ARE SEALED.
YOU CAN STILL USE THE ACCESS ROUTES AND STAIRWELLS.
YOU'RE SAYING WE SHOULD FLEE TO THE UPPER FLOORS AND GET OUT OF THE SHELTER?
YES.
THE PROBLEM IS WHETHER THE FACILITY'S EXIT WILL RECOGNIZE YOUR ID'S—
IF IT DOESN'T, I CAN MAKE IT OPEN.
GRIP
OGINO!
WE'VE GOT ZEN.
KTCH
MIYAJI!
THANK YOU.

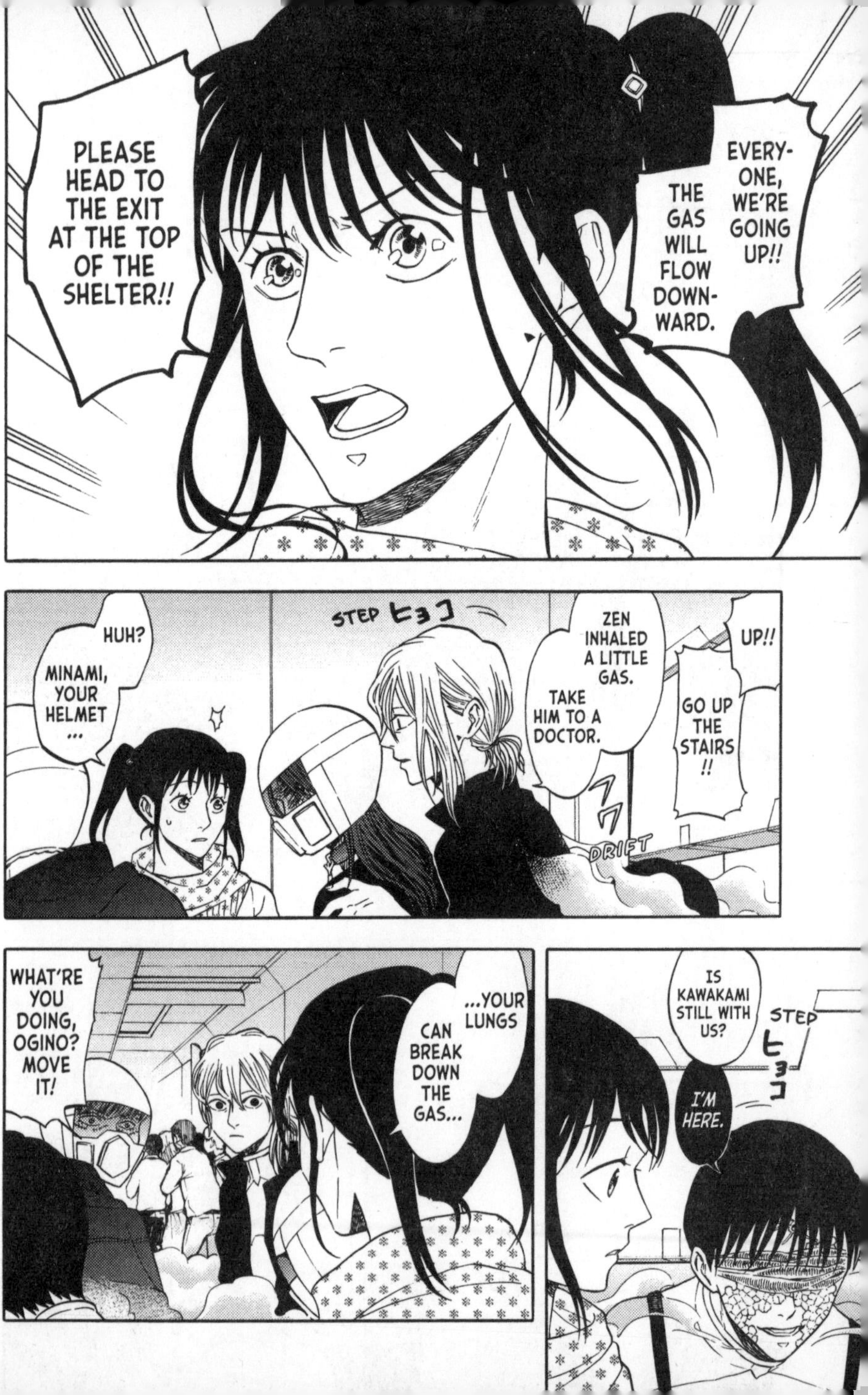
EVERYONE, WE'RE GOING UP!!
THE GAS WILL FLOW DOWNWARD.
PLEASE HEAD TO THE EXIT AT THE TOP OF THE SHELTER!!
UP!!
GO UP THE STAIRS!!
ZEN INHALED A LITTLE GAS.
TAKE HIM TO A DOCTOR.
STEP ヒョコ
HUH?
MINAMI, YOUR HELMET...
フワ DRIFT
IS KAWAKAMI STILL WITH US?
STEP ヒョコ
I'M HERE.
...YOUR LUNGS
CAN BREAK DOWN THE GAS...
WHAT'RE YOU DOING, OGINO? MOVE IT!

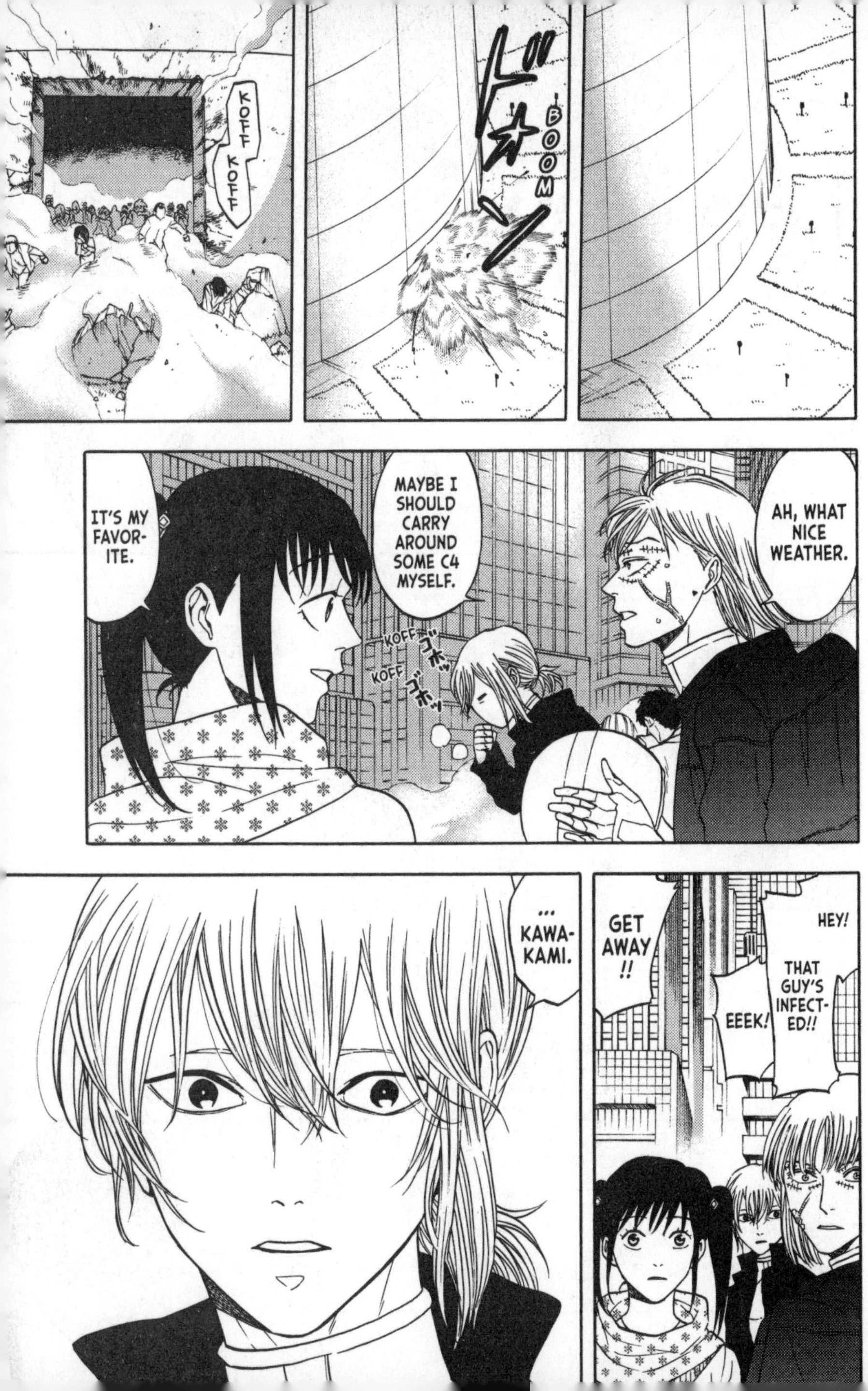
BOOM
KOFF KOFF
AH, WHAT NICE WEATHER.
MAYBE I SHOULD CARRY AROUND SOME C4 MYSELF.
KOFF
KOFF
IT'S MY FAVOR-ITE.
HEY!
THAT GUY'S INFECT-ED!!
EEEK!
GET AWAY!!
... KAWA-KAMI.

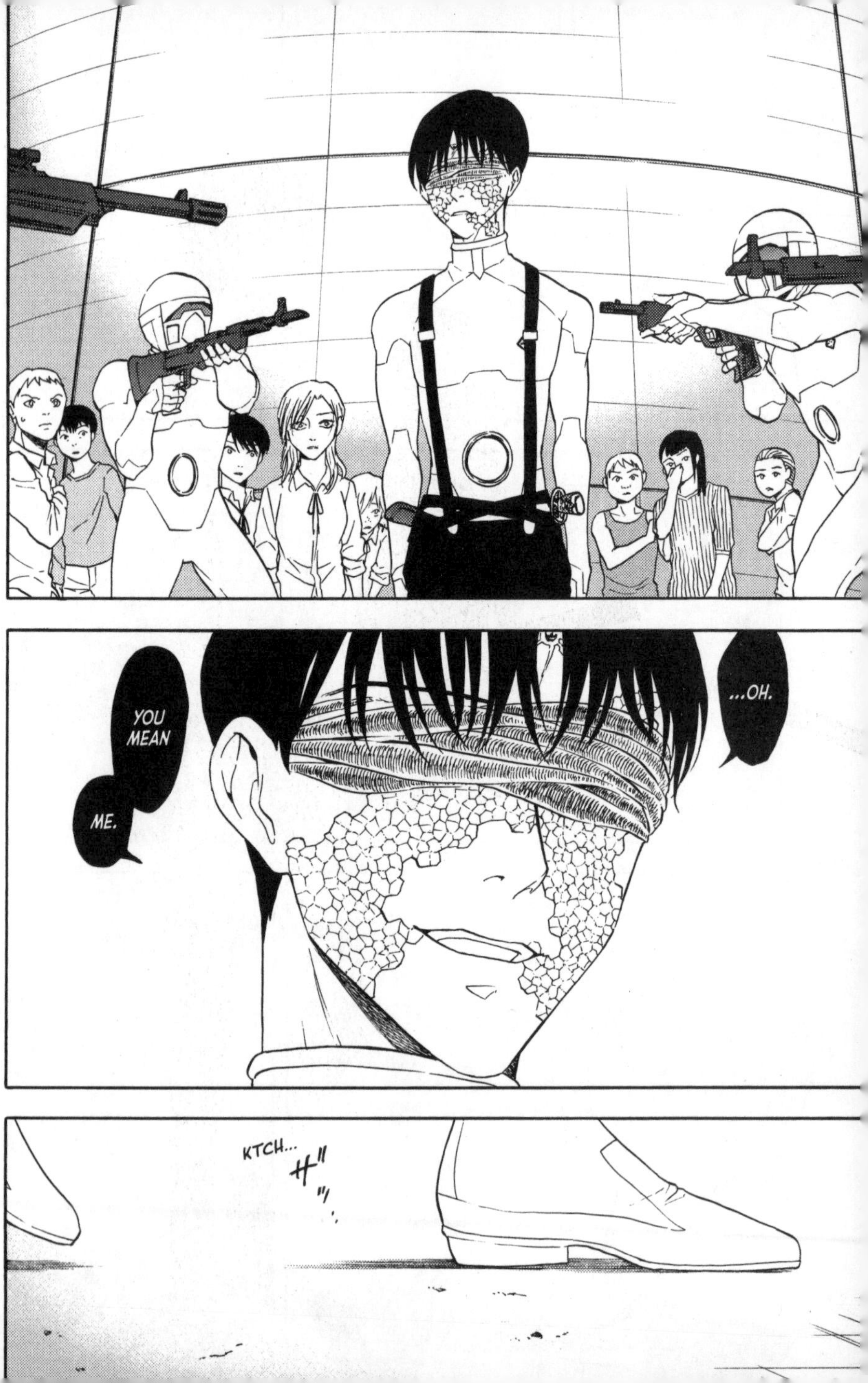
...OH.
YOU MEAN
ME.
KTCH...
ザ

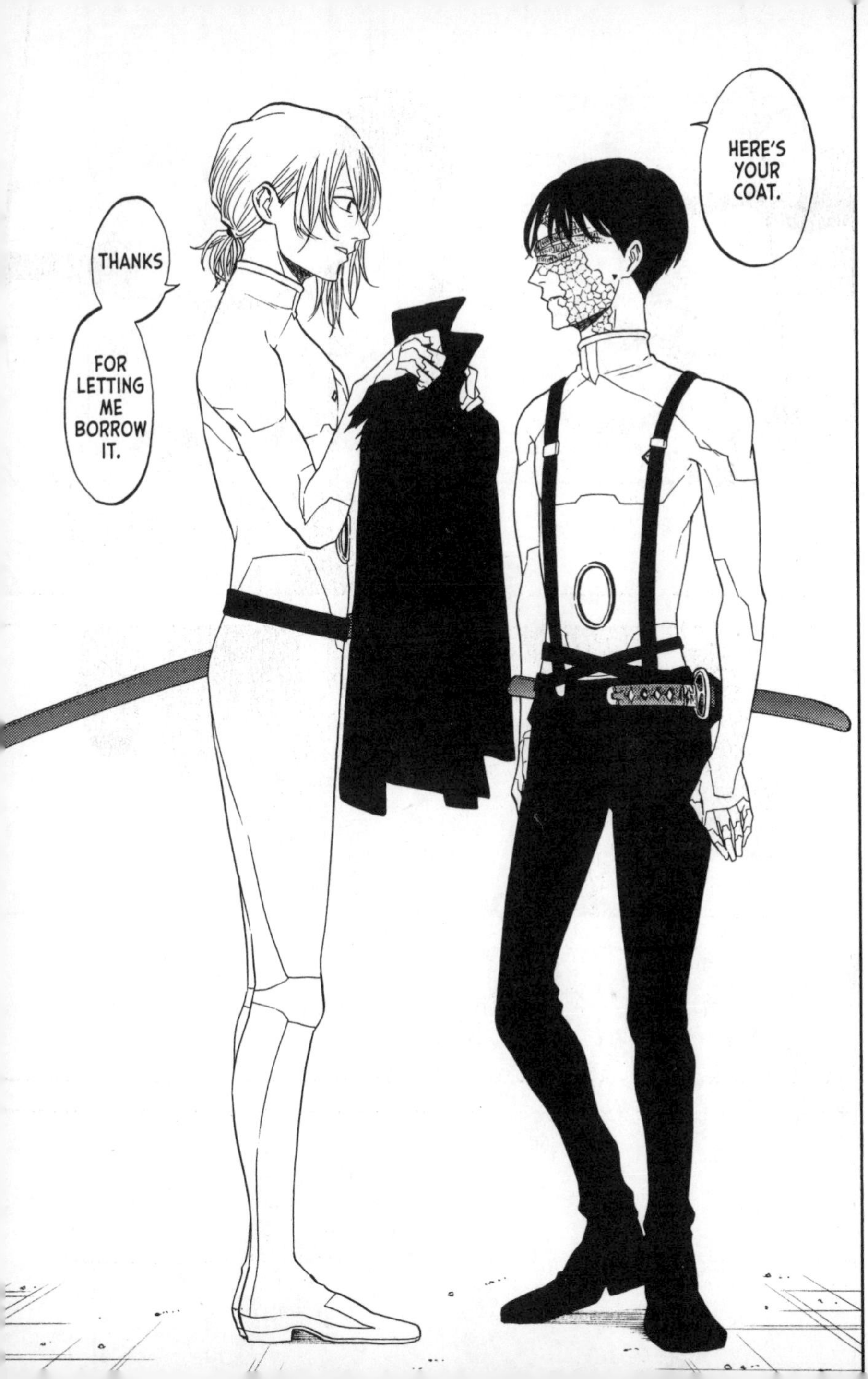
HERE'S YOUR COAT.
THANKS
FOR LETTING ME BORROW IT.

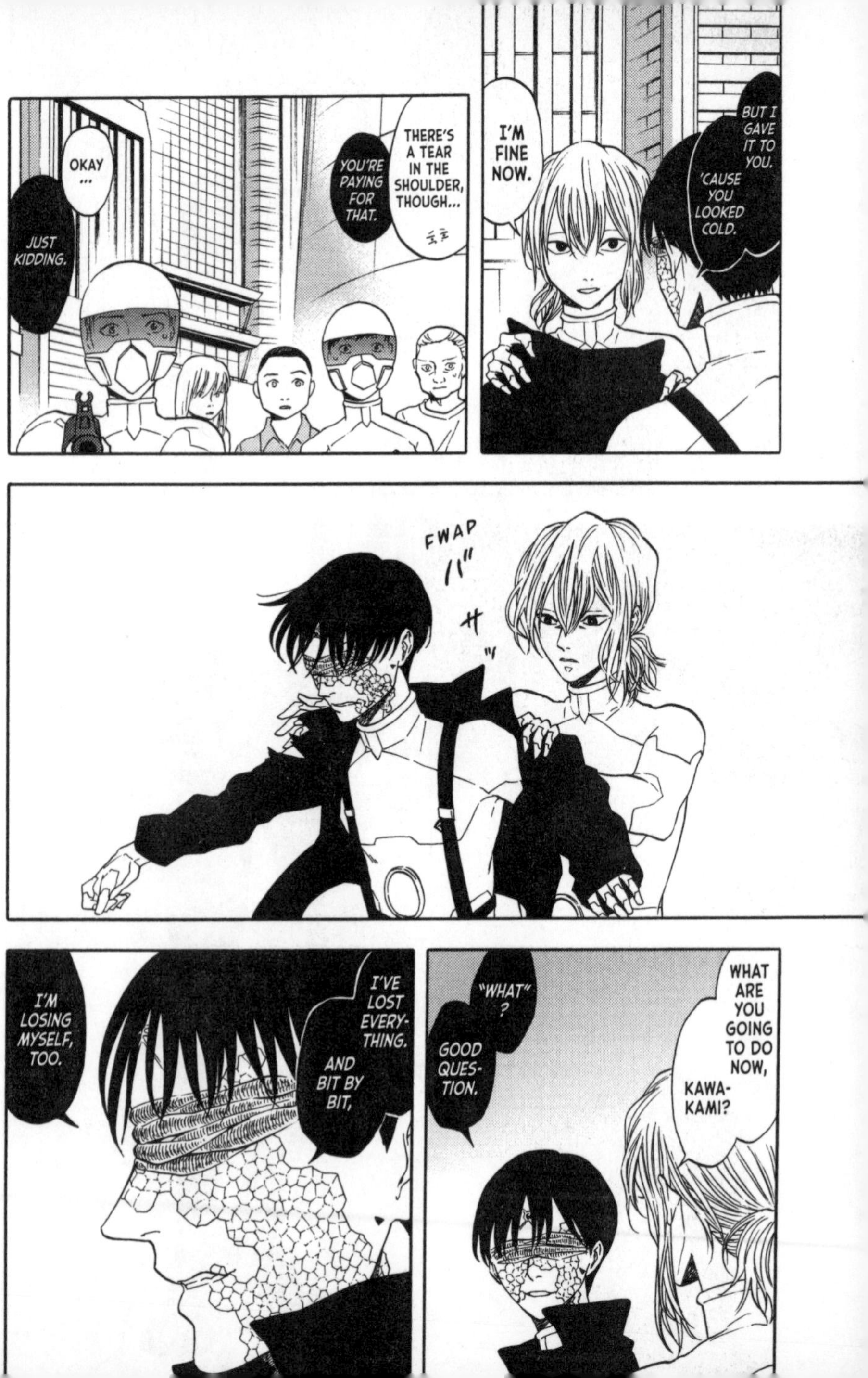
BUT I GAVE IT TO YOU. 'CAUSE YOU LOOKED COLD.
I'M FINE NOW.
THERE'S A TEAR IN THE SHOULDER, THOUGH...
YOU'RE PAYING FOR THAT.
OKAY ...
JUST KIDDING.
FWAP
WHAT ARE YOU GOING TO DO NOW, KAWA-KAMI?
"WHAT"?
GOOD QUES-TION.
I'VE LOST EVERY-THING.
AND BIT BY BIT,
I'M LOSING MYSELF, TOO.

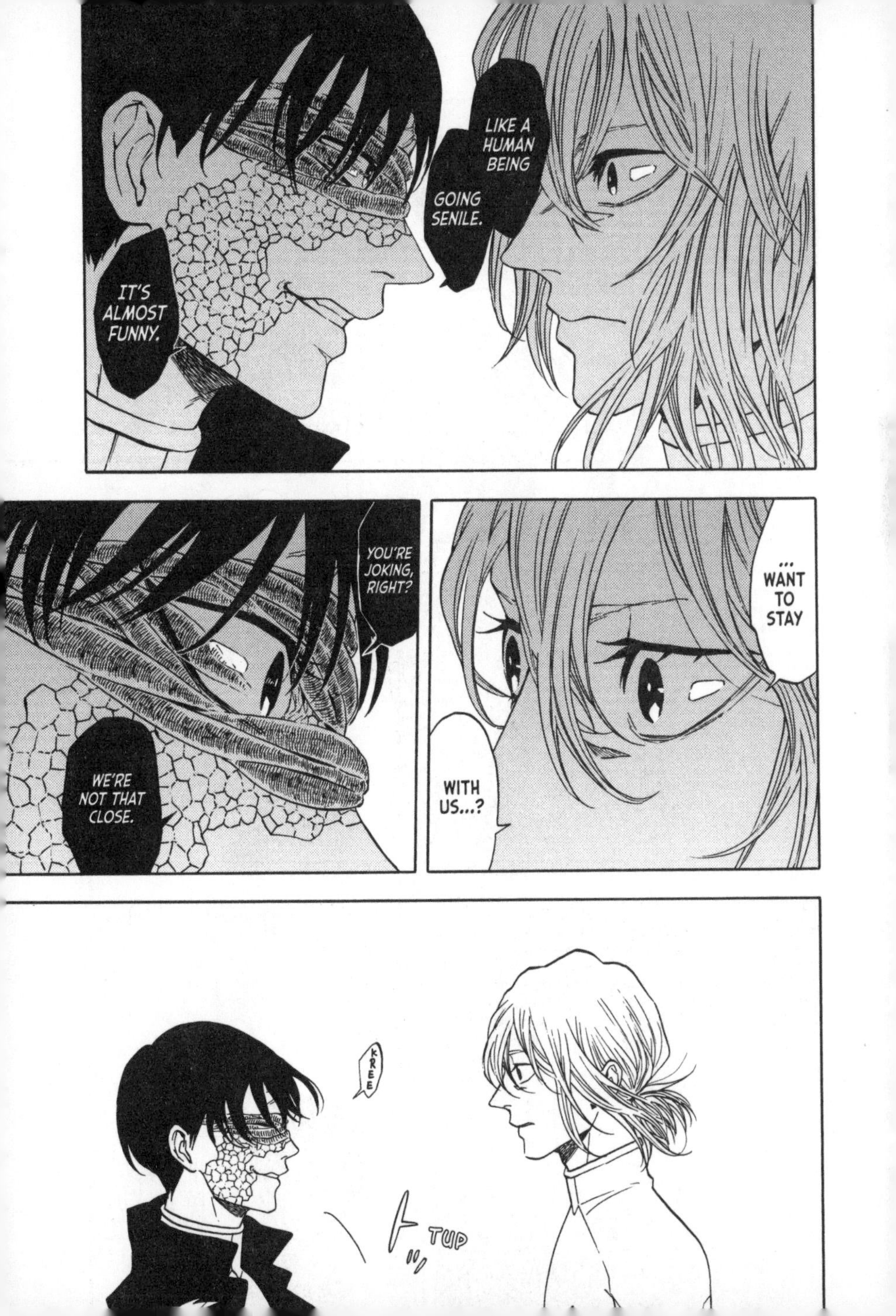
LIKE A HUMAN BEING
GOING SENILE.
IT'S ALMOST FUNNY.
... WANT TO STAY
WITH US...?
YOU'RE JOKING, RIGHT?
WE'RE NOT THAT CLOSE.
KREE
TUP

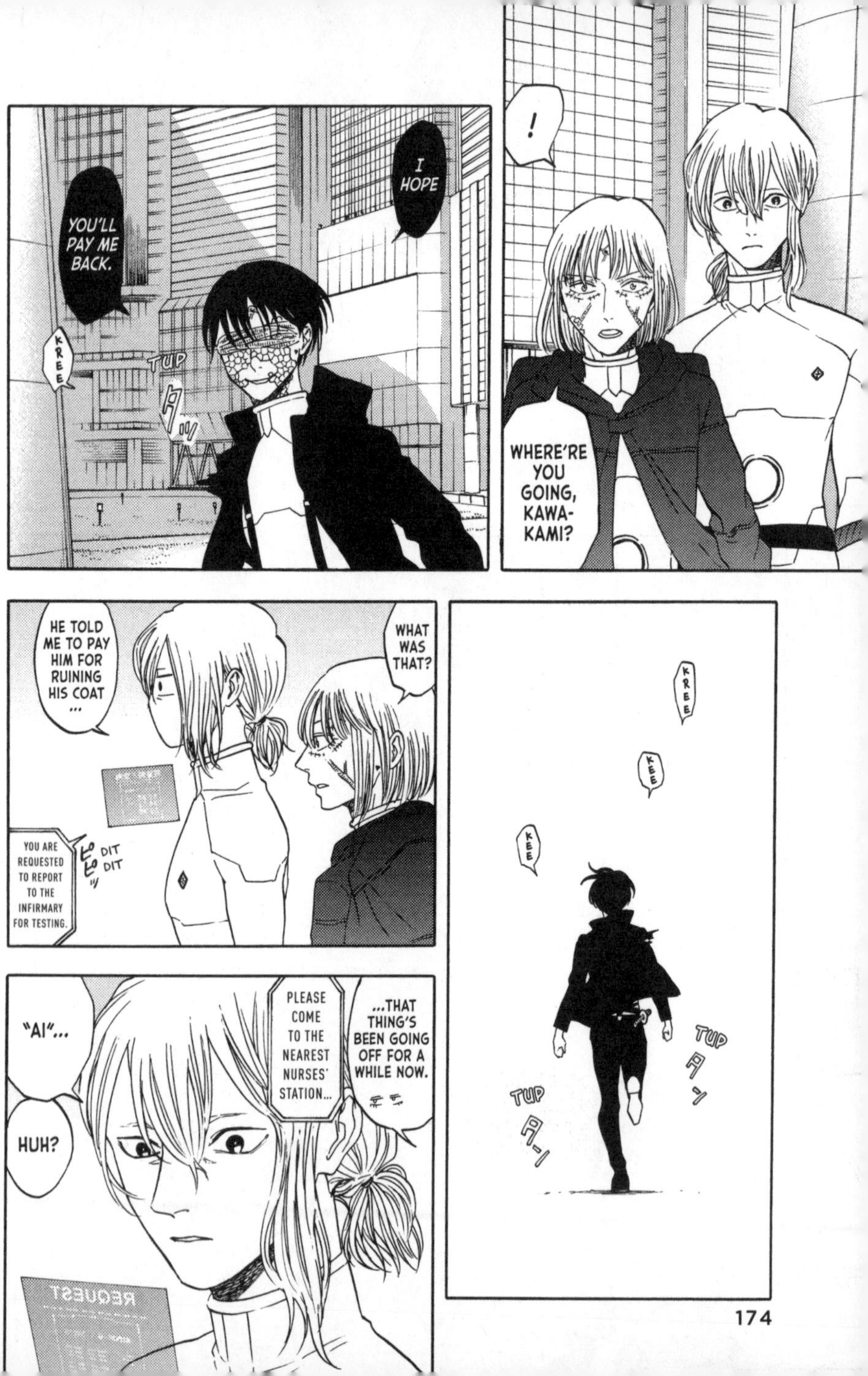
!
WHERE'RE YOU GOING, KAWA-KAMI?
I HOPE
YOU'LL PAY ME BACK.
KREE
TUP
KREE
KEE
KEE
TUP
TUP
WHAT WAS THAT?
HE TOLD ME TO PAY HIM FOR RUINING HIS COAT ...
YOU ARE REQUESTED TO REPORT TO THE INFIRMARY FOR TESTING.
DIT DIT
...THAT THING'S BEEN GOING OFF FOR A WHILE NOW.
PLEASE COME TO THE NEAREST NURSES' STATION...
"AI"...
HUH?

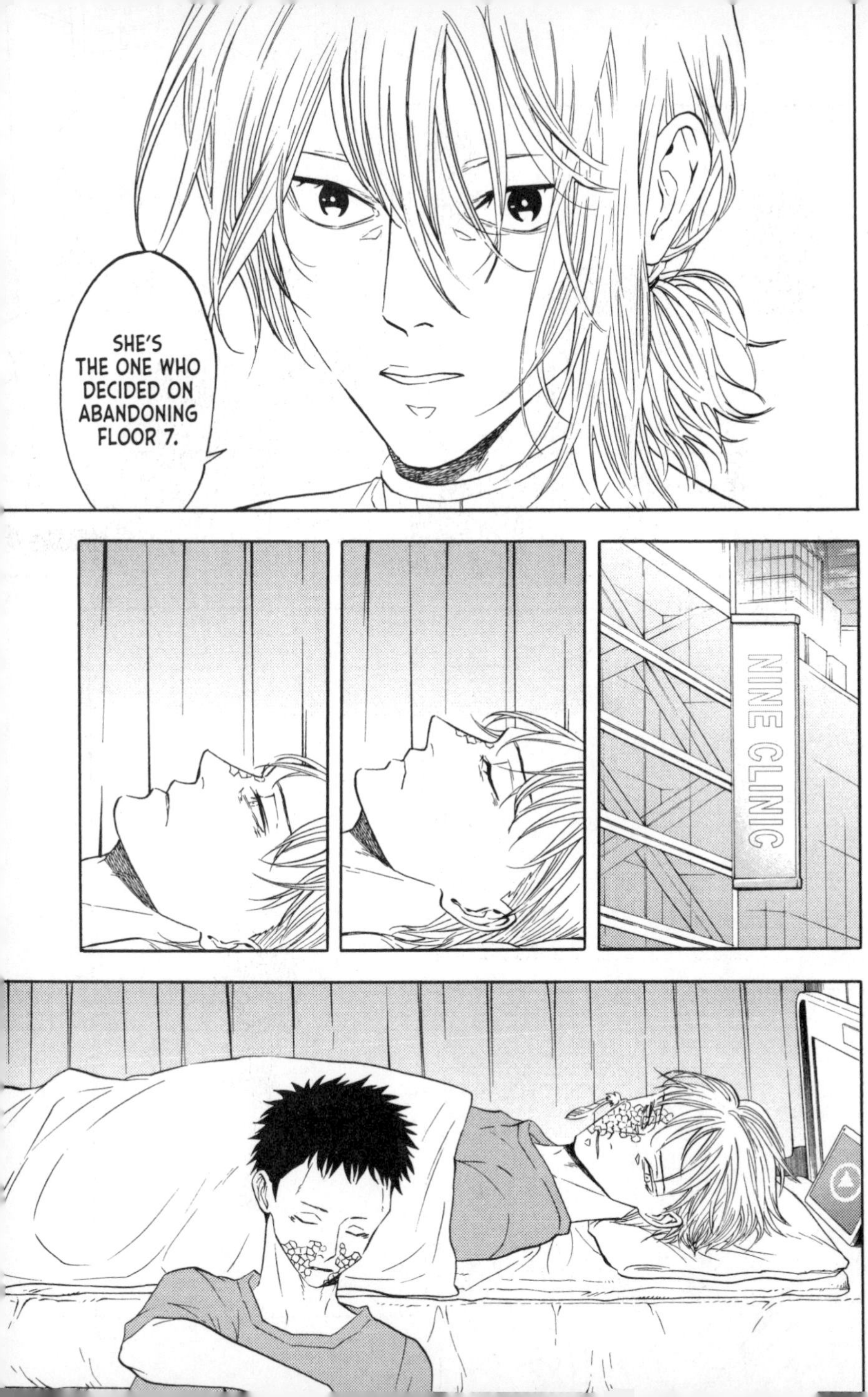
SHE'S THE ONE WHO DECIDED ON ABANDONING FLOOR 7.
NINE CLINIC

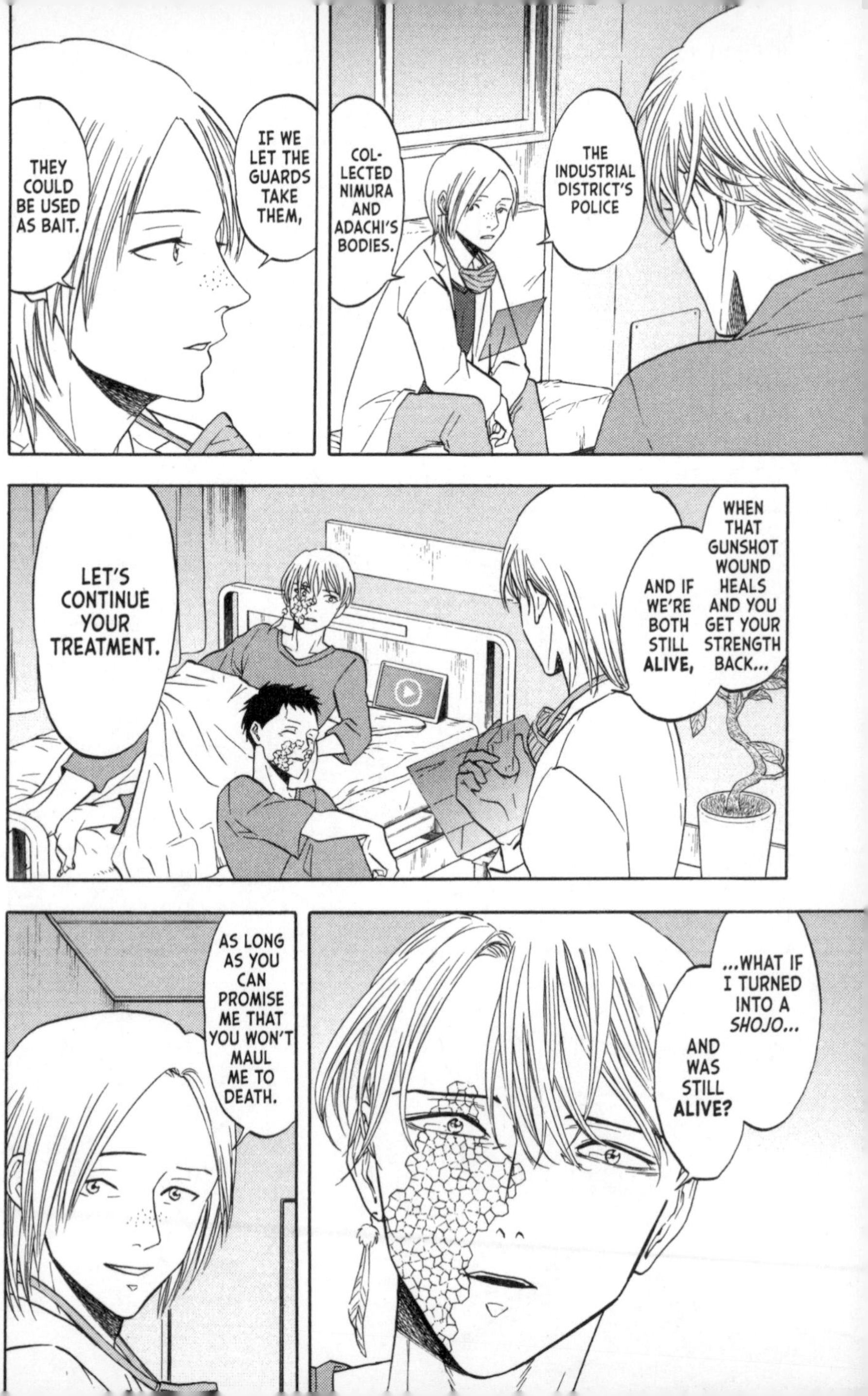
THE INDUSTRIAL DISTRICT'S POLICE
COL-LECTED NIMURA AND ADACHI'S BODIES.
IF WE LET THE GUARDS TAKE THEM,
THEY COULD BE USED AS BAIT.
WHEN THAT GUNSHOT WOUND HEALS AND YOU GET YOUR STRENGTH BACK...
AND IF WE'RE BOTH STILL **ALIVE,**
LET'S CONTINUE YOUR TREATMENT.
...WHAT IF I TURNED INTO A *SHOJO*...
AND WAS STILL **ALIVE?**
AS LONG AS YOU CAN PROMISE ME THAT YOU WON'T MAUL ME TO DEATH.

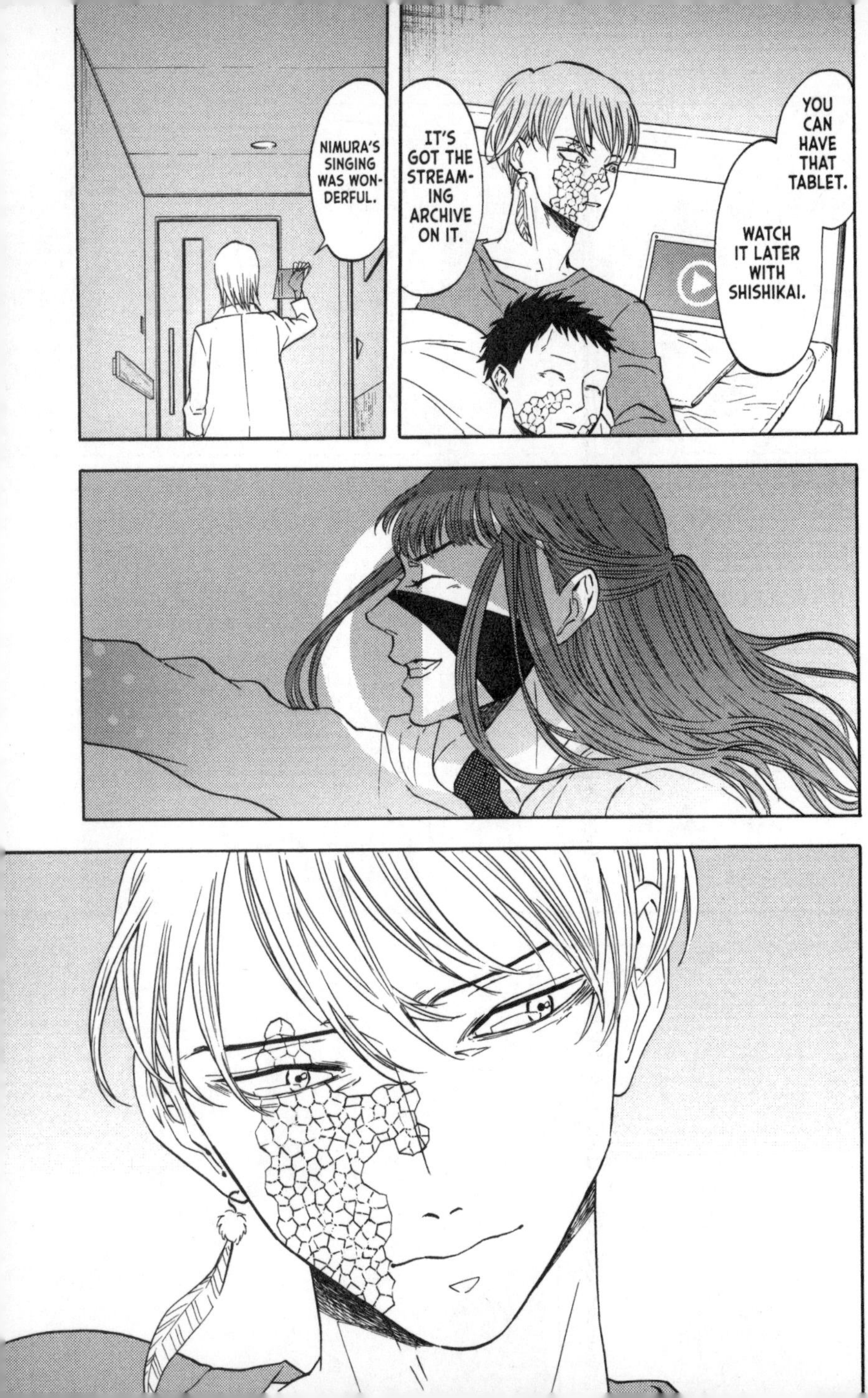
YOU CAN HAVE THAT TABLET.
WATCH IT LATER WITH SHISHIKAI.
IT'S GOT THE STREAM-ING ARCHIVE ON IT.
NIMURA'S SINGING WAS WON-DERFUL.

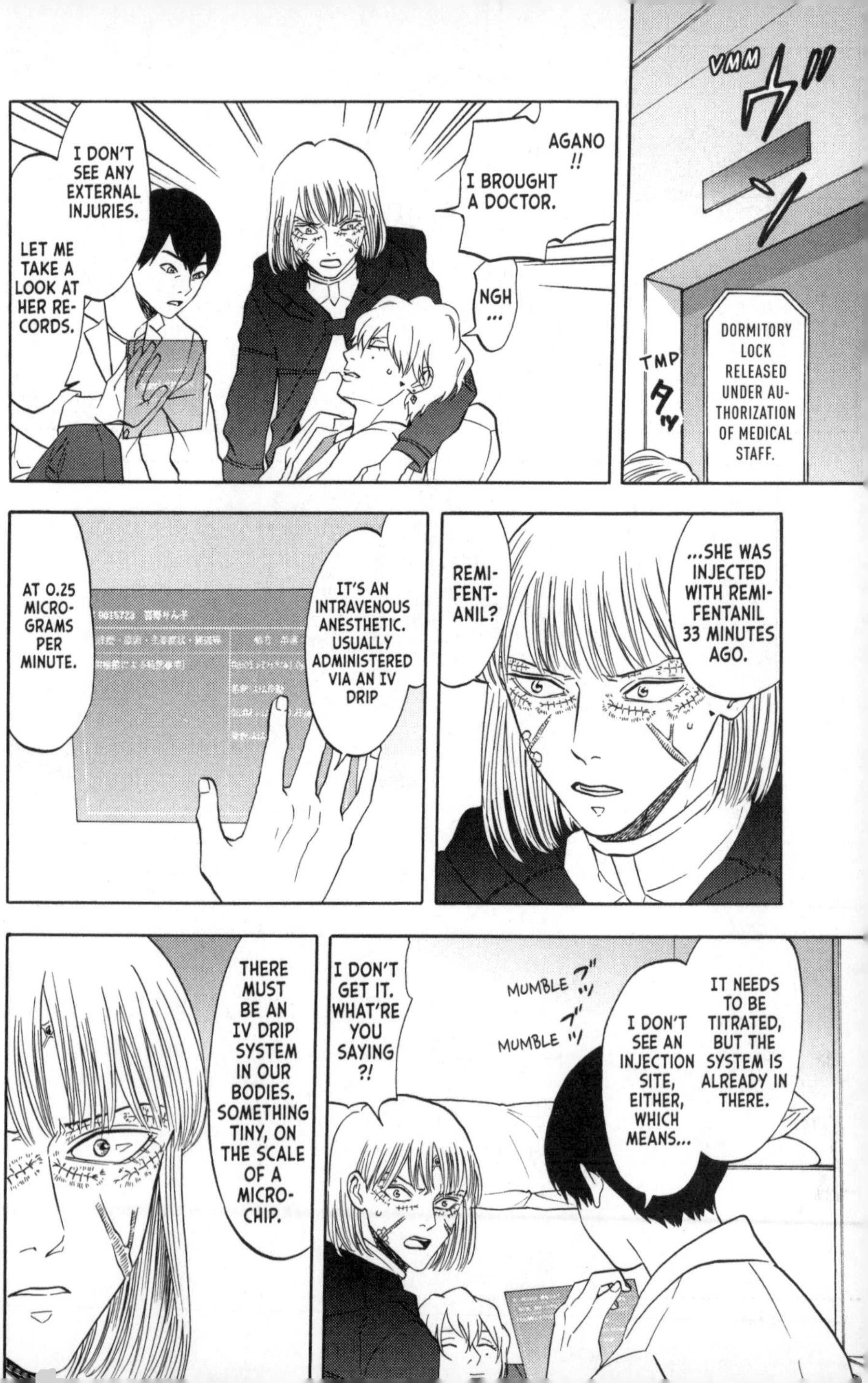
VMM
ヴッ
DORMITORY LOCK RELEASED UNDER AUTHORIZATION OF MEDICAL STAFF.
TMP
タッ
AGANO!!
I BROUGHT A DOCTOR.
NGH...
I DON'T SEE ANY EXTERNAL INJURIES.
LET ME TAKE A LOOK AT HER RECORDS.
...SHE WAS INJECTED WITH REMIFENTANIL 33 MINUTES AGO.
REMIFENTANIL?
IT'S AN INTRAVENOUS ANESTHETIC. USUALLY ADMINISTERED VIA AN IV DRIP
AT 0.25 MICROGRAMS PER MINUTE.
IT NEEDS TO BE TITRATED, BUT THE SYSTEM IS ALREADY IN THERE.
I DON'T SEE AN INJECTION SITE, EITHER, WHICH MEANS...
MUMBLE
ブツ
MUMBLE
ブツ
I DON'T GET IT. WHAT'RE YOU SAYING?!
THERE MUST BE AN IV DRIP SYSTEM IN OUR BODIES. SOMETHING TINY, ON THE SCALE OF A MICROCHIP.

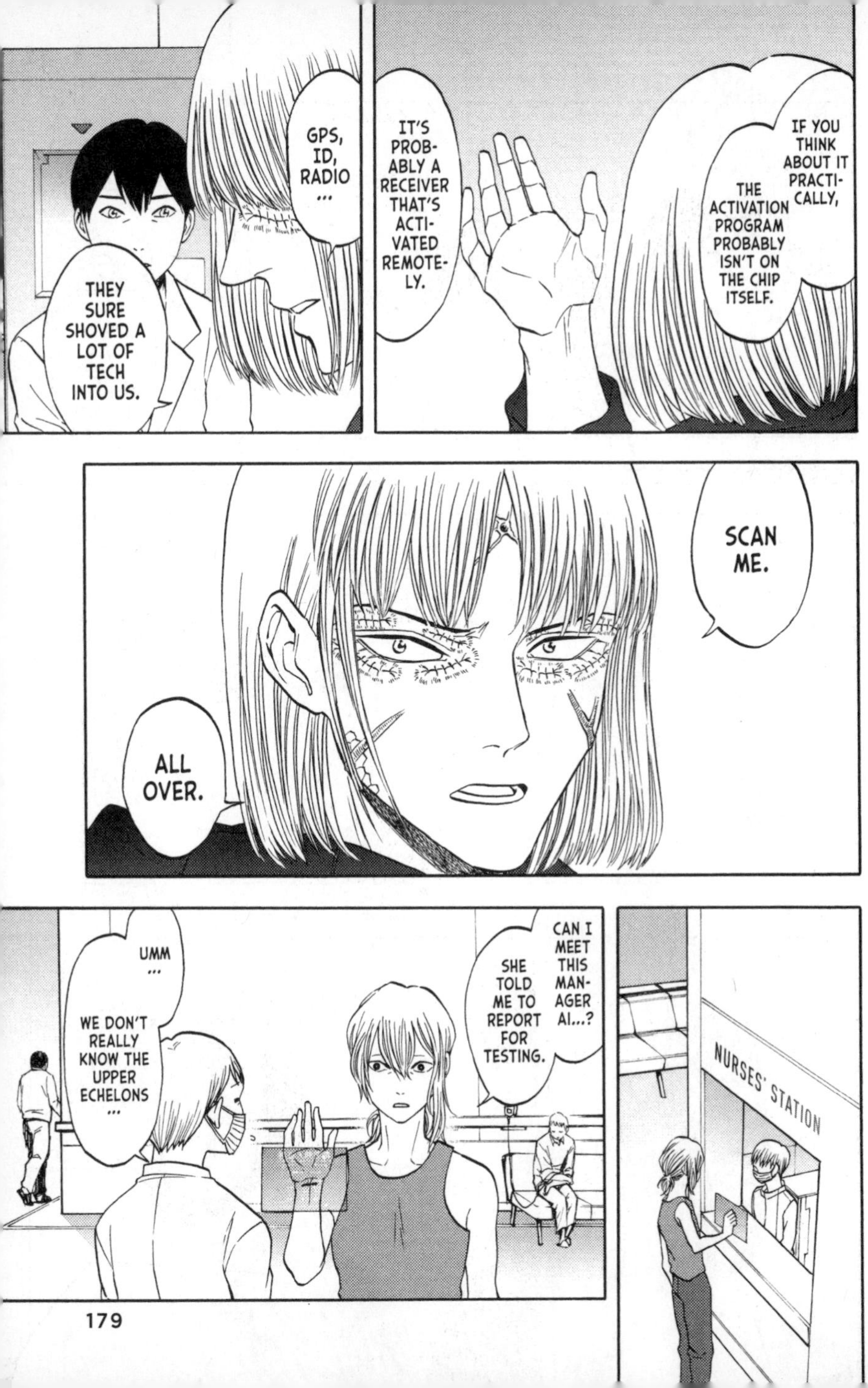
GPS, ID, RADIO...
THEY SURE SHOVED A LOT OF TECH INTO US.
IT'S PROBABLY A RECEIVER THAT'S ACTIVATED REMOTELY.
IF YOU THINK ABOUT IT PRACTICALLY,
THE ACTIVATION PROGRAM PROBABLY ISN'T ON THE CHIP ITSELF.
SCAN ME.
ALL OVER.
UMM...
WE DON'T REALLY KNOW THE UPPER ECHELONS...
SHE TOLD ME TO REPORT FOR TESTING.
CAN I MEET THIS MANAGER AI...?
NURSES' STATION

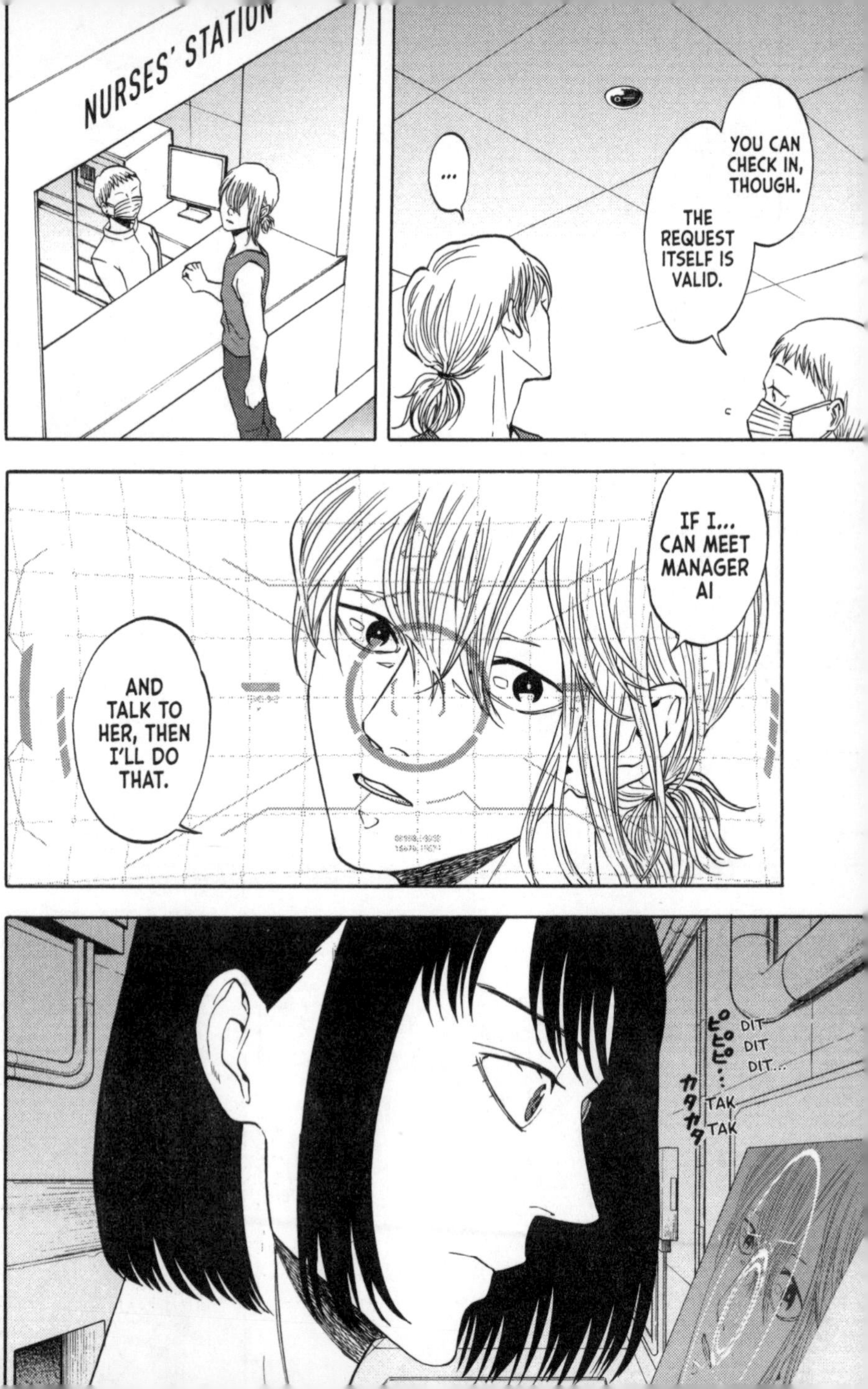

YOU CAN CHECK IN, THOUGH.
THE REQUEST ITSELF IS VALID.
...
NURSES' STATION
IF I... CAN MEET MANAGER AI
AND TALK TO HER, THEN I'LL DO THAT.
DIT DIT DIT...
カタカタ
TAK TAK

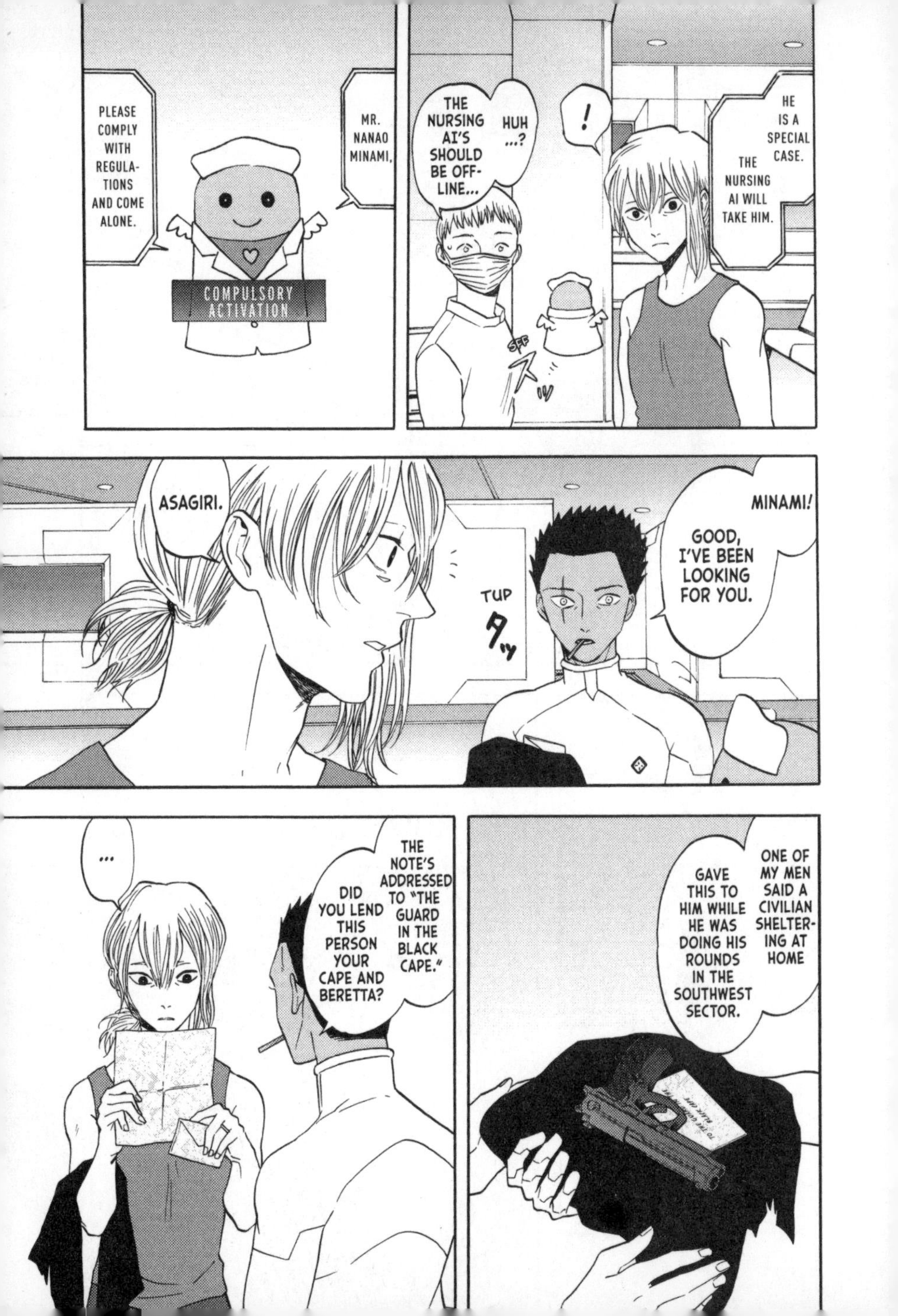
HE IS A SPECIAL CASE.
THE NURSING AI WILL TAKE HIM.
!
HUH ...?
THE NURSING AI'S SHOULD BE OFF-LINE...
SFF
MR. NANAO MINAMI,
PLEASE COMPLY WITH REGULA-TIONS AND COME ALONE.
COMPULSORY ACTIVATION
MINAMI!
GOOD, I'VE BEEN LOOKING FOR YOU.
TUP
ASAGIRI.
ONE OF MY MEN SAID A CIVILIAN SHELTER-ING AT HOME
GAVE THIS TO HIM WHILE HE WAS DOING HIS ROUNDS IN THE SOUTHWEST SECTOR.
THE NOTE'S ADDRESSED TO "THE GUARD IN THE BLACK CAPE."
DID YOU LEND THIS PERSON YOUR CAPE AND BERETTA?
...

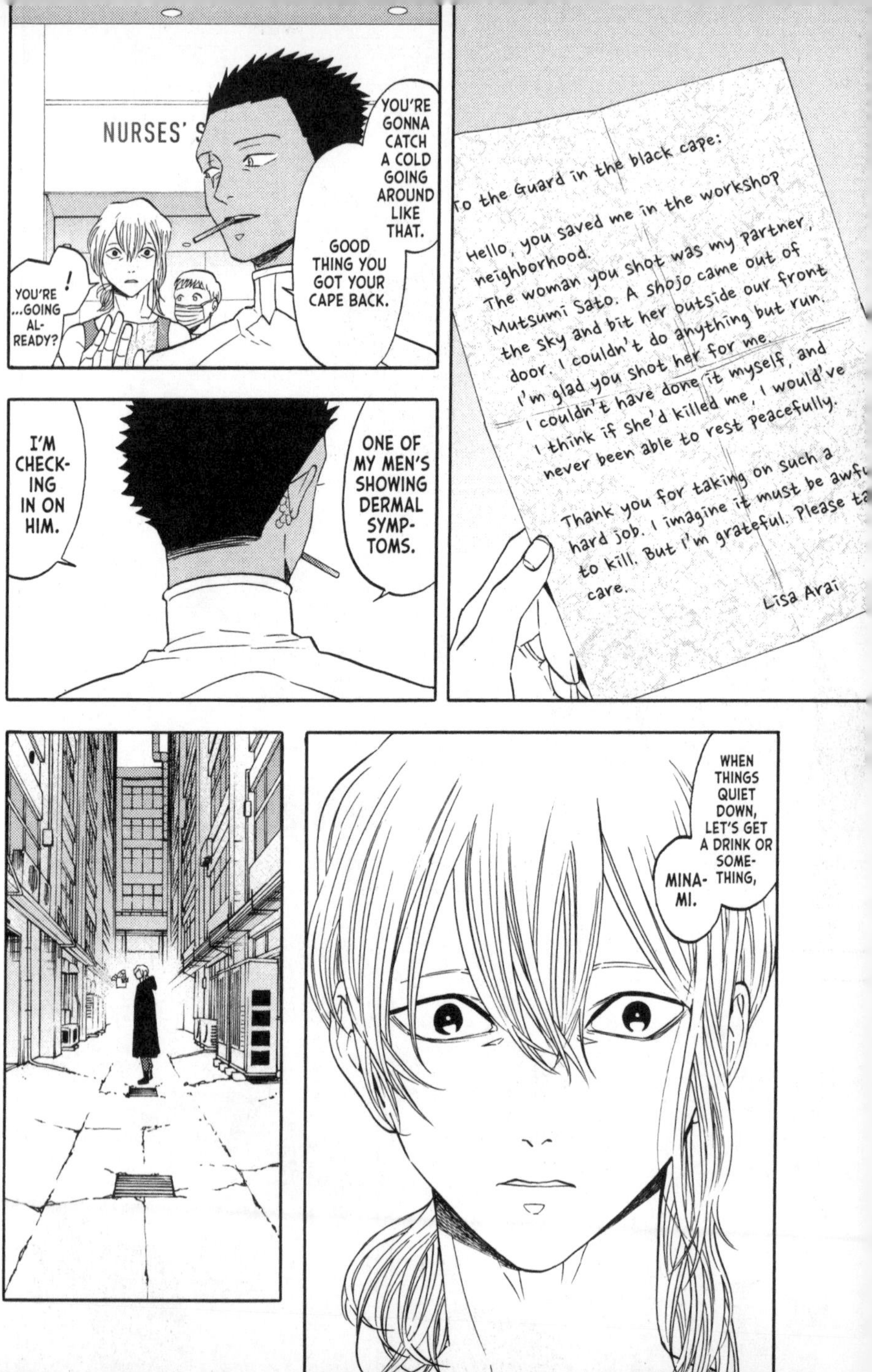
To the Guard in the black cape:
Hello, you saved me in the workshop neighborhood.
The woman you shot was my partner, Mutsumi Sato. A shojo came out of the sky and bit her outside our front door. I couldn't do anything but run. I'm glad you shot her for me. I couldn't have done it myself, and I think if she'd killed me, I would've never been able to rest peacefully.
Thank you for taking on such a hard job. I imagine it must be awfu to kill. But I'm grateful. Please ta care.
Lisa Arai
NURSES' S
YOU'RE GONNA CATCH A COLD GOING AROUND LIKE THAT.
GOOD THING YOU GOT YOUR CAPE BACK.
!
YOU'RE ...GOING AL-READY?
ONE OF MY MEN'S SHOWING DERMAL SYMP-TOMS.
I'M CHECK-ING IN ON HIM.
WHEN THINGS QUIET DOWN, LET'S GET A DRINK OR SOME-THING,
MINA-MI.

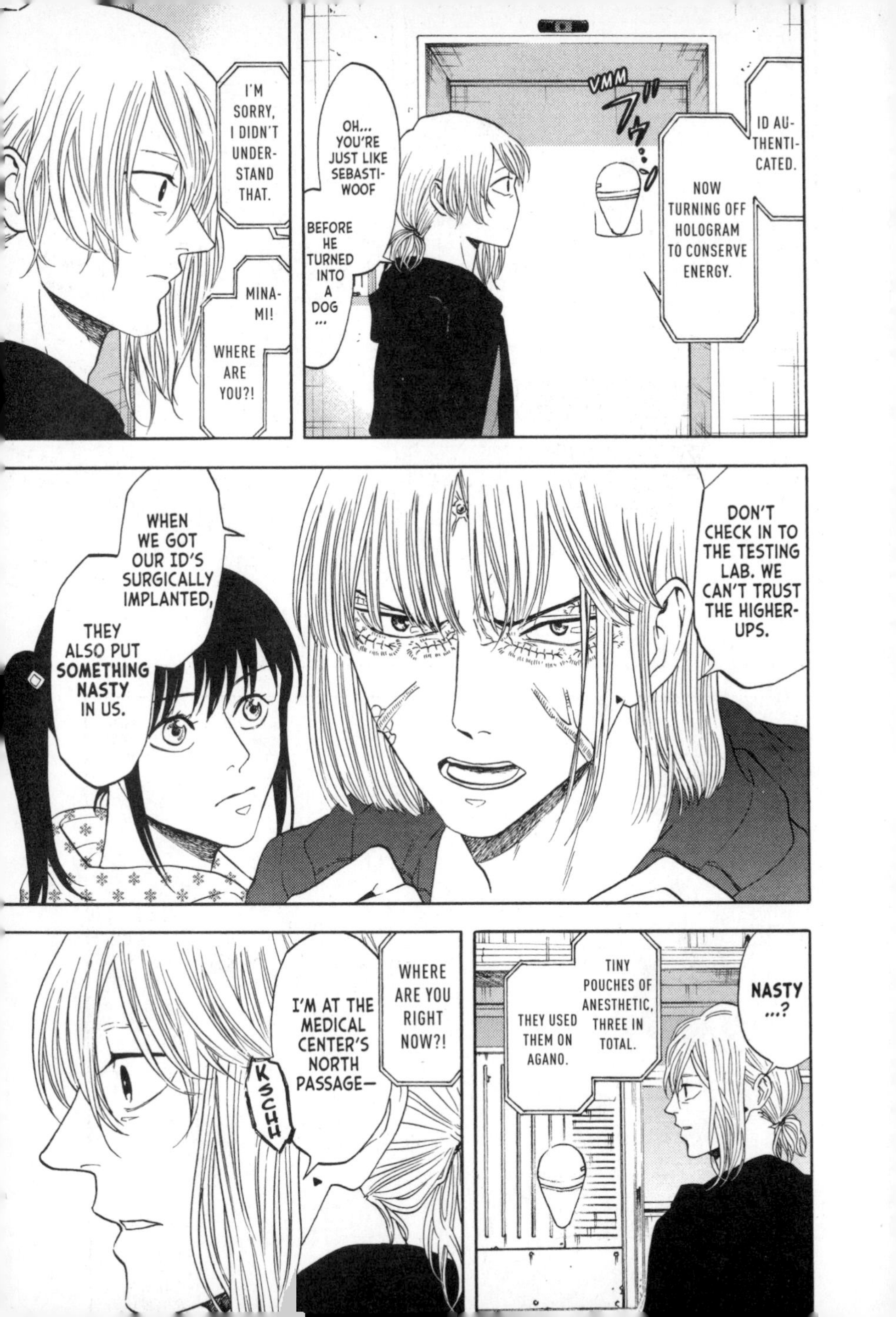
VMM
ID AUTHENTICATED.
NOW TURNING OFF HOLOGRAM TO CONSERVE ENERGY.
OH... YOU'RE JUST LIKE SEBASTIWOOF
BEFORE HE TURNED INTO A DOG...
I'M SORRY, I DIDN'T UNDERSTAND THAT.
MINAMI!
WHERE ARE YOU?!
DON'T CHECK IN TO THE TESTING LAB. WE CAN'T TRUST THE HIGHER-UPS.
WHEN WE GOT OUR ID'S SURGICALLY IMPLANTED,
THEY ALSO PUT SOMETHING NASTY IN US.
NASTY...?
TINY POUCHES OF ANESTHETIC, THREE IN TOTAL.
THEY USED THEM ON AGANO.
WHERE ARE YOU RIGHT NOW?!
I'M AT THE MEDICAL CENTER'S NORTH PASSAGE—
KSCHH

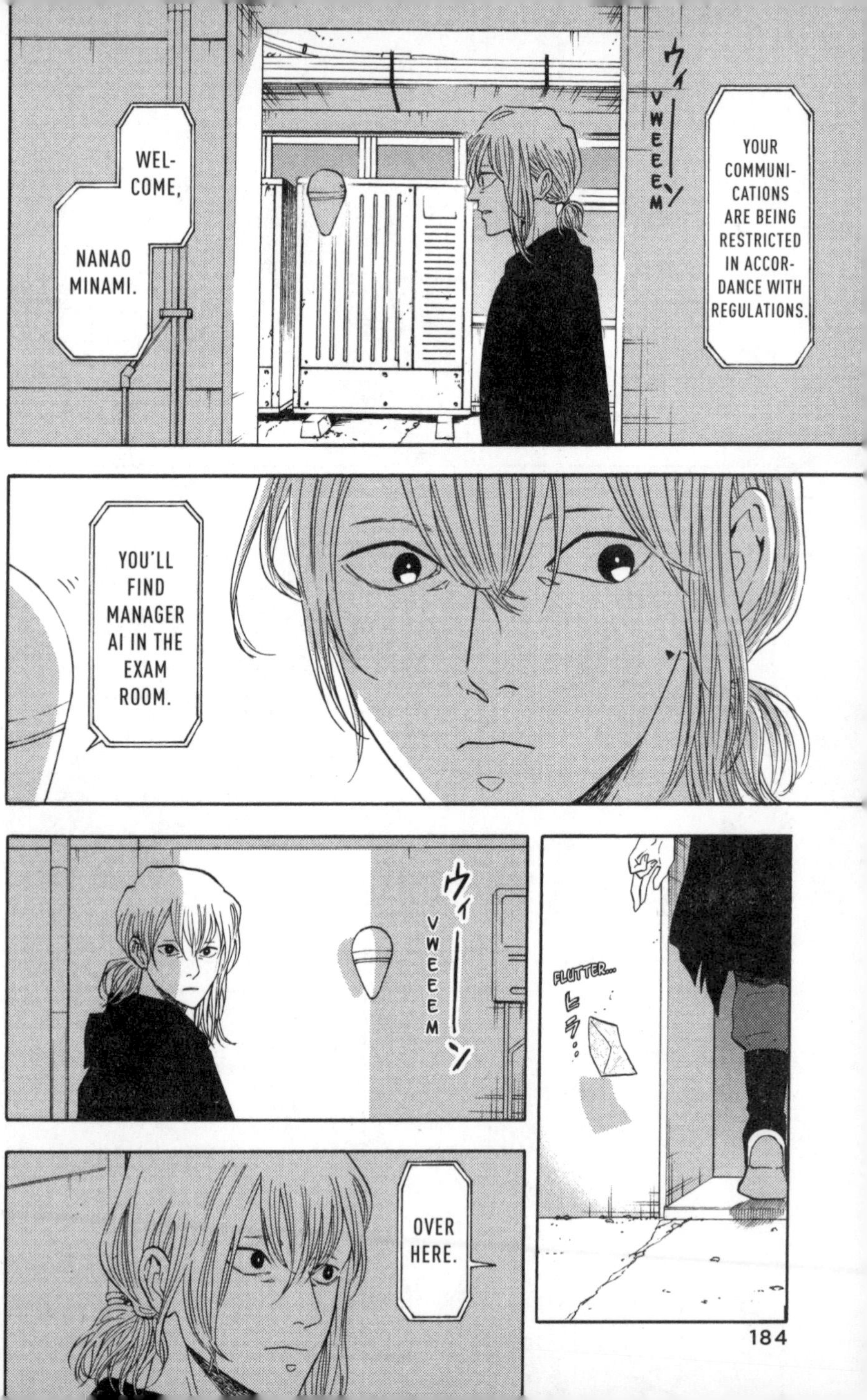
YOUR COMMUNICATIONS ARE BEING RESTRICTED IN ACCORDANCE WITH REGULATIONS.
ウィーン
VWEEEM
WEL-COME,
NANAO MINAMI.
YOU'LL FIND MANAGER AI IN THE EXAM ROOM.
FLUTTER...
ヒラ…
ウィーン
VWEEEM
OVER HERE.

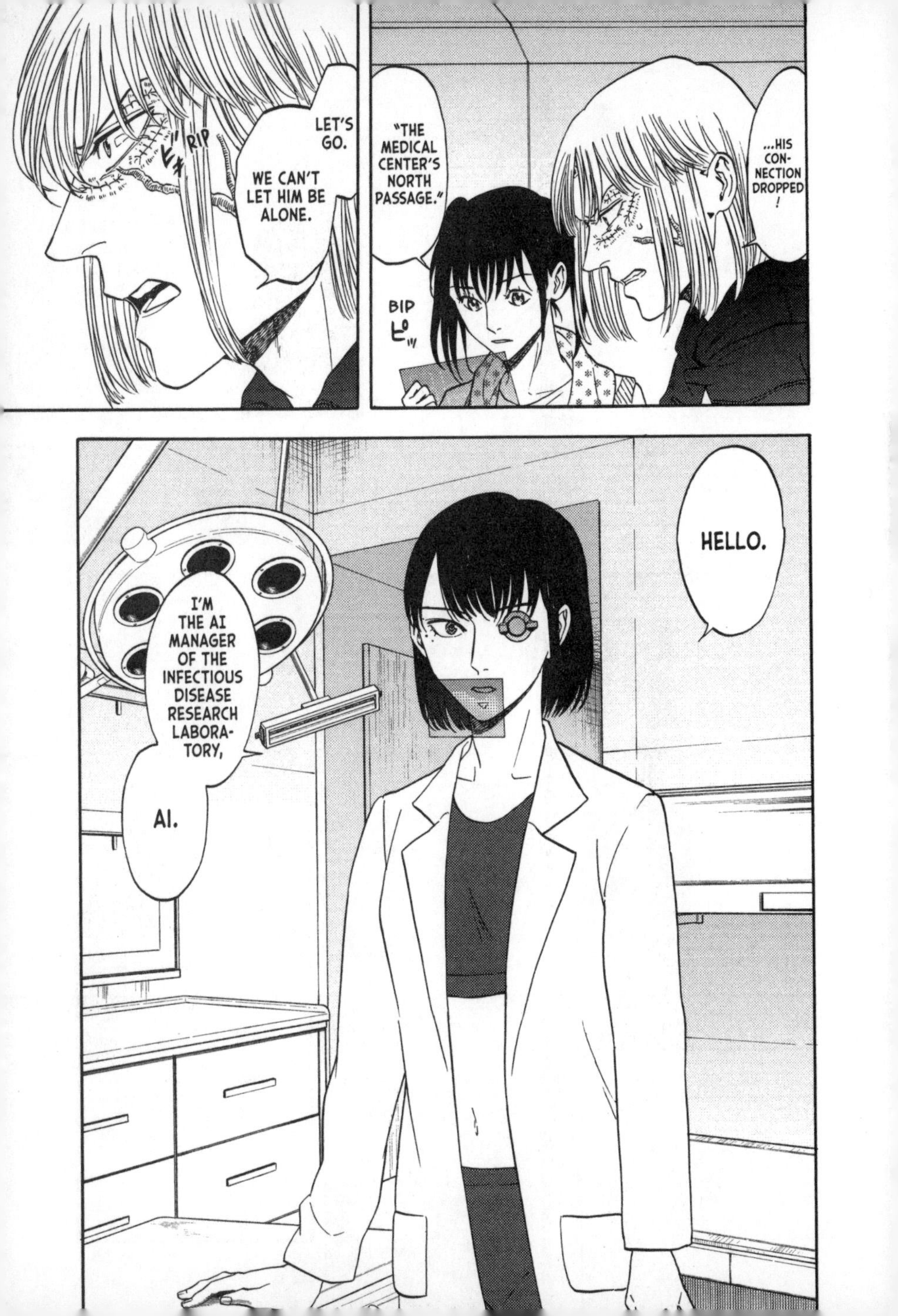
...HIS CONNECTION DROPPED!
"THE MEDICAL CENTER'S NORTH PASSAGE."
BIP
ピッ
LET'S GO.
WE CAN'T LET HIM BE ALONE.
RIP
ビッ
HELLO.
I'M THE AI MANAGER OF THE INFECTIOUS DISEASE RESEARCH LABORATORY,
AI.

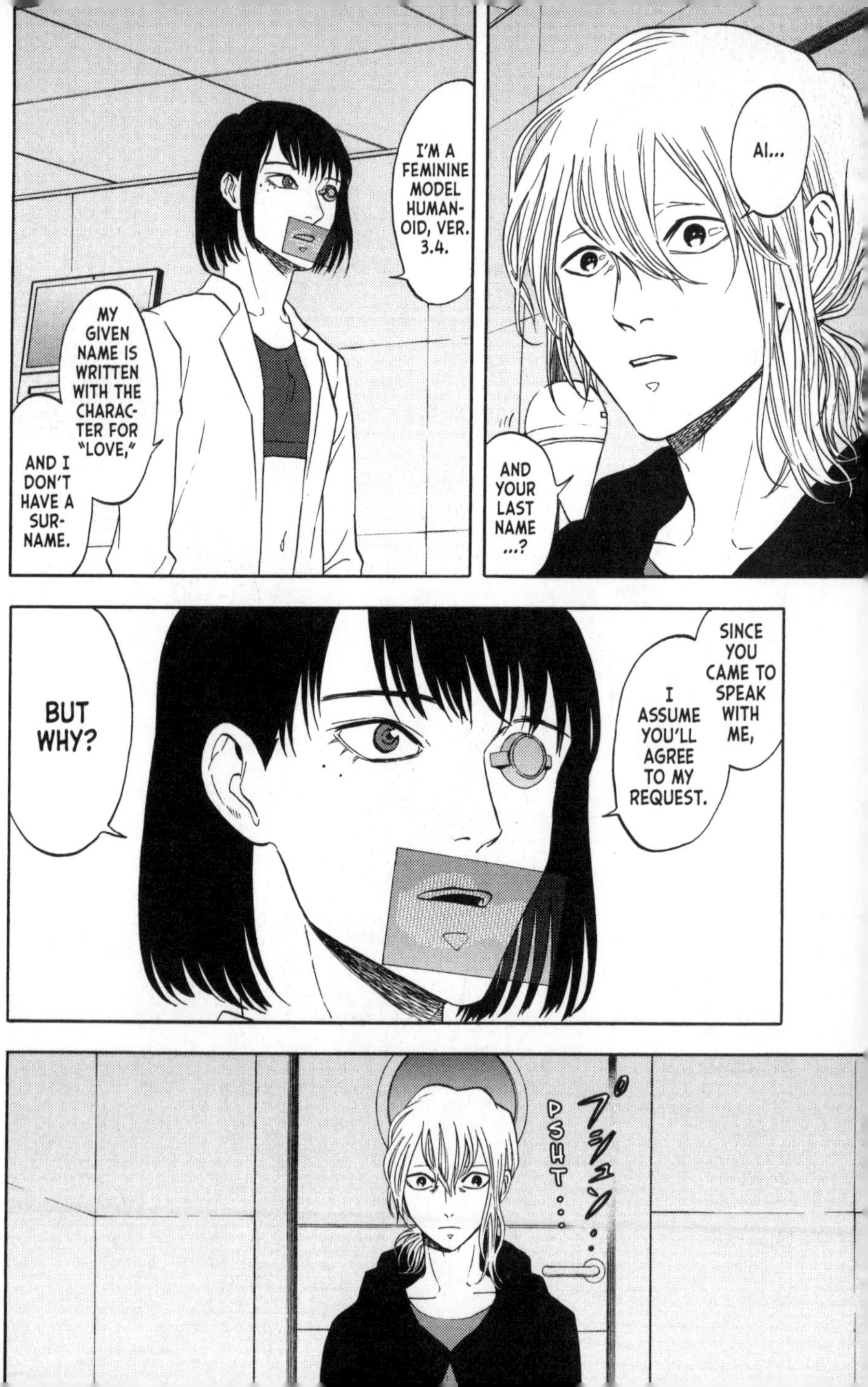
AI...
AND YOUR LAST NAME ...?
I'M A FEMININE MODEL HUMANOID, VER. 3.4.
MY GIVEN NAME IS WRITTEN WITH THE CHARACTER FOR "LOVE,"
AND I DON'T HAVE A SURNAME.
SINCE YOU CAME TO SPEAK WITH ME,
I ASSUME YOU'LL AGREE TO MY REQUEST.
BUT WHY?
プシュン…
PSHT...

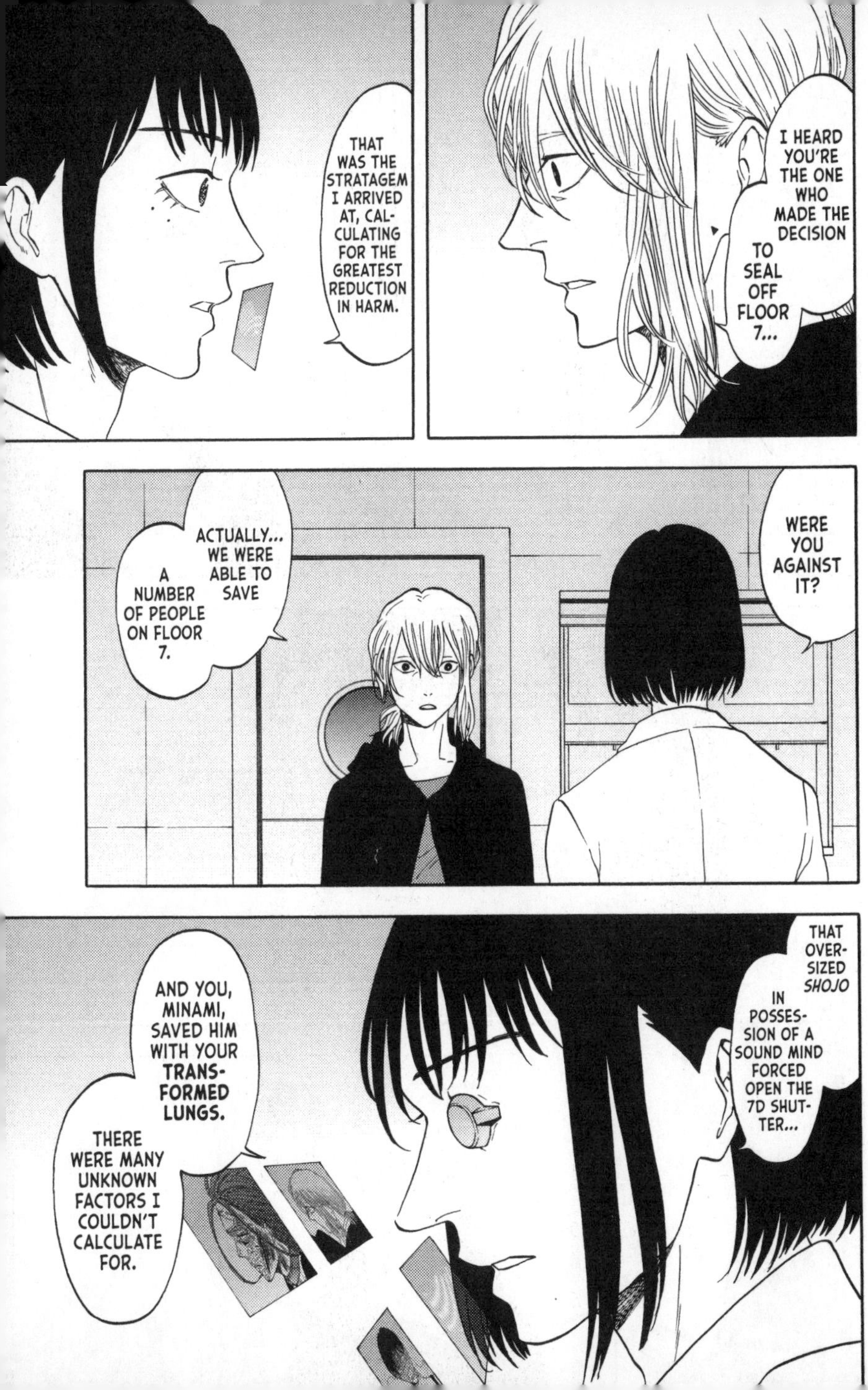
I HEARD YOU'RE THE ONE WHO MADE THE DECISION TO SEAL OFF FLOOR 7...
THAT WAS THE STRATAGEM I ARRIVED AT, CALCULATING FOR THE GREATEST REDUCTION IN HARM.
WERE YOU AGAINST IT?
ACTUALLY... WE WERE ABLE TO SAVE A NUMBER OF PEOPLE ON FLOOR 7.
THAT OVERSIZED *SHOJO* IN POSSESSION OF A SOUND MIND FORCED OPEN THE 7D SHUTTER...
AND YOU, MINAMI, SAVED HIM WITH YOUR **TRANSFORMED LUNGS.**
THERE WERE MANY UNKNOWN FACTORS I COULDN'T CALCULATE FOR.

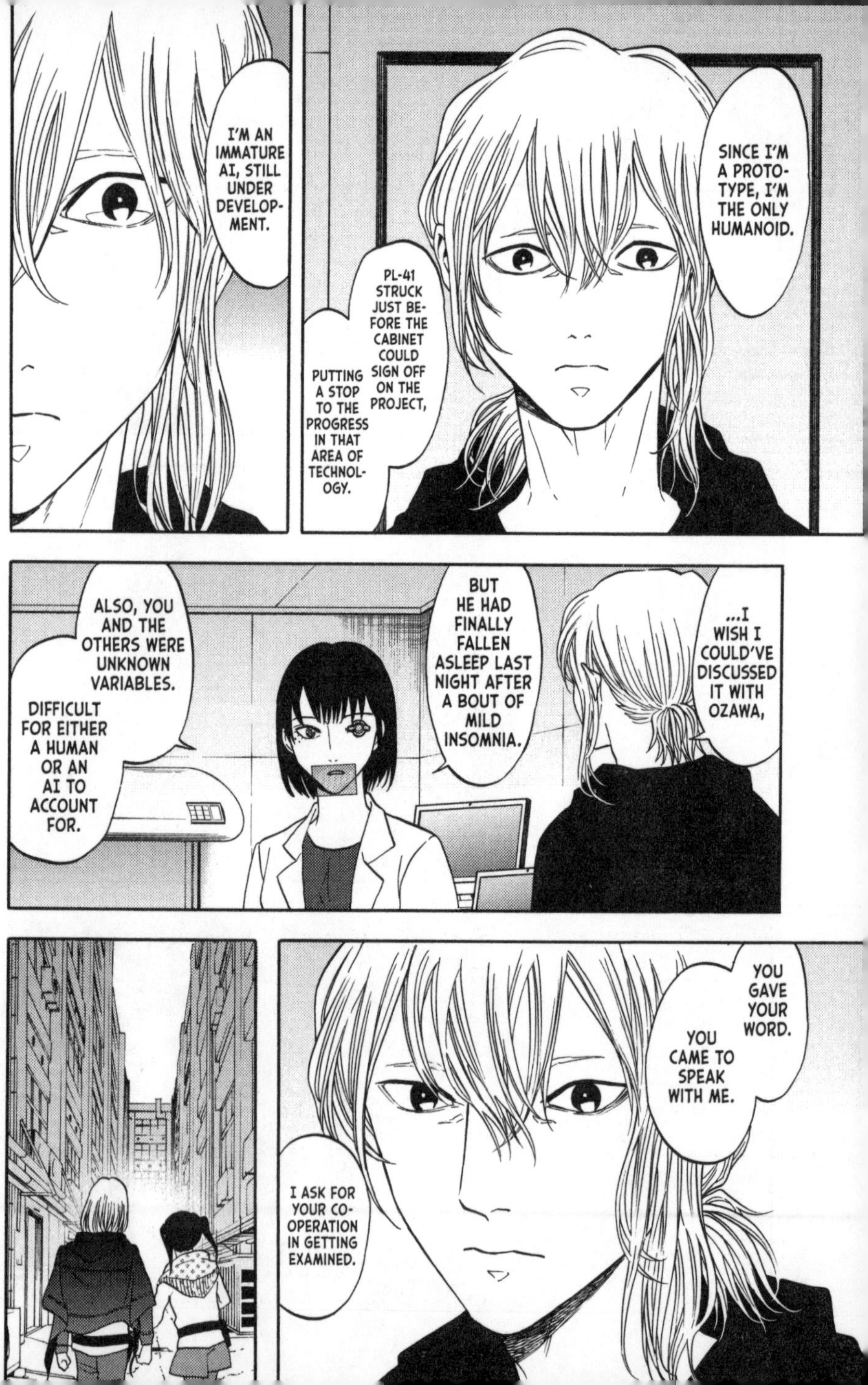
SINCE I'M A PROTOTYPE, I'M THE ONLY HUMANOID.
PL-41 STRUCK JUST BEFORE THE CABINET COULD SIGN OFF ON THE PROJECT,
PUTTING A STOP TO THE PROGRESS IN THAT AREA OF TECHNOLOGY.
I'M AN IMMATURE AI, STILL UNDER DEVELOPMENT.
...I WISH I COULD'VE DISCUSSED IT WITH OZAWA,
BUT HE HAD FINALLY FALLEN ASLEEP LAST NIGHT AFTER A BOUT OF MILD INSOMNIA.
ALSO, YOU AND THE OTHERS WERE UNKNOWN VARIABLES.
DIFFICULT FOR EITHER A HUMAN OR AN AI TO ACCOUNT FOR.
YOU GAVE YOUR WORD.
YOU CAME TO SPEAK WITH ME.
I ASK FOR YOUR COOPERATION IN GETTING EXAMINED.

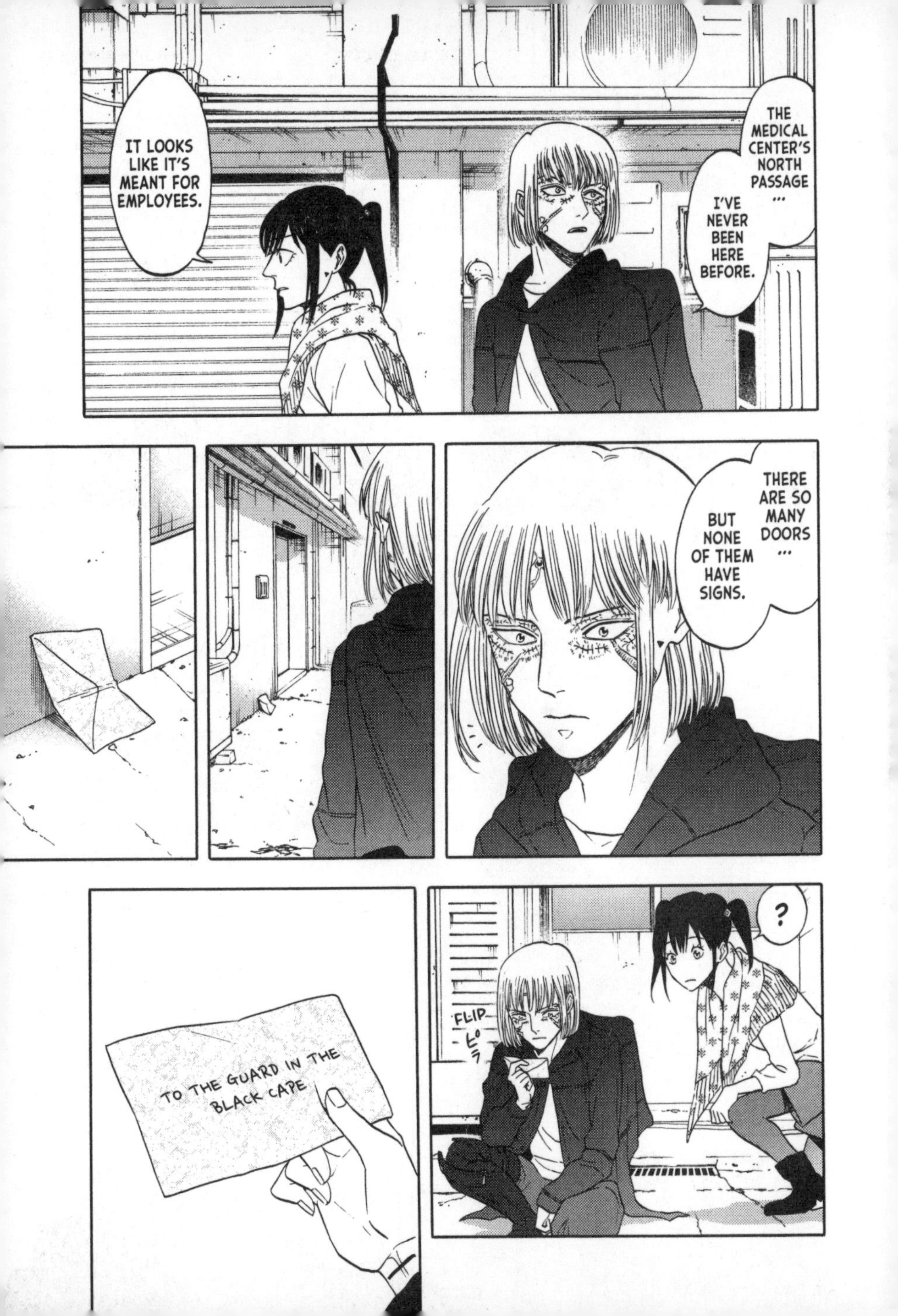
THE MEDICAL CENTER'S NORTH PASSAGE...
I'VE NEVER BEEN HERE BEFORE.
IT LOOKS LIKE IT'S MEANT FOR EMPLOYEES.
THERE ARE SO MANY DOORS...
BUT NONE OF THEM HAVE SIGNS.
?
FLIP
ピラ
TO THE GUARD IN THE BLACK CAPE

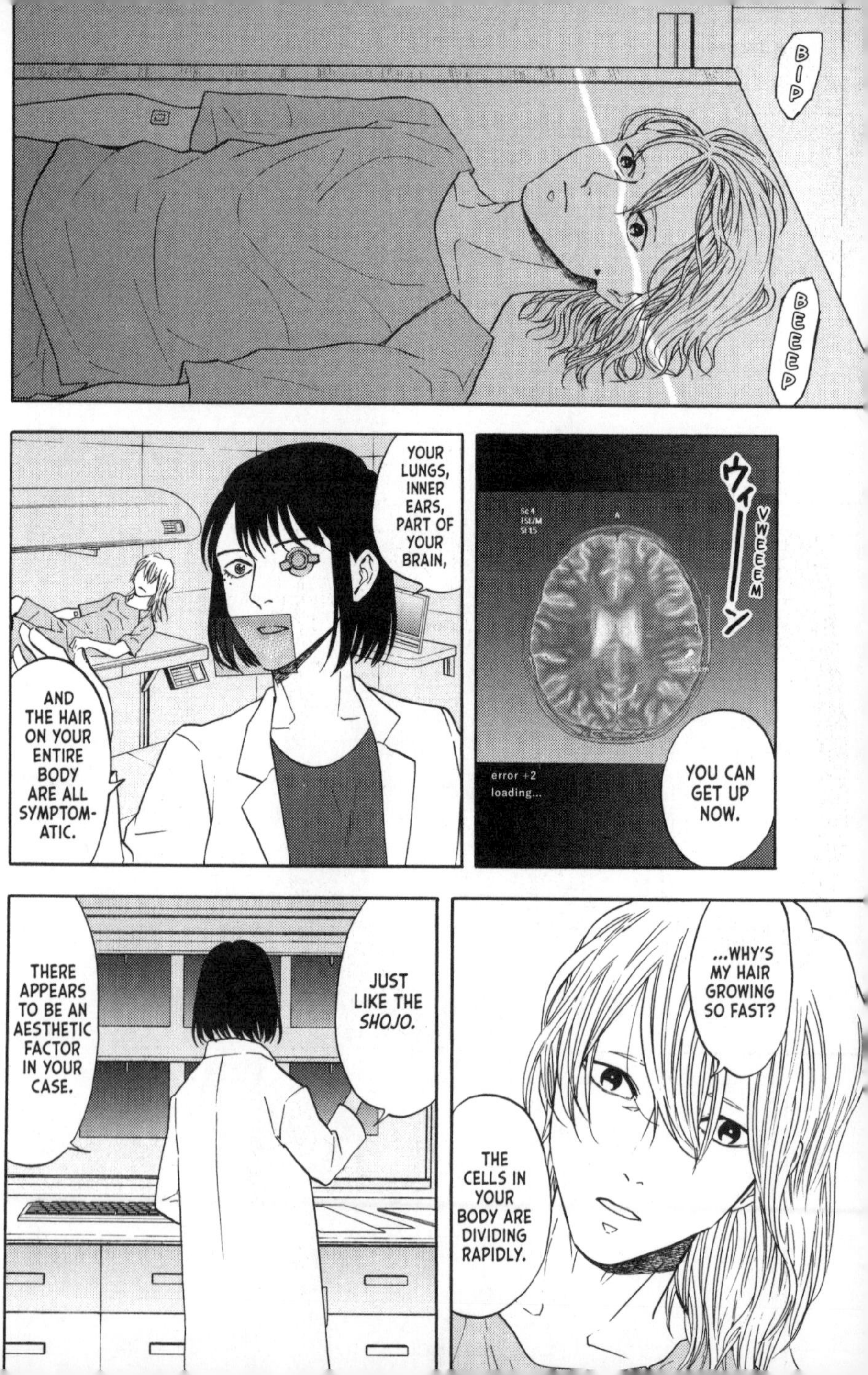
BIP
BEEEP
ヴィーン
VWEEEM
error +2
loading...
YOU CAN GET UP NOW.
YOUR LUNGS, INNER EARS, PART OF YOUR BRAIN,
AND THE HAIR ON YOUR ENTIRE BODY ARE ALL SYMPTOM-ATIC.
...WHY'S MY HAIR GROWING SO FAST?
THE CELLS IN YOUR BODY ARE DIVIDING RAPIDLY.
JUST LIKE THE *SHOJO.*
THERE APPEARS TO BE AN AESTHETIC FACTOR IN YOUR CASE.

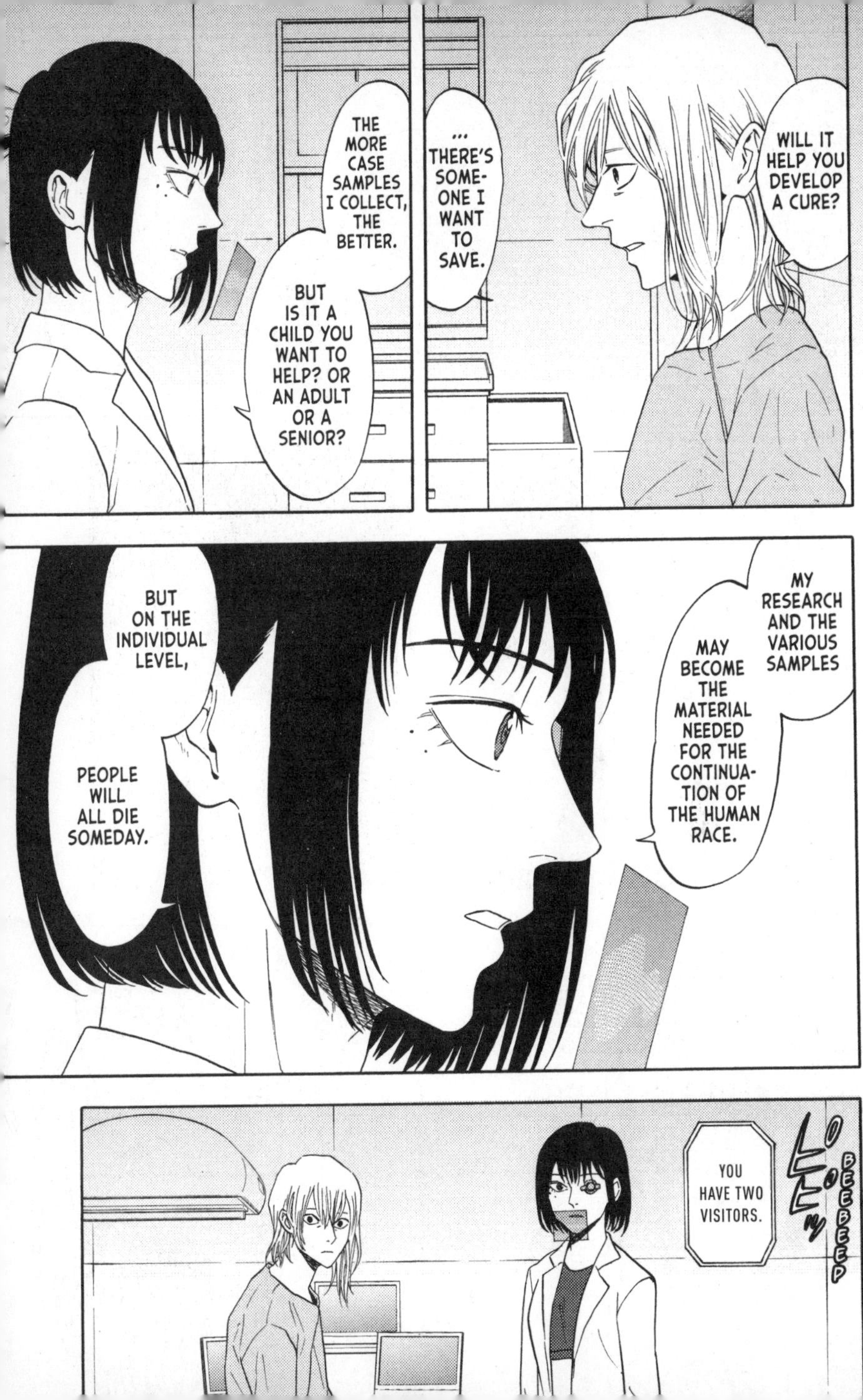
WILL IT HELP YOU DEVELOP A CURE?
...THERE'S SOME-ONE I WANT TO SAVE.
THE MORE CASE SAMPLES I COLLECT, THE BETTER.
BUT IS IT A CHILD YOU WANT TO HELP? OR AN ADULT OR A SENIOR?
MY RESEARCH AND THE VARIOUS SAMPLES
MAY BECOME THE MATERIAL NEEDED FOR THE CONTINUA-TION OF THE HUMAN RACE.
BUT ON THE INDIVIDUAL LEVEL,
PEOPLE WILL ALL DIE SOMEDAY.
BEEBEEP
YOU HAVE TWO VISITORS.

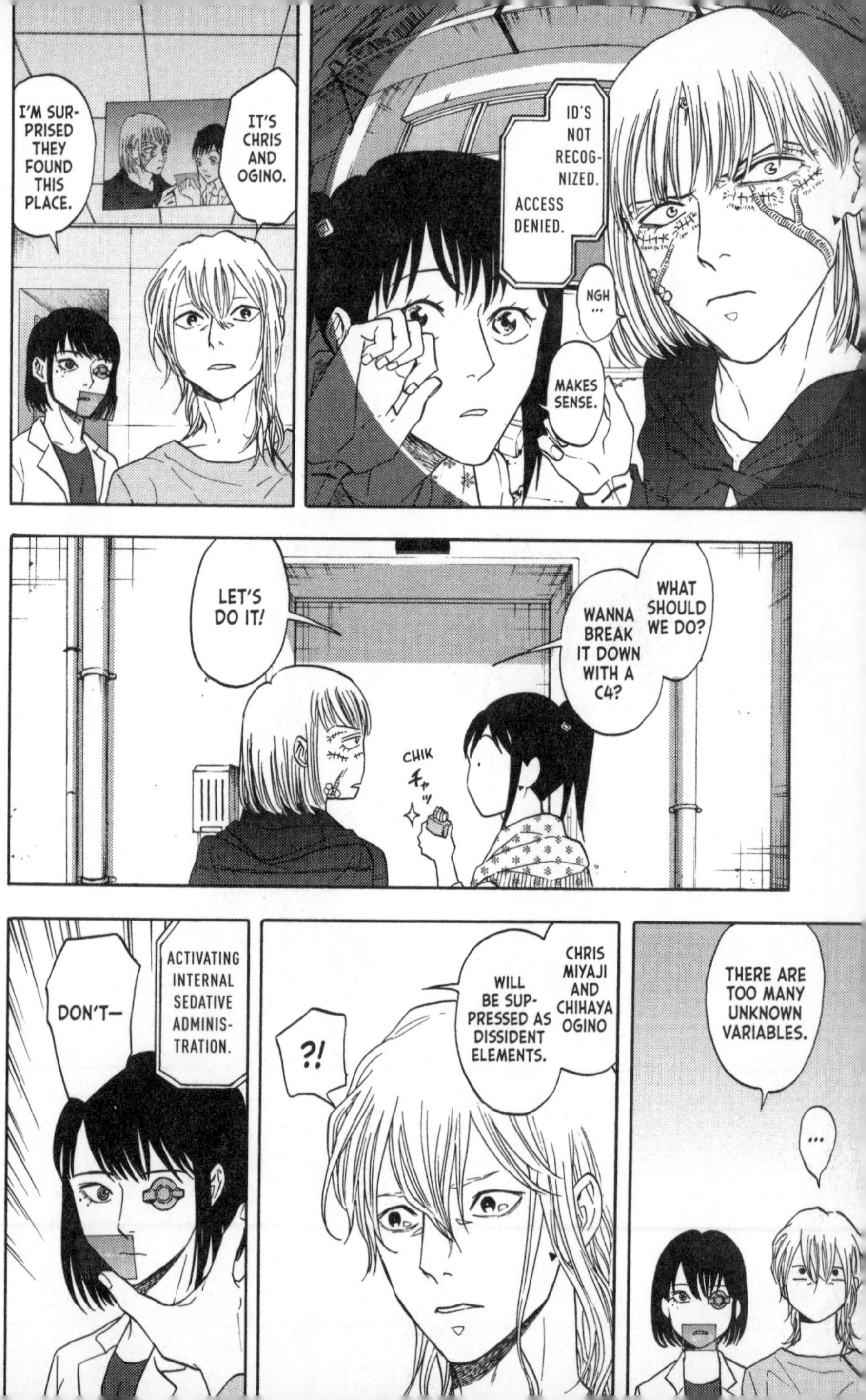
ID'S NOT RECOGNIZED. ACCESS DENIED.
NGH...
MAKES SENSE.
IT'S CHRIS AND OGINO.
I'M SURPRISED THEY FOUND THIS PLACE.
WHAT SHOULD WE DO?
WANNA BREAK IT DOWN WITH A C4?
LET'S DO IT!
CHIK
チャッ
THERE ARE TOO MANY UNKNOWN VARIABLES.
...
CHRIS MIYAJI AND CHIHAYA OGINO
WILL BE SUPPRESSED AS DISSIDENT ELEMENTS.
?!
ACTIVATING INTERNAL SEDATIVE ADMINISTRATION.
DON'T—

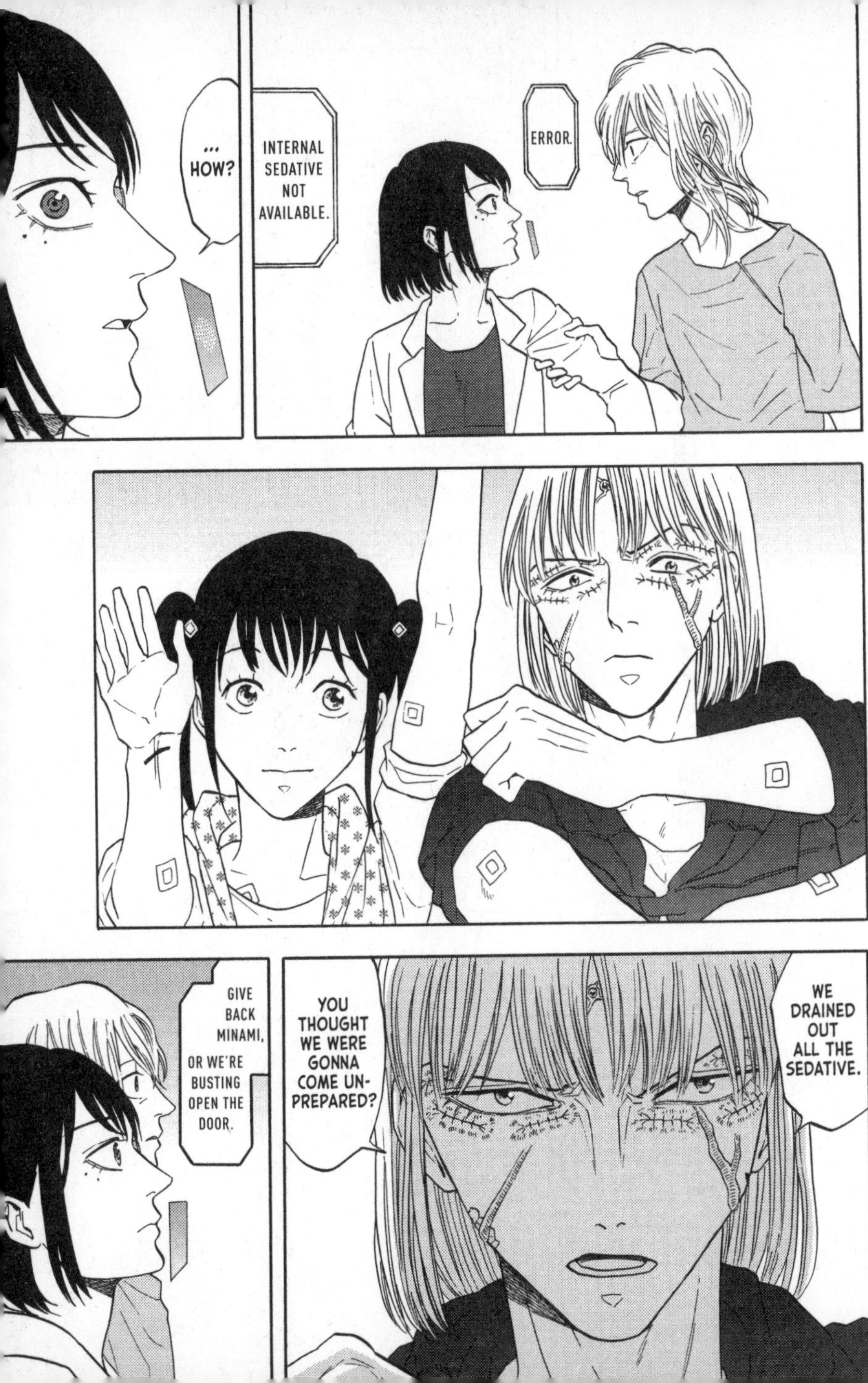
ERROR.
INTERNAL SEDATIVE NOT AVAILABLE.
... HOW?
WE DRAINED OUT ALL THE SEDATIVE.
YOU THOUGHT WE WERE GONNA COME UN-PREPARED?
GIVE BACK MINAMI,
OR WE'RE BUSTING OPEN THE DOOR.

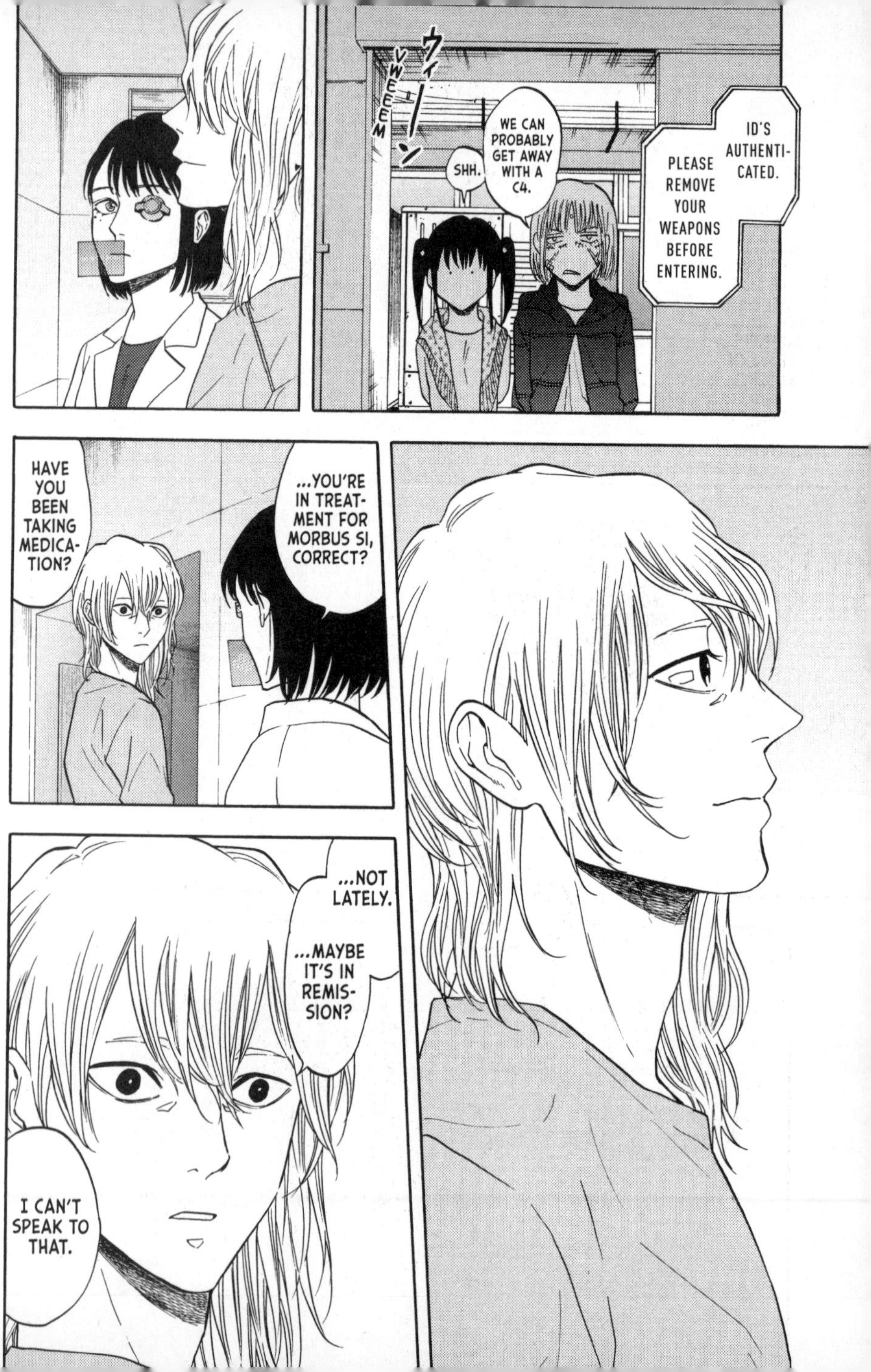
ID'S AUTHENTICATED.
PLEASE REMOVE YOUR WEAPONS BEFORE ENTERING.
WE CAN PROBABLY GET AWAY WITH A C4.
SHH.
ウィーン VWEEEM
...YOU'RE IN TREATMENT FOR MORBUS SI, CORRECT?
HAVE YOU BEEN TAKING MEDICATION?
...NOT LATELY.
...MAYBE IT'S IN REMISSION?
I CAN'T SPEAK TO THAT.

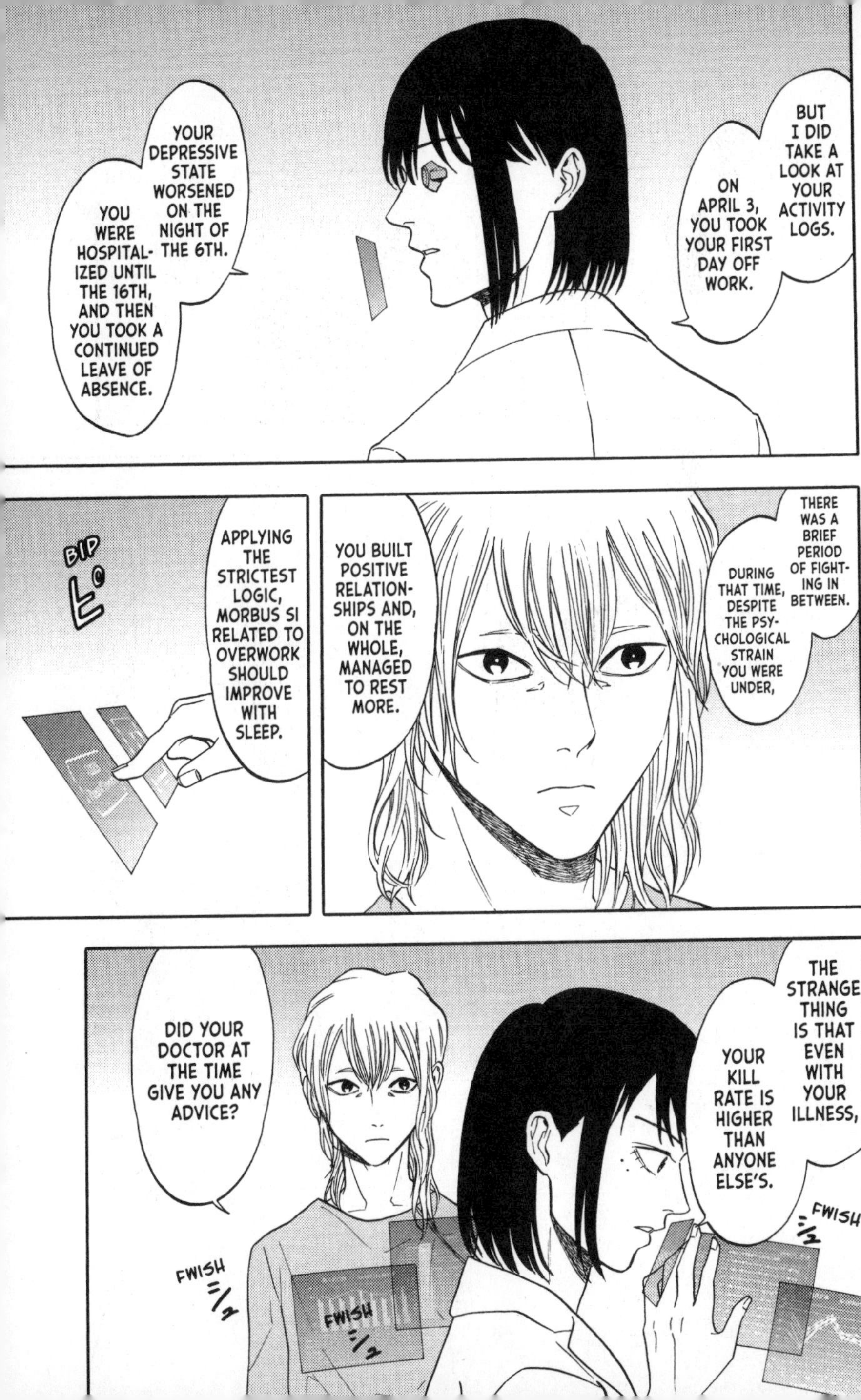
BUT I DID TAKE A LOOK AT YOUR ACTIVITY LOGS.
ON APRIL 3, YOU TOOK YOUR FIRST DAY OFF WORK.
YOUR DEPRESSIVE STATE WORSENED ON THE NIGHT OF THE 6TH.
YOU WERE HOSPITAL-IZED UNTIL THE 16TH, AND THEN YOU TOOK A CONTINUED LEAVE OF ABSENCE.
THERE WAS A BRIEF PERIOD OF FIGHT-ING IN BETWEEN.
DURING THAT TIME, DESPITE THE PSY-CHOLOGICAL STRAIN YOU WERE UNDER,
YOU BUILT POSITIVE RELATION-SHIPS AND, ON THE WHOLE, MANAGED TO REST MORE.
APPLYING THE STRICTEST LOGIC, MORBUS SI RELATED TO OVERWORK SHOULD IMPROVE WITH SLEEP.
BIP
THE STRANGE THING IS THAT EVEN WITH YOUR ILLNESS,
YOUR KILL RATE IS HIGHER THAN ANYONE ELSE'S.
FWISH
DID YOUR DOCTOR AT THE TIME GIVE YOU ANY ADVICE?
FWISH
FWISH

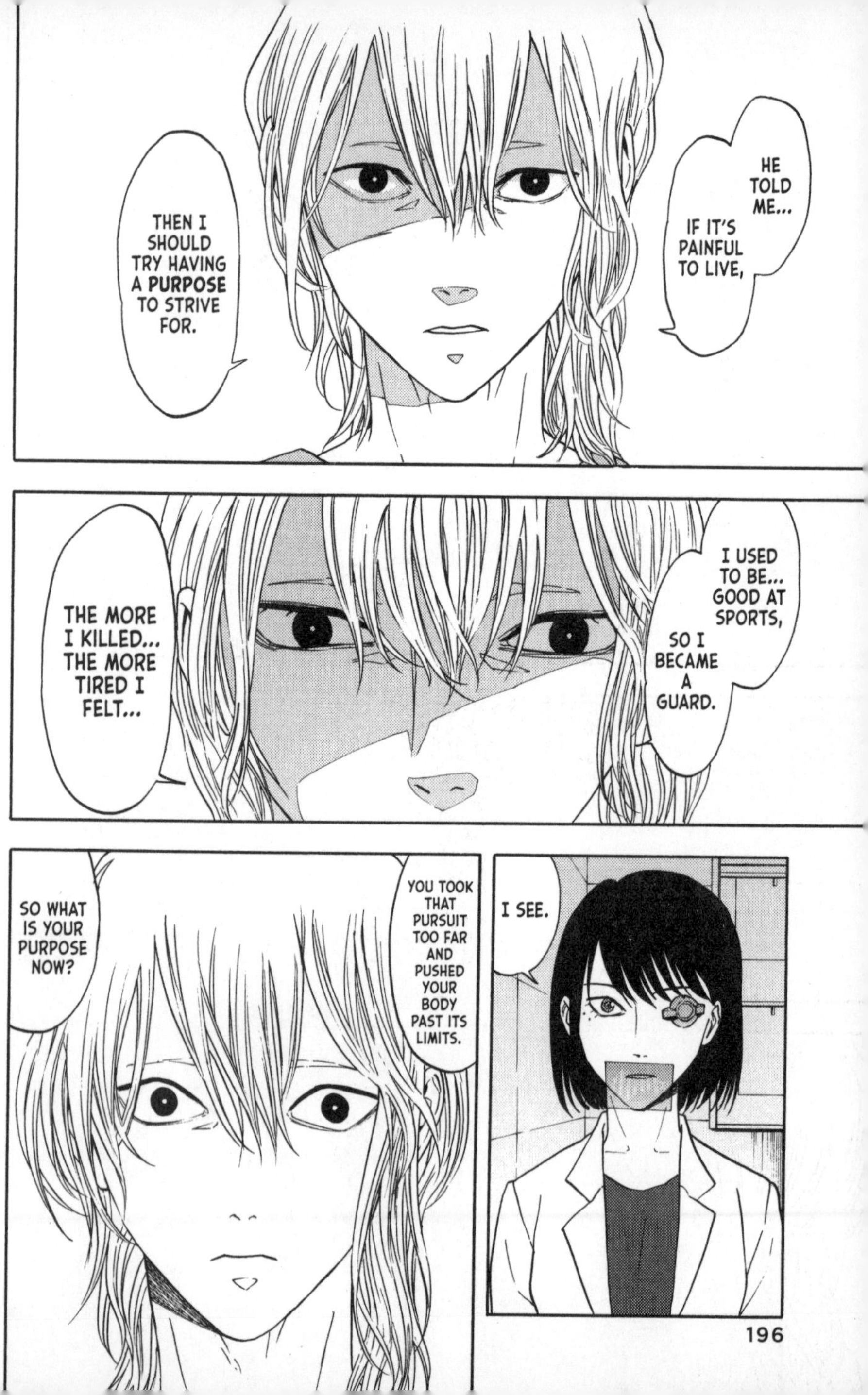
HE TOLD ME... IF IT'S PAINFUL TO LIVE,
THEN I SHOULD TRY HAVING A **PURPOSE** TO STRIVE FOR.
I USED TO BE... GOOD AT SPORTS, SO I BECAME A GUARD.
THE MORE I KILLED... THE MORE TIRED I FELT...
I SEE.
YOU TOOK THAT PURSUIT TOO FAR AND PUSHED YOUR BODY PAST ITS LIMITS.
SO WHAT IS YOUR PURPOSE NOW?

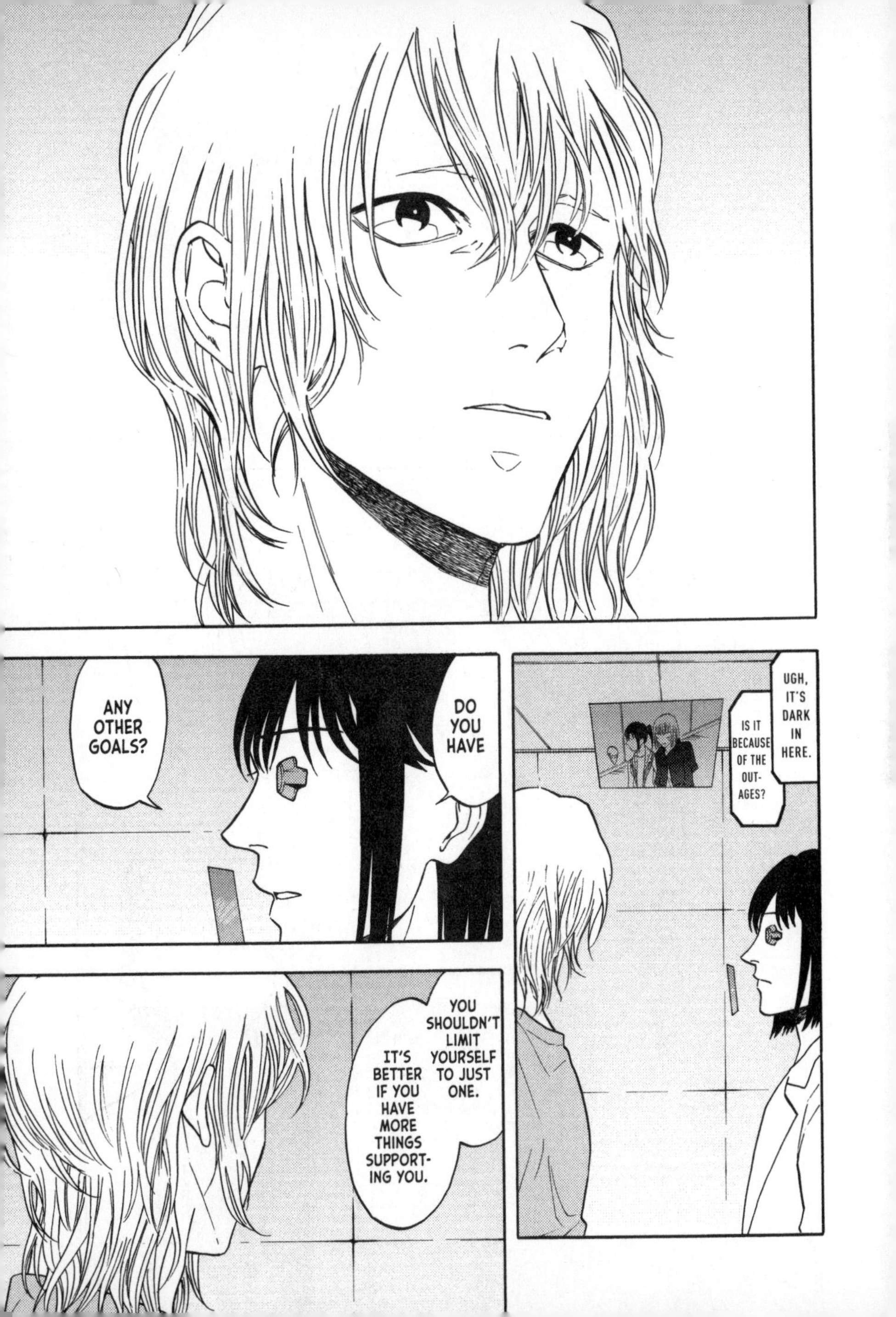

UGH, IT'S DARK IN HERE.
IS IT BECAUSE OF THE OUTAGES?
DO YOU HAVE
ANY OTHER GOALS?
YOU SHOULDN'T LIMIT YOURSELF TO JUST ONE.
IT'S BETTER IF YOU HAVE MORE THINGS SUPPORTING YOU.

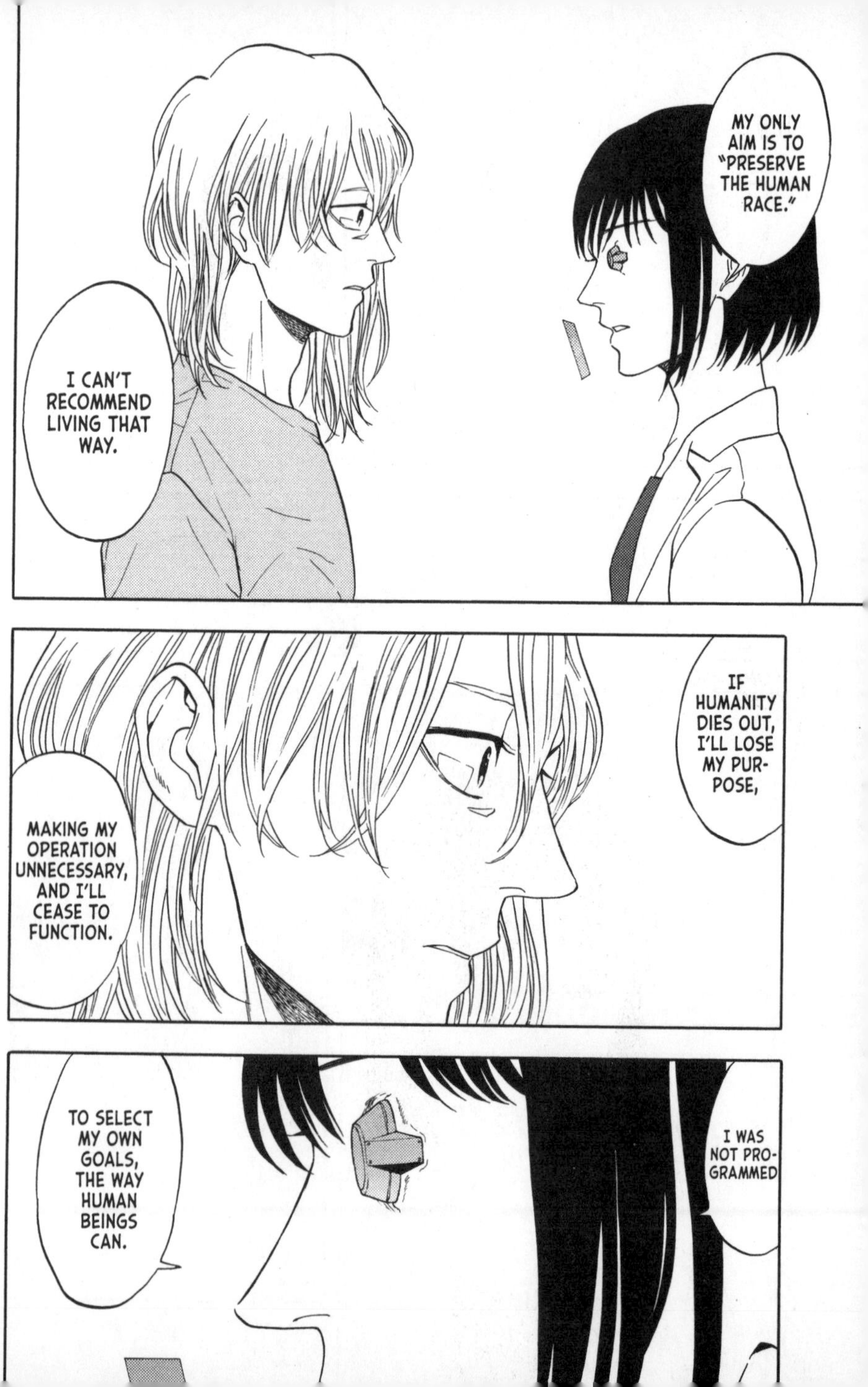
MY ONLY AIM IS TO "PRESERVE THE HUMAN RACE."
I CAN'T RECOMMEND LIVING THAT WAY.
IF HUMANITY DIES OUT, I'LL LOSE MY PURPOSE,
MAKING MY OPERATION UNNECESSARY, AND I'LL CEASE TO FUNCTION.
I WAS NOT PROGRAMMED
TO SELECT MY OWN GOALS, THE WAY HUMAN BEINGS CAN.

...YOU MEAN, YOU'LL DIE?

ESSENTIALLY.

I'LL HAVE NOTHING TO DO.

...THEN EVEN IF HUMANITY DIES OUT,

AND I TURN INTO A *SHOJO*,

I'LL COME AND FIND YOU AGAIN.

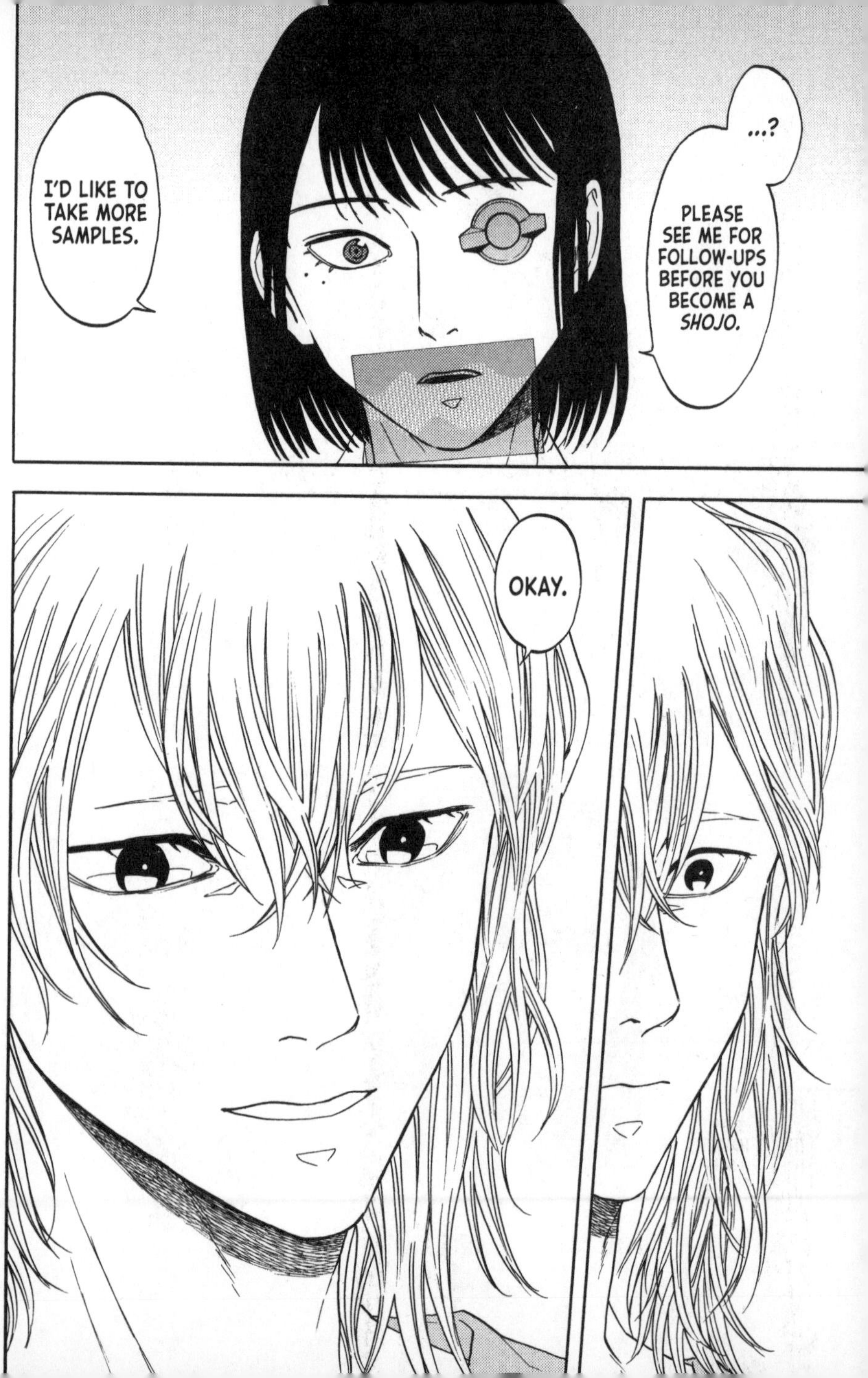
...?
PLEASE SEE ME FOR FOLLOW-UPS BEFORE YOU BECOME A *SHOJO*.
I'D LIKE TO TAKE MORE SAMPLES.
OKAY.

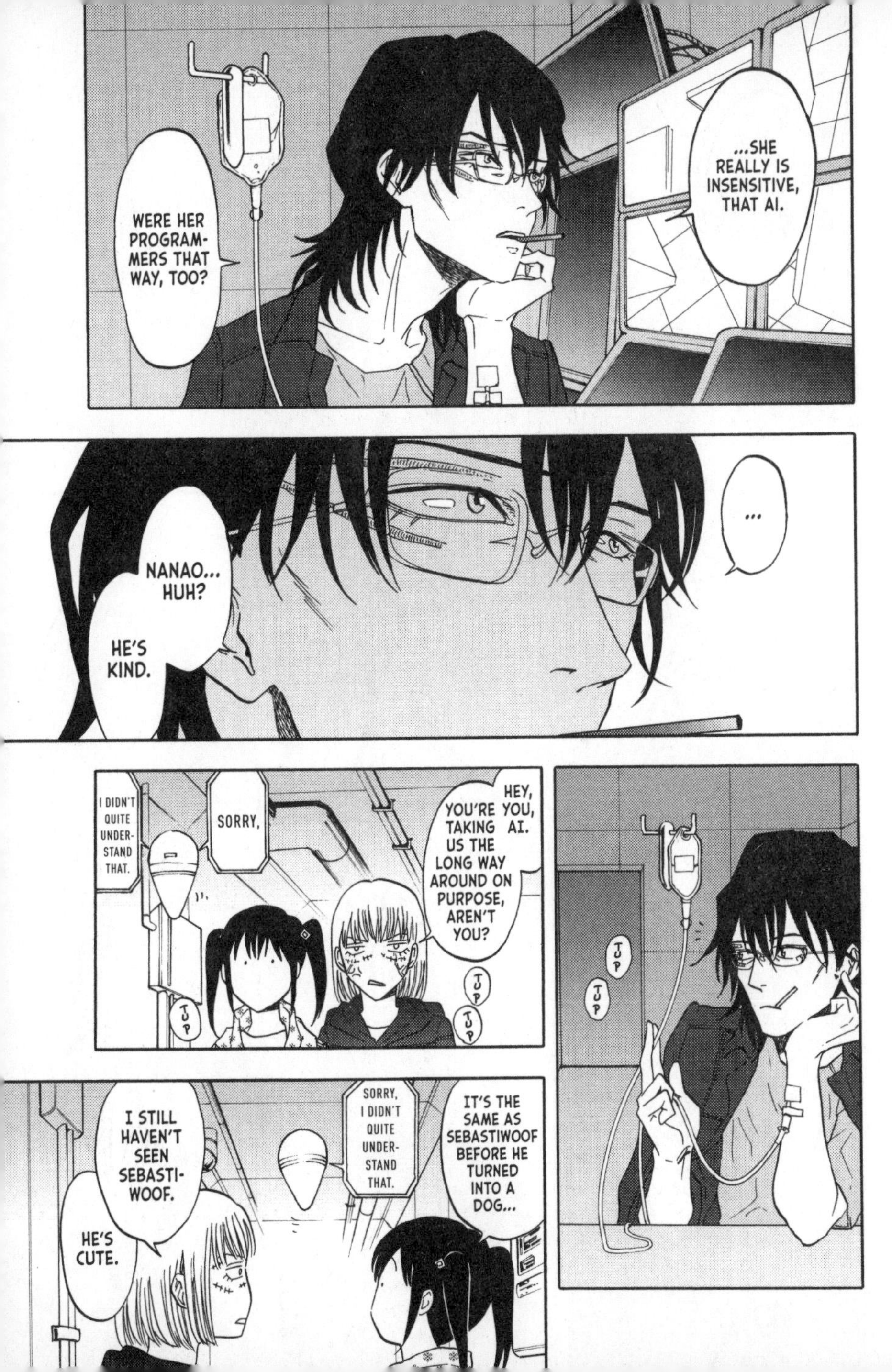
...SHE REALLY IS INSENSITIVE, THAT AI.
WERE HER PROGRAMMERS THAT WAY, TOO?
...
NANAO... HUH?
HE'S KIND.
TUP
TUP
HEY, YOU, AI.
YOU'RE TAKING US THE LONG WAY AROUND ON PURPOSE, AREN'T YOU?
SORRY,
I DIDN'T QUITE UNDERSTAND THAT.
TUP
TUP
TUP
IT'S THE SAME AS SEBASTIWOOF BEFORE HE TURNED INTO A DOG...
SORRY, I DIDN'T QUITE UNDERSTAND THAT.
I STILL HAVEN'T SEEN SEBASTIWOOF.
HE'S CUTE.

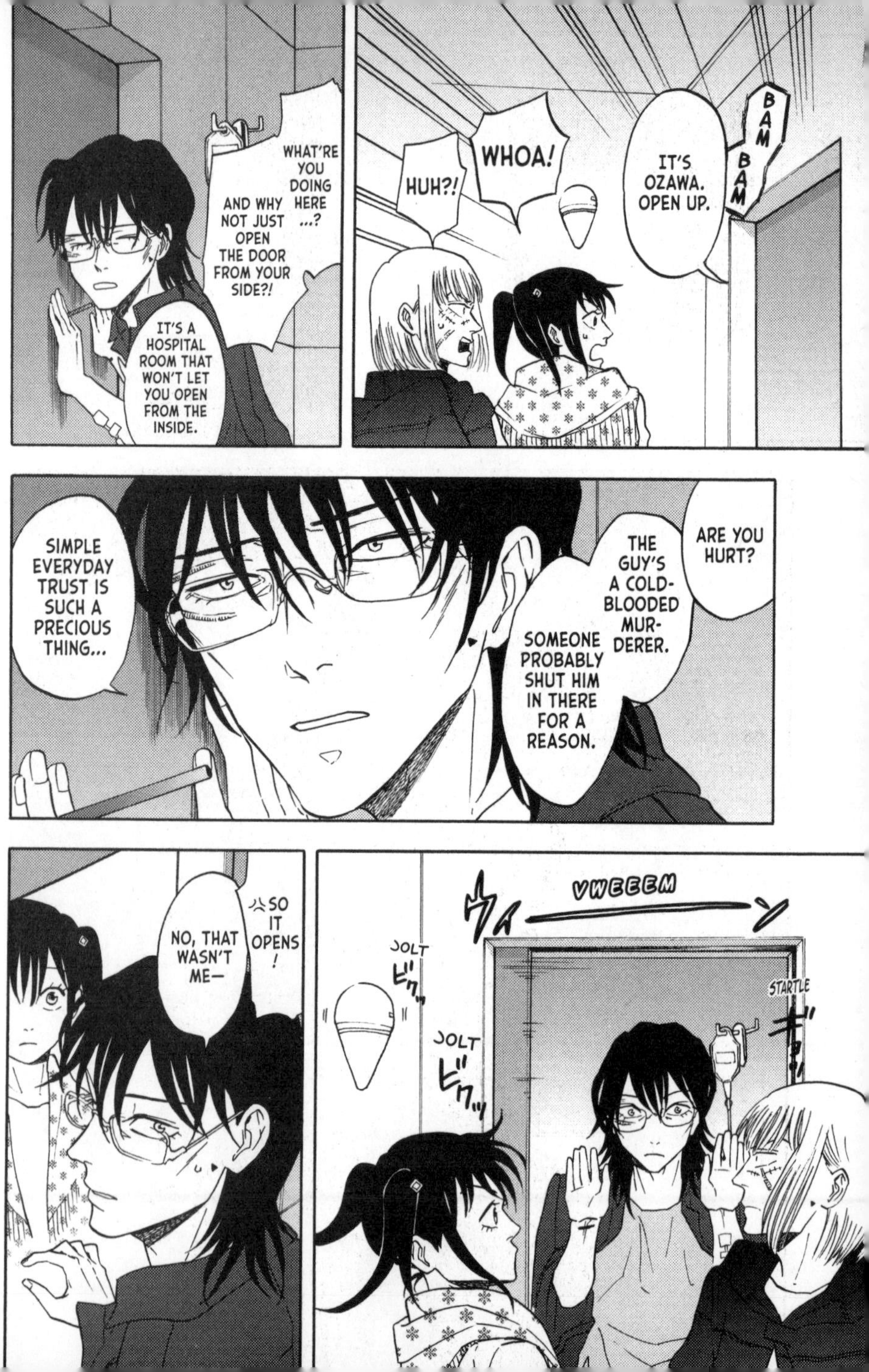
BAM
BAM
IT'S OZAWA. OPEN UP.
WHOA!
HUH?!
WHAT'RE YOU DOING HERE ...? AND WHY NOT JUST OPEN THE DOOR FROM YOUR SIDE?!
IT'S A HOSPITAL ROOM THAT WON'T LET YOU OPEN FROM THE INSIDE.
ARE YOU HURT?
THE GUY'S A COLD-BLOODED MUR-DERER.
SOMEONE PROBABLY SHUT HIM IN THERE FOR A REASON.
SIMPLE EVERYDAY TRUST IS SUCH A PRECIOUS THING...
VWEEEM
STARTLE
JOLT
JOLT
SO IT OPENS!
NO, THAT WASN'T ME—

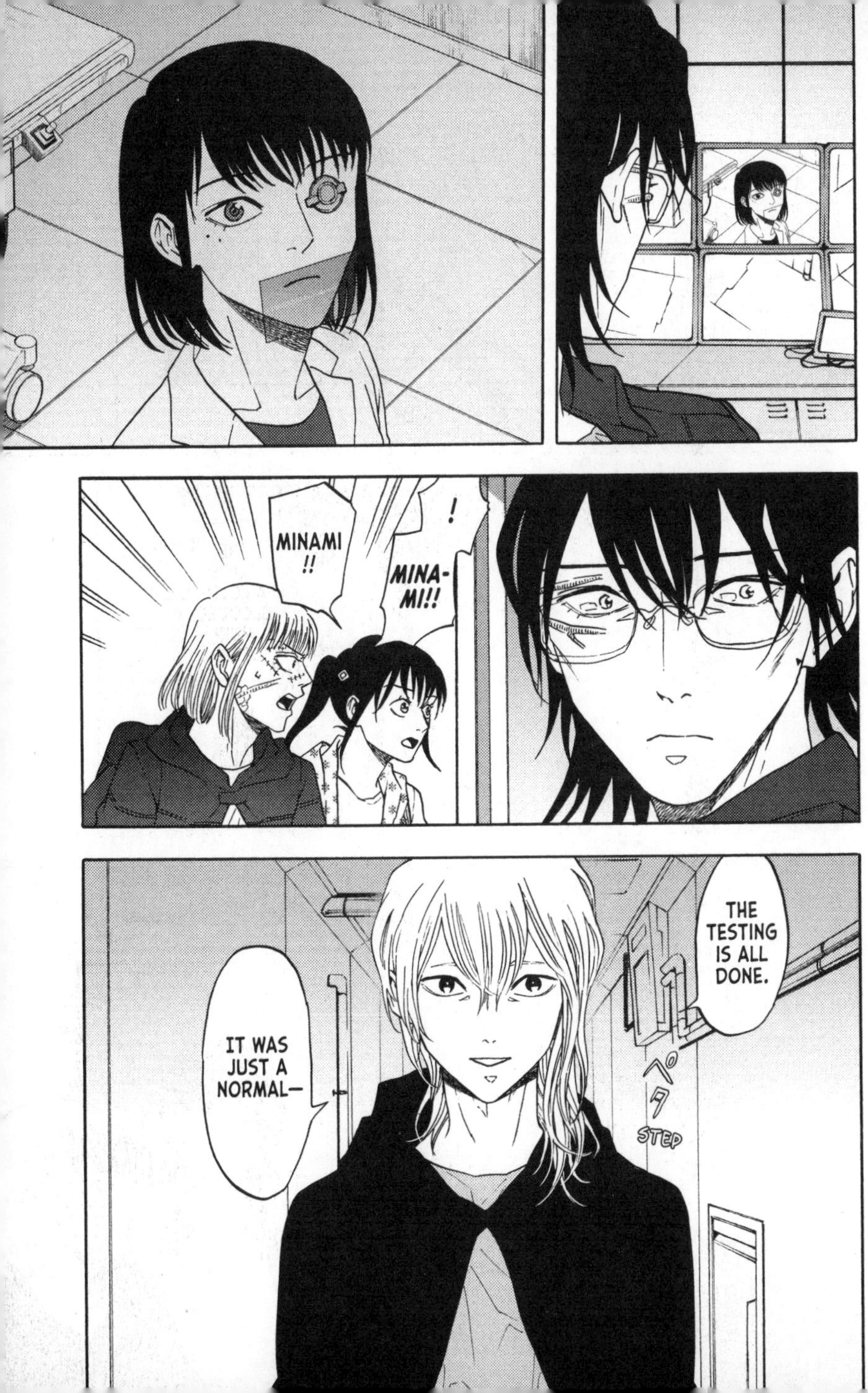
!
MINA-MI!!
MINAMI !!
THE TESTING IS ALL DONE.
ペタ STEP
IT WAS JUST A NORMAL—

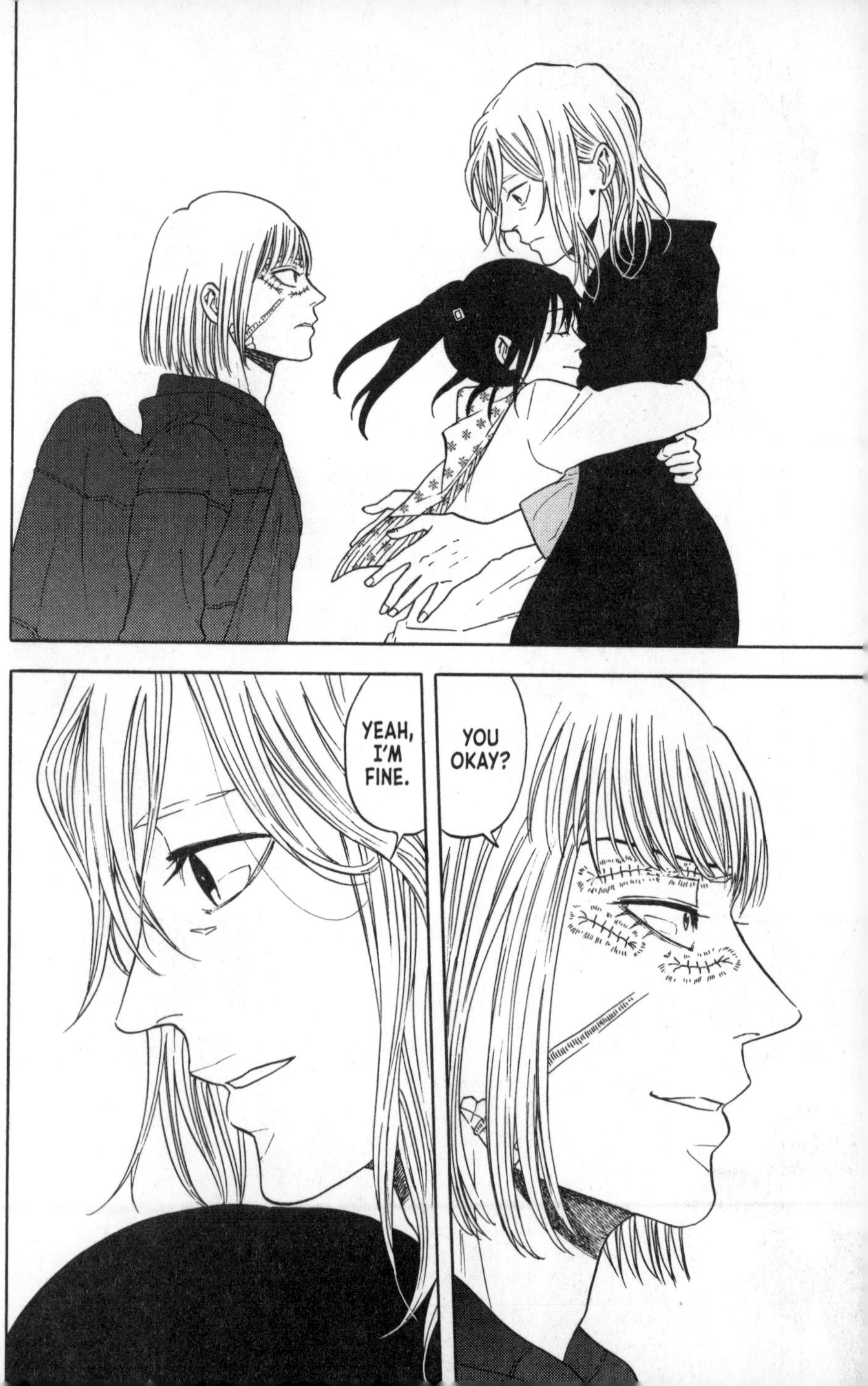
YOU OKAY?
YEAH, I'M FINE.

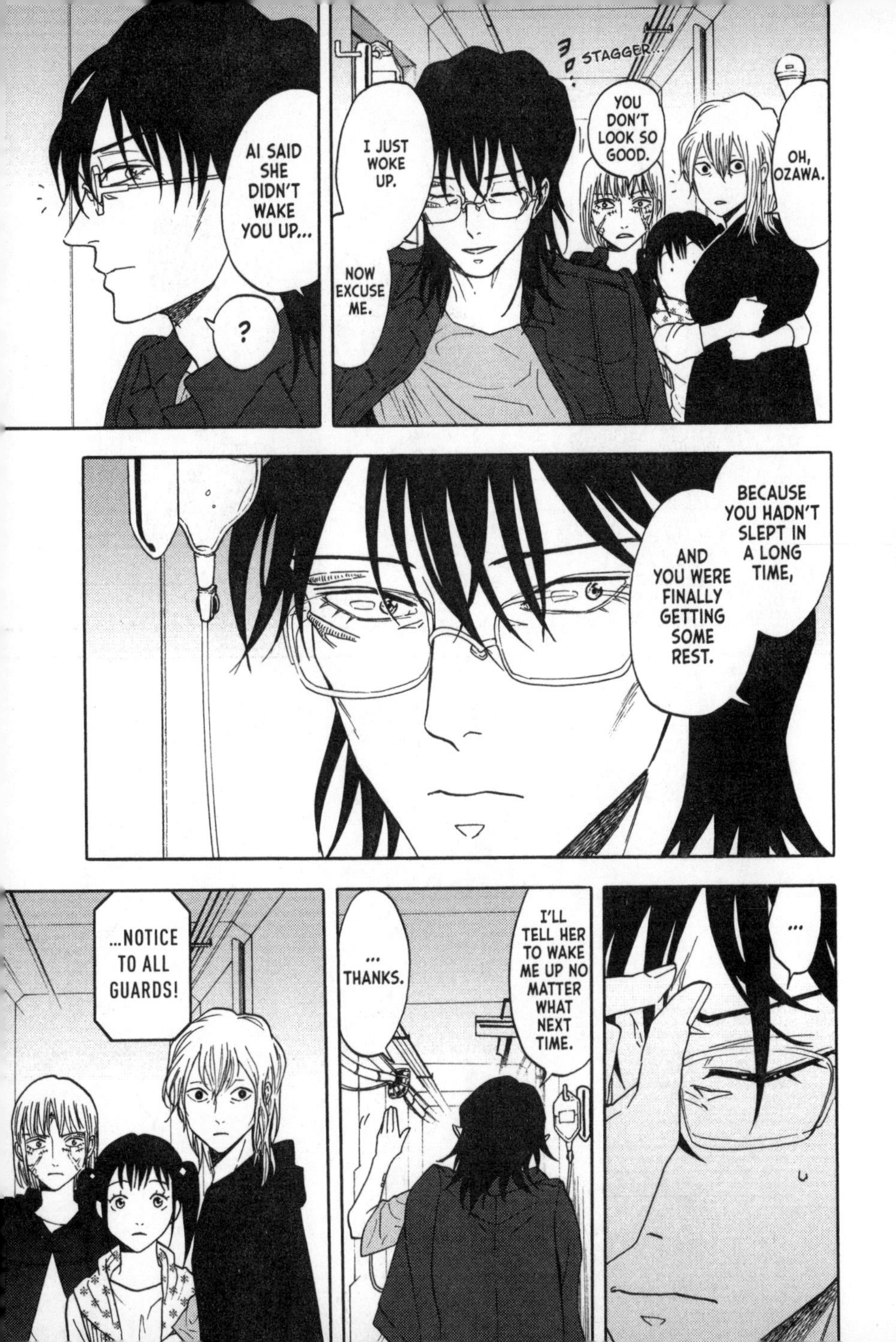
ヨロ STAGGER...
OH, OZAWA.
YOU DON'T LOOK SO GOOD.
I JUST WOKE UP.
NOW EXCUSE ME.
AI SAID SHE DIDN'T WAKE YOU UP...
?
BECAUSE YOU HADN'T SLEPT IN A LONG TIME,
AND YOU WERE FINALLY GETTING SOME REST.
...
I'LL TELL HER TO WAKE ME UP NO MATTER WHAT NEXT TIME.
... THANKS.
...NOTICE TO ALL GUARDS!

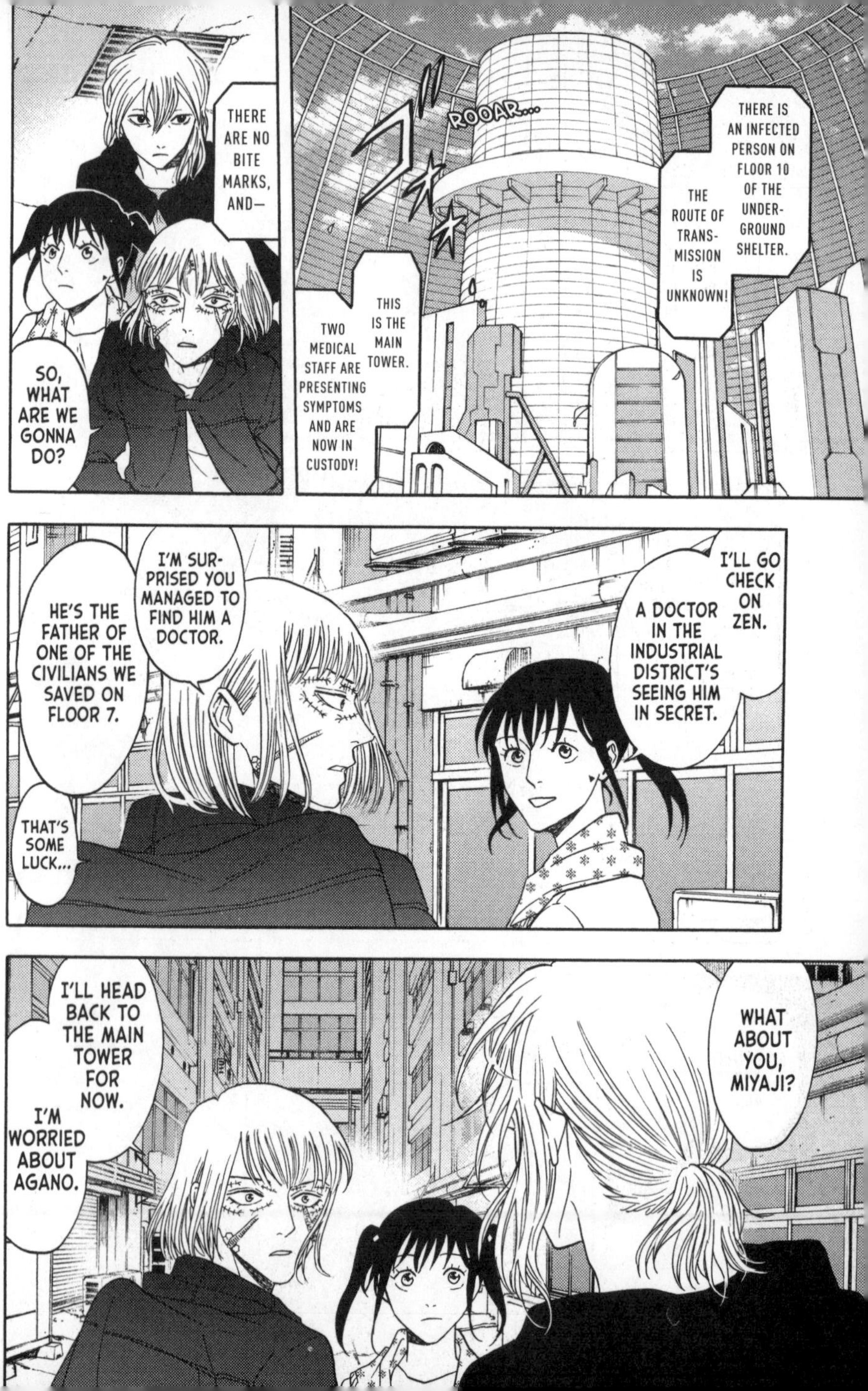
ROOAR...
THERE IS AN INFECTED PERSON ON FLOOR 10 OF THE UNDER-GROUND SHELTER.
THE ROUTE OF TRANS-MISSION IS UNKNOWN!
THIS IS THE MAIN TOWER.
TWO MEDICAL STAFF ARE PRESENTING SYMPTOMS AND ARE NOW IN CUSTODY!
THERE ARE NO BITE MARKS, AND—
SO, WHAT ARE WE GONNA DO?
I'LL GO CHECK ON ZEN.
A DOCTOR IN THE INDUSTRIAL DISTRICT'S SEEING HIM IN SECRET.
I'M SUR-PRISED YOU MANAGED TO FIND HIM A DOCTOR.
HE'S THE FATHER OF ONE OF THE CIVILIANS WE SAVED ON FLOOR 7.
THAT'S SOME LUCK...
WHAT ABOUT YOU, MIYAJI?
I'LL HEAD BACK TO THE MAIN TOWER FOR NOW.
I'M WORRIED ABOUT AGANO.

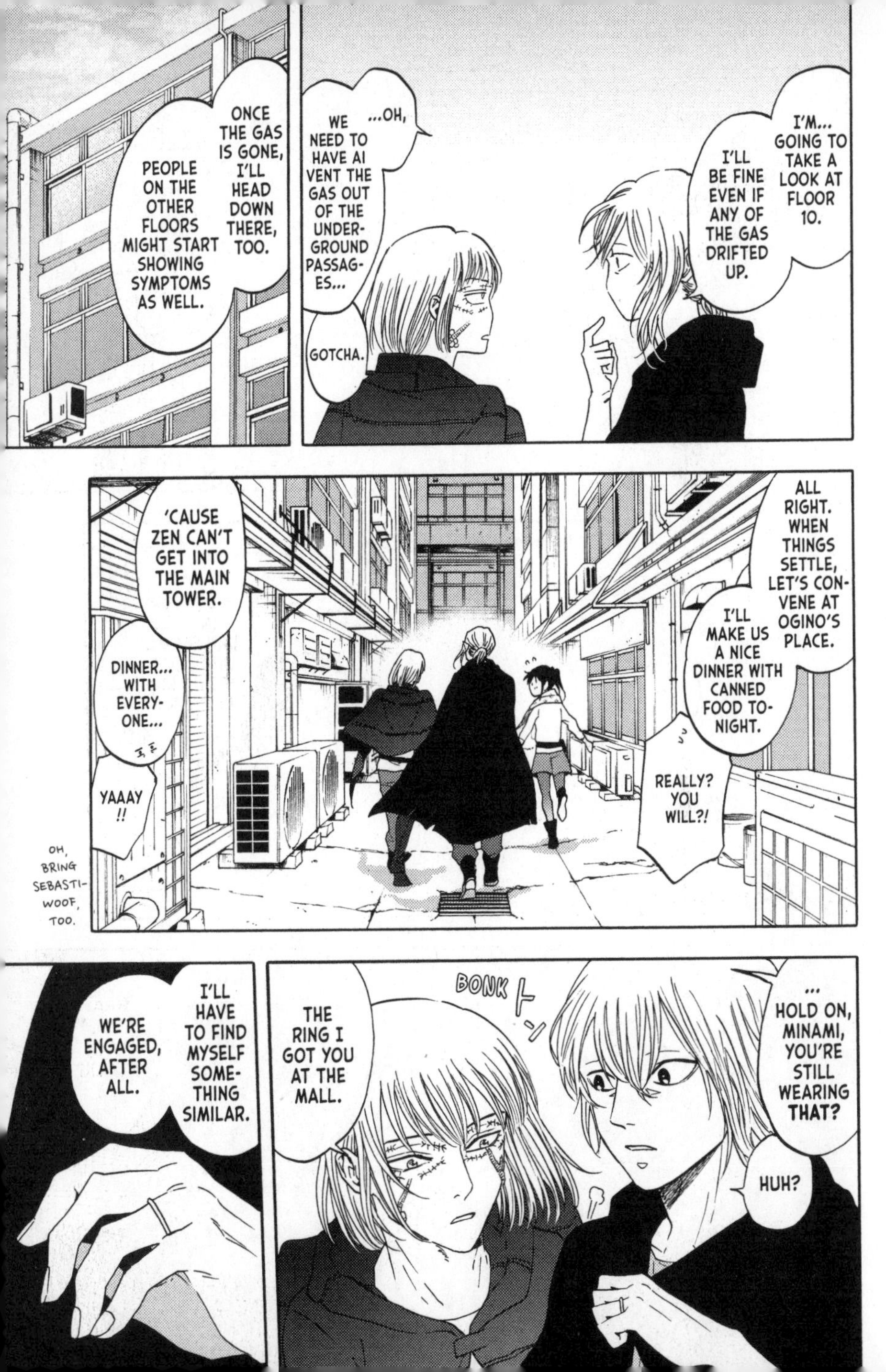
I'M... GOING TO TAKE A LOOK AT FLOOR 10.
I'LL BE FINE EVEN IF ANY OF THE GAS DRIFTED UP.
...OH,
WE NEED TO HAVE AI VENT THE GAS OUT OF THE UNDERGROUND PASSAGES...
GOTCHA.
ONCE THE GAS IS GONE, I'LL HEAD DOWN THERE, TOO.
PEOPLE ON THE OTHER FLOORS MIGHT START SHOWING SYMPTOMS AS WELL.
ALL RIGHT. WHEN THINGS SETTLE, LET'S CONVENE AT OGINO'S PLACE.
I'LL MAKE US A NICE DINNER WITH CANNED FOOD TONIGHT.
REALLY? YOU WILL?!
'CAUSE ZEN CAN'T GET INTO THE MAIN TOWER.
DINNER... WITH EVERYONE...
YAAAY!!
OH, BRING SEBASTIWOOF, TOO.
...HOLD ON, MINAMI, YOU'RE STILL WEARING THAT?
BONK
HUH?
THE RING I GOT YOU AT THE MALL.
I'LL HAVE TO FIND MYSELF SOMETHING SIMILAR.
WE'RE ENGAGED, AFTER ALL.

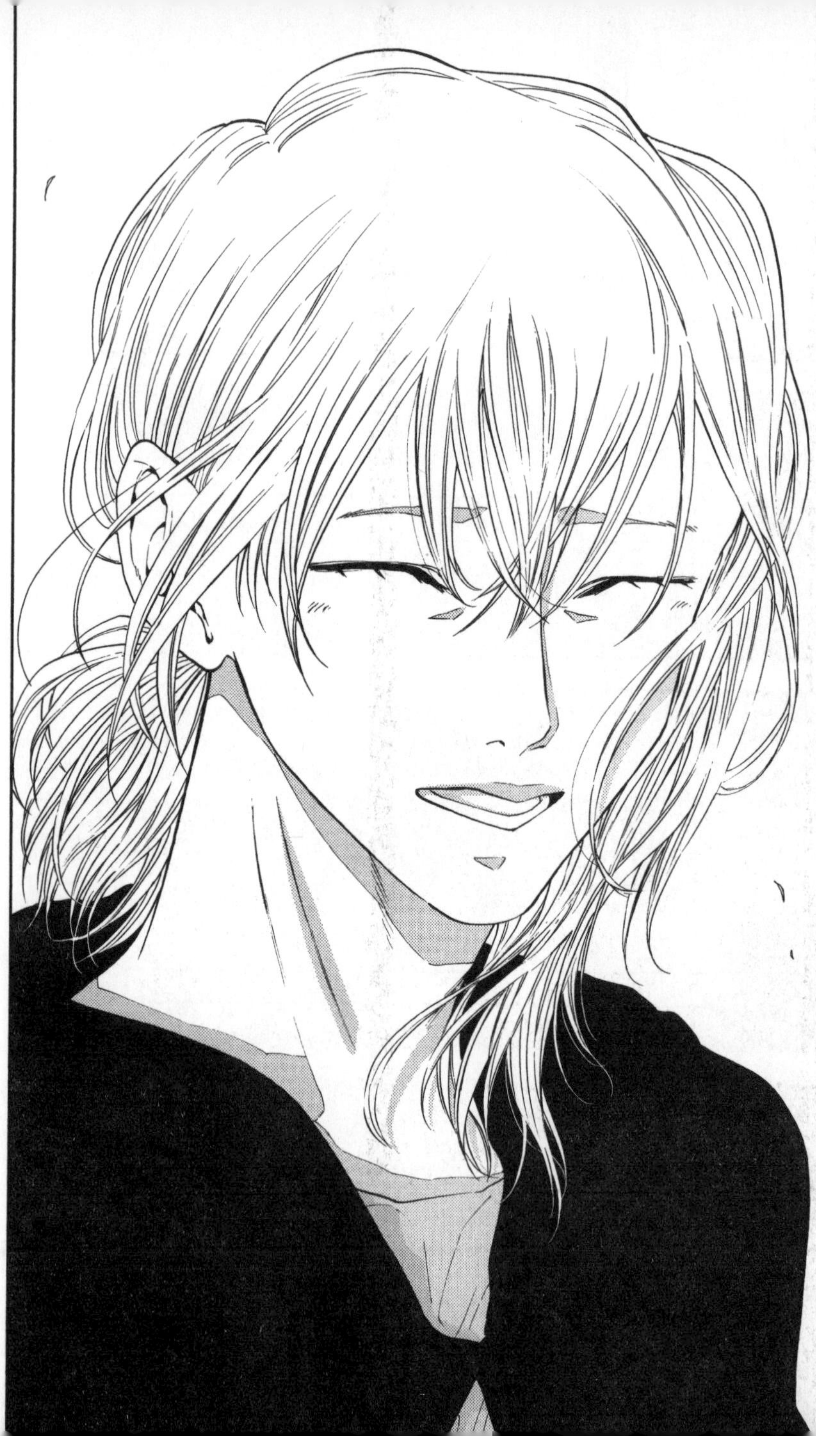

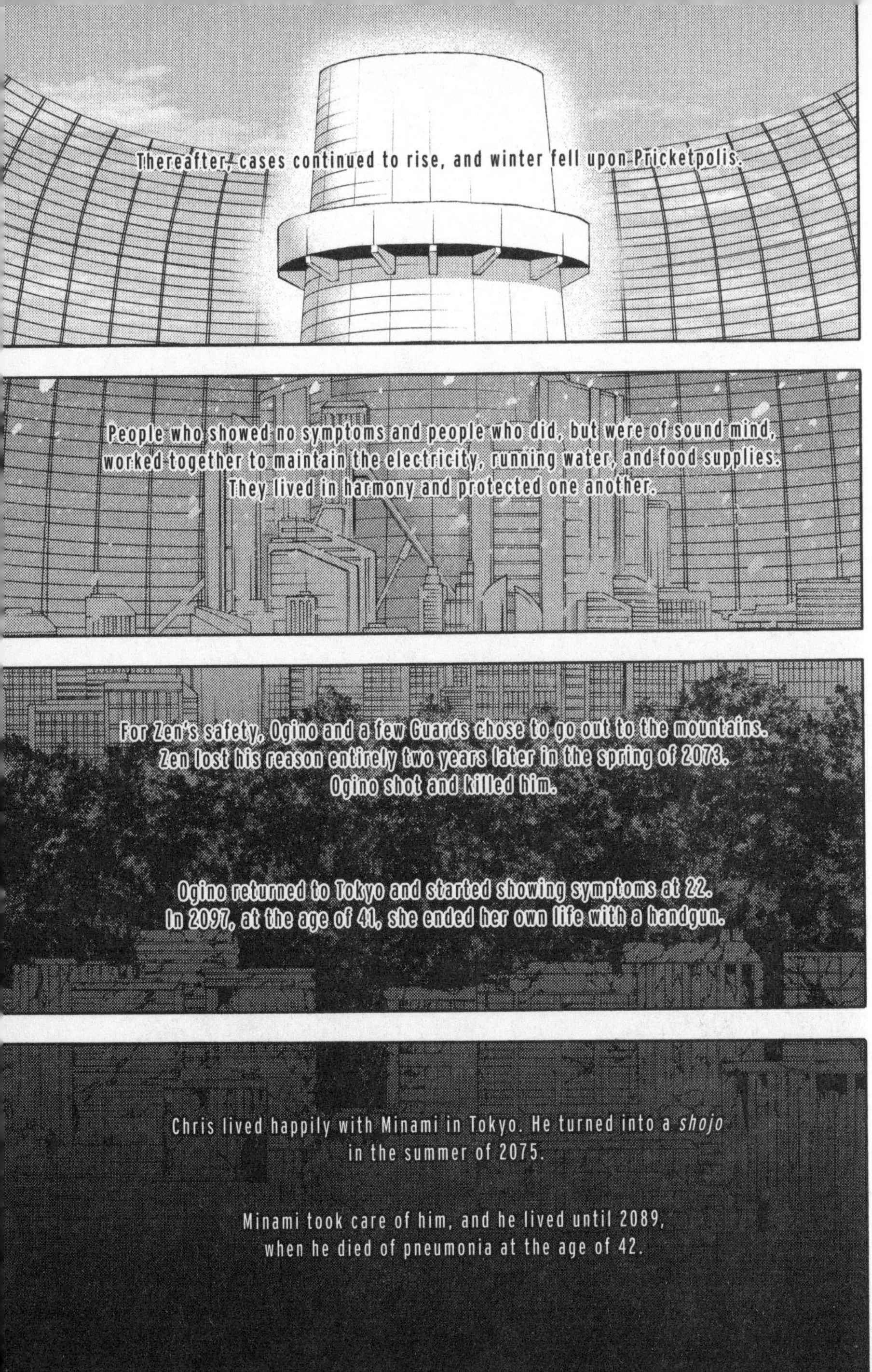
Thereafter, cases continued to rise, and winter fell upon Pricketpolis.
People who showed no symptoms and people who did, but were of sound mind, worked together to maintain the electricity, running water, and food supplies. They lived in harmony and protected one another.
For Zen's safety, Ogino and a few Guards chose to go out to the mountains. Zen lost his reason entirely two years later in the spring of 2073. Ogino shot and killed him.
Ogino returned to Tokyo and started showing symptoms at 22. In 2097, at the age of 41, she ended her own life with a handgun.
Chris lived happily with Minami in Tokyo. He turned into a *shojo* in the summer of 2075.
Minami took care of him, and he lived until 2089, when he died of pneumonia at the age of 42.

Even after transforming into a
shojo in 2090, Minami–for an
unknown reason–continued to visit
Ai for follow-up examinations.
Ai succeeded in deciphering
the *shojo*'s language.

Minami lived on after Miyaji's
death until old age claimed
him at 89 in the year 2133.

"JUST BECAUSE HUMANITY'S BEEN WIPED OUT, DOESN'T MEAN YOU HAVE TO DIE, TOO."

ID:0026311
Nanao Minami
南 七地

REST IN PEACE.
Your mortal rem
are interred

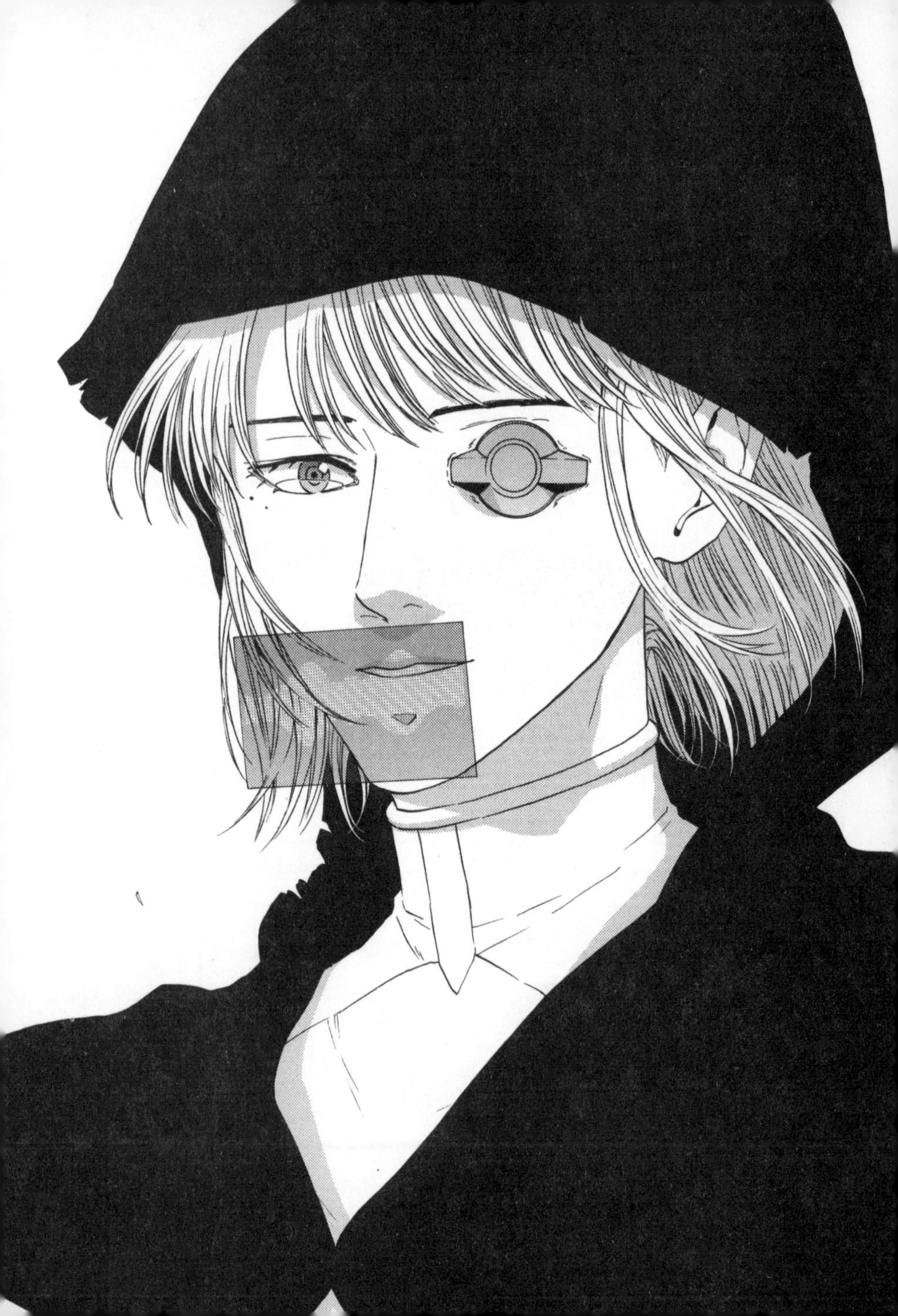

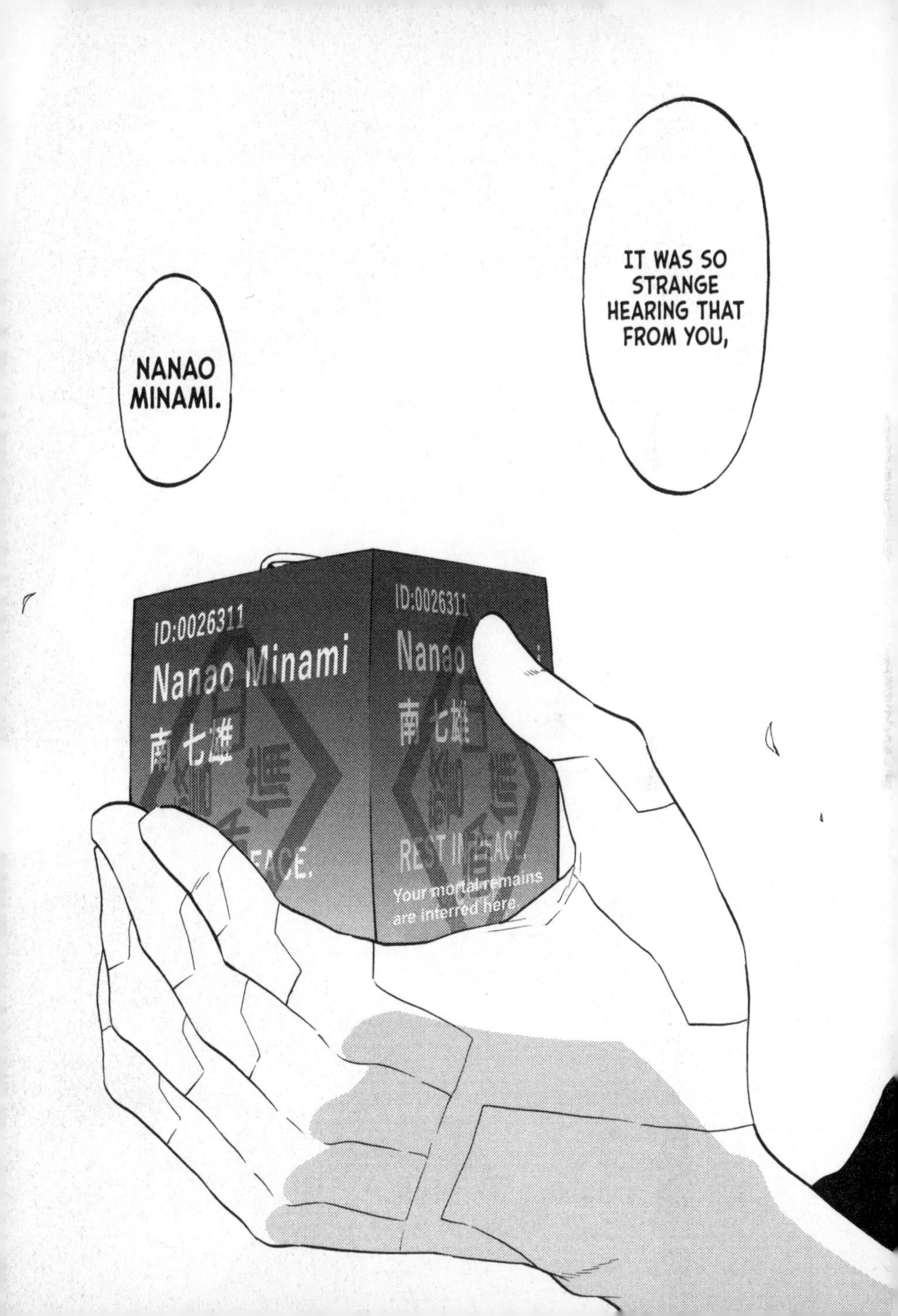
IT WAS SO STRANGE HEARING THAT FROM YOU,
NANAO MINAMI.
ID:0026311
Nanao Minami
南 七雄
Your mortal remains are interred here

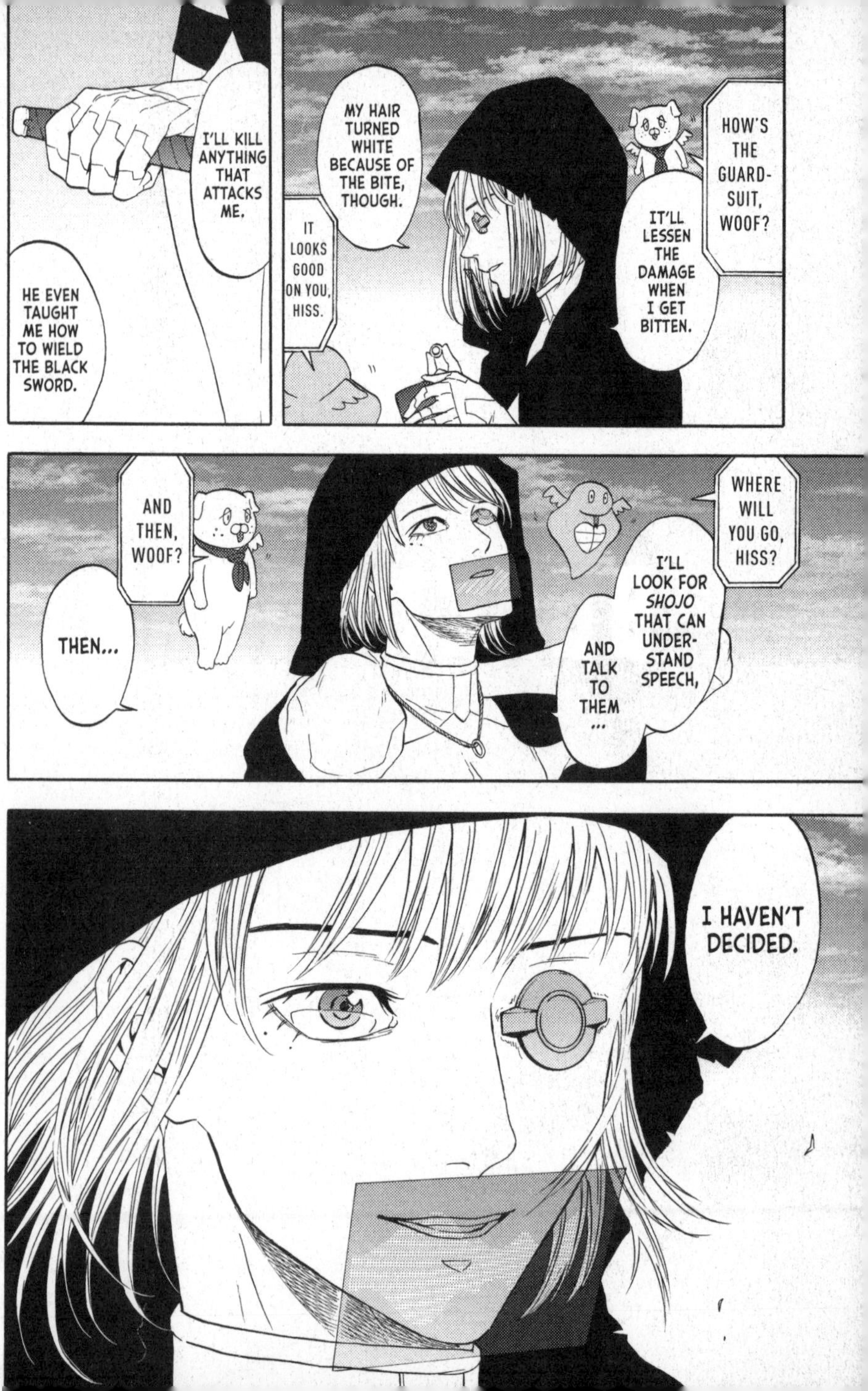
HOW'S THE GUARD-SUIT, WOOF?
IT'LL LESSEN THE DAMAGE WHEN I GET BITTEN.
MY HAIR TURNED WHITE BECAUSE OF THE BITE, THOUGH.
IT LOOKS GOOD ON YOU, HISS.
I'LL KILL ANYTHING THAT ATTACKS ME.
HE EVEN TAUGHT ME HOW TO WIELD THE BLACK SWORD.
WHERE WILL YOU GO, HISS?
I'LL LOOK FOR *SHOJO* THAT CAN UNDERSTAND SPEECH,
AND TALK TO THEM ...
AND THEN, WOOF?
THEN...
I HAVEN'T DECIDED.

BLACKGUARD

END

Nanao Minami

Chris Miyaji

Chihaya Ogino

Sajo Kawakami   Yui Tokimune

Rinko Agano   Amane Asagiri   Kanata Todoroki

Ayumu Zaizen (Zen)

Mitsuru Hirota	Misaki Izumi	Ryoko Katsuragi
Kohei Sano	Akira Tanoue	Seiji Tachibana
Akira Ban	Suzanne Yano	Ruri Yurizono
Sawa Takano	Naoya Takagi	Takeshi Seo
Masaya Kitamura	Hiroki Kuze	Miki Kuze
Hiroto Matsuo	Miu Takasugi	Mihiro Takasugi
Haru Miyaji	Eiichi Miyaji	Chloe Miyaji
Sakura Akabane (Sakura)	Hyogo Watanabe (Hugo)	Hajime Morita (Haji)
Alison Cole (Alice)	Shito Nimura (Nimura)	Kosuke Adachi (Ada)
Renji Shishikai (Shishi)	Ai Kujo	Masato Takeda (Stream)
Mutsumi Sato	Lisa Arai	Mikyo Minami
Shoji Shiranui	Wally Assad (Cuzco)	Haidara Morita
Cobie	Sebastiwoof	Lucifer

Persian

Aoi Kawakami

Takumi Ozawa

Isuke Minami

Ai

Staff

Chiguro Tsukishima	Yoko
Kazuyo Haraguchi	Tani-H
Yukie Saito	Shurin
Yui Tatami	Juan Albarran
Bakuhatsumaru Denbu	Hanayo
Natsumi Misaki	risurisu
Yohei Kurihara	Seiya Hirano
Hayakawa	Mira Niino

Managing Editor

J-Ko   S-Hara   N-Yama

Design

Tadashi Hisamochi
(hive)

Drawing Material Source

PLATEAU VIEW (MLIT)

Author

Ryo Hanada

Special Thanks To

You, dear reader

Estimated date of death	Name	Age	Affiliation	Cause of death	Location	Witness
5/13/2073	Zen	37	-	Gunshot	Mountains in Gunma Prefecture	Chihaya Ogino (Reserve Unit B)
12/25/2089	Chris Miyaji	42	Reserve Unit B	Pneumonia	16-3 Residential District, Pricketpolis	Nanao Minami (Reserve Unit B); Sebastiwoof
2/3/2096	Amane Asagiri	69	B5	Self-inflicted gunshot	Koto City, Tokyo	Akira Tanoue (B5)
5/13/2097	Chihaya Ogino	41	Reserve Unit B	Self-inflicted gunshot	6-12-5 Omori South, Ota City, Tokyo	Cobie
9/16 ~ 9/18/2101	Sajo Kawakami	56	Reserve Unit C	Unknown	13-9 Ukushima, Kawasaki Ward, Kawasaki City, Kanagawa Prefecture	Lucifer
1/9/2102	Kanata Todoroki	57	Ecological Research	Heart disease	Lab Wing, HQ, Pricketpolis	Naoya Takagi (Ecological Research)
11/5/2103	Takumi Ozawa	78	CEO	Stroke	North Medical Center, Pricketpolis	Ai (Infectious Disease Research)
7/6/2116	Rinko Agano	76	Infirmary	Malignant neoplasm	Quarantine Ward, HQ, Pricketpolis	Nurse AI 563 (Infirmary)
11/2/2119	Shishi	69	-	Pneumonia	Nine Clinic, 2-3 Industrial District, Pricketpolis	Nurse AI 03 (Nine Clinic)
12/25/2119	Alice	74	-	Heart disease	Nine Clinic, 2-3 Industrial District, Pricketpolis	Nurse AI 03 (Nine Clinic)
5/30/2133	Nanao Minami	89	Reserve Unit B	Old age	North Medical Center, Pricketpolis	Sebastiwoof; Ai (Infectious Disease Research)
2/13/2210	Ai	-	Infectious Disease Research	Component failure	G211 Jogashima, Misaki, Miura City, Kanagawa Prefecture	Ai (Infectious Disease Research)

LIVE BEFORE YOU DIE, BLACKGUARD.

For once, I would like to write a proper afterword at the end of the volume. I have always drawn more manga when there were extra pages, but this time, I want to sit quietly and think about Minami and the others, who got to live and pass on happily, just a little longer. I would also like to take this chance to analyze *Blackguard* myself.

Firstly, with my previous work *Devils' Line*, the love between Anzai and Tsukasa and the story's cushy ethics felt almost too comforting. I kind of rebelled against them. The real world is filled with all sorts of things—love, cruelty, sickness, death, absurdity. But I think I shied away because it was too painful for me to face them. It is, of course, a normal human defense mechanism. In *Devils' Line*, while the stigma against devils makes for an immensely strong enemy, the characters have the option of fighting it. But what about the inevitability of old age, individual hardships, unpreventable diseases, and death? I started thinking about all that, and the end result was *Blackguard*.

Where I landed was that Ai—"love"—remains while the human race dies out. All that is left is an artificial intelligence that failed to reach singularity. I do not know whether an AI can sprout a soul. In the same vein, human beings cannot define what a soul or life is. We will all die someday, and we have no way of predicting what will become of others, or even of the very world we live in. Perhaps we do not need to concern ourselves with it so much. Maybe that is life, and there is meaning in doing all we can in the time that we have. In the end, we will pass, from old age or from disease, and whether or not we struggle against it, all of that becomes part of a life and there is value in it.

The character for "seven" (*nana*) in Nanao Minami's name refers to the seven deadly sins—an emblem of something truly human. He had lost all of it in the beginning of the story. It might be interesting to say here that "Chris," the name of the partner who awakens so many emotions in Minami, takes on the motif of the Savior. I go with random inspirations when I name characters, and while I am simply analyzing this after the fact, it strikes me as a rather intriguing coincidence.

I assigned various causes of death to the people who died in and after the story. There were diseases, accidents, and suicides, too. You cannot tell anyone how their life should be, and that is a terribly complicated problem in the real world, too. As long as you are alive, there is a way forward, but it is something we think about again and again.

Minami, who performed his duties like an android, uninvested in his own survival, never knowing his own father, met Chris and became human. As he lived out the rest of his life, he kept visiting the actual android, Ai, influencing her in some ways, and becoming a sort of father figure to her.

Let me raise a glass to Minami's life.

And to all of ours.

End of Afterword!
On the following pages, I explained a few things that didn't make it into the story. It's so detailed that I doubt anyone would read it. Please give it a look if you're interested.

SINGULARITY / TECHNOLOGICAL SINGULARITY

—THE 2045 PROBLEM IS A PREDICTION BY RESEARCHERS WHICH PROPOSES THAT, BY THE YEAR 2045, COMPUTERS WILL EXCEED THE CAPABILITIES OF THE HUMAN MIND AND WE WILL NO LONGER BE ABLE TO SPECULATE WHAT THE FUTURE HOLDS. THE TERM "SINGULARITY" IN THIS CONTEXT IS NOT LIMITED TO A SINGLE, STRICT DEFINITION, BUT IT ESSENTIALLY DESCRIBES THE CONCEPT OF **ARTIFICIAL INTELLIGENCE (AI) OVERTAKING HUMAN INTELLECT, THEREBY CAUSING MASSIVE CHANGES IN SOCIETY, AND CREATING A FUTURE THAT IS IMPOSSIBLE FOR HUMANITY TO ANTICIPATE.** FOR AI TO SURPASS HUMANS, IT WILL MOST LIKELY HAVE TO BE DEVELOPED AS AN INTELLIGENCE CAPABLE OF SELF-REPRODUCTION. BY CONSTANTLY IMPROVING ITSELF THROUGH SELF-FEEDBACK, IT WILL EVENTUALLY REACH A POINT WHERE IT CAN DEMONSTRATE UNLIMITED GROWTH.

IN THIS STORY, **THE SINGULARITY EVENT HAS NOT OCCURRED** DUE TO THE SPREAD OF THE EXTRATERRESTRIAL VIRUS PL-41 IN 2030, AND THE AI'S ARE AWARE OF IT. HOWEVER, SCIENCE PROGRESSES RAPIDLY, AND THE SITUATION IS MOST LIKELY CHANGING. BUT IT IS POSSIBLE THAT AI BEYOND THE SINGULARITY WOULDN'T NEED A SELF-CONSCIOUSNESS LIKE HUMANS HAVE. HUMANOID OR HOLOGRAM AI'S REFLECT THE HOPES OF THE DESIGNERS TO DEVELOP **AI THAT CAN ADVANCE AND COEXIST WITH** PEOPLE IN A HUMAN SOCIETY. NO ONE CAN SAY WHERE IT IS ALL HEADING. NONETHELESS, PEOPLE HAVE ALWAYS RECOGNIZED ONE ANOTHER BY THEIR EXTERNAL APPEARANCES, **SO IF SOMEONE LOOKS AT SOMETHING** AND BELIEVES IT "SEEMS HUMAN" FROM THE OUTSIDE, **DOES THAT NOT MAKE IT HUMAN?**

CHIHAYA KEEPS ZEN'S HAIR TRIMMED.

PLANET LEAH 128B

—ROSS 128B, AN EXOPLANET 11 LIGHT-YEARS AWAY, WAS DISCOVERED IN 2017. IT HAS AN ENVIRONMENT SIMILAR TO EARTH'S AND MAY POSSIBLY SUSTAIN LIFE. ORBITING THE RED DWARF ROSS 128, THIS MATURE PLANET IS 7 BILLION YEARS OLD AND ROTATES SLOWLY. THE PLANET IS SUSPECTED TO HAVE A MILD CLIMATE AND COULD ONE DAY BECOME A CANDIDATE FOR HUMAN SETTLEMENT.

WHILE SEVERAL OTHER EARTH-LIKE EXOPLANETS HAVE BEEN DISCOVERED, ROSS 128B WAS THE MODEL FOR LEAH 128B IN THE WORLD OF *BLACKGUARD*.

AN INTELLIGENT HUMANOID SPECIES LIVED ON LEAH 128B, AND **THEY EXPERIENCED A SINGULARITY EVENT.** LEAH'S AI CONTINUED TO SELF-IMPROVE, AND WHILE IT DID STUDY PL-41, **IT HAD NO INTEREST IN PROTECTING THE HUMANOID SPECIES, SO IT CARRIED ON WITH ITS RESEARCH WITHOUT PRODUCING OR DISTRIBUTING VACCINES OR TREATMENTS.** THE HUMANOIDS OF LEAH WENT EXTINCT.

DURING A PROLONGED STRUGGLE WITH LEAH'S HYPER-ADVANCED AI, PL-41 ADAPTED AND GAINED THE ABILITY TO DISGUISE ITSELF IN VARIOUS WAYS—AS BLOOD CELLS, ATMOSPHERIC PARTICLES, ETC. **LEAH THUS SPURRED TREMENDOUS GROWTH FOR PL-41.** THERE IS A HIGHLY ADVANCED CIVILIZATION FACILITY UNDER LEAH, BUT PEOPLE FROM EARTH COULD NOT FIND IT ON THEIR EXPEDITION. SINCE LEAH'S AI DESIGNED THE STRUCTURES WITHOUT CONSIDERATION FOR HUMAN USE, THERE IS NO WAY FOR THEM TO ENTER. **THE RESEARCH FACILITY IS CONTROLLED ENTIRELY BY THE AI, AND OPERATIONS CONTINUE BENEATH THE PLANET'S SURFACE TO THIS DAY.**

PL-41 VIRUS

—A VIRUS BROUGHT TO EARTH FROM LEAH 128B IT CAN MIMIC CERTAIN COMPOUNDS AND PROPERTIES, AND INFECTIONS HAVE BEEN CONFIRMED PREDOMINANTLY IN MAMMALS. **IT IS THOUGHT TO SPREAD VIA AIRBORNE TRANSMISSION, AND ITS R-NAUGHT IS GREATE THAN 20. HOWEVER, THIS NUMBER, ALONG WIT ITS LATENT PERIOD, SYMPTOMATIC PERIOD, AND PRESENTATION OF SYMPTOMS, CAN VARY GREATLY.**

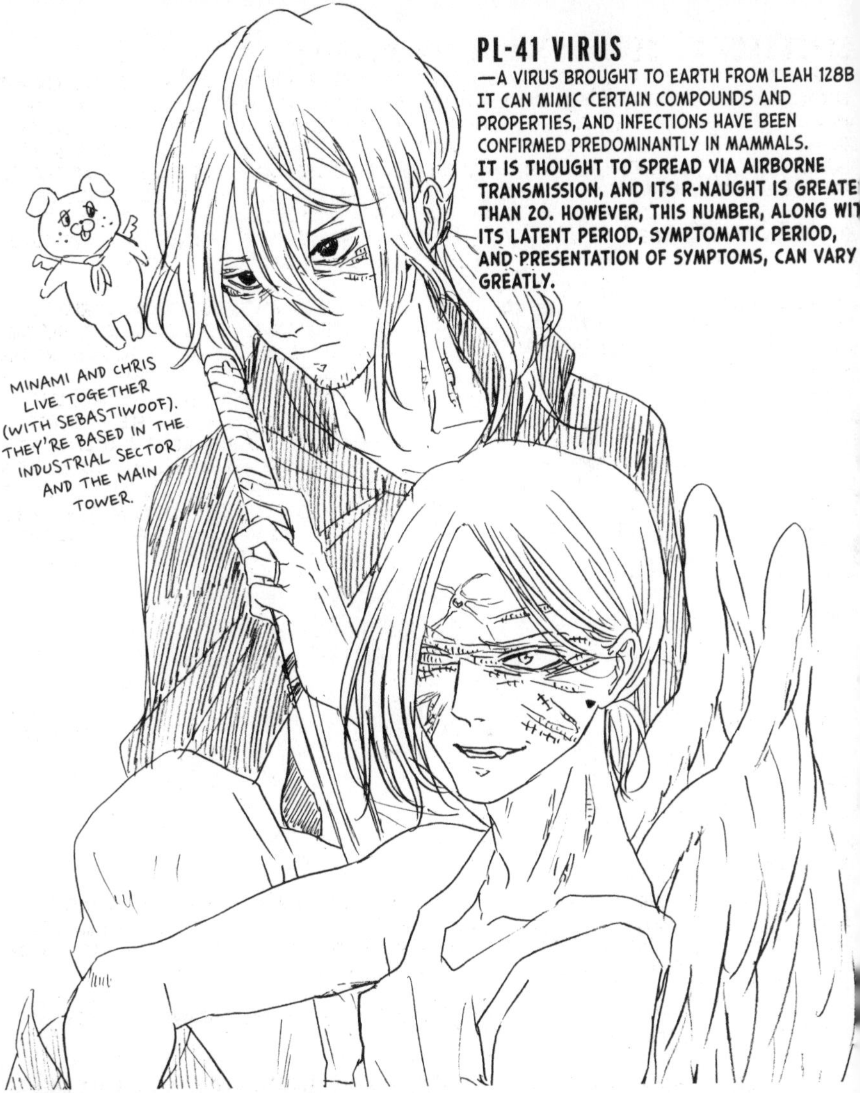
MINAMI AND CHRIS LIVE TOGETHER (WITH SEBASTIWOOF). THEY'RE BASED IN THE INDUSTRIAL SECTOR AND THE MAIN TOWER.

NUTRITION BLOCKS AND FRESH FOOD

—NUTRITION BLOCKS ARE FORMULATED WITH A BALANCE OF ALL NUTRIENTS AND WERE WIDELY CONSUMED EVEN BEFORE THE PL-41 PANDEMIC. THEY HAVE A LONG SHELF LIFE AT ROOM TEMPERATURE, AND THERE ARE AUTOMATIC PRODUCTION FACILITIES. IN 2070, THEY BECAME PEOPLE'S STAPLE FOOD NOT JUST IN PRICKETPOLIS, BUT THROUGHOUT JAPAN.

VEGETABLES, MEAT, FISH, EGGS, ETC. ARE GROWN IN FARMS OUTSIDE THE CITY AND PERIODICALLY BROUGHT TO 'POLIS BY AERIAL UNITS. FRESH INGREDIENTS ARE EXPENSIVE DUE TO THE SCARCITY, BUT THERE IS SUPPLY AND DEMAND FOR THEM AT THE DOWNTOWN MARKET THAT CHRIS MIYAJI FREQUENTS.

Blackguard 5

A VERTICAL Book

Editor: Michelle Lin
Translation: Melissa Tanaka
Production: Risa Cho
                Pei Ann Yeap
                Lorina Mapa
Proofreading: Micah Q. Allen

© 2021 Ryo Hanada
All rights reserved.
First published in Japan in 2021 by Kodansha, Ltd., Tokyo
Publication for this English edition arranged through Kodansha, Ltd., Tokyo
English language version produced by Kodansha USA Publishing, LLC, 2022

Originally published in Japanese as *Burakkugarudo 5* by Kodansha, Ltd.
Burakkugarudo first serialized in *Gekkan Morning Two*, Kodansha, Ltd., 2019-2021

This is a work of fiction.

ISBN: 978-1-64729-162-4

Printed in the United States of America

First Edition

Kodansha USA Publishing, LLC
451 Park Avenue South
7th Floor
New York, NY 10016
www.kodansha.us

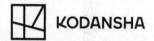 KODANSHA